It is hard to overestimate the importance of Augustine's work and influence, both in his own period and in the subsequent history of Western philosophy. Until the thirteenth century, when he may have had a competitor in Thomas Aquinas, he was the most important philosopher of the medieval period. Many of his views, including his theory of the just war, his account of time and eternity, his understanding of the will, his attempted resolution of the problem of evil, and his approach to the relation of faith and reason, have continued to be influential up to the present time. In this volume, sixteen scholars provide a wide-ranging and stimulating contribution to our understanding of Augustine, covering all the major areas of his philosophy and theology.

THE CAMBRIDGE
COMPANION TO
AUGUSTINE

THE CAMBRIDGE
COMPANION TO
AUGUSTINE

EDITED BY

ELEONORE STUMP
St. Louis University

AND

NORMAN KRETZMANN

CAMBRIDGE
UNIVERSITY PRESS

PUBLISHED BY THE PRESS SYNDICATE OF THE UNIVERSITY OF CAMBRIDGE
The Pitt Building, Trumpington Street, Cambridge, United Kingdom

CAMBRIDGE UNIVERSITY PRESS
The Edinburgh Building, Cambridge CB2 2RU, UK   www.cup.cam.ac.uk
40 West 20th Street, New York, NY 10011–4211, USA   www.cup.org
10 Stamford Road, Oakleigh, Melbourne 3166, Australia
Ruiz de Alarcón 13, 28014 Madrid, Spain

First published 2001

Printed in the United Kingdom at the University Press, Cambridge

Typeface Sabon MT 10/13pt   *System* QuarkXPress™   [SE]

A catalogue record for this book is available from the British Library

ISBN 0 521 65018 6 hardback
ISBN 0 521 65985 X paperback

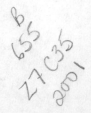

CONTENTS

CONTRIBUTORS

MARY T. CLARK, RSCJ is Professor Emeritus of Philosophy at Manhattanville College. Among her books on Augustine are *Augustine, Philosopher of Freedom*; *Augustinian Personalism*; *Augustine, An Introduction to His Thought*. She also wrote the Analytical Introduction to and translation of *Marius Victorinus: Theological Treatises on the Trinity*. Her articles on Augustine have been published in *Augustinian Studies*; *Revue des etudes Augustiniennes*; *Augustinus*; and *Studia Patristica*.

BONNIE KENT is an Associate Professor of Philosophy at Syracuse University and the author of *Virtues of the Will: The Transformation of Ethics in the Late Thirteenth Century*. Her articles include "Moral Provincialism" and "Moral Growth and the Unity of the Virtues."

CHRISTOPHER KIRWAN is Emeritus Fellow in Philosophy at Exeter College, Oxford. He is author of *Augustine* in the *Arguments of the Philosophers* series, and his articles include "Augustine on Souls and Bodies" and "Avoiding Sin: Augustine against Consequentialism."

SIMO KNUUTTILA is Research Professor in the Academy of Finland and Professor of Theological Ethics and the Philosophy of Religion at the University of Helsinki. He is the editor of *The New Synthese Historical Library* and the author of *Modalities in Medieval Philosophy* and many articles on the history of logic, semantics, the philosophy of mind, and philosophical theology.

SCOTT MACDONALD is Professor of Philosophy and Norma K. Regan Professor in Christian Studies at Cornell University. His many publications in medieval philosophy include "Primal Sin" and "Aquinas's Incompatibilist Account of Free Choice," and he has recently co-edited (with Eleonore Stump) *Aquinas's Moral Theory*. He edits the journal *Medieval Philosophy and Theology*.

WILLIAM E. MANN is Professor of Philosophy at the University of Vermont. He has written extensively on topics in medieval philosophy and the philosophy of religion. His recent articles include "Inner-Life Ethics" (on Augustine) and "Duns Scotus on Natural and Supernatural Knowledge of God" in *The Cambridge Companion to Duns Scotus*.

GARETH B. MATTHEWS is Professor of Philosophy at the University of Massachusetts, Amherst. He is the author of *Thought's Ego in Augustine and Descartes* and the editor of *The Augustinian Tradition*.

GERARD O'DALY is Professor of Latin at University College London. He is the author of *Plotinus' Philosophy of the Self*, *Augustine's Philosophy of Mind*, *The Poetry of Boethius*, and *Augustine's 'City of God': A Reader's Guide*, and is on the editorial board of the *Augustinus-Lexikon*.

JAMES J. O'DONNELL is Professor of Classical Studies and Vice Provost for Information Systems and Computing at the University of Pennsylvania. He is author of a three-volume edition of and commentary on the *Confessions* and more recently of *Avatars of the Word: From Papyrus to Cyberspace*.

JOHN RIST is Professor Emeritus of Classics and Philosophy at the University of Toronto. He is author of various books and articles mostly on ancient philosophy and patristics, including *Eros and Psyche*, *Plotinus: The Road to Reality*, and *Augustine: Ancient Thought Baptized*.

M. W. F. STONE is Lecturer in the Philosophy of Religion, King's College London. He is the editor with Jill Kraye of *Humanism and Early Modern Philosophy* and author of the two-volume work, *The Subtle Arts of Casuistry*. He has published articles on late medieval philosophy and early modern scholasticism.

ELEONORE STUMP is the Robert J. Henle, S.J., Professor of Philosophy at Saint Louis University. She has written extensively on various topics in medieval philosophy as well as in philosophy of religion and metaphysics. Her books include *Boethius's De topicis differentiis*, *Boethius's In Ciceronis Topica*, and *Dialectic and Its Place in the Development of Medieval Logic*. Her recent articles include "Ockham on Sensory Cognition," in the *Cambridge Companion to Ockham*, "Aquinas on Justice," and "Saadya Gaon and the Problem of Evil."

ROLAND TESKE, S.J., is Professor of Philosophy at Marquette University in Milwaukee. He is author of *Paradoxes of Time in St. Augustine* and of many articles on Augustine and on William of Auvergne. He has also translated six volumes of the works of Augustine, including all the anti-Pelagian writings.

PAUL WEITHMAN is Associate Professor of Philosophy at the University of Notre Dame. He has published articles in medieval political theory, contemporary political philosophy, religious ethics, and medical ethics. He is the editor of *Religion and Contemporary Liberalism* and the co-editor, with Henry Richardson, of the five-volume *The Philosophy of Rawls*.

JAMES WETZEL is Associate Professor of Philosophy and Religion at Colgate University. His publications include *Augustine and the Limits of Virtue*, "Snares of Truth: Augustine on Free Will and Predestination," in *Augustine and his Critics*, ed. Robert Dodaro and George Lawless, and "Time After Augustine."

THOMAS WILLIAMS is Assistant Professor of Philosophy at the University of Iowa. His work in medieval philosophy includes articles on John Duns Scotus and translations of Augustine's *On Free Choice of the Will* and Anselm's *Proslogion* and *Monologion*.

PREFACE

When this project was conceived, Norman Kretzmann had had multiple myeloma for a long time; but he and I were fairly confident that he would live long enough to hold the finished book in his hand. As it turned out, that did not happen. The disease took a sudden turn for the worse, and he died on 1 August, 1998. His death was a great loss for the field of medieval philosophy, as well as for philosophy of religion, where his influence was also widely felt. His death was an incalculable loss for me. He was my teacher, my mentor, and my friend; and everything I did, I did better because of him. Although I finished this project without him, it is entirely fitting that his name should appear on the book as co-editor. He and I shared in conceiving and launching the project, and his stamp and influence are apparent everywhere in it. No doubt the final product would have looked different if he had been able to participate in all its stages; but I think that, if he could have seen it, he would have been very pleased with this volume as it stands.

More ordinary debts also need to be acknowledged here. Hilary Gaskin, the Cambridge University Press editor for this series, was helpful at every stage of the process of production, and the volume is much better for her input to it. My secretary Betty Andrews is responsible for whatever organization there was in the process that begins with commissioning chapters and finishes with the acknowledgment of the final drafts. Bryan Cross suffered with the task of producing harmony across chapters in the citations of Augustine's works, and Chris Pliatska labored at the bibliography and the proofs. I am very grateful for all these contributions to the volume.

The final stages of this volume were completed at the National Humanities Center, where I was a Lilly Foundation Fellow for the academic year 1999 2000. It is hard to imagine a more pleasant environment in which to work, or one more conducive to research, than the National Humanities Center, and I am grateful to the Center and to the Lilly Foundation for my year there.

Eleonore Stump

Series

CCSL	Corpus Christianorum, Series Latina
CSEL	Corpus Scriptorum Ecclesiasticorum Latinorum
PL	*Patrologia Latina*

Titles of Augustine's works

Adnotat. in Job	*Adnotationes in Job*
Conf.	*Confessiones*
C. Acad.	*Contra Academicos*
C. ep. Pelag.	*Contra duas epistolas Pelagianorum*
C. ep. fund.	*Contra epistulam Manichaei quam vocant fundamenti*
C. Faust.	*Contra Faustum Manichaeum*
C. Gaud.	*Contra Gaudentium Donatistarum episcopum*
C. Max.	*Contra Maximinum Arianorum episcopum*
C. Mend.	*Contra Mendacium*
C. Prisc. et Orig.	*Ad Orasium contra Priscillianistas et Origenistas*
C. Secundinum	*Contra Secundinum Manichaeum*
De civ. Dei	*De civitate Dei*
De cons. evang.	*De consensu evangelistarum*
De corrept. et gratia	*De correptione et gratia*
De doct. christ.	*De doctrina christiana*
De dono persev.	*De dono perseverantiae*
De Gen. ad litt.	*De Genesi ad litteram libri duodecim*
De Gen. c. Man.	*De Genesi contra Manichaeos*
De immor. anim.	*De immortalitate animae*
De lib. arb.	*De libero arbitrio*
De mag.	*De magistro*
De nat. boni c. Man.	*De natura boni contra Manichaeos*

De nat. et gratia	*De natura et gratia*
De nat. et orig. anim.	*De natura et origine animae*
De ord.	*De ordine*
De pecc. merit. et remis.	*De peccatorum meritis et remissione*
De praed. sanct.	*De praedestinatione sanctorum*
De quant. anim.	*De quantitate animae*
De serm. Dom. in monte	*De sermone Domini in monte*
De spir. et litt.	*De spiritu et littera*
De Trin.	*De Trinitate*
De util. cred.	*De utilitate credendi*
De vera relig.	*De vera religione*
Enarr. in Ps.	*Ennarrationes in Psalmos*
Ep.	*Epistulae*
Ep. ad Gal. expos.	*Epistolae ad Galatas expositio*
Ep. ad Rom. incoh. expos.	*Epistolae ad Romanos inchoata expositio*
Quaest. evang.	*Quaestiones evangeliorum*
Retract.	*Retractationes*
Sol.	*Soliloquia*

Introduction

It is hard to overestimate the importance of Augustine's work and influence, both in his own period and in the history of Western philosophy after it. Patristic philosophy and theology, and every area of philosophy and theology in the later medieval period, manifest the mark of his thought. In fact, at least until the thirteenth century, when he may have had a competitor in Thomas Aquinas, Augustine is undoubtedly the most important philosopher of the medieval period. Furthermore, although his influence is somewhat less after the medieval period, it is still important. Many of his views, including, for example, his theory of the just war, his account of time and eternity, his understanding of the will, his attempted resolution of the problem of evil, and his approach to the relation of faith and reason, have continued to be important up to the present.

He was born around 354 AD in north Africa to Monica, who was fervently Christian, and Patricius, who was a non-believer for most of his life. His family was not especially wealthy or distinguished, but they were able to afford a good education for him of the sort common at the time, focusing on rhetoric. His family's plan, with which he initially concurred, was that he should marry well and make his way in the world by means of his skill in rhetoric. While he was waiting to make a suitable marriage, he took a concubine who bore him a son, Adeodatus. When Augustine sent his concubine away, Adeodatus stayed with him. The boy seems to have been remarkably bright, as he is described in Augustine's treatise *De magistro,* which also gives us an interesting witness to the relations between Augustine and his son. Adeodatus did not live to manhood; he died not long after the time of the dialogue portrayed in *De magistro*.

Augustine's mother Monica was determined that Augustine should become a Christian, but initially he joined the Manichaeans instead. Although most of Augustine's life was lived in Africa, in 383 AD he went to Italy, where he made the aquaintance of Ambrose, bishop of Milan, himself one of the most forceful and important Christian thinkers of the time. Many influences, including that of Ambrose, came together to bring about Augustine's conversion, and he was baptized in 387 AD. Moved by stories of desert ascetics that were then popular,

Augustine also committed himself to a life of celibacy, a decision made famous by his moving description in the *Confessions* of the process leading up to it. In 391 AD he was ordained priest, and a few years later he became bishop of the African town of Hippo, an office he held until his death in 430 AD.

As bishop, he exercised a widespread influence. He was especially vigorous in combatting Manichaeism and the Christian heresies of Donatism and Pelagianism. His controversies with these three common Patristic theological views shaped his philosophy on such issues as free will and the problem of evil. In addition to his pastoral and administrative duties as bishop, he managed to write extensively. His surviving works include roughly two hundred letters, five hundred sermons, and a hundred philosophical and theological works.

His life spanned a turbulent period in the Church and in the Roman empire. He lived through the sack of Rome in 410 AD, and there were barbarian armies outside Hippo when he was dying. The Church during this period was also often in tumult. It was hammering out not only the shape of orthodoxy but also its relations to the state, and theological quarrels tended to become entangled with political strife. The tenor of the time and the difficulties of understanding Augustine's life in its historical context are laid out in detail in the chapter which opens this volume, James J. O'Donnell's "Augustine: his time and lives."

Augustine made important contributions to every area of philosophy, and there are many appropriate ways of ordering the various topics on which he wrote. Furthermore, in Augustine's work – much more than in the work of a medieval philosopher such as Aquinas, for example – disparate topics are interwoven in such a way that trying to disentangle them would do violence to the thought. So, for instance, Augustine wrote a great deal on the nature of the will, but his views on the will are also integral to his position on the relation of faith to reason, his account of virtues and vices, his attempted refutation of Pelagianism, and a host of other issues. There is, then, ineluctably some overlap among the topics discussed in the chapters of this volume.

Augustine himself would certainly have put first, in importance to himself and to a philosophical comprehension of the world, an understanding of the nature of God and God's relations to the world. Consequently, after O'Donnell's introduction to Augustine's life and time, the volume opens with a series of chapters on philosophy of religion.

John Rist's chapter, "Faith and reason," examines Augustine's view of human reasoning and its relation to religious belief, which has been taken as a charter for Christian philosophy from Augustine's time to our own. Faith is an epistemic starting point, in Augustine's view, especially for religious truths, but it is not the ending point. The role of reason is to bring a person who believes to understand what he believes. Although faith is necessary for understanding, it is not sufficient; reason is necessary as well.

William E. Mann's chapter, "Augustine on evil and original sin," and James Wetzel's chapter, "Predestination, Pelagianism, and foreknowlege," examine Augustine's contribution to particular topics in philosophy of religion, including the problem of evil and the apparent incompatibility of divine foreknowledge with human free will. In the process, each chapter also touches on a variety of related topics. Mann examines Augustine's account of the nature of goodness and its relation to being; he also explains Augustine's interpretation of the doctrine of original sin, which plays a role in Augustine's understanding of the problem of evil. Wetzel considers Augustine's theory of divine knowledge, including knowledge of the temporal future, and he shows the connection between this theory and Augustine's position on two closely associated theological topics: divine predestination and the role of divine grace in human salvation.

The last chapter in this section, Thomas Williams's "Biblical interpretation," serves as a useful guide to Augustine's biblical commentaries and his exegetical theory. Augustine wrote a large number of biblical commentaries, and some of his most important philosophical and theological positions are hammered out in them. In addition, Augustine thought extensively about what it is to interpret a text, especially a text taken to constitute divine revelation, and his views on this subject are instructive not only for their approach to the subject of biblical interpretation but also for their contribution to the topic of hermeneutics.

The next three chapters are on metaphysics and theology. These are intimately connected for Augustine and cannot readily be separated from each other. This fact is made plain by the first chapter, Scott MacDonald's "The divine nature." As MacDonald explains, Augustine finds his way into Christianity by means of a certain metaphysics which is heavily indebted to Platonism. This metaphysics includes a ranking of natures, with matter nearer the bottom of the hierarchy and immaterial minds closer to the top. At the very top is the divine nature itself. God's nature is the foundation for all the others, not only because God is the creator of everything in the world, but also because God is the highest good and being itself.

Mary T. Clark's chapter, "De Trinitate," considers the way in which this metaphysics is interwoven with the specifically Christian doctrine of the Trinity. In the process of elucidating Augustine's interpretation of the doctrine, Clark also takes up various metaphysical issues, such as the concept of substance, which are foundational for Augustine's thought, as well as some elements in Augustine's philosophy of mind that he uses to illustrate his view of the relations among the persons of the Trinity.

Finally, Augustine's view of God as the atemporal creator of a temporal creation is at the heart of his philosophical theology, and Simo Knuuttila addresses this view of Augustine's in his chapter, "Time and creation in Augustine." Knuuttila explains Augustine's account of time and eternity, which was very influential in the later medieval period. He also discusses Augustine's understanding of various other divine attributes, including divine freedom, omnipotence, and omniscience. A certain theory of modality and its connection to the actualization of possibilities in time is crucial to this part of Augustine's thought as well, as Knuuttila brings out.

The next section, Augustine's philosophy of mind, begins with Roland Teske's "Augustine's theory of soul." Augustine accepted an account of the soul as intimately connected to the body and yet incorporeal and able to exist without the body. Augustine's views on this subject are influenced by Platonism; but, in his mature thought, he emphasizes that a human being is one substance constituted of body and soul. Teske also explores Augustine's speculations regarding the soul's origins, its creation and/or propagation, and its destiny after death.

The next chapter, my "Augustine on free will," is concerned with Augustine's struggle to understand the nature of the freedom to be found in the will. There is widespread controversy over this part of Augustine's thought, so much so that it is sometimes hard to believe the participants in the controversy can be reading the same texts of Augustine's. I argue that part of the problem stems from the fact that contemporary theories about free will have formed the lenses through which scholars have read Augustine's texts, and that these theories are inadequate to capture his position. For this reason, the chapter begins with a careful consideration of theories of freedom of the will in order to outline a theory not canvassed in contemporary philosophy but more illuminative of Augustine's position. With this theory in hand, it is possible to produce a more or less irenic compromise among competing interpretations of Augustine's account of free will.

The section concludes with Teske's chapter "Augustine's philosophy of memory." As Teske points out, it is not possible to present Augustine's theory of memory without bringing in his whole philosophy of mind, because for Augustine memory is intimately connected with all the other powers of the mind, including sense perception, intellectual cognition, and emotion or affection. Augustine is at pains to understand the way in which memory retains not only previously acquired information and previous experiences but also previously felt emotions; and he puzzles over the fact that it is possible, for example, to remember the experience of feeling joyful without feeling joyful while remembering. In his early work, he entertains the notion that memory preserves knowledge from a previous state of existence, but in the end he rejects this idea. Finally, the concept of memory is also important for Augustine's philosophical theology. The relations among the persons of the Trinity can be modeled, on Augustine's view, by considering the relations among human understanding, memory, and will; and the modeling elucidates Augustine's views of the mind as well as his interpretation of the doctrine of the Trinity.

The next section, Augustine's theory of knowledge, begins with Gerard O'Daly's "The response to skepticism and the mechanisms of cognition." O'Daly's chapter sets Augustine's views on human cognition in their historical context by showing how they developed in response to a kind of skepticism popular in his period. At an early point in his career, as he was becoming alienated from Manichaeism, Augustine gave serious consideration to the skepticism of the Academics, who held that nothing can be known for certain. Augustine's earliest surviving work is a dialogue that attempts to refute this Academic position, and he returned to the subject several times in later works. In the course of developing his position against skepticism, Augustine worked out his views about the way in which human cognitive faculties make contact with extra-mental reality and achieve knowledge of all sorts. His theory of sensation is based on the biology of his day, and it is surprisingly sophisticated.

Gareth B. Matthews's "Knowledge and illumination" focuses on Augustine's understanding of the nature of knowledge. Augustine's theory of knowledge is forged from different elements in his thought. His attempt to refute skepticism is certainly one; his struggle to understand language acquisition is another. In elucidating Augustine's account of perceptual knowledge, Matthews also examines Augustine's theory of sensation, but his conclusions are in disagreement with those of O'Daly. O'Daly argues for a claim that Matthews disputes, namely, that for Augustine the objects of perception are images of the objects perceived. One uncontroversial hallmark of Augustine's theory of knowledge is his insistence on the need for divine illumination. Matthews investigates the objects of divine illumination and Augustine's reasons for taking illumination to be requisite for knowledge.

For each of the remaining sections except the last, one contributor to the volume has taken on the task of expounding an entire area of Augustine's philosophy. Christopher Kirwan's essay "Augustine's philosophy of language" considers Augustine's view of the nature and uses of language. Kirwan argues that Augustine's theory of language is largely derivative, and he examines the extent to which Augustine's views were shaped by Stoic as well as Aristotelian theories of language. Augustine takes words to be signs, which are significative of things, although he is aware that there are different kinds of words and that some kinds of words do not readily fit this model. Kirwan also discusses Augustine's notion of an inner word and the role of an inner word in human communication through language.

Bonnie Kent undertakes the daunting job of examining Augustine's rich and complicated ethics. This part of his work includes his account of the nature of human beings and human happiness, and this topic in turn leads unavoidably into certain theological matters. Kent considers Augustine's much-discussed dictum that only God is to be loved for his own sake and other human beings are to be loved only for the sake of God. To contemporary readers, this line can sound as if Augustine were recommending that we treat human beings as means to some theological end, but Kent explains the line differently. On Augustine's theory of value, every created thing has the value it does, however great that value, only in relation to the Creator. An important part of Augustine's ethics is built around his recognition that the will can be divided against itself, and Kent shows the way in which Augustine struggled to reach a philosophical under-standing of conflict within the will. Augustine's philosophical understanding of the will is interwoven with his interpretation of such theological doctrines as original sin and what he takes to be the correct doctrine of grace and free will, and so Kent considers Augustine's controversy with the Pelagians in this context. The chapter concludes with a discussion of Augustine's theory of virtues and vices.

Paul Weithman's chapter, "Augustine's political philosophy," deals with those elements in Augustine's writings that make a contribution to what we now call political philosophy. Although Augustine did not write any treatise specifically in this area of philosophy, certain of his positions have been very influential in the history of political philosophy. In one or another philosophical or theologi-cal context, Augustine wrote about slavery, property, the nature of justice, the purposes of human government, the relations between Church and state, and the conditions for just war, among other such topics. His political theory is based on his foundational notion of the world as divided into the city of God and the earthly city, which are identifiable on the basis of the loves that move the people in them. Augustine's theory of the distinction between Christian and pagan virtues also plays a role in his theory of the two cities, and Weithman shows the way in which Augustine's rejection of pagan virtues is connected to his theolog-ical views of human happiness.

The final section is an exploration of Augustine's influence in the later medie-val period and afterwards. M. W. F. Stone's chapter, "Augustine and medieval phi-losophy," shows the variety of influences that Augustine had on philosophy in the Middle Ages. Boethius, Eriugena, Anselm, and philosophers important in the twelfth-century renaissance of Neoplatonic philosophy were all heavily indebted to Augustinian thought, not only for particular theological and philo-sophical positions but also for his advocacy of the role of reason in human understanding. Augustine is also often seen as the source of a thirteenth-century school of thought, popular especially among the Franciscans, which was hostile to the reception of Aristotle. Stone argues that this scholarly commonplace is in some ways a caricature of a much more complicated reality. As Stone points out, even such leading proponents of Aristotelianism as Albert and Aquinas fre-quently cite Augustine and take his views as authoritative. Stone goes on to con-sider the various attitudes taken towards Augustine's thought in the fourteenth century, where there is a distinctive neo-Augustinian movement, and in the early Reformation period, where Augustine was an important influence on humanist thinkers.

Matthews's "Post-medieval Augustinianism" concludes the volume with a discussion of Augustinian concepts and views (whether explicitly recognized as Augustinian or not) in modern philosophy. Matthews argues that Descartes was thoroughly Augustinian in his approach, particularly in his focus on a first-person perspective, as well as in certain of his philosophical views, such as his view of the mind. Malebranche was explicit about his debt to Augustine, especially for his theory of knowledge. Others, such as Grotius, were more influenced by Augustine's theory of just war. Leibniz acknowledged himself indebted to Augustine for certain views in philosophy of religion, including the problem of evil. Matthews goes on to canvass an array of other philosophers, including Mill, Berkeley, Wittgenstein, and Russell, arguing that in one respect or another these philosophers show the continuing power of Augustine's thought.

Augustine's thought is so rich and the scholarship on it is so diverse that capturing it adequately in one short volume is not possible. But the sixteen scholars whose work is presented in this volume have provided a stimulating contribution to our understanding of Augustine. Their chapters constitute a provocative next step in the on-going project of comprehending, critically assimilating, and making use of Augustine's deep and insightful legacy to Western philosophy.

NOTE

I am grateful to Scott MacDonald and Marjorie Woods for comments on an earlier draft of this introduction.

I

JAMES J. O'DONNELL

Augustine: his time and lives

Our knowledge of Augustine's world has transformed itself in the last generation. Ever since the work of Gibbon, at least, the fourth and fifth centuries had
been marginalized in the historical imagination even of specialists. Gibbon
described the decline of the Roman empire as "the triumph of barbarism and
religion" (in the form of Christianity). This was too good a story to disregard,
and the evidence was overwhelming and unambiguous.

But from the 1960s onward, the concept of "late antiquity," born earlier in the
century, was used to transform our grasp of the period. French Catholics, Italian
Marxists, and German philologists all had a part to play, but late antiquity's
most persuasive apologist and the real shaper of the revolution is the liminal
figure of Peter Brown – an Irish-born Protestant on whom, as an infant, the
emperor Haile Selassie laid ecclesiastically potent hands claiming descent from
Solomon. Brown made his mark as Augustine's biographer and leads, thirty
years later, the continuing reimagination of Augustine's age. The diversity of that
world and the ambiguity of its transformations are painted in richer and richer
colors, and with each few years new tracts of space and time are infused with
fresh vitality. The barbarians and the Christians of the age now appear to have
had more in common with each other and with their fellow Romans than we
once thought, and the many cultures of that Roman world now stand out in
greater and more differentiated relief.

Old conventionalisms about Augustine are quite true. He was born in the reign
of Constantius II, in a Roman world flea-bitten at its borders by outside armies
but fundamentally secure, and he died in the reign of Theodosius II in a part of
the empire that no longer recognized Constantinople's sway, in a city surrounded
by besieging armies that all agreed were "barbarian" in origin and that would
capture his city and his province shortly after his death. In the world of his youth,
it was still easy to imagine a world without Christianity; in the world of his old
age, it was beginning to be impossible to do so. Augustine continued to live in
the imaginary world of his youth and never fully realized the implications of a
Christianized society. He lived most of his life as a member of one religious

minority or another, and yet his writings have had wide influence among his followers in ages when they were in an unchallenged position of dominance.

Augustine's physical world was far smaller than the whole of the Roman empire. Apart from a few years in Italy in the 380s, he lived his life chiefly in three places: Tagaste, Hippo, and Carthage. His trips elsewhere in north Africa were few and limited. Though his words traveled widely, his spatial limitations are important to remember, not least because they kept him chiefly in the more urbanized and coastal north of Africa, away from the high plains and the frontier, away from the districts where a rougher form of life and perhaps a more native form of religion held sway.[1]

Augustine himself is a figure whose life we know too well.[2] He has offered us such a variety of materials, of such high quality, for reconstructing his life that it would be almost impossible not to use them, gratefully, to good advantage. But if we would use them, it is equally almost impossible not to use them to tell the story in the way he would have us tell it – and therein lies the danger.

The evidence of the danger lies in the biographies of Augustine, on large canvas or small, that accumulate in our libraries. In the case of Brown, fully 40% of the book is taken up with the narrative of Augustine's life before his ordination as bishop – before he achieved the position that made it possible for him to exercise a significant influence in his lifetime and after. Narratives of briefer compass regularly find it impossible to restrain the narrative of early life into even so little as 40% of their bulk.

The reason for this preoccupation is famously not far to seek. The *Confessions* are not, indeed, an autobiography in any useful sense of the word, as those of us who write on them regularly aver. But they contain autobiographical narrative and vignettes whose power no recounter of Augustine's life can resist. Consider the episode at the end of *Conf.* 2 in which Augustine tells how he and a few youthful friends stole pears from a neighbor's tree and threw them to the pigs. An hour at most, ten minutes more likely, in the life of a man who lived near half a million waking hours, but the episode is unavoidable, even for those (the majority of readers today) who are baffled or disapproving at finding the episode at all or at finding it made much of.

The *Confessions* are the chief instrument by which Augustine shaped the narratives of his life. The achievement of that self-presentation lies in the way the narrative is made to revolve around a defining moment of conversion, localized to a specific place and time and dramatized in a particular way. From infancy to age 18 and again from age 27 until his death, any reasonable person who knew Augustine and was asked his religious affiliation would have said "Christian." For the intervening nine years, many would still have said the same, while others would have named a group, the Manichees, that non-Christians would have distinguished from Christianity at large only with difficulty. And yet Augustine has persuaded us that the religious drama of the years 386–387, when he decided to accept Christian baptism at the hand of Ambrose, is the interpretive key to his whole life. The issue has generally been not whether he is right in the frame he gives his narrative, but rather whether we have adequately tested his narrative in detail at all points against the other facts.

But he is virtually our sole source of facts. Even those documents of Augustine's life that come from other pens usually reach us because he allowed them to. We have today some five million words from Augustine's pen, vastly more than we have from any of the famous writers of antiquity. None of that material survives against Augustine's will. Though from time to time we hear of scandalous accusations made against him, we hear of them only from him, or if he quotes them to take polemical advantage.

Augustine shaped his own survival with great care. Late in life[3] he compiled a catalogue of his own written works under the evasive title *Retractationes* ('Reconsiderations').[4] Each work was listed with some description of the circumstances of its composition and its purpose, as well as corrections or explanations of difficult or controversial passages. The work does not so much record changes of mind as dig defensive trenches around things said imprudently, or simply in a different spirit, when he was young. The result is a catalogue of Augustine's authentic works, reinforced by the survival of a hand-list from Augustine's library, written by his disciple and authorized biographer Possidius (bishop of Calama, not far from Hippo, and a lifelong follower of Augustine).[5] Possidius' list not only includes "books" but also lists sermons and letters. Augustine left for the afterlife with a vastly better than average chance that his works would survive, be collected, and be read as his. The survival of so much of what he wrote is extraordinary.[6] (At least we may be sure that the surviving books are his. Judicious skepticism will stand alongside piety in the presence of the relics of his body presented to view in Pavia.)

The purposes of the modern student of Augustine may best be served if we come to the personal core of his life from the outside, working in. Accordingly, this essay will present Augustine's life not as a conversion narrative but as the unfolding of a dazzling piece of origami. We will begin with the textual Augustine who lies heavy on our shelves, proceed through the public Augustine (or rather the several Augustines known to different publics in his lifetime), and come only at the end to the man and his ultimate self-presentation. Such an approach gives more value to the social context within which he worked and more value to his social interactions with others. It will remain an open question how far the imperial individualism that Augustine practices and implicitly teaches is a useful discipline, whether for self-presentation or for historical analysis.

Augustine's books range from the highly personal and polemical to the lofty and abstract, but even the loftiest and most abstract are charged with a clear idea about where error lies and how it is to be opposed. For modern philosophical readers, the most important titles are well known: *Confessiones*, *De civitate Dei*, *De Trinitate*, *De Genesi ad litteram libri duodecim*, and the brace of early works written during and after Augustine's post-conversion winter of 386/387 – *De Academicis* (also known as *Contra Academicos*), *De ordine*, *De beata vita*, *Soliloquia*, and *De libero arbitrio voluntatis*. Philosophers today generally quail before, but then reluctantly plunge into, the late works against the Pelagians, looking for but not often finding solid ground on which to assess Augustine's views on free will and predestination. But the most generous armload of accessible and interesting works, available in translation and regularly read today, still adds up to only a small fraction of the surviving œuvre. Least well represented in modern readings of Augustine are his letters (by happenstance of bulk and relative rebarbativeness – the annotation needed for each letter and its moment of pedagogy or polemic can be annoying) and his sermons (because of their bulk, running to approximately one-third of the surviving œuvre, and their short and scrappy focus on issues of pastoral urgency).

Augustine today, moreover, dances for us behind numerous veils. His Latin is correct and clear, but can be read effortlessly by few today. Accordingly, he penetrates contemporary thought in ways conditioned by the history of his translations, and there is no modern language that has yet seen a translation of his *complete* works.[7] The prestige of French scholarship on Augustine has been undoubtedly enhanced by the fact that French Augustinians published, beginning in the 1950s, an extraordinarily valuable series of editions of Augustine's works, with Latin text and French translation, accompanied by learned and helpful notes. They remain a vital path into Augustine's work and thought for serious readers, even while they implant in those readers a style of interpretation characteristic of that particular Paris.

Augustine's books are for the most part today presented to us by those in the contemporary world who see themselves as his co-religionists. Modern Augustinian scholarship was in its formative decades overwhelmingly baptized, and indeed baptized Roman Catholic. It remains extraordinary that a provincial religious writer and churchman of sixteen centuries ago should be so fortunate as to have his works presented to our world by a relatively homogeneous and sympathetic body of interpreters. Here again, as with the *Confessions*, we know him too well. If we could forget that he is "Christian," and if we could forget the story he tells us of his own life, what would we think of him?

Here is one way to answer that question. Who was Augustine to his contemporaries in his lifetime? Beyond a circle of friends and colleagues, he came to public attention in a series of roughly concentric or at least overlapping circles.

Augustine the bane of "Pelagianism"

This Augustine was known farthest and widest, beginning in the early 410s, when he was nearing 60. This renown was both good and bad for him, in that it propagated his name but won him influential and ferocious enemies. He ended his life in a futile and dispiriting literary combat with a learned Christian bishop from Italy, Julian of Eclanum, with whom he sparred endlessly before a Christian literary public on all Latin-speaking shores of the Mediterranean. At the end of his life, his reputation had penetrated erratically into the Greek Church and an invitation was sent for him to attend the council of Ephesus – but he had died before it could reach him in Africa.

The controversy in which Augustine found this fame was largely factitious. The "Pelagianism" that he attacked was a construct of his own, founded on his imputations of implications and logical conclusions to a writer who disowned most of them. When Pelagius was himself examined for his beliefs by a relatively independent and unbiased ecclesiastical court, in Palestine in 415, he came away vindicated.[7] Augustine could not accept this and pounded away for a few years more on Pelagius himself, winning the Pyrrhic victory of papal approval for some of his own condemnations. The victory backfired when, in his last decade, Augustine found himself under fire for it from the doctrinaire Julian (who was willing to accept some of the conclusions that Pelagius himself shied from), and from devout Christian ascetics to whose belief and practice Augustine would have ordinarily been closely attuned. These last (some of them in Africa, rather more in Gaul) saw defeatism in Augustine's ideas and feared that his view of predestination denied value to their ascetic achievements. Although Augustine's most extreme ideas were hotly confuted in these circles, he himself was rarely condemned as a heretic and his opponents were strikingly reluctant to mention him by name, so great was the prestige he had created for himself.

Augustine the literary lion

That prestige had come in good measure from long years of assiduous literary self-promotion. Beginning in the early 390s, while not yet himself a bishop, Augustine had carefully built for himself a choice audience of readers for his works beyond his homeland. Though his works doubtless circulated in Hippo and Carthage, we know he had found ways of bringing them to the attention of distinguished literary Christians elsewhere. Paulinus of Nola, in particular, a retired Christian gentleman in Italy, poet and literary man, seems to have been one conduit for Augustine's reputation and for his works themselves.[9] More strikingly, we have a fairly full record of Augustine's correspondence with Jerome in Bethlehem, showing a fierce but repressed competition of egos between the two ambitious men.[10] Though Jerome was a clergyman of the second rank, he had carved out a position of authority based on his learning and his status as impassioned and persuasive writer. Augustine came on the scene years after Jerome and set out to achieve a similar kind of reputation. Writing to Jerome in the early 390s was a way of calling himself to the older writer's attention and entering into the literary public that Jerome dominated. Over the years that followed, Augustine's books became well known outside Africa in upper-class Christian circles.

His time in those circles led to one of his two most famous and lasting books, *De civitate Dei*.[11] The ostensible point of departure of that work is "pagan" reaction to the sack of Rome by Visigoths in 410 AD and the learned debates of upper-class refugees in Carthage. What if, so they supposedly argued, the fate of the city of Rome is due to our impiety toward the ancient gods and to our adhesion to the new Christian god? Should we perhaps revive ancient practices? Augustine overwhelms those arguments in the first five books of *De civitate Dei*, which he wrote within a couple of years of the controversy's eruption, but he then continued for another decade and more to add another 17 books to the work, going far beyond what the moment of controversy called for. The work in the end outlines a large view of human history, from creation to apocalypse, and situates Roman, and indeed all Mediterranean, history within that perspective. It refutes every form of "paganism" that Augustine cared about, but chiefly the Neoplatonism that he understood from what he knew of Plotinus and Porphyry. The style of the first books shows that Augustine could play the part of the learned traditionalist to a fare-thee-well and take pleasure in using a pastiche of quotations from the most classical of Latin authors to demolish the pretensions of Roman religion.

Augustine the anti-Donatist

Augustine's most widely known public persona, however, was one that requires a distinct effort of historical construction for us today. Augustine the anti-Pelagian has been made current to many following generations by the timelessness of the debates over grace and free will that he instigated and guided. Augustine the anti-"pagan" makes a case against a straw man enemy that moderns understand readily, so familiar are we with the glib juxtaposition of "pagans" and Christians in the Roman world.[12]

But Augustine the anti-Donatist is a figure who has spoken directly only to a few moderns and, I venture to suggest, to none of our contemporaries. The most notable example of a modern resonating with Augustine on these points is Newman, who quoted a line of Augustine's directed against the Donatists as though it were his own mantra of conversion.

Augustine found the widest (if not always receptive) public for his writing and speaking as an opponent of Donatism.[13] He surely spent more of his energies as bishop of Hippo on this one issue than on all the other controversies of his career combined. After the last wave of official persecution of Christianity in the early 300s had ebbed, Christians in North Africa fell into two camps. To name them is to take sides, but perhaps one may characterize them as rigorist and latitudinarian. The rigorist camp held that those who had in any way compromised the ferocity of their Christian allegiance in time of persecution had thereby exiled themselves from the Christian community and required sacramental initiation in order to re-enter. Particular hostility was directed towards clergy who had handed over the books of scripture to the Roman authorities to be burnt. *Traditores* ("traitors," lit. handers-over) they were called, and they were thought to have disqualified themselves as clergy by that act. Ordinary faithful who had fallen in similar ways were to be rebaptized, and clergy, if such there were, who had fallen and sought clerical status again would have to be reordained.

The latitudinarian camp took no less harsh a view of the betrayals of the time, but took a higher view of the sacraments of the Church. Baptism could only be administered once for all. If you lapsed from grace after baptism, then only by a tedious ritual of repentance could you, in principle, be readmitted to communion. This may not sound latitudinarian, indeed is in some ways even more rigorist in theory than the other position, but in practice this community pursued lapses with less fervor and was more inclined to let bygones be bygones.

To make matters more complicated, the whole fourth century in Africa was punctuated by arguments over who the *traditores* had really been. Had the first bishops of the post-persecution latitudinarians really been themselves *traditores*? Or on the other hand (as was alleged, with good evidence), had the leaders of the rigorist faction themselves included some who had fallen away and never been rebaptized? Each side accused the other of bad faith and bad behavior at every level, most persuasively.

But the rigorist faction inherited the traditions and practices of the church of Africa, and throughout the fourth century it dominated African life, despite numerous attempts by the latitudinarian party to invoke imperial authority against it. When Augustine became priest and then bishop at Hippo, he was a member of the minority community there. Moderns debate the social roots of both communities, cautiously concluding that the rigorists were more broadly planted in African society at a variety of levels (including the highest), while the latitudinarians tended to be confined to the more Romanized and urbanized segments of society.

Augustine made it his business as bishop of Hippo to fight for the latitudinarians against the rigorists – hence for the "catholic" Church (he uses the adjective in its root meaning of "universal", and he made much of the fact that *his* church was in communion with churches all over the Roman world) against the "Donatists" (so-called after a charismatic founding figure). He made common cause with Aurelius, his faction's bishop in Carthage, and for twenty years they were a tireless team, working together for the defeat of their opponents. Augustine wrote book after book, and together they pulled every lever of government influence. Eventually they prevailed by the latter route, when the emperor sent a commissioner to convene a hearing and resolve the issue. The commissioner, Marcellinus, was a devout layman who immediately fell in with Augustine. There was never any doubt at the conference, held in the baths at Carthage in June of 411 (we have the stenographic transcript of most of the three days of the conference), that he would find for Augustine's catholic party, and he did so. From that day onward, "Donatism" had no legal standing in Africa and effectively vanished from history.

In all this period, Augustine often spent half his year in Carthage, preaching, writing, and debating against the Donatists. Those audiences saw a learned and fluent preacher with a taste for the kind of debater's tricks of language and argument that audiences loved. They knew about his books and they knew about his influence with powerful people, and some of them encountered those books and that influence more directly. But he was pre-eminently a public and visible figure. Augustine always traveled reluctantly, but he took his anti-Donatist persona on the road from time to time, debating with Donatist leaders and seeking converts. When he came to one or another small city, it was very much as a publicly recognized visiting dignitary, absorbed in the high politics of the moment. Many of those who knew him this way loathed him as a powerful figure in a party they abhorred, but such is the pathology of celebrity that the loathing was part of his power. This Augustine reached the most people, however superficially, and this Augustine shaped the impressions of Africans about all the other Augustines.

Augustine at Hippo

For all that Augustine made himself known to a wider world through his writings and his involvement in the affairs of the day, he still spent more of his time, from 391 until his death in 430, at home in Hippo than anywhere else. There he invented and struggled to define his role as bishop and leader of his community and there he performed the sacramental acts in which he and his followers believed that divine power flowed through his hands. (He tried to be in Hippo every year for the most sacred rituals of Easter, when new members were initiated to the community and received baptism.) He appeared serene before his congregation as they stood, row on row, straining to hear his voice. It troubled him that they venerated him so, for he was acutely aware of his own failings – even to the point of what later churchmen would call scrupulosity. Did he delight to a fault in the beautiful music of the church service? When his mind wandered from prayer, did he return to the task promptly *enough*? He judged himself against a high standard and found himself wanting, and so felt unworthy in the eyes of his congregation. The writing of the *Confessions* was, among many other things, an attempt at self-understanding that would permit him to continue as bishop with this acute consciousness of imperfection.[14]

But it is unlikely that Augustine's congregation shared his sense of those imperfections. To them he was a hieratic figure, dispenser of God's word and God's sacrament, but judge and jury as well. In increasing numbers, they came to him, divinely authorized and reliable, to settle their petty legal cases, in an age when Roman justice was more remote, more expensive, and more unreliable than ever. He expressed his frustration at the time he spent on this kind of business and finally, in his early seventies, designated a successor in order to hand over the worldly business of the bishopric so that he, Augustine, could retire to his study and his studies.

Those studies took place in a privileged space that Augustine carved out for himself. It is conventional but anachronistic to call it a "monastery": Augustine used the word *monasterium* a few times, specifically to speak of the little community he created in Hippo, but the word was so new and he used it so infrequently that it must have rung far more strangely on his contemporaries' ears than it does on ours. The word and the thing would have been unfamiliar: a household of men without women, men without social status (or at least without property), dressed in a way that set them apart, pursuing activities of marginal social value – study and prayer. The ethos of the ascetic who separated himself from civil society was still a novelty in Africa, and the choice to set himself apart in *this* way from civil society made Augustine relatively unusual among clergy of the time. Augustine's choices in Hippo made him more visible and better known and at the same time more remote than a more conventional cleric would have been.

The young Augustine

Augustine came to Hippo when he was almost 37 years old. He lived another 39 years and from that period come most of the five million words that survive of his œuvre for us. Half the ordinary life of a man on this earth he passed before he came to the city where he would make his lasting reputation. It is that half of his life that he tells us about in his *Confessions,* and about which we know less than we know about the later years.

For the years in Hippo, from 391 to his death in 430, are amply attested in his own voice, year by year, in his letters, sermons, and books. And in many ways such a self-presentation is more reliable than the retrospective and self-serving narrative of the *Confessions*. We know by name, moreover, no contemporary reader of the *Confessions* who was persuaded by its narrative.[14] (In the *Retractationes* [2.6, ed. Mutzenbecher] Augustine suggests that there were other readers who thought the book a great success, but he does not tell us their names and we have no way to interrogate them.) Of most interest are the two readers, one a Manichee, the other a member of a small sect that broke off from the Donatists, who both knew Augustine when he was a young man on the make. He recalls himself as a libertine: they recall him as a prig.[16] Augustine's narrative leaves them unmoved.

Can we recover a true narrative of Augustine's early years? No. The most we can do is hold to the elements of his narrative that are most likely to have been verifiable to his contemporaries. No reader will long resist the power of the *Confessions*, but for as long as we can maintain it, resistance is far from futile. What do we learn if we resist?

Augustine was born on the margins of gentility. To the poor, he was an aristocrat, to aristocrats, he was a scion of a provincial, down-at-heel family. His father had connections who were wealthier and who could be drawn upon shamelessly to support, for example, the son's education. One scholar has astutely seen, indeed, in the way Augustine's father pressed to find resources for his son's education what he calls a "Balzacian novel before its time": a family that chose to invest heavily in the education of one precocious older son (there were at least two other children, one son and one daughter) in whose career the whole family would advance.[17]

Because Augustine invests the story of his schooling with philosophical and religious narrative (reading Cicero he somehow falls among the Manichees, and he is reading Cicero again 15 years later when he is about to fall among the orthodox Christians), modern readers linger over the personal side of the story and pay little attention to the familial. In brief, the story is that Augustine left home at a very early age to pursue his schooling, pursuing it eventually with vigor and success all the way to Carthage. A year's rustication in his home town as a teacher was prologue to a bright near-decade teaching in Carthage and then a daring leap first to Rome and then to Milan to seek the heights of his profession. No sooner did he land, on his feet, in Milan, exalted at the age of 30 as imperial professor of rhetoric, called on to deliver formal court panegyrics and with every hope of a political career, than his whole family – his mother, his brother, his sister, and at least one or two other junior relatives and hangers-on – turned up in Milan, looking to hitch their wagons to his star. Their hopes began with, but were not limited to, a lucrative governorship. Had he ascended higher still, the profit for his retinue would have multiplied itself.

But in Milan Augustine's philosophical and religious interests derailed his self-interest. Controversy has raged for a century and more about just what happened in Milan and, since we have only Augustine's retrospective and self-serving narrative of a decade later to go by, we are unlikely to achieve certainty. He came under the influence of bishop Ambrose[18] and became convinced that his own personal well-being depended on abandoning a worldly career and devoting himself to God in a special way – not just joining the Christian Church (though he did that formally in Milan in 387, taking baptism at the hands of Ambrose) but renouncing the life of the flesh and in particular abandoning the quite ordinary sexual life he had led with one quite respectable common-law wife (and mother of his child) and then with a somewhat less respectable "mistress" (the term is anachronistic: he took up temporarily with a lower-status woman when he was engaged to a higher-status fiancée). Nothing about Christianity required him to abandon sexual activity in order to be baptized, but Augustine sought something higher: the life of a Christian philosopher, separate and distinct from the ordinary run of Christian and excelling the most ascetic and ethereal of non-Christian philosophers.

Having made this choice of celibacy and science in the fall of 386, not yet baptized, Augustine took his household to the country for the winter – there perhaps to test his sexual resolve in a setting less tempting than the cosmopolitan capital, and there certainly to pursue his philosophical studies. From those months at the country estate of Cassiciacum we have the earliest books surviving from his pen, dialogues written (and indeed enacted by himself and his friends and family) in a consciously Ciceronian vein. The first of them, *De Academicis* (usually and wrongly titled *Contra Academicos*), takes up the radical skepticism to which Cicero himself was more than tempted and finds in it the basis for a mystical philosophy of Christianity. Certain knowledge is impossible, Augustine accepts from the Academics, and so one must give oneself over in faith to the fount of true knowledge who is (as it is revealed on the last pages of an otherwise quite secular book) Christ.

The philosophy to which Augustine gave himself at this moment in his life was one he eagerly sought in later years to assimilate to orthodox Christianity. Believing that Christianity could rival the ancients in every way, Augustine pursued a philosophy that got its doctrine from scripture, interpreted that doctrine in the light of Plotinus, and hedged it around with mystical expectations that mixed Plotinian intellectualism[19] and ritual purification. To us today, this particular mixture of ideas is difficult to grasp and seems remote and artificial, but to Augustine it was indeed the new-age religion and philosophy for a truly elite intellectual of his time, more appealing even than Manichaeism – his first new-age enthusiasm – had been.

And so it made perfect sense that he retired from his public career, retired from Milan, and went back home to become a more refined version of his father. He settled in Tagaste, the little town he came from, residing on the family property there, discharging the obligations of a gentleman and pursuing a life of philo-sophical leisure, writing contentious books and exchanging letters with like-minded friends. There he stayed for three years, from 388 to 391.

Why Augustine ever left Tagaste we will never know. The assumption of pious biographers has always been that his religious interests were consistent and per-sistent and that it was chance that took him in 391 to Hippo where chance again seized him and made him a clergyman: for so he tells the story himself, to the congregation at Hippo 35 years later.[20] But it is remarkable that he did not leave the isolation of Tagaste and did not think of accepting a life elsewhere until after his son had died – until, that is, the worldly hopes of his family had been extin-guished and until there was no son to whom to leave the property he had himself inherited from his father. Only with his son's death was Augustine properly root-less, only then eligible to take up easily the disconnected life of the monk.

Even then, he seems to have resisted. A letter by Augustine to his new super-ior, Valerius the bishop of Hippo, was clearly written a few months after his ordi-nation – forced ordination to hear him tell it – at Hippo. It seems to be a letter of request to Valerius for permission to spend some time away from Hippo pur-suing the study of scripture.[21] Modern readers have seen in this the devoted and studious Augustine of whom they are fond, casting a fresh eye on the Christian scriptures he was now bound to obey and preach. But there are several odd things about the letter, and a more credible interpretation would see it as a piece of politic revisionism. The subtext is this: seized and ordained a priest at Hippo, Augustine's natural impulse had been to flee, and he followed that impulse back to Tagaste. Once there, regretting his choice, perhaps fearing divine retribution, he wrote the letter to his bishop (to whom he would not have needed to *write* this request if both were in Hippo, and if there were no reason for a public declara-tion about his whereabouts and activities), putting a good face on what he has done and thus implicitly promising to return. And return he did, to become the Augustine of history. It could have been otherwise.

But even if that speculation about reluctance is ill-founded, it is worth under-lining just how much the Augustine of 387–391, the man who had abandoned his worldly career and returned to Africa, was ready to disappear from view as a mild-mannered country squire with philosophical and literary interests. The role of a Paulinus of Nola is the most to which he might have aspired there, and nothing in his literary product of those years suggests that he would have had even that renown. It was only with his clerical ordination that he took up epis-tolary utensils to enter the eye of a broader Christian literary public, and only with the *Confessions* that he succeeded in producing work of a sort that would merit broad and lasting attention. Augustine of Tagaste in 390 is one of the great might-have-been-a-has-beens of world history, his father's son in more ways than one.

The Augustine of the *Confessions*

But if we trace the Augustines whom his contemporaries knew – the bishop known for his books, the bishop known for his politics, the bishop known by his flock, and the young man who disappeared from view when the clergyman appeared – it must be admitted that the Augustine of the *Confessions* does not disappear from history. Augustine the son of Monica, Augustine the confessor, is one of the greatest creations of self-presentation that our literary past has to offer. And he holds and shapes the attention of readers more than the historical Augustine ever could.

The Augustine of the *Confessions* can be spoken of in various almost-too-familiar ways. He invents (if Marcus Aurelius did not already invent it) a textual self whose interiority is not only on public display but seems to be the chief object of the narration. Events of past life are recounted and circumstances of present life are examined in order to reveal the inner man. But who is speaking in this narrative? Is it the inner man himself? Or is the inner man the object of attention of some subject lurking more deeply within the person? To ask those questions is to enter into the spirit of the book almost too wholeheartedly. At any rate, he provides a model, unexampled in antiquity and unrivaled until at least Aelred of Rievaulx (and perhaps we must wait for Pascal or Montaigne), of self-presentation through meditative analysis of thoughts, emotions, and memories in a swirling and impressionistic dance of words. The ease with which twentieth-century readers have leapt to their Freudian task, quite sure that Augustine's narrative of his relations with his mother offers the key to his character, is a sign of the power of the text. A conscientious analyst would recognize this text not as the unself-conscious revelation that the Freudian couch seeks to elicit but rather as something closer to the first narrative that the anlaysand tells, defensive and disarming, diverting and deceiving, on entering the analysts's care. Breaking down that narrative and finding insight is a task that still remains to be done.[22]

A central feature of the narrative lies in Augustine's creation of himself as a man driven by philosophy, persuadable by Cicero's dictum (*De finibus bonorum et malorum* 1.2.3) that the true student of philosophy never goes by half-measures but pursues truth relentlessly and endlessly. He shows us that philosophical urge turned into Christian faith but still undiminished, and generations of intellectualizing Christians have found comfort and example in that. The philosopher's Augustine takes three particular directions from the *Confessions*.

First, it is the book of memory. Book 10 of the *Confessions* famously divagates into a consideration of memory and its workings that has been widely influential if curiously under-studied throughout modern philosophical history.[23] Augustine blends metaphors of space and of interiority in a persuasive and vivid portrayal of a huge and capacious hall, rich in furnishings, and yet so vast that valuable contents often go missing, contained in memory but somehow not present. Memory, moreover, seems at times in that account almost to *become* the self, and many readers find this persuasive – we are the concatenation of our own experiences, present to ourselves. There are grave difficulties for Augustine's view to be derived from cognitive psychology, but he remains so sympathetic a figure that we forgive him his difficulties and admire his imagination.

Second, the *Confessions* are the book of time. The eleventh book no less famously pursues the question of a definition of time through scriptural and Plotinian byways, ending with a definition of time as a "distension of the mind" – a strikingly mentalistic reading. Here too, Augustine is quoted, admired, and rarely criticized directly – so great is his prestige.[24]

Third, and in a different vein, the *Confessions* provides a narrative within which to read the self-indulgent and sometimes pretentious dialogues of Cassiciacum – *De Academicis, De beata vita, De ordine* – and the associated works, especially *Soliloquia* and the fragmentary and frustrating *De immortalitate animae*. In the winter after his determination to renounce sexual activity once for all, Augustine and his students, friends, and family retired to a country villa to re-create Ciceronian philosophical leisure. They read Virgil of a morning, and of an afternoon would play-act the philosophical dialogue. The books report that stenographers took down their every word and swear that the texts represent debate as it really was. Modern readers have doubted that dialogue could naturally have unfolded so neatly, but omit to recognize (1) that the dialogues are carefully-sewn-together segments of conversation – out of several months' residence in the country, barely two weeks of time turn up represented in the texts of these works; and (2) that the people who participated in these dialogues were quite consciously playing parts, recreating Cicero's Tusculum, whose texts they knew only too well. The books remain interesting as sophisticated readings and reapplications of Ciceronian thought and method in a Christianizing context. If nothing else from Augustine survived, these texts would be minor classics, of the order of the works of Minucius Felix or the emperor Julian, but the fact of Augustine's later career and the persuasive reading offered for them by the *Confessions* have given them a special place as charter texts in Augustine's way of thinking. For all that they were written by an unbaptized rhetorician going through a bout of something approaching depressive withdrawal, they loom large in modern readers' attention to Augustine because of their authorized place in the autobiographical narrative.

The Augustine of the *Confessions* has also given rise in modern times to the most lasting and ferocious of quarrels over his philosophical ancestry and affiliation. The text of the *Confessions* explicitly tells us of his discovery of the "books of the Platonists" in Milan in 385 and the powerful influence those books exercised. Now, the text in which the discovery is reported tells us with no apology that what Augustine thought he found in those books was identical with the content of the first words of John's Gospel.[25] There are various ways to interpret that assertion, but behind it clearly lie some distinct acts of reading. Particularly since Pierre Courcelle's epoch-making book of 1950, much modern Augustinian scholarship has concentrated on identifying the nature of those books and the time and place of Augustine's various readings of them (presumably, at the outset, under the influence of Ambrose).[26] After a half-century of scholarship, debate still rages. There are two chief questions:

1. What did he read and when did he read it? The "what" question centers on the proportions of Platonic material that came to Augustine in the words of Plotinus and of Porphyry. Given that Augustine read the texts in Latin translations that had to be (given the difficulty of the Greek originals) exceedingly difficult and frustrating, finding the exact mix of Plotinus and Porphyry has been impossible. (Since Porphyry was Plotinus' disciple, biographer, editor, and abridger – in the work under his own name called "Sentences" – it is also likely that Augustine found some things that *he* thought were Plotinian but that were in fact Porphyrian.) The "when" question tries to trace Augustine's readership through 385 and 386 most closely, but is also concerned to know what later readings, particularly of Porphyry, occurred. The Augustine of 386 seems not to have known that Porphyry had notoriously written "Against the Christians" – a work lost to the intolerance of his enemies. By about 399, Augustine seems to have discovered Porphyry's hostility, and that becomes a leitmotif of his later discussions of Platonism, notably those in Books 8–10 of the *De civitate Dei*.

2. A different kind of debate has centered on Augustine's reception of Plotinian ideas and has pitted scholars against one another. Robert O'Connell, S.J., has held out *contra mundum* for over a generation for the position that Augustine was through most of his life a crypto-Plotinian, espousing a doctrine of the soul that he received from Neoplatonism according to which the souls of human beings had entered matter by a "fall" from the purity of uncorporeal existence. Human life was hence a struggle to free the soul of corporeality. A broader consensus of scholars holds that Augustine's frequent protestations of his inability to determine an answer to the question of the soul's origin can be taken at face value. O'Connell's story requires us to complicate the traditional narrative of conversion with an inner conflict of lingering attachment to a central piece of unconverted doctrine through the years of Augustine's public profession as bishop. To be sure, Augustine is noticeably marked as he grows older by his fear of his own past, and he externalizes that fear: he attacks the Platonists in *De civitate Dei* and then strikingly turns his quarrel with Julian of Eclanum into a reprise of his attack on the Manichees. The last

words of the last book Augustine wrote – was working on when he fell ill to die – are part of a slanging match in which Augustine and Julian take turns accusing the other of crypto-Manichaeism.[27] O'Connell's view suggests bad conscience about Plotinus: a minority view, but one that needs to be given serious attention.

What other Augustines are there yet undiscovered? I will close by suggesting that there are two, at least.

The first may perhaps just be coming into view. This is the Augustine who revealed himself at vast length in his letters and sermons, texts which constitute over 45% of the bulk of his surviving works. These texts have been mined for facts that fit the pre-determined structure of biographical narrative, but have received far too little attention for their literary and philosophical content. Some new studies have begun to take these texts seriously, but it is striking that even these still tend to come from European Catholic scholars essentially accepting the portrait we have received. The impetus from the new Divjak letters and Dolbeau sermons (see note 6) will prove most fruitful if it broadens to include reconsideration of these long-known but under-studied masses of text.

The second Augustine I have tried to sketch here, one whose life is not defined by the narrative he himself supplies. This Augustine does not succeed in imposing his interiority upon us, does not succeed in making his own interpretation of his religious history the armature of everything we are to know about him. We cannot escape from the Augustine of the *Confessions*, but we owe him and ourselves the effort to see him in other lights, to find other ways of reading his narrative. When we do, he becomes less the extraordinary figure who wrote dazzling books and more readily understood as a man of his time and place. In important ways, this then makes it easier to give proper respect to the thinker and the writer.

Beyond and behind even those Augustines was a man whose privacy we never penetrate. His earliest biographer closed with an account of the dying Augustine asking to have the seven penitential psalms written out and posted on the walls of his chamber, then asking to be left alone with those sobering words for his last hours and days.[28] Many structures of interpretation could be erected around such a report, but we should not fail to see the image presented, of an old man who knows he is dying, choosing to be alone with words that come from his God and that tell him insistently, and that are meant to let him tell himself, how far he falls short of divinity. Our last impression of Augustine is of a man who never made things easy for himself.

NOTES

1 Perler 1969 is a meticulous guide to Augustine's movements and evokes some of the flavor of his Africa.

2 For readers seeking to consult this essay as a source of information or to refresh memories, I supply here a few key dates in Augustine's life.

13 November 354: born at Tagaste. Parents Patricius and Monica.

360s–370s: studied at Madauros and Carthage, taught at Tagaste, then at Carthage again; while in Carthage, his father died and Augustine took a common-law wife and had a child.

384: pursued his teaching career to Rome, thence in the same year to Milan.

386/87: abandoned teaching career, produced first surviving literary works, was baptized, and determined to return to Africa, and did so in 388. Monica died while he was in Italy.

388–391: lived life of gentleman of literary and philosophical leisure at Tagaste; death of his son.

391: was pressed into service as *presbyter* (roughly = "priest") of the church of Hippo Regius.

395/96: ordained bishop of Hippo.

397: *Confessions*.

411: final public defeat of Donatism; beginning of work on *City of God* and beginning of Pelagian controversy.

28 August 430: died at Hippo.

Brown 1967 is so masterly a narrative that I have annotated only specific references and matters where Brown's book might not serve as an adequate guide. The freshest recent recounting of Augustine's life is Wills 1999, with especially fresh and effective translations from Augustine. I have written at length on many of the issues here in my commentary on the *Confessions* (O'Donnell 1992).

3 But he had been thinking about it for 15 years: *Ep.* 143.2–3.

4 Englished as *Retractations*, trans. Bogan 1968.

5 Never translated to my knowledge; Latin text available in *Miscellanea Agostiniana* 1930, 2.149–233.

6 In the last two decades, two precious finds have added to the corpus. Johannes Divjak brought to light over two dozen letters never before published and François Dolbeau a like number of sermons. The best approach to the new letters is Divjak 1987, in the series "Bibliothèque Augustinienne," vol. 46B, with text, French translation, and notes; English translation by Eno 1989. The sermons have been published as Dolbeau 1996; translated by Hill (1997).

7 The French Bibliothèque Augustinienne (described in the text here: now published by the Institut des Etudes Augustiniennes in approximately four dozen volumes) has come closest, but is now being rivaled by the English "A Translation for the Twenty-First Century," under the general editorship of John Rotelle, OSA; but both sets are far from complete at the present writing.

8 On this period and the gap between Augustine's imagination and Pelagius' teachings, see Wermelinger 1975.

9 Courcelle 1963, 559–607.

10 Hennings 1994.

11 Dyson 1998 is the newest version; Brown 1967, 287–329, is still the best introduction to the circumstances of writing.

12 That familiarity lubricates our reading of *De civitate Dei*: a little less familiarity might bring greater understanding, howbeit at the price of greater effort. The notion of "pagan," making no sense except as a Christian theological category, hurries us

into thinking in ways quite alien to the period. See O'Donnell 1979.

13 Frend 1985 is still the best connected narrative of the sect's history, but is marked by a certain partisanship that must be kept in mind.

14 Books 10–13 of the *Confessions* (see O'Donnell 1992 passim) show Augustine struggling with the role he had undertaken and the inadequacies he felt.

15 The skeptics represent the breadth of Augustine's polemical opponents: Secundinus the Manichee (object of Augustine's *Contra Secundinum*), Pelagius (described reacting to *Conf.* 10 at *De dono persev.* 20.53), Vincent the Rogatist (*Ep.* 93.13.51), and Julian of Eclanum.

16 The Manichee was Secundinus (*Epistula Secundini* 3 – transmitted with Augustine's *C. Secundinum*), the renegade Donatist Vincent (see previous note).

17 Lepelley 1987.

18 McLynn's *Ambrose of Milan* (1994) is a first-rate study and in many ways the best new book on *Augustine* in many years.

19 Augustine wrote, in the habit of that period, books of the "liberal arts" during that winter and spring of 387, books meant to purify the mind from earthly matters by showing it the eternal patterns through which one could ascend from language to number to the heavens and then to peace beyond. See Hadot 1984.

20 *Sermon* 355.

21 *Ep.* 21.

22 On the Freudian reading and misreading of the *Confessions* and of Augustine, see O'Donnell 1992, 1.xxx–xxxi, esp. n. 32. The best modern essay on the topic is Fredriksen 1978.

23 See O'Daly 1987.

24 See Meijering 1979 and Sorabji 1983.

25 *Conf.* 7.9.13, and see O'Donnell 1992 *ad loc.*

26 Courcelle 1950; see O'Donnell 1992 on *Conf.* 7.9.13 for a summary of the issues.

27 *Contra Julianum opus imperfectum* 6.41.

28 Possidius, *Vita Augustini* 31.

2

JOHN RIST

Faith and reason

"Since the blindess of our minds is so great, by reason of the excesses of our sins, and the love of the flesh . . .
They try to overcome the most stable foundation of the well-established Church by the name and appeal of apparent reasoning."

(*Ep.* 118.5.32)

If there is a God, it is possible that he cannot be known by our reason. If reason could attain to religious truths, faith would be unnecessary. If faith is needed, reason is somehow inadequate. But why? Either because the human mind cannot comprehend the mysteries of God in whole or in part, so that (at least some) religious truths – such as the Resurrection or the Day of Judgment, according to Augustine (*De vera relig.* 8.14, cf. *De Trin.* 4.16.21) – are inaccessible to unaided reason; or because such truths cannot be demonstrated and can only be shown to be more or less plausible or possible; or because our minds are now damaged and need to be habituated – by faith, by the practice of the virtues or by both – to reason more effectively, and above all not merely to rationalize.

Augustine normally holds that in this life we can know a certain amount about God by reason alone, but not enough for happiness and salvation;[1] that our consequent need for faith, that is for true belief, in matters of religion can be compared with our need for – and reliance on – *belief* in other areas of our lives; and that our weakened capacity to reason, and consequent ignorance, must be explained as a result of the original sin of "Adam."

Three problems can be immediately identified. First, it is misleading to see Augustine directly engaged with the problem of faith *versus* reason, since he normally discusses the relationship between reason and authority.[2]

Secondly, in a late text, Augustine defines believing as "thinking with assent,"[3] but since this formulation represents his standard position, we can ask – without fear of producing a false synthesis of his views – what he means by "assent," examining in particular the relationship between willing, wanting, loving, intending, and determining, and hence his understanding of the "will" (*voluntas*). Finally, since Augustine thinks within a tradition going back to Plato, we must consider the relationship between Augustinian "faith" and Platonic "belief," since in Augustine's view – but not in Plato's – faith (a variety of belief) seeks and understanding finds (*De Trin.* 15.2.2).

The modern problem of faith *versus* reason – as developed since the seventeenth century – is part of a discussion of the nature of philosophy itself, hence the concern whether Augustine should even be called a philosopher – or whether, despite his description of Christianity as a philosophy,[4] he ceased to be a philosopher when he converted. The modern problem is supposed to arise because philosophy, exclusively concerned with argument and argued conclusions, can allow no room for faith and authority, while Augustine holds that the philosophers fail to recognize the limits of reason and, from his conversion, gives authority a certain priority: he tells us (*C. Acad.* 3.20.43) that he will never depart from the authority of Christ, but that he will investigate his beliefs with the most sophisticated reasoning in the hope of advancing to understanding.[5] Later, in the same spirit, writing in 410 or 411 to a certain Dioscorus (*Ep.* 118.5.33), he observes that when the school of Plotinus flourished at Rome, some of them were depraved by their indulgence in magic but others realized that Christ is the sum of authority and the light of reason: authority and reason are compatible.

Not for everyone – indeed not for Augustine himself – a simple unreasoning faith. For all Augustine's occasional deprecation (as in *De quant. anim.* 7.12) of what is called "reasoning" but which in fact is mere noxious opinion about the faith, he is prepared to endure the long circuitous paths which reason demands,[6] urging that reason not be abandoned because of its frequent abuse (*Ep.* 120.1.6). Still, conventional philosophy is wrong in one important respect: it claims always to *start* with reason,[7] whatever the subject-matter. Such an apparently reasonable claim, Augustine wants to show, is irrational.

Long before returning to his mother's Catholic Christianity Augustine had been inspired to philosophy by Cicero's *Hortensius*; then, believing himself to be throwing off his fear of enquiry (*De beata vita* 1.4), he joined the Manichaeans; when they no longer satisfied, he turned, in the steps of Cicero and Varro, to the Skepticism of the New Academy. Both moves were undertaken in the belief that reason alone could lead to the truth, even if the truth is that nothing can be known for certain. Augustine always insists that the Manichaeans claimed – falsely as he later believed – to rely on reason alone. He told Honoratus that they declared that they would lay aside all awesome authority and by pure and simple reason bring to God those willing to listen to them (*De util. cred.* 1.2). The Catholics, in their view terrified by superstition, were bidden to believe rather than reason, while they themselves pressed no one to believe unless the truth had been discussed and unraveled.[8] Their claim, however, faltered over astrology, though for a while Augustine preferred the authority of that pseudo-science to the skepticism of his friends Vindicianus and Nebridius (*Conf.* 4.3.6).[9]

With his loss of confidence in the Manichaeans, Augustine almost lost confidence in reason itself,[10] returning to Ciceronian Skepticism. He was in no doubt that assent – as the Stoics had it – should be given to the truth, but who was to show him the truth (*C. Acad.* 3.5.12)? Perhaps to reach it is beyond the capacity of the human mind. Yet *some* forms of knowledge are possible: there is a certain knowledge of disjunctive propositions. We know that either p or not-p is the case (3.10.23), and we have certain knowledge in mathematics. And we have what has been dubbed "subjective knowledge": "When a man tastes something, he can swear in good faith that he knows that this is sweet to his palate . . . and no Greek sophism can deprive him of that knowledge" (3.11.26).[11] Such claims confound the *global* versions of Skepticism normal in antiquity. If some knowledge is possible, perhaps religious and metaphysical truth can be obtained.

Augustine never loses confidence that there is "truth"; the problem, as he sees it, lies with human capacity. The example of sense-knowledge suggests that firsthand experience is a possible route to knowledge, but there is a huge range of possible knowledge neither "subjective" nor mathematical nor logical; religious claims fall outside these limits, and after the Manichaean debacle, though inclined to despair, Augustine persisted in seeing the possibility of progress:

> Often it seemed to me that truth could not be found . . . but often again, as I reflected to the best of my ability how lively was the human mind, how wise, how penetrating, I could not believe that the truth must lie undetected. Possibly the manner of seeking truth might be hidden and would have to be accepted from some divine authority. (*De util. cred.* 8.20)

From such thoughts springs to Augustine's regular recourse to Isaiah 7.9 (in the Latin translation of the Septuagint), "Unless you believe, you will not understand"[12] – and the early *De moribus ecclesiae catholicae* indicates a similar approach (2.3; cf. 7.11): the mind is weak and needs the guidance of authority; human wickedness clouds the light of truth. As yet, however, Augustine offers no more radical explanation in terms of the "ignorance" resulting from original sin and its accompanying weakness of will (*difficultas*).

Yet the latter as much as the former is to provide Augustine with the resources to explain the present limited power of the human mind. We fail to understand not only because "now we see through a glass darkly" (1 Cor. 13.12), but because we do not always *want* to know, or even want to want to know, what is good and true. A classic example, for Augustine, is strict atheism;[13] in antiquity it was rare, and Augustine suggests that denial of God's existence is often due to the moral corruption of atheists: being slaves of desire, they do not want to believe in goodness or recognize the truth.[14] Even if they "know" the truth, their wickedness may choose other "riches." Augustine himself did not want to know too much about chastity, lest he should feel impelled to it (*Conf.* 8.7.17).[15] But for a thinker in the Platonic tradition, reflection on the limits of our knowledge could only promote a re-evaluation of the low status of belief and consequent concern to identify credible authorities.[16]

Skepticism about the ability of human reason to attain to knowledge, combined with a belief in truth itself, led Augustine to conclude that belief or faith is the only way forward. Accordingly he offers an analysis of different types of *credibilia*: facts to be believed.[17] First, we have historical truths which can *only* be believed since we have no first-hand knowledge of them. In *De util. cred.* Augustine notes that we know on Cicero's own authority of the execution of the Catilinarian conspirators. This authority is sound, as is that on which we know who are our parents; our mothers identify our fathers, and various midwives and other servants corroborate the claims of our mothers. It would be grotesque to refuse reverence for our parents on the grounds that we do not *know* who they are (*De util. cred.* 12.26).[18] Augustine is impressed by the fact that some of the most basic human relationships – the love of a child for its parents and the closeness of friends and married couples – can only depend on trusting beliefs.[19]

Next, Augustine speaks of those epistemic situations where belief and understanding go hand in hand: we believe in the truths of logic and mathematics only when we understand what we believe. Finally come those beliefs – only theological beliefs such as belief in the Trinity are cited – where belief is a necessary precondition for understanding, but no guarantee of it. How does that cohere with his conviction that the Platonists have formulated – and obviously believe – true propositions in the philosophy of religion, such as a belief in the intelligible world, indeed in the existence of God? The answer is that the Platonists understand only incompletely what they profess to know.

In theory, they are in a position to proceed to understanding, but their arrogance (*superbia*) prevents them from so doing even to the limited degree possible for human beings in the present life. They do not understand the intelligible world; hence they give a picture of it which is incomplete, liable to degenerate into error, indeed prone to promote it – particularly in their inferences as to how to live the philosophical life. While making proper inferences about God, they fail to understand their theoretical and practical import. In part this is to be explained by the fact that their "philosophical" experience of God is not first hand, for (as Augustine argues in a Platonic spirit, not least in *De mag.*)[20] if we are to *understand* the world rather than believe things about it, we must experience it at first hand. Miracles and special graces aside, a non-Christian, lacking faith, cannot reasonably hope for the type of experience necessary for a proper understanding of the Christian God.

Augustine's rhetoric can mislead us about belief, as at times it may have misled its author. In some passages he suggests a more radical contrast between reason and faith than he strictly intends, claiming baldly that faith starts from authority while reason may refuse to do so (*De ord.* 2.5.16;[21] 2.9.26; cf. *De Trin.* 4.16.21, etc.). Yet he is well aware of the need for discernment among authorities,[22] and discernment is a function of reason: reason does not desert authority when we consider who is to be believed (*De vera relig.* 24.45). Between this position and any more radical contrast between faith and reason there is a tension which perhaps can be resolved only if reason's universal claims – themselves unreasonable – are toned down; a proper responsibility of reason is to recognize its limitations.

When sharply contrasting it with "faith," Augustine seems to think of "reason" as strict demonstration, perhaps as a simply deductive process. In the discernment of authorities, of course, no such logical certainty can be attained. Something more empirical and at best inductive is appropriate – and judgment rather than deduction. Here is a different use of our rational capacity.

In the first instance it is part of reason's role to identify who is worthy to be believed; the first step towards a resolution of the problem of the relationship between reason and religious belief is the recognition not just of authority but of credible authority. If, for example, unaided reason is liable to lead us, as it led Augustine, into the chaos of Manichaeanism or the despair of Skepticism, perhaps insistence on the autonomy of reason guarantees a false starting point. Augustine regularly claims to seek only knowledge of God and the soul – a range of interests less restricted than might at first appear – but God and the soul cannot be the objects of the kinds of *knowledge* Augustine identifies in *C. Acad.*; rather they must be the objects of faith, that is, of *religious* belief. Augustine certainly claims that belief that God exists is importantly like other kinds of belief, such as that Cicero executed the Catilinarian conspirators, though, as we have noticed, he wants to say not that *all* knowledge is preceded by belief, but that all *theological* understanding arises from a preceding belief. Apparently wherever Augustine claims that belief is a prerequisite for understanding (*intellectus*), he is thinking of some theological proposition.[23] He may be mistaken in limiting himself so strictly – or perhaps the sense of "theological" can be expanded.

As some sort of Platonist, it was incumbent on Augustine, proclaiming the usefulness of belief in general and of theological faith in particular, to spell out and justify his novel position. Plato had claimed in the *Republic* that we cannot have true beliefs about Forms. Of Forms only knowledge or ignorance is possible, because one of the prerequisites of knowledge is first-hand experience;[24] we have already noticed the importance of first-hand experience in Augustine. Augustine, however, has learned from Scripture that now we see God by faith; only in heaven will we pass beyond faith and see him face to face (*Sol.* 1.7.14).

So a major difference between Plato and Augustine is that Augustine has lost confidence in our comprehending and understanding the Good in this life; our mind, he insists, is now inadequate. And while admitting that the Platonists advance true metaphysical propositions, above all about the existence of the immaterial world, he observes in the *Confessions* (7.20.26) that he was fortunate to meet the Platonism of Plotinus before converting to Christianity. The reverse order would have been unfortunate; he would have failed to recognize the difference between presumption and "confession."

Having indicated where Augustine thinks belief to be a necessary prerequisite for understanding, we should consider whether he is correct in limiting this to directly theological propositions. In fact, he makes no such formal limitation himself; the limitation has been supplied by scholars who have pointed out that in all cases where Augustine cites belief as a prerequisite for understanding the context is theological. Part of the reason for this is that some beliefs – and certainly religious beliefs – must be affectively experienced as well as cognitively grasped, and Augustine held more generally that where beliefs have affective associations, the two can only be separated conceptually. Hence if religious beliefs are to lead to understanding, they must be held with a specifically religious affectivity. In Augustinian language, if a belief is to lead to a specifically religious understanding, it must be accompanied by a specific disposition of the "will" – to retain that popular if inaccurate representation of the Latin *voluntas*. For the moment we may leave the "will" aside, merely asking whether Augustine was right to limit the prior beliefs required for understanding to strictly theological propositions.

Other candidates might be proposed, the most obvious being ethical beliefs. In the last analysis Augustine might include these under the theological rubric, maintaining that no proper ethics (or aesthetics) is possible without metaphysical, indeed theistic foundations. Furthermore, effective ethical beliefs – as the practical ineffectiveness of Platonism showed – have to be accompanied by a proper ordering of the emotions; they cannot be merely cognitive states. And since God as love is the foundation of Augustine's ethics,[25] ethical schemata devoid of that belief must be theoretically inadequate and practically empty; indeed God is to be seen not merely as love, but in the light of love as understood in the scriptures and Catholic tradition. We conclude that even if all Augustine's examples of propositions where affective belief may lead to full understanding are propositions in "systematic theology," he could easily accommodate himself to a longer list, itself determined by the identification of those areas of philosophy where affective belief bears on our judgments: especially, that is, in aesthetics and ethics – including meta-ethics. For Augustine the human mind should typically be used for the discernment of authorities; it is inadequate and irrational to identify certain major theological, and probably also ethical and aesthetic, truths without such authorities. Augustine claimed that he would not have believed the Gospels without the authority of the Catholic Church (*C. ep. fund.* 5.6). But he is also aware that human discernment is impoverished, and he blames the Fall for such impoverishment. How then does he know that he has discerned his authorities correctly? Of course, he does not *know*, but he claims true belief or faith. Insofar as his discernments are correct, this correctness has been achieved through the grace and aid of God – which can often be identified retrospectively. God works in history to show which individuals and which institutions are worthy of theological belief, and in the individual to enable him to see that to which he may normally be blind. As Augustine increasingly put it after 412, citing Proverbs 8.35, the "will is prepared by God."

At this point we touch on (but cannot linger over) Augustine's theory of illumination: he is puzzled (for example) as to why when once he looked at the scriptures, he could read the words and know what they meant, but he did not understand them (*De Trin.* 11.8.15).[26] After he has believed, however, or rather in learning to believe,[27] he is in a state to benefit further from divine illumination: here indeed faith has been the prerequisite to understanding. In treating of illumination, of course, Augustine does not limit himself to the understanding of theological propositions. Unless we are illumined, any teacher can bombard us with truths which we cannot take in and understand.

Faith – necessarily associated with hope and love[28] – is required as a prerequisite to understanding, not only because an affective belief – say, about God – would indicate a different mentality from its theoretically non-affective equivalent,[29] but also because Augustine must explain why, though the Christian God is Truth, there are non-believers, some of them philosophically competent. His not infrequent reply, as we have seen, is that the non-believer is morally underdeveloped or corrupt, or – more philosophically – that his moral and spiritual disposition is poorly attuned to reality; he is inadequately formed – either because he has rejected the opportunity for Christian belief or because he has had no such opportunity. In either case he is unable (morally or spiritually) to assent to certain true propositions; he simply does not (or cannot) *want* to believe. In explicating this claim we both learn more about the kind of "faith" which Augustine holds to be prerequisite for theological understanding and are brought up against the second of the problems we identified at the outset: that of willing and assenting.

Augustine's identification of belief as "nothing other than thinking with assent" (*De praed. sanct.* 2.5) sounds Stoic, but it will turn out to indicate a Stoicism transformed.[30] The Stoics had introduced the concept of assent into ancient accounts of action so effectively that even hardened Aristotelians, like the great second-century commentator Alexander, assumed that it was already a feature of Aristotle's *Nicomachean Ethics*.[31] But the notion of assent is in itself far from transparent. What does it mean to "assent"? For the Stoics, the answer is clear: we assent to propositions, and this assent is a good or bad judgment. But Augustine's view is more complex and richer – expanded on what he could find in Cicero or even in Seneca, the Stoic who on this topic is his most plausible source. Let us begin with a passage of *De spir. et litt.* (34.60): "To yield our consent . . . or to withhold it is the function of our *voluntas* – if we function properly." Which means that to understand "assent" we need to understand *voluntas*. If we want to translate *voluntas* as "will," then we need to determine Augustine's account of the will – which may or may not be ours, or that of the medievals, or that of the Stoics. If we understand "will," we may understand more of Augustine's concept of assent, and if we understand his concept of assent we may understand why – in many important matters – his account of belief as a prerequisite for the most important forms of understanding is both intelligible and challenging.

Augustine's concept of *voluntas* is best approached through the Stoic ideas with which he was familiar.[32] Recognizing these ideas as both resembling and differing from his own, we shall see how, in the concept of *voluntas* as elsewhere, he transposes much inherited Stoicism into a form of Platonism, highlighting the fundamental orientation of each human being and emphasizing love over both want and obligation in his account of moral agency and of the virtues – and explaining how no merely "cognitive" knowledge of God, but a pure heart,[33] a loving faith, and a personal experience of God are prerequisites both for the good life and for the highest metaphysical enquiries – those, that is, about God himself. In a brief treatment of the Stoics, we should consider texts from Seneca and Epictetus (the latter of whom Augustine had not read), since in view of the limited survival of Old Stoic material in Greek – which in any case Augustine did not use – and of the comparative lack of relevant material in Cicero, these provide the most readily accessible points of comparison. The Epictetan Greek term with substantial similarities to *voluntas* is *prohairesis*.[34]

For Epictetus our *prohairesis* (moral character) is opposed to our *sarx* or carnal self.[35] To have the right moral character is to have the correct moral beliefs, and it is up to us, as moral agents, whether we give our own moral well-being the proper primacy in our thoughts, plans, and desires. If we do, we shall intend the right, whatever the consequences, and we shall demand a similar attitude in others. A few examples will make the thesis clearer: "Nothing has power over our *prohairesis* except itself" (1.29.12); "It was not Socrates who was taken off and given the hemlock. It was not Socrates' *prohairesis* but his body which suffered in this way" (1.29.16ff.); "You will fetter my leg but not even Zeus can conquer my *prohairesis*" (1.1.23). From Augustine's point of view such texts display several moral errors, but we shall concentrate on just one. According to Epictetus, arguing in orthodox Stoic fashion, man's basic nature is pure (and mere) reason. Thus to behave morally is no more than to behave in accordance with right reason – which is very different from saying that moral behavior is (*inter alia*) rational. And the "will" (the *prohairesis* or *voluntas*) is to be seen in terms of a settled capacity and determination of the reason to make judgments of whatever sort: in ethics the ability both to make second-order judgments about wanting to want to do right, and to form and want to persist in moral (i.e. rational) intentions and rational decisions.

As with Epictetus, so with Seneca: in the latter *voluntas* is usually best translated as "intention" or "purpose," or, more literally, as what we want to do.[36] Certainly it indicates more than mere cognition (or recognition), indeed something which we would call volitional, but for the Stoics volition itself, if properly activated, is a kind of single-minded showing forth of a correct judgment, arising, as Seneca puts it (*Epistulae morales* 95.57) from a right disposition of mind. In Seneca there is no special *faculty* of the will. If I will X, I show the direction in which my "reason" takes me (rightly or wrongly).

According to the later Stoics, when we make a moral mistake, or exhibit weakness of will, our reason somehow acts unreasonably or against right reason. In their technical language, our assent to the relevant proposition is "weakly given." When reason acts irrationally, it gives way to the accumulated weight of past mistaken beliefs which have formed bad habits. We yield to such habits like animals, our habits being themselves a set of beliefs, and our "mind-sets" (*voluntates*) – or the intentions or purposes which result from such mind-sets – being beliefs and desires particularized as judgments determinative of action. Thus, when we are cowardly, it is just that, because of our bad habits, beliefs and desires, we assent to the false proposition that death is to be feared.

Unlike most Stoics, Epictetus believes that he needs innate ideas to get moral talk off the ground. We all have a general idea (a *prolepsis*) of good and evil; our problems arise when we try to apply that *prolepsis* to individual circumstances. Some grasp of the formal significance of good and evil (that is, without specific understanding of what is in fact good and evil) seems necessary for moral discussion at all – as was part of Aristotle's point when he put goodness outside the categories – but according to Epictetus our innate grasp of good and evil – which is more than what may be loosely called "formal" – is such that if we live in accordance with it we best preserve our moral character (*prohairesis*).

That best *prohairesis* will be informed by some grasp or understanding of what is the case about the universe: above all that – like it or not – there is a god, a source of providence, which we defy or deny at our peril. Our *prohairesis*, at its best and properly tended, is thus realized as a form of rational comprehension so that insofar as we are moral agents, we turn out to be impersonal but normally beneficent spirits.[37] If we translate *prohairesis*, or see *prohairesis*, with reference to the "will," as does C. H. Kahn, then the Epictetan "will" itself is to be identified (at its best) as a simple, "impersonal" judgment-making and judgment-enacting capacity.

These claims find their parallel in certain forms of Kantian and post-Kantian ethics. An apparent objection to all of such ethics, whether ancient or modern, has been expressed in terms of the following question: If you were seriously ill, would you prefer to be looked after by someone motivated by impersonal duty or by someone whose sense of duty is bound up with affection and love? Most people would prefer the latter, holding the man of duty to have an insufficiently broad understanding of the requirements of morality, while Epictetus would surely hold the broader view to be less moral but more sentimental. In contrasting the Stoics with Augustine, however, we are less concerned about the importance in morality of duty or of altruism as such than about the moral importance of emotional and affective commitment – which carries corollaries about the nature and importance of persons as individuals, and probably also the implication that unless we are concerned with others in a non-impersonal way, our proper concern for the well-being of our own *prohairesis* is misguided in that it is doomed to be ineffectual.

Like the Epicureans – though Stoic solutions are less brutal – the Stoics are aware of a moral demand for commitment, while remaining – again like the Epicureans – very conscious of its dangers. It is what I do for someone else, and not at all the degree to which I also empathize with him, that is the measure of my faithfulness to him (and faithfulness, for Epictetus especially, is a primary virtue); I must help him without risking emotional disturbance to myself. Now the claim of those critics – and they would include Augustine – who point out that we would prefer to be helped by a committed friend rather than a faithful Stoic is that, without commitment and affection, care, however effective, remains empty duty, indeed inhuman and conceivably hypocritical.

For Augustine it is not enough to build the concept of *voluntas* simply on assent to propositions, on a combination of belief and desire, on intentions, decisions and judgments, or even on persistence in wanting. Such an analysis is incomplete, too negligent of the relation between our moral beliefs and determinations on the one hand and our most basic loves and hatreds on the other. Augustine maintains – not in the Stoic, but in the Platonic tradition, contradicting Cicero (*De civ. Dei* 2.21.2) – that by their loves and hates, by their orientation either to God or the Devil, we can identify the nature of both individuals and societies. It is two loves which have formed two cities, that is, the secular city and the City of God (14.28). It is by assenting to our loves and hates – not even simply to our "wants"; that would be insufficiently personal and human – and by the habit of such assent that we develop, each one of us, a mind-set: what *he* thinks of as a *voluntas*. Augustine's *voluntas*, certainly influenced by Stoic ideas, is to be seen as formed not only by beliefs and desires but primarily by our love of God or lack of it.

Leaving the world of Epictetus and Seneca (let alone the earlier Stoics), we conclude that Augustine uses the word and concept "*voluntas*" not only to point to beliefs and wants, but to do some of the work of the word and concept "*eros*" – the love of the good and the Beautiful, and the perversions of that love – in the Platonic tradition. Hence we should not be surprised that *voluntas* is often interchangeable with *amor* and in its perfect form identified with it: that is, as the Holy Spirit (*De Trin.* 15.17.31; 15.20.38; 15.21.41). An essential feature of Augustine's account of God, and therefore – through the notion of man as an image – of the ideal human person, is that God (or the good man) not merely does not intend to do wrong, does not plan to do wrong, does not determine to do wrong, but that he cannot *want* to do wrong, since he cannot *love* to do wrong – indeed *cannot* love to do wrong.

If we translate *prohairesis/voluntas* as "will," we have to say that Augustine's account of the will and/or of the moral person – and therefore of assent itself – is far richer than his definition of belief as thinking with assent might seem to suggest. To understand Augustine's view – in contradistinction to that of the Stoics (even of Seneca) – we revert to that typical definition of the virtues found in the early treatise *De moribus ecclesiae catholicae*. Virtue, says Augustine (1.15.25), is "nothing other" than the supreme love of God. In brief, while for the Stoics all forms of virtue are modes of right reason and intentionality, for Augustine they have become modes of love: rational, of course, but far more than that. According to Augustine, among human beings – all of whom are incomplete in virtue – women are superior in emotional strength, that is in love, to men. Which is why Mary Magdalene was able to be the first witness of the Resurrection of Jesus[38] – and why the cleverest philosophical reasoners may be far from salvation.

In the *Discourses* (1.29.16ff.) Epictetus remarks: "Nothing has power over our *prohairesis* except itself." In *De lib. arb.* (1.12.26) Augustine commits himself to "What is so much in the 'will' as the will itself" ("Quid enim tam in voluntate quam ipsa voluntas sita est"). Both thinkers maintain that human beings can, or ought to be able to, act well, but the nature of the proper state of the *voluntas/prohairesis* – and therefore of the soul – is widely different. Epictetus is concerned with the failure of our judgment to distinguish good from evil, while Augustine would be quite dissatisfied with what he would perceive as the superficial incompleteness of such an explanation.

In Augustine's view we do not hold false moral and theological beliefs because of some mere error in our rationality. We do not assent "weakly" merely after some failure in rational calculation or in our rational habits, but often because we "love to" hold such and such a belief. Assent is not only a determining judgment, but a determining love. Consider someone who succumbs to peer-pressure – as Augustine tells us in the *Confessions* he succumbed over the famous theft of

pears (2.4.9; 2.8.16, etc.). He may have believed that since other people are perverse, he was licenced to be perverse too; but the actions to be performed are in
some sense "wanted," even "loved." Augustine, it may be said, both loved to do
wrong and loved to be popular with his friends, rather as Adam, according to *De
Genesi ad litteram libri duodecim* (11.42.59), wanted to be popular with Eve
when he ate the apple.

The Stoic analysis of the relation between moral belief and affectivity is seriously flawed. While correctly counting assent as substantially dependent on
habit, the Stoic account of habit-formation neglects the fact that we are not what
we believe (perhaps the original Stoic view), nor what we want (perhaps the supplementary view of Seneca), but what we love (*In Johannis epistulam ad Parthos
tractatus* 2.14): "Do you love earth?" Augustine asks. "You will be earth. Do you
love God . . .?" When "will" is more intense, it is called love. In God, as we have
seen – and therefore in our fully purified and unified selves – genuine love and the
"will" are identical.[39]

We return directly to faith and reason. We have seen how the ability to form
and understand theological (and probably other) propositions ultimately
depends on identifying and following the correct authorities, our reason being
aided by God, and that our beliefs about such authorities – themselves dependent on what we are, on our mind-set or *voluntas* – cannot depend on mere cognitive acts. That is not the kind of beings we are; such are not the motives which
drive us. To be able to believe in God, to have faith in him, is to have something
of the love of God (itself a gift of God) – that loving belief being the prerequisite to further moral and theological understanding. There can be no merely
rational substitutes. If we are to understand that belief is thinking with assent,
Augustine holds that we must know in the case of each belief the conditions
under which such assent can be secured. In religion (widely conceived) thinking
the truth cannot be separated from loving the truth, and in our present world
loving the truth cannot be separated from faith.

In about 410 Augustine exchanged letters (119–120) with a certain Consentius,
perhaps a monk of Lérins and the future recipient of his treatise *Contra
Mendacium*. In reply to Consentius' claim that theological truth must come
from faith *rather* than reason – otherwise only the wise could be happy – and
that one must simply follow the authority of the saints, Augustine sets out his
position once more, in a text often considered definitive of his mature views.
Correcting what he sees as Consentius' fideism, he urges that the goal of religious thought must be to see by reason (properly understood) what we now hold
by faith. Isaiah's "If you will not believe, you will not understand" would have
summed it up once more. Once again faith is not religious understanding but
only the necessary prerequisite to it, for, continues Augustine, God forbid that
he should hate in us that faculty by which he made us superior to all other living

beings. It is wrong to adopt the kind of belief which wishes to exclude the light of understanding. The scriptures themselves urge us to think about the Trinity (2.12).

Since we are rational beings, it would be absurd to suppose that the prerequisite that faith precede reason is irrational – and we have now seen in what way it is eminently rational. The unbeliever, who asks for a reason for what he cannot understand without prior belief, is in an impossible situation, but the believer will eventually find himself capable of understanding. It is loving faith which *prepares* the mind for reason to be able fully to perform its proper and most important functions. By such faith the philosopher can develop the love which builds on the foundation of humility which is Christ Jesus and which leads to understanding and the good life (*Conf.* 7.20.26).[40, 41]

NOTES

1 "Normally" indicates that whatever his early hesitations, Augustine through the major part of his career as Christian thinker would defend the views, if not always the specific formulations, given roughly systematic form below. For a general introduction to questions of Augustine's development see Rist 1994, 13–19.

2 So Gilson 1960, 33.

3 *De praed. sanct.* 2.5.

4 Cf. *De vera relig.* 1.1.5; *Contra Julianum* 4.14.72, etc.

5 Even in the Cassiciacum dialogues (as this passage of the C. *Acad.* indicates) reason must always be subordinated to authority. Scholars have sometimes argued that in early Augustine re ison by itself (at least for a few) is a possible way to salvation. Even if this were correct, Augustine soon changed his mind.

6 Note already the tone of *De ord.* 2.9.26: "I do not know how I could call those happy who . . . content with authority alone . . . apply themselves constantly only to good ways of living and to prayer." Cf. *De ord.* 2.5.16.

7 So *De ord.* 2.5.16; *De Trin.* 4.16.21.

8 Cf. *De util. cred.* 9.21; 11.25; *De vera relig.* 1.4; *Conf.* 3.6.10. See Russell, 1975, 14–15 and Burnaby 1938, 74.

9 Cf. Van Fleteren 1973, 36.

10 For his disillusionment see *Conf.* 6.4.6. For the continuing caution which the experience engendered see *De ord.* 2.5.17.

11 See Kirwan 1989, 37.

12 *De mag.* 11.37; *De lib. arb.* 1.2.4, 2.2.6; *Sermons* 118.1, 126.1.1; *Ep.* 120.1.3; *De Trin.* 7.6.12, 15.2.2; *In Joannis evangelium tractatus* 29.6, 45.7; *C. Faust.* 1.46, etc.

13 Strict atheism would be the denial of the existence of God or the gods; more common in antiquity – and still called atheism – was the denial of providence.

14 *De vera relig.* 38.69; *In Joannis evangelium tractatus* 106.4; *Enarr. in Ps.* 53(52).2; cf. *De Trin.* 8.3.4.

15 More generally see Crawford 1988, 291–302.

16 Further early texts on reason and authority include *De ord.* 2.5.16; *De vera relig.* 7.12.

17 *De diversis quaestionibus octoginta tribus* 48; cf. *Ep.* 147.6–8. Cf. Markus 1967, 350.

18 Cf. *Conf.* 6.5.7; *De civ. Dei* 11.3.

19 *De util. cred.* 12.26; see *De fide rerum invisibilium* (1.2) on friendships and 2.4 on stable marriages.

20 See Burnyeat 1987.

21 For the limited success of philosophy even among the philosophers, note "Philosophia rationem promittit et vix paucissimos liberat." See Madec 1970, 179–186.

22 *De ord.* 2.9.27; *De vera relig.* 25.46; *De util. cred.* 9.21.

23 See Kretzmann 1990, 15.

24 Cf. *Meno* 97Aff.; *Theaetetus* 201BC.

25 Note the definition of the virtues as early as *De moribus ecclesiae catholicae* 1.15.25: they are "nothing other" than forms of the supreme love of God.

26 Cf. Coward 1990, 26. Note that "heretics" too accept the scriptures as authoritative, but still do not understand them (*Ep.* 120.3.13).

27 To understand how Augustine thinks God prepares the will, we need to understand his account both of *voluntas* itself and of its relationship to "cognition" and "assent." See pp. 35–37 below and more generally Sage 1964.

28 *Enchiridion de fide, spe et caritate* 2.8; cf. Kretzmann 1990, 25.

29 In theology, metaphysics, and ethics Augustine, we have suggested, would deny the "real" existence of non-affective beliefs. If our beliefs about God were not affectively "informed" by Christianity, they would be informed by other, hence damaging, affectivities.

30 Cf. *De spir. et litt.* 31.54 ("Quid est enim credere nisi consentire verum esse quod dicitur?"). The Stoicism is noted by Holte 1962, 81.

31 Alexander, *Quaest.* 3.13, 107.18; see Dobbin 1991, 123.

32 My account of the "will" is necessarily curtailed; no adequate treatment yet exists. It is often (wrongly) assumed that Augustine's views became standard; it would be nearer the truth to say that deformed versions of them became standard. For Seneca see Inwood (unpublished).

33 Only the pure in heart can understand the divine: *De diversis quaestionibus octoginta tribus* 48; 68.3; cf. *Ep.* 120.1.3–4 and *Sermones* 43.10.10 on the cleansing power of faith.

34 Kahn 1988, 234–259, drew attention to many similarities between Epictetus and Augustine on the "will," but neglected the important differences to be discussed below. See also Rist 1994, 186–188.

35 Modern treatments of Epictetus' notion of moral character still depend much on Bonhoeffer 1890.

36 Cf. *Ep.* 34.3, 71.36.

37 Thus we may wish to restrain the enthusiasm of Kahn 1988, 253 ("Theoretical reason is essentially impersonal"), who argues that the Stoic emphasis on *practical* reason, and in particular Epictetus' identification of himself "not with reason as such but with the practical application of reason" is "a momentous one for the evolution of the idea of person and selfhood."

38 For Augustine's doctrine of deification see *Sermons* 192.1.1: "Deos facturus qui homines erant, homo factus qui Deus est", with Bonner 1984.

39 *Sermo Guelf.* 14.1–229L.1; 45.5; 51.2.3; 232.2.2; 244.2; 245.2; *De Trin.* 4.3.6; *In Joannis evangelium tractatus* 121.1.

40 *De Trin.* 15.20.38; 15.21.41; cf. *Enarr. in Ps.* 122(121).1; *Conf.* 13.9.10; *De civ. Dei* 11.28; cf. Burnaby 1938, 94, note 1; Holte 1962, 243.

41 My thanks to Eleonore Stump for constructive comment on an earlier version of this chapter.

3

WILLIAM E. MANN

Augustine on evil and original sin*

Before his conversion to Christianity, Augustine conceived of God as a supremely good being who is "incorruptible, inviolable, and immutable" (*Conf.* 7.1.1). At the same time, he was aware of the existence of evil in the world, evil that can be divided into two major classes. First, physical objects have limitations and defects. In particular, the limitations of living things result in hardship, pain, illness, and death. Secondly, there are people who behave wickedly and whose souls are characterized by such vices as pride, envy, greed, and lust.

It would seem that a supremely good God would prevent or eradicate as much evil as he possibly could. The problem of evil, then, is to see whether and how it might be both that God exists and that evil exists. Before his conversion, Augustine grappled with this problem for a number of years and found some intellectual satisfaction in the solution offered by Manichaeism. Manichaeism taught that the world is an arena in which two opposing cosmic forces incessantly contend, one good, the other evil. If one concentrates on the attributes of incorruptibility, inviolability, and immutability, it does not seem impossible that there be *two* beings having those attributes in common while occupying opposite ends of the moral spectrum. Manichaeism thus offered a straightforward solution for the problem of evil: God is doing the best he can against evil, but finds himself facing an independent opponent as formidable as he.

Although Manichaeism is dualistic, the dualism is confined within a thoroughgoing materialism. Goodness is identified with corporeal light; evil with physical darkness. The youthful Augustine found this feature of Manichaeism unobjectionable because he antecedently had had difficulty understanding how anything could exist without being corporeal (*Conf.* 5.10.19, 7.1.1–2). It was, he says, as if God were a boundless ocean completely permeating the finite sponge of the created world (*Conf.* 7.5.7). Taking the metaphor a step further, we can offer on behalf of the Manichaeans the observation that the same sponge is also awash with a supremely toxic fluid – indeed, that the two fluids together not only permeate but *constitute* the sponge.

With his conversion to Christianity Augustine came to think that a proper solution to the problem of evil must depart radically from the Manichaeans in its conceptions of God and evil. Augustine came to think that God is a spiritual, not a corporeal, being. Augustine thus rejects Manichaeism's materialistic dualism but embraces a different dualism between corporeal and spiritual beings, with God, angels, and human souls falling into the latter class.

God's incorporeal nature is not sufficient to dispel Manichaeism, for a persistent Manichaean might hold that there is still an ultimate, invincible source of evil, be it corporeal or incorporeal. This alternative is denied by Augustine's insistence that God is rightfully *sovereign* over all other beings. Even if the attributes of incorruptibility, inviolability, and immutability do not preclude their multiple instantiation in antagonistic forces, sovereignty does: no being can be supremely sovereign if there is another being over which it cannot prevail.

God's sovereignty over all other things is grounded in the fact that he *created* them. Two features of Augustine's account of creation are especially important to his resolution of the problem of evil: that God creates *ex nihilo*, out of nothing, and that everything that God creates is good. It is instructive to distinguish Augustine's claims about creation from Plato's influential account.

In the Platonic dialogue bearing his name, Timaeus argues that the demiurge or divine artisan creates because not to create would betoken a character fault – envy – that a perfect being cannot possess. But freedom from envy does not dictate what kind of universe the demiurge will create. Being supremely good, the demiurge cannot tolerate creating anything less than the best; he wants everything to be as much like himself as possible. So the demiurge imposes order on initially discordant matter, producing a universe that is as good as the nature of its matter allows (Plato, *Timaeus*, 29e–30b). There are three components of Plato's account to which Augustine does not give allegiance.

The first feature flows naturally from the artisan analogy that governs Timaeus' creation account; it also comports with Parmenidean strictures against non-being. Matter existed in some inchoate form before the process of creation, providing the raw material on which the demiurge worked. The demiurge's creative performance was thus constrained by the nature of the raw material at hand, about which the demiurge had no say. Augustine rejects this account of creation as fabrication because of its presupposition that matter is coeval with God. In creating the world God brought into existence not only its material inhabitants but also the very material of which they are made.

1. For they [your works] have been made by you out of nothing, not out of you, not out of something that is not yours or that existed previously, but out of "concreated" matter, that is, matter created simultaneously by you, since you gave form to its formlessness without any interposition of time. For although the matter of heaven and earth is one thing and the form of heaven and earth

another, you nevertheless made both of them simultaneously – the matter, indeed, entirely out of nothing, but the world's form out of unformed matter – in such a way that form followed matter with no gap in time. (*Conf.* 13.33.48)

2. Thus when I ask of you, from whence the whole of creation has been made, which, even though good of its kind, is nevertheless inferior to the creator – so that the one is always immutable and the other mutable – you will not speak falsely if you respond that you confess it to be made entirely from non-being. (*C. Secundinum* 8)

These passages enunciate the doctrine of creation *ex nihilo*. They also imply that God cannot create anything equal to himself. Because every created thing has its origin in non-being, it is mutable. But God is essentially immutable, and any immutable being is superior to any mutable being.

The second and third components of the *Timaeus* account of creation arise from these two questions. Why did the deity create *anything*? Why did the deity create *this* universe? Plato's answer to the first question is "An essentially flawless being cannot be envious" and to the second question, "A supremely good being cannot create anything less than the best." The two responses do not present equivalent doctrines. The first does not entail the second. The demiurge is free from the charge of envy so long as he creates something and is not subsequently envious of what he creates. If that standard of performance is all that is required, then a cynical demiurge might fill the bill by creating a crew of miserable creatures envied by no one. Plato's second response sets a much higher standard. Only the best will do for a supremely good being. Even so, the second response does not entail what the first entails, for the second response does not entail that the demiurge will create anything. The first response supplies that ingredient. The two responses together entail that the demiurge created this world and that this world is the best world the demiurge could have created.

Augustine endorses neither of these views. We can examine Augustine's doctrines by seeing what he has to say about God's will in creating and about the goodness of the created world. Concerning God's will, this text is important:

3. Thus if they were to say "What determined God to make heaven and earth?" one should respond to them that those who desire to become acquainted with God's will should first learn about the power of the human will. For they seek to know the causes of God's will when God's will itself is the cause of all the things there are. For if God's will has a cause, it is something that takes precedence over (*antecedat*) God's will, which is sinful to believe. Therefore to one who says "Why did God make heaven and earth?" one should respond "Because he willed." For God's will is the cause of heaven and earth, and thus God's will is greater than heaven and earth. But one who says "Why did God

will to make heaven and earth?" seeks something that is greater than God's will; but nothing greater can be found. (*De Gen. c. Man.* 1.2.4)

This passage relies on a causal principle – every cause is superior to its effects – that, together with the thesis that nothing is superior to God's will, precludes God's will from having any cause. For Augustine the explanatory buck stops here. To put it another way, Augustine finds nothing in God's nature that entails that God must create.

It is not evident that Augustine thinks that if God decides to create, then God must create the best world that he can. Creation is indeed very good (*De Genesi ad litteram imperfectus liber* 1.3, echoing Genesis 1.31), created out of the "fullness of [God's] goodness" (*Conf.* 13.2.2; 13.4.5). Augustine adds that God will not create a thing unless he *knows* that it is good (*De civ. Dei* 11.21). At the same time, however, Augustine offers the following observations. No *created* being had a claim against God to be created (*Conf.* 13.2.2–3). If Augustine endorses the more general thesis that *no* being, actual or possible, had such a claim, then it follows that God would have wronged no actual being in omitting to create it and that God has wronged no potential but non-actual being in omitting to create it. God did not create out of any need, nor to perfect any deficiency in himself (*Conf.* 13.4.5). God thus knowingly creates a good world, but Augustine's remarks do not entail the *Timaeus* thesis that this world is as good a world as God could create. Perhaps naively, perhaps slyly, Augustine characterizes Plato's doctrine simply as the doctrine that the most accurate explanation for the world's creation is that good works are made by a good God (*De civ. Dei* 11.21). Aquinas would later distinguish between a world's being composed of the best possible parts and a world's having the best possible order among its parts, even if the parts themselves are not the best. Aquinas argued that the created world must be as good as possible in terms of the order imposed on it by God, but that it need not be populated by the best possible components.[1] I have not found Aquinas' distinction in Augustine's writings. If Augustine does regard the created world as best in either of Aquinas' senses, that regard is not a prominent part of his philosophy.

But Augustine does insist that every creature is good insofar as it exists (*De nat. boni c. Man.* 1). How then, is there evil?

Augustine deploys his answer in two stages. First, although every creature is good, some creatures are better than others. That every creature is good Augustine regards as a consequence of God's creative activity. Insofar as corporeal things exist at all, God has bestowed upon them some degree of measure, number (or form), and order (*De lib. arb.* 2.20.54; *De nat. boni c. Man.* 3). Organisms and artifacts possess these features to a high degree, but even the comparatively simpler materials out of which they are composed have some degree of measure, number, and order: if that were not so, these raw materials would be literally non-existent (*De lib. arb.* 2.20.54). So for Augustine the predicate "good" is not like the predicate "average." Even if all the children of Lake Wobegon are above average, it is mathematically impossible for *everyone* to be above average. Yet everything can be and is good in virtue of having measure, number, and order.

Some good things are better than others (*De civ. Dei* 11.22). Augustine sometimes seems prepared to regiment all cases of *x*'s being better than *y* into cases of *x*'s having more measure, number, and order than *y* (*De nat. boni c. Man.* 3). But he leaves the project's details mostly blank. Thus, for example, he is eager to put forward the thesis that some things, even when corrupted, are still better than other things that remain uncorrupted. According to human estimation, at least, corrupted gold is better than uncorrupted silver, and corrupted silver is still better than uncorrupted lead (*De nat. boni c. Man.* 5). It may be that Augustine believes that human estimation is capricious in this matter. But there is nothing capricious, in his estimation, about the claims that a rational spirit corrupted by an evil will is still better than an uncorrupted irrational spirit, and that any spirit, no matter how corrupted, is better than any uncorrupted body (ibid.). In support of the latter claim Augustine says that as a runaway horse is better than a stationary stone and a drunken sot is better than the excellent wine he imbibed, so the lowest, most depraved soul is better than light, the noblest of corporeal things (*De lib. arb.* 3.5.12–16).

This is the imagery of a rhetorical master. More prosaic minds seek instruction about how to justify the claim behind the images. The trio of measure, number, and order suggests that betterness might track increased structural integrity or complexity. But since many of us find our paradigm examples of structural integrity and complexity in material objects, many of us will need guidance on how to apply the trio to sustain Augustine's comparative judgments *between* spiritual and material beings. The situation is especially puzzling because Augustine regards God, the supreme spiritual being, as supremely *simple*, having no metaphysical complexity whatsoever.

No creature, then, is evil, in spite of the fact that some creatures are worse than others (*De nat. boni c. Man.* 14). The word "evil," when predicated of creatures, refers to a *privation*, an absence of goodness where goodness might have been (*Conf.* 3.7.12). If we are audacious enough to enquire why God allows such privations to occur, we are apt to be reminded of the following points. First, creatures have a natural tendency towards mutability and corruption, an unavoidable liability of their having been created *ex nihilo*. Secondly, we are subject to perspectival prejudices, failing to see how local privations, especially the ones that affect us, contribute to the good of the whole. The distinctive twist that Augustine puts on this now-familiar point is that for him the assessment of the good of the whole is more diachronic than synchronic. One who laments the passing away of particular ephemeral things should realize that to wish that they might last forever is to wish that not they but some other kind of being existed. Moreover, their passing away ushers in new, good creatures. Finally, there is order and beauty to be found in this very dynamic passage, analogous to the way in which speech is made possible by the coming to be and passing away of phonemes, or music by the sequential production of notes (*De lib. arb.* 3.9.24–25; 3.15.42–43). Thirdly, "God owes nothing to anyone" (ibid. 3.16.45). On the contrary, anything that exists owes its entire existence to God's grace.

But "evil" is sometimes predicated of the choices and actions of creatures possessing reason. The second stage of Augustine's treatment of the problem of evil begins here, presupposing, however, the results of the first stage.

4. As I have said, therefore, sin is not a desire for naturally evil things, but an abandonment of better things. And this itself is evil, not that nature which the sinner uses evilly. For evil is to use a good evilly. (*De nat. boni c. Man.* 36)

5. But perhaps you are going to ask: since the will is moved when it turns away from an immutable good to a mutable good, from whence does this movement arise? It [the movement] is actually evil, even though a free will is to be counted among the good things, since without it no one can live rightly. For if that movement, that is, the will's turning away from the Lord God, is without doubt a sin, how can we say that God is the author of the sin? Thus that movement will not be from God. From whence then will it come? If I respond thus to your querying – that I do not know – perhaps you will be disappointed – but nevertheless I would respond truly. For that which is nothing cannot be known. (*De lib. arb.* 2.20.54)

Sin is not a desire for naturally evil things, according to passage (4). Augustine's claim must be interpreted *de re* – there are no naturally evil things that could serve as objects of sinful desires – rather than *de dicto*. For *de dicto*, there might well be benighted souls who desire what they take to be naturally evil things, and such a desire would be sinful for Augustine. Passage (4) leaves unexplained what might constitute a case of abandonment of better things. Even if gold is intrinsically better than silver, my desiring a silver chalice over a gold one could hardly count as sinful. Augustine sometimes stipulates that the thing desired must be forbidden to the desirer by justice (*De Genesi ad litteram imperfectus liber* 1.3). Since justice is derived from God's eternal law (*De lib. arb.* 1.6.50), an object of a sinful desire is something in fact forbidden to the desirer by God's edicts. On some occasions Augustine takes pains to say that the sinfulness of the desire resides not in the desire itself but in one's *consent* to it (*De continentia* 2.3–5), where consent involves either forming an intention to act in accordance with the desire or, at a minimum, failing to suppress the desire.[2]

As passage (5) indicates, Augustine is fond of describing sin as the will's turning away from God, a culpable rejection of the infinite bounty God offers in favor of an infinitely inferior fare. Passage (5) also conveys the message that what makes the rejection culpable is that it is freely chosen by the agent's will. Described as the free rejection of an infinite good, however, the sin is not just culpable. It is staggeringly irrational; from a cost–benefit viewpoint, the worst deal imaginable. Attracted by the Platonic thesis that all error is due to ignorance, one might then probe for some cognitive defect in the anatomy of every sin. On many occasions we might find a cognitive defect, but it is no part of Augustine's brief that we always will.

Retrieve the last sentiment expressed in passage (5), namely, that the cause of the will's movement away from God is unknowable non-being. Compare it with the remark in passage (3) that "those who desire to become acquainted with God's will should first learn about the power of the human will." We may extract the following parallels. Just as God's will in creating has no cause, so a human's will in sinning has no cause. This feature is one aspect of the power of the human will, but perhaps not the only one. If God can knowingly choose to create a world that is not the best world he might have created, in either of Aquinas' senses mentioned above, then one can argue analogously that humans can have a clear perception that one good is superior to another, yet freely choose the inferior good. In some cases, perhaps, such as choosing silver over gold, the choice may lie below the threshold of sinfulness. In other cases, however, involving the choice of what justice forbids, the threshold is knowingly and culpably passed. Another aspect of the power of the human will is to reject the verdict of reason.[3]

One might wonder whether the latter "power" is more liability than asset. Augustine offers the following answer. Material objects, as a class, are good but can be put to evil use and are not necessary for living rightly. In contrast, some spiritual goods, namely the virtues of justice, prudence, fortitude, and temperance, are necessary for living rightly and cannot be used wrongly. There is another class of goods, intermediate between material goods and the virtues, which are spiritual, necessary for living rightly, but capable of being used wrongly. In this class are the faculties of will, reason, and memory (De lib. arb. 2.18.49–2.19.52). A genuinely free will necessarily carries with it the liability to sin. But without having freedom of choice, with its built-in liability, humans would lack the capacity to choose to live rightly.

There are two cases of sinful choice that dramatize for Augustine the sheer willfulness of sin, the Devil's defection from the ranks of the angels and Adam and Eve's choosing to eat the forbidden fruit in the Garden of Eden. The Devil's case serves as a template to which the psychology of many human sins conforms. In answer to the question why the Devil rejected the blessed life open to all angels, Augustine cites the motive of *pride* (*superbia*), which he defines as "the love of one's own excellence" (*De Gen. ad litt.* 11.14.18) and a "desire for per verse elevation" (*De civ. Dei* 14.13).

Pride is also the initial evil impulse behind the fall of Adam and Eve (*De Gen. ad litt.* 11.5.7; *De civ. Dei* 14.13). The Devil's tempting of Adam and Eve did not coerce their fall, for if the temptation had been coercive, then their punishment would be unjust. Adam and Eve voluntarily succumbed to the temptation because of their prideful fascination with the thought that they would become like God. Augustine takes this similarity between the two cases to warrant the claim that sin entered the created world through pride. At the same time he is careful to insist that pride is not a component in all sins; as he points out, some sins are committed in ignorance or desperation (*De natura et gratia* 29.33).[4]

Adam and Eve's fall ushered into the world *original sin*, which is not an event but rather a condition (*De pecc. merit. et remis.* 1.9.9–1.12.15). It is the condition imposed by God as punishment on Adam and Eve for disobedience. According to Augustine the condition includes dispossession from a naturally perfect environment, the loss of natural immortality and the acquisition of susceptibility to physical pain, fatigue, disease, aging, and rebellious bodily disorders, especially sexual lust (*De Gen. ad litt.* 11.32.42; *De civ. Dei* 14.16–19). The condition is not only pathological, it is inherited, infecting every descendant of Adam and Eve. The condition is innate, not acquired; as Augustine puts it, it is transmitted by propagation, not imitation (*De pecc. merit. et remis.* 1.9.9–1.12.15). Augustine's view, then, is that our first ancestors squandered their patrimony and our inheritance and – as if that were not bad enough – thereby contracted a suite of infirmities that is passed on to all their progeny.

The infirmities are physical: Augustine appears not to think that the penalties of original sin include any intrinsic diminution of the soul's active abilities, such as the abilities to reason and to will. Although he nowhere considers the point, Augustine has reason to reject that possibility. One can argue that an alteration of the soul's native abilities would be tantamount to the creation of a new species. It is awful enough to be told that we are at present disadvantaged because of the misdeeds of our ancestors. It would be monstrous to be told that our kind was created as a punishment for misdeeds perpetrated by superior beings of a different species. Even so, the physical infirmities have made it harder for humans to exercise their souls' abilities correctly. According to Augustine, all sinful souls suffer from two penalties, ignorance and difficulty (*De lib. arb.* 3.18.52). Ignorance, not inborn stupidity: humans now lack the kind of noetic intimacy with God enjoyed by Adam and Eve, an intimacy, however, insufficient to guarantee the maintenance of righteousness, in either Adam and Eve's or the Devil's case. Difficulty, not impossibility: it is no part of Augustine's message that humans have been *shattered* by the fall.[5] A full reconnaissance of this terrain would have to include an excursion into Augustine's anti-Pelagianism. But, as

Augustine makes clear in the *Retractationes* (1.9.6), he takes his anti-Pelagianism to be fully consistent with this analogy. Suppose that our blessedness consisted in eloquence, so that every grammatical gaffe were a sin. Even then no one would fault an infant for initial ignorance, for the infant has not yet either culpably neglected eloquence or culpably allowed it to be lost once acquired. Nor would we fault an adult who continues to find eloquence difficult. We would reserve censure for those who do not even make the effort and for those who, having achieved some proficiency, backslide into inarticulateness (*De lib. arb.* 3.22.64).

NOTES

* Research on this essay was supported by a University of Vermont Summer Research Grant, hereby gratefully acknowledged.
1 See Kretzmann 1983 and Kretzmann 1991 for citations and discussion.
2 See Mann 1999 for a discussion of the role of consent in Augustine's ethics.
3 See MacDonald 1999 and Eleonore Stump's essay in this volume for further discussion of Augustine on the will.
4 For a different account of the origin of sin in a good world, see MacDonald 1999.
5 For a fuller discussion of these issues and their historical consequences, see Quinn 1999.

4

JAMES WETZEL

Predestination, Pelagianism, and foreknowledge

Looking ahead: predestination and foreknowledge

It is not hard to determine what Augustine meant by predestination. In one of his last works, written for those who opposed him mainly on the issue of predestination, he has this to say about his doctrine: "This is the predestination of the saints, nothing else: plainly the foreknowledge and preparation of God's benefits, by means of which whoever is to be liberated is most certainly liberated."[1] His doctrine has a dark corollary. If you are not one of the saints – one of those looked after by God – you are most certainly lost; your lot in life is to remain part of a ruined race, squandered in sin (*massa perditionis*). The doctrine of predestination and its corollary, the inevitable ruin of those not predestined to be redeemed, fairly encapsulate a career's worth of theological reflection on Augustine's part. He had arrived at a relentlessly God-driven account of human redemption, and if his own assessment of his development can be credited, he had begun from a place not too dissimilar.[2] I will be marking some of the turns in Augustine's trek to his doctrine of predestination, at least in passing, but the question I most have in mind is less one of how he gets there than why he bothers. What moves him so to emphasize God's role in redemption that to even some of his own most loyal supporters, he seems to have all but obliterated the human part?

In assessing Augustine's motives for holding a position, it is sometimes hard to sort out what he holds in response to an opponent from what he would have held regardless of opposition. His career as a bishop was burdened by near-constant controversy, and much of his theology of grace was articulated in response to someone else's – usually a Pelagian or a Pelagian sympathizer's – supposed mistake. Ideally Augustine never would have defended a view whose truth he would seriously question outside of a polemical context. Even granting Augustine a large claim to this ideal (as I am inclined to do), it would still be misleading to reduce his account of predestination to his defense of it. Both in his own day and thereafter, Augustine's opponents have tended to either overlook or discount the importance of key elements in his doctrine. They have tended to see relatively little, for instance, in Augustine's favorite illustration of predestination. "There is," he writes, "no more illustrious example of predestination than the Mediator himself."[3]

In the Gospels, Augustine finds his clearest example of a human being – Jesus of Nazareth – whose humanity is pleasing to God. It is pleasing, claims Augustine, not because Jesus overcame the temptations of the flesh and thereby earned God's favor, but because at heart he was never other than the person God intended him to be.[4] A way of being human, conceived in God's eternity, takes incarnate form when Jesus is born of Mary. The grace at work in his predestination – making Jesus into the man who would never be moved to live other than as God's son – is closely bound up in Augustine's mind with the mystery of incarnation, the mystery of mortal and yet sinless flesh. The case of Jesus proves to be the most illuminating for pondering predestination because his is presumably the one case where there is a perfect convergence between what God foreknows and what God predestines.[5] For the rest of us, elect and damned alike, there is always some divergence – the effect of an all-too-human disposition to sin.

Taken in the abstract, the distinction between foreknowledge and predestination is straightforward: what is predestined is foreknown, but not all that is foreknown is predestined. Augustine made use of the abstract distinction when he was seeking to disentangle divine foreknowledge from what he took to be pagan notions of fate and divination. Cicero, he knew, had rejected any suggestion that the future could be perfectly foreknown, for that possibility would seem to imply a fixed order of events and an absence of freedom in all but appearance. Although Augustine was no fan of divination (he had a particular animus against astrology), he refused to compromise the integrity of God's knowledge. In *De civitate Dei*, largely in response to Cicero's *De fato* and *De divinatione*, he offers that "our wills are contained in the order of causes, an order that is fixed for God and contained in his foreknowledge."[6] Augustine's idea is that regardless of whether a particular expression of will is foreknown, the will retains its character as a cause of action; if a will can be foreknown as such, foreknowledge implies no impediment to free will. This idea, which is apt to sound question-begging to those who worry about the compatibility between foreknowledge and free will, never gets developed in Augustine. Instead he assumes its truth and uses his assumption to navigate a different kind of complexity: God predestines some wills, but only foreknows others. Those whose lives are foreknown but not predestined inevitably come to a bad end. The rest are made holy and redeemed.

The polemical context: a question of initiative

"There is only this difference between grace and predestination, that predestination is the preparation for grace, while grace is the giving of the gift (*donatio*)."[7]

Augustine wrote those words for malcontent monks in and around Lérins and Marseilles in Southern Gaul. Late in his career as bishop, he was discovering that his uncompromising stance on predestination and his insistence on God's pre-emption of all human initiative for self-betterment were not playing too well in ascetic communities. About a year prior to the outbreak of controversy in Southern Gaul, Augustine addressed the incomprehension of monks nearer to home, in Hadrumetum on the North African coast. One of their number – a monk named Florus – had returned from a trip with a copy in hand of Augustine's letter to Sixtus;[8] in it Augustine exhorted the then Roman presbyter, who would later become pope, to rest firm in his condemnation of the Pelagian heresy. Pelagius and his supporters had just been decisively condemned by Zosimus, bishop of Rome; the year was 418. When the African monks read of Augustine's case against Pelagianism some nine years later, in the letter brought to them by Florus, some of them concluded that there was no point in a monk accepting the rebuke of his abbot. If the monk were meant to be better, God would make him so; otherwise, the monk would remain in sin and error despite his abbot's best efforts. Augustine sent off two treatises to correct the misinter-pretation of his letter. When one of these, *De correptione et gratia*, reached the monks of St. Victor at Marseilles, on the other side of the Mediterranean, it fueled opposition to Augustine's theology in Southern Gaul.

The various treatises and letters associated with Augustine's attempt to win monastic support for his doctrine of predestination have commonly been referred to as his writings against the semi-Pelagians. This is a misleading desig-nation, as now nearly all scholars of Augustine and his times agree. In the first place, his African and Gallic audiences could hardly be said to constitute a unified movement, semi-Pelagian or otherwise. The Africans never questioned the authority of Augustine's teaching; they argued over its implications and allowed Augustine to resolve their dispute. The monks in Gaul had greater expo-sure to the theological traditions of the Greek East, and they had their own lumi-naries, such as John Cassian, to guide them. Although they certainly did not discount Augustine's authority, they were less beholden to it than were their African counterparts.[9] What the African and Gallic ascetics did have in common was a rejection of Pelagianism. This brings up the other, more important way, in which the designation "semi-Pelagian" misleads. It suggests that Augustine's more or less loyal opposition needed to be persuaded not to be Pelagians.

Pelagianism itself is not well defined as a historical movement.[10] Its eponymous founder the lay ascetic Pelagius, a native of Roman Britain, was active in Rome in the years prior to Alaric's sack of the city in 410; there Pelagius was exhorting Christians to transcend the moral mediocrity of indifferent times and hold them-selves to an exemplary standard of perfection, a message that was winning an audience principally among lay men and women of aristocratic lineage. Pelagius

THE CAMBRIDGE COMPANION TO AUGUSTINE

fled Rome when the city was threatened and sojourned for about a year in North Africa while en route to the Holy Land. It was his disciple, Caelestius, a Roman aristocrat, who first aroused the ire of the North African bishops. While in Carthage, Caelestius raised questions about the practice of infant baptism, suggesting it could be supported (as he in fact did support it) without having to appeal to an original sin which tainted every human birth. For the Africans, this was to question a hard-won dogma, and they denounced him in synod. Pelagius briefly escaped guilt by association when he was cleared of heresy at the synod of Diospolis, presided over by a council of bishops from Palestine in December 415. But in the years following his acquittal, the Africans, now led by Augustine, rallied their forces and eventually persuaded pope Zosimus to condemn the heresy of Pelagius. After 418 Pelagianism continued as a reactionary movement led by Julian of Eclanum, one of 18 Italian bishops to protest the condemnation. Julian was probably the best theologian of the Pelagian lot, certainly the most effective controversialist; he managed to embarrass Augustine by associating his defense of the doctrine of original sin with the heretical Manichaean view of the flesh as inherently evil. (Augustine had once been a Manichee, although never one of the adepts.) Regardless of the lengthy and rather vituperative exchanges between Augustine and Julian, Pelagianism ceased to be a viable theological alternative in the Latin West once its early proponents were either officially denounced or forced to take up residence in the East.

There is another story of Pelagianism, tangentially related to movements, personalities, and politics, but mostly about the mind of Augustine himself and the ability of that mind to shape and anticipate the agenda of Western theological enquiry. In *De dono perseverantiae*, he neatly reduces Pelagianism to three grave errors: to think that God redeems according to some scale of human merit; to imagine that some human beings are actually capable of a sinless life; to suppose that the descendants of the first human beings to sin are themselves born innocent.[11] His Gallic readers would have readily recognized the errors as grave and rejected them as such. Their quarrel was with Augustine's doctrine of predestination, not with his doctrine of original sin, nor with his sense of the necessity and generosity of God's grace. Still Augustine pressed them as if they were incipient Pelagians. It was apparently possible to reject the letter of Pelagianism but still be seduced unawares by its spirit. The spirit of Pelagianism as Augustine wrestled with it has been difficult for even his admirers to grasp, let alone exorcise; all the same it exerts its influence on Augustine's legacy, leaving to his heirs and enemies alike a sense of human destiny that can seem, in the blink of an eye, wildly hopeful or darkly despairing.

His tone in *De dono perseverantiae* and its companion piece, *De praedestinatione sanctorum*, is irenic, even sympathetic – not at all like the combative rhetoric of the work he would soon take up but never finish against Julian, an avowed Pelagian. His major work just prior to these works, the *Retractationes*, had been a review of his own long list of literary productions, not exhaustive but substantial. Something about the doubts and confusions of the Gallic monks further encouraged his retrospection. In *De dono perseverantiae*, he speaks admiringly of his *Confessiones*, the work of his that had first irked Pelagius,[12] and defensively of *De libero arbitrio*, the one work of his that had won Pelagius' approval.[13] In *De praedestinatione sanctorum*, he confesses that he too once thought too little of grace. In an early exegesis of Romans 9, where Paul discusses God's favoring of Jacob over Esau, Augustine had assumed that election must be based on foreknowledge of faith; God could see that Jacob, and not Esau, would one day put his strength in the Lord.[14] It was not the error of Pelagius. Augustine never thought of himself as having ever been Pelagian. But it was close enough, an error in the spirit of Pelagius; now the monks were caught by it. In both works for their benefit, he commended his brethren to consult another work of his on Paul, written at the request of his friend and mentor, Simplician, successor to Ambrose in the See of Milan.[15]

In the second part of his first book of responses to Simplician, Augustine revises his earlier reading of Romans 9 and concludes, somewhat to his own amazement, that Paul could not have been speaking there of an election based on foreknown faith; that would be too close to the idea that divine favor is dispensed on the basis of what some human beings do better than others.[16] In the case at hand, Jacob would be better than his brother at faithfulness. Augustine had before been convinced that Paul rejects works-based election; what had yet to occur to him was how broadly the notion of a work should be interpreted. In his revised reading of Paul, he decides that election and the means of conveying it – God's grace – must be utterly gratuitous. If God favors Jacob over Esau, one of two brothers formed in the same womb, then God has decided, for reasons known only to God, to make Jacob into the brother worth choosing.[17] In other words, God both foreknows and predestines Jacob's redemption. For anyone who is similarly favored by God, the call to redemption is given in such a way as to elicit a faithful response; God never has to wait for human faith to come of its own. As for the ones not favored – the condemned heap (*massa damnata*) – they, like Esau, are simply never called in the right way.[18]

Doubtless Augustine's replies to Simplician signaled, as he himself indicated, a new turn in his theology, his first fateful step towards a predestinarian theology. He thought that he had disposed of Pelagianism then and there, before ever hearing of Pelagius or having to convince monks of the pre-emptory power of grace. His interpreters have been less sure of what *De diversis quaestionibus ad Simplicianum* can be said to anticipate. I follow Patout Burns in thinking of the work as unsettled.[19] There is the revolutionary rereading of Romans 9, which gives Augustine an exegetical basis for insisting on the gratuity of grace, but this rereading sits uncomfortably next to what he has had to say in the previous section, where he ponders Paul's avowals of distress in Romans 7, such as 7.18: "Wanting the good, that I am near to, but doing the good, no."[20] At this point in his understanding of Paul, Augustine has yet to imagine that even the apostle of the resurrected Christ can be graced with divine favor and sometimes lack the ability to act out of his better nature; he assumes that Paul must be speaking out of character in Romans 7, affecting the persona of someone who despairs of his own strength and longs for grace. About a quarter of a century later and well into his conflict with the Pelagians, Augustine alters his reading of Romans 7 and insists that Paul speaks there in his own voice.[21]

Two developments in Augustine's thought have intervened. He has come to think that no one has a desire for God – not a scintilla of it – who has not been predestined by God to have it. In stark contrast, desire that originates with human beings is always the dark, ungodly desire of ungraced freedom. He has further come to think that this latter kind of desire, in light of its human origins, is what damns humanity. To be born human is to be born judged. Those predestined to be spared are shown unaccountable mercy. Whether these two arguably parallel lines of thought were dictated by Augustine's turn in *De diversis quaestionibus ad Simplicianum* or merely suggested by it, they convey quite evidently the difficulties of squaring his doctrine of predestination with divine justice and human responsibility.

Adam and Christ: a question of priority

Adam had a certain amount of grace, but it was not enough to carry him through his most desperate choice. Eve had taken her taste of forbidden fruit – knowledge of good and bad, in a form she found hanging from a tree – and now she was offering what she had picked to him. On one side of his choice was Yahweh, who had breathed life (*spiritus*) into wet clay and made Adam, a creature of the earth, into a living being, and on the other was the partner Yahweh had intended him to have, flesh of Adam's flesh, bone of his bone. He could choose his flesh over his spirit or his spirit over his flesh, if either of these choices can be imagined humanly sustainable. The writer of Genesis does not tell us how Adam himself imagined his choice. We are simply told that the woman gave the fruit to her husband, and he ate of it (Genesis 3.7).

Augustine's Adam is an ambiguous figure, something like a human crossroads. In his original flesh, he is neither mortal nor immortal, but the living embodiment of the choice between life eternal and a way to die. Augustine rejected the Pelagian exegesis of Genesis, which had made Adam out to be mortal from the beginning, and in its place set the notion of a conditional immortality: "If he had not sinned, he would have had to have been changed into a spiritual body and passed into the incorruptibility which is promised to the saints and the faithful."[22] It does not take a Pelagian to wonder, Changed from what? Can there be a natural alternative to the spiritual body that is not naturally mortal? Adam's choice does not so much resolve the ambiguity of his nature as pass it on to his descendants; in the best of times, the saints and the faithful experience in themselves a temporary ascendancy of spirit over flesh, but never without some reminder of an unintegrated flesh – a nagging desire to seek fulfillment apart from spirit, or what Augustine normally dubs 'concupiscence' (*concupiscentia*). Human flesh seems incapable of forgetting whatever had moved Adam to choose as he did; the apostles themselves, says Augustine, were dogged by concupiscence to the end of their days.[23]

Adam is in us in some mysterious and mythic way, but he is not, for Augustine, the paradigm of what it means to be human. The most important difference between Adam and the rest of us is that we no longer have – if we ever did – his original choice. He could either serve the desires of his flesh or not. We can either serve dispirited flesh, having no other motive to guide us, or be led inexorably by the spirit to lose all motive for serving the flesh. There is no middle way. If as a son or daughter of Adam, you feel yourself torn between spirit and flesh, and your struggle is genuine (not a trick of the flesh), you are already graced in a way unknown to Adam. He was free to part from God and die; you are bound to die, but are not free to part from God. In your struggle against the flesh, you are already claimed by spirit – predestined, that is, to incarnate incorruptible flesh, that of the resurrected body. When Augustine insists that no desire for God is uninspired by God, he has in mind this pre-emption of Adam's choice. The ones whom God wants to keep, God never loses to corruptible flesh.[24]

The notion that Adam could be the original human being but not paradigmatic of humanity has caused no end of trouble for Augustine's interpreters. The Pelagians were the first to be put off. If the descendents of Adam were not free as individuals to make a choice between good and bad, spirit and flesh, then what was making Augustine think that a human being could still be responsible for becoming one kind of person rather than another? The monks who would later become known as semi-Pelagians were similarly vexed. Granting that the original power of choice is only a shadow of what it once was, is there not still some remnant of choice left, at least enough to allow a humbled monk to turn his freedom willingly over to God? In response to broadly Pelagian worries, Augustine would try to undercut nostalgia for Adam's condition; whatever freedom can be said to be present in Adam's original choice, it has to be less, he says, than what the saints are getting through Christ.[25] The saints are being led in life into the freedom of new flesh, still mortal like the old but freed from sin and therefore fit to be resurrected; it is an experience of the flesh that is impossible to contemplate while still facing Adam's kind of choice or regretting the loss of it.

What misleads in Augustine's response is his tendency to contrast the freedom of the saints with the loss of freedom in those supposedly not predestined in Christ and therefore bound to sin. In one breath, he invokes Adam's original choice of sin to explain why the freedom *only* to sin is justly punishable in all of Adam's descendants; in the next he refuses to have Adam's original freedom not to sin count in any way in the election of some to saintliness. The Pelagians were understandably confused. If Adam never had Christ's kind of freedom, and if this is the freedom that makes people pleasing to God, why is the loss of Adam's kind of freedom at all relevant to the issue of what makes people responsible for sin?

I do not believe that Augustine ever had a good answer to this question, and yet it is, in a number of different forms, the question that his critics have most wanted him to resolve. When he is relieved for a moment of this burden, his doctrine of predestination shows a different face. Christ's kind of freedom – the freedom of a pure heart – is no longer an indictment of an originally human failing, but a reminder and offer of the humanity that human beings were originally intended to have. The doctrine of predestination becomes, in essence, the claim that Christ's humanity is prior to Adam's, even though Jesus of Nazareth, like any descendant of Adam, is born into historical time and has a genealogy. In Jesus Christ, time and eternity have conjoined; for those who are his heirs, there is no longer a need to reckon the human incarnation of spirit a failure. When flesh and spirit war, as they seem inevitably to do in life, that is a birth pang rather than a death throe. Adam may have obscured the difference between living and dying by choosing flesh in the way in which he chose it. Who is in a position to throw stones? The one who could chose not to, and the result is that life is still before us.

If Augustine were to have kept to this face of predestination, he might still have had something important to say about human responsibility for sin, but nothing, I think, that would have led him back to his terrible doctrine of reprobation. Augustine accords reprobates, or those not predestined to be redeemed, a double punishment. The reprobate soul, disposed to deprive itself of God in order to satisfy the flesh, gets half its wish: it is deprived of God. Then, when physical death has sundered soul from its needy body, the soul awaits final judgment. Its body is destined to be returned to it, as a vehicle for its punishment. Pain is heaped upon deprivation.[26] This is the view of the same Augustine who believes that as the soul is the life of the body, so is God the life of the soul.[27] If God were truly to abandon a soul, or let a soul deprive itself fully of spirit, there would be nothing living left to punish. Hell is not what you find in a God-forsaken life; it is what you find on the way there.

Conclusion: the lesson of incarnation

Christ and the saints partake of the same predestination, but with this difference: Christ is predestined to be the head of humanity, the saints the limbs. The image, which is taken from *De praedestinatione sanctorum*, suggests the reconstitution of a body.[28] It recalls in a telling way Augustine's own experience of conversion in the *Confessiones*. In Book 8, we hear of an Augustine torn between spirit and flesh, wanting to lead a life of service to God, but still strangely bound to a discredited carnality. The resolution to his immediate crisis comes in a moment of illumination, when he takes up a book of scripture, reads where his eyes first land, and responds to this command: "clothe yourself in the Lord Jesus Christ and make no provision for the flesh in carnal desires (*concupiscentiis*)."[29] Although the Latin term, *concupiscentia*, clearly has the connotation of robust sexual appetite, the contrast implied in the command is between two ways of wearing the flesh; not all desires for the flesh, then, are trouble. Augustine has confessed up to this point that he has had a great deal of trouble with sexual desire, but his trouble has come not from sex *per se*, but from the odd way in which satisfying his mundane desires, the sexual ones especially, has left him feeling empty rather than fulfilled. He seeks communion and finds alienation instead. From Christ he hopes to learn a better way of seeking. In Augustine's moment of illumination, he catches a glimmer, I suspect, of the difference between love and desire. It is in any case the cardinal distinction of his lifetime's confession.

The difference between love and desire, though familiar to most of us, is notoriously painful to learn. In Augustine's life and thought the lesson takes on a peculiar urgency. He sees himself and all the rest of us as caught up in sin; that is, we are born disposed to deprive ourselves of the good in a vain attempt to serve our individual happiness. The end of this seeking, if left unchecked, is consummate deprivation – the void at sin's heart. Would God – the good that we are missing – allow this to happen? The hope that underwrites Augustine's doctrine of predestination suggests not. We are never forsaken in the lesson we have to learn about love, even should God have to meet us in the void. If that sounds too easy, Augustine would have us remember that no saint while walking the earth ever quite shakes off the lure of loveless desire; if it sounds too contrived, he would have us know that even with the help of Christ, the best of teachers, the lesson is still ours to learn.

NOTES

1 *De dono persev.* 14.35.
2 Augustine reviews himself in his *Retractationes*. Although there he is not at all averse to flagging his errors, he never imagines himself to have been other than deeply respectful of divine initiative – even in his early works against Manichees, where he often felt bound to underscore human responsibility for sin.
3 *De dono persev.* 24.67.
4 Here is another, mildly paradoxical way of making Augustine's claim: Christ's

humanity is uniquely and fully responsive to divine grace, and it is divine grace that has made Christ's humanity what it is. See *De praed. sanct.* 15.30–31. For an account of Augustine's christology that goes well beyond what I can sketch in my essay, I recommend the one in TeSelle 1970, pp. 146–176.

5 I leave to the side the exceptional, but possibly parallel case of Mary. Augustine never questions her immaculate conception and exemplary life, but her sinless status is for him a reflection of her son's. See *De nat. et gratia* 36.42.

6 *De civ. Dei* 5.9; cf. *De lib. arb.* 3.2.4–3.4.11.

7 *De praed. sanct.* 10.19.

8 *Ep.* 194.

9 The historical and theological intricacies of semi-Pelagianism are well reviewed in Harden 1996.

10 On the shape and significance of Pelagianism as an historical movement, I am much indebted to the Otts lectures of Gerald Bonner, Bonner 1992 and 1993.

11 *De dono persev.* 2.4.

12 Ibid. 20.53.

13 Ibid. 11.27.

14 *De praed. sanct.* 3.7; *Expositio quarundam propositionum ex epistola ad Romanos* 60–62.

15 *De praed. sanct.* 4.8; *De dono persev.* 21.55.

16 *De diversis quaestionibus ad Simplicianum* 1.2.5–7.

17 It is, of course, contradictory to assert both that redemption is given gratuitously and that God has some reason, albeit unfathomable, for redeeming one person rather than another (e.g., Jacob rather than Esau). Augustine is willing to tolerate this contradiction in order to preserve the appearance of God's justice.

18 *De diversis quaestionibus ad Simplicianum* 1.2.13–14.

19 Burns 1980.

20 *De diversis quaestionibus ad Simplicianum* 1.1.11. I have translated Paul from Augustine's Latin citation of him.

21 *C. ep. Pelag.* 1.8.14; 1.10.22.

22 *De pecc. merit. et remis.* 1.2.2.

23 *C. ep. Pelag.* 1.11.24.

24 The locus classicus for the reading of Augustine I have just sketched is *De correptione et gratia* 11.31–12.35. In those chapters, he contrasts the grace whereby Adam was able not to sin (*posse non peccare*) with the grace that Christ had not to be able to sin (*non posse peccare*). The saints are taken up into the grace of Christ.

25 *De corrept. et gratia* 12.35.

26 *De civ. Dei* 21.3.

27 *Conf.* 3.6.10; cf. *De civ. Dei* 13.2.

28 *De praed. sanct.* 15.31.

29 *Conf.* 8.12.29; the citation is from Romans 13.14.

5

TIIOMAS WILLIAMS

Biblical interpretation

Augustine's exegetical writings

Augustine began writing commentary on scripture not long after his conversion. His first such work, meant as a counterblast to Manichaean attacks on the creation account, was *De Genesi contra Manichaeos* (388–390). In many ways it sets the tone for much of his later work: Augustine admits an allegorical sense but warns against overenthusiasm for allegory and denigration of the literal sense; we see also from the outset Augustine's interest in scripture as a controversialist and polemicist. After his ordination to the priesthood in 391, he seems to have gone through something of a writer's block,[1] starting but leaving incomplete a treatise on exegetical theory (*De doctrina christiana*, begun 396 but not completed until 427), another commentary on Genesis (*De Genesi ad litteram imperfectus liber*, 393–394), and an exposition of Romans (*Epistolae ad Romanos inchoata expositio*, 394–395). He did manage to finish a verse-by-verse commentary on Galatians, giving the literal sense (*Epistolae ad Galatas expositio*, 394–395) and a commentary on the Sermon on the Mount (*De sermone Domini in monte*, 393–396). His *Expositio quarundam propositionum ex epistola ad Romanos* (394) derives from conversations with the monks at Hippo, who recorded his answers to their questions about Romans; Augustine tells us later that he missed what he eventually came to see as the main point of the epistle.

Augustine found his voice when he came to write the *Confessions* (397), of which Books 11–13 are an extended commentary on Genesis 1. It is often described as an allegorical commentary, but wrongly so: most of it is quite literal by Augustine's standards, which are unlike ours. Only in Book 13, chapter 12, does the real allegory begin: Augustine sees in the story of the divine making of the formless world another story about the divine remaking of the sinful soul. After the *Confessions* came two works not intended as sustained commentary: *Quaestiones evangeliorum* (399–400) is a loose collection of replies to a correspondent's questions about Matthew and Luke; and the *Adnotationes in Job* (399) were compiled and published, not very skillfully, by others. *De consensu evangelistarum* (399–400), by contrast, was a product of more careful composition; in it Augustine discusses the authority and nature of the Gospels and attempts to reconcile apparent contradictions between them.

The greatest of Augustine's exegetical writings, mostly long works composed over the course of many years, came between 400 and 420. *De Genesi ad litteram libri duodecim* (401–415) is a wide-ranging and open-ended work intended to show the consistency of scripture with the science of the day; polemic against the Manichees no longer figures in the title, but it is by no means forgotten. Perhaps his greatest work on scripture is the *In Joannis evangelium tractatus* (406–421; the dates are much disputed), a collection of sermons treating the whole text of the Gospel. It is a masterly blend of literal and allegorical exegesis, philosophical speculation, moral exhortation, and theological polemic. The commentary on First John (*In Johannis epistulam ad Parthos tractatus*, 406–407) is another collection of exegetical sermons, as is the highly allegorical *Enarrationes in Psalmos*, which Augustine began in 392 and put in final order around 417. (A number of the sermons in the *Enarrationes*, however, were composed specially for the work and were never preached.) Augustine's other *Sermons* (392–430) are also generally exegetical. An *Expositio epistolae Jacobi ad duodecem tribus*, probably written around 412, is no longer extant.

In 419 Augustine wrote two commentaries on the first seven books of the Bible. *Locutiones in heptateuchum* deals with obscurities in the Latin text that arise from peculiarities of Hebrew or Greek idiom; *Quaestiones in heptateuchum* offers more developed exposition of difficult passages. Near the end of his life Augustine made a collection of moral injunctions in the *Speculum Scripturae* (*Mirror of Scripture*, 427).

De octo quaestionibus ex veteri testamento is of uncertain date, and its authenticity is controversial.

Exegetical practice

Augustine's exegetical practice defies easy generalization. A reader who wishes to get a feel for his style as a biblical commentator can do no better than to follow him through a few representative passages. Here I provide an introduction to that task by exhibiting Augustine's approach to Genesis 1.1–2a in *Confessions* 11.3–12.13. The first thing one notices is that Augustine has squeezed some 9000 words of commentary from a text that runs (in his version) to a mere 17 words. He is not always so prolix, of course, but Augustine finds a great deal in his chosen texts – partly because, being thoroughly convinced of their divine authority, he *expects* to find a great deal in them. He is no cautious scholar, afraid to commit himself beyond the evidence, trained to a dreary skepticism that scours the gloss off the greatest of texts; he brings to his exegesis the full measure of Christian belief. His goal, moreover, is not merely to inform us but to help us see things differently. So he does not (for example) merely offer a quick definition of some difficult term in scripture and then move on; he asks his readers to look within until, by teasing out the implications of some quite ordinary experience or idea, he brings us to see for ourselves what the term means. And he often breaks off for praise to God and exhortation to his readers – these not being digressions, in his mind, but an integral part of the exegete's task. These procedures, however, do not make for short commentaries.

"In the beginning God made heaven and earth." In Augustine's view, the change and variation of created things is itself evidence that they have their existence from some source other than themselves. Moreover, the beauty, the goodness, indeed the very existence of heaven and earth points to the perfect beauty, goodness, and being of their Creator, whom they mimic in their fragmentary and defective way. So heaven and earth were made, and it was God who made them: but how? He cannot have used any pre-existing material in order to make them, because all such material is itself part of heaven and earth. Thus, purely rational argument shows that God created *ex nihilo*, and Augustine often relies on such philosophical argument in his commentaries. But rational argument has left us with an unanswered question: "*How* did God create heaven and earth?" To find the answer, Augustine relies on another favorite exegetical technique: he uses one part of scripture to illuminate another. For scripture itself tells us how God made heaven and earth: "He spoke and they were made" (Psalm 33.9) and "By the word of the Lord were the heavens established" (Psalm 33.6). What sort of word was this? It could not have been a word produced by a physical voice and having temporal duration, for there were as yet no physical voices and no time. It must have been an eternal word – in fact, the Word of which John the Evangelist wrote. "And so you call us to understand the Word, God with you, O God, the Word that is uttered eternally and by which all things are uttered eternally" (*Conf.* 11.7.9). This Word, as Truth itself, is rightly called the Beginning, since "if he did not abide when we went astray, there would be nowhere for us to return to. Now when we return from going astray, we certainly return through knowing; and in order that we might know, he teaches us, since he is the Beginning and also speaks to us"[2] (*Conf.* 11.8.10).

So "in the beginning" means "in the co-eternal Word." Since the Word is eternal, the divine act of creation is eternal, and there is no room for questions like "What was God doing before he made heaven and earth?" Augustine accordingly embarks on a long explanation of the nature of eternity and time,[3] all aimed at showing the folly of such questions and providing us with some insight, inevitably dim and partial, into a mode of existence utterly different from our own life in this realm of beginnings and ends.

Having explained "In the beginning," Augustine moves on to "God created

THE CAMBRIDGE COMPANION TO AUGUSTINE

heaven and earth." Here he relies on a passage from the Psalms (115.15–16) where scripture itself comments on scripture: "May you be blessed by the Lord, who made heaven and earth. The heaven of heaven is the Lord's, but the earth he gave to the children of men." Here, "heaven" is identified with the heaven of heaven, and earth means the whole visible creation – including what we conventionally call the heavens (the skies). Augustine understands the "heaven of heaven" to be some sort of intellectual creature that ceaselessly contemplates God and is everlastingly happy in that contemplation. Although it is capable of change, it does not in fact change – so that it is not bound by time.[4]

Then we are told something about the earth (that is, the whole material creation): "The earth was invisible and unformed." That is, the first step of material creation is formless matter: "Was it not you, O Lord, who taught me that before you gave form and variety to this formless matter, it was not anything: not color, not shape, not body, not spirit? And yet it was not altogether nothing; it was a sort of formlessness, devoid of all beauty" (*Conf.* 12.3.3). It is not that God actually created formless matter first and then proceeded to form it; this is not a case of temporal succession but of logical priority. Rational analysis shows that underlying all change from one form to another there must be some "stuff" that itself has no form but is capable of taking on form; this is the formless matter of which Augustine speaks.

This formless almost-nothing is timeless, because time is present only where there is change in form. The temporality of creatures means mutability, which is in a sense a limitation; but it is also the sphere in which God can work by forming them. The heaven of heaven is also not temporal, because although changeable, it is never in fact changed. Hence, there is no mention of "day" when "God created the heaven [i.e. of heaven] and the earth [i.e. unformed matter]," because neither of these creations is temporal. We get days only when God starts to form matter in various ways.

Exegetical theory: epistemological dimensions

Again, this is what Augustine considers literal exegesis – for he is reading the creation story as a creation story, not as (for example) the story of the Church or of individual salvation, and so he is not reading it allegorically. But even in literal commentary the exegete is free to draw material from altogether different parts of scripture and from the best of philosophy. The approach is not scholarly in the modern sense – no self-respecting biblical scholar in our day would offer a reading of Genesis that depended heavily on Saint John the Evangelist and Plato – and the results are often anything but commonsensical. Augustine is aware that the reading he has just given will strike some people as strange: "Others, admirers of the book of Genesis and not fault-finders [he is thinking of the Manichees in the latter group], say, 'The Spirit of God, who wrote these words through his servant Moses, did not intend for them to be understood in this way; he did not mean what you say, but something else – what we say'" (*Conf.* 12.14.17).

In his response Augustine lays out the theory that legitimates his exegetical practice. He begins by stating some things he is quite sure of, things that "Truth says to me with a strong voice in my inward ear" (*Conf.* 12.15.18). Now he had used this expression three times in 12.11, where he was laying out his exegesis in the first place, except there it was "You, Lord, have said to me with a strong voice in my inward ear." Note two crucial differences in the expression as it appears here. First, it has changed from second person to third; the subject now is 'Truth,' which to Augustine means specifically God the Son. Second, it is no longer perfect tense ("you have said") but present ("Truth is saying"). These changes hint at some significant elements of the theory that will emerge. What we learn from scripture is learned from Truth himself. And Truth is not past but present, always accessible. It is in intellectual "memory," where we see not the images of past realities that are now gone (as is the case with sense memory) but the present – in effect timeless – realities themselves.

There is a careful parallelism in Augustine's invocation of what is said to him "with a strong voice in [his] inward ear." In 12.11 he uses that expression to introduce a discussion of (a) God's eternity, then of (b) the relationship between God and creatures, then of (c) the heaven of heaven; he then adds, independently of that expression, a discussion of (d) the timelessness of unformed matter. The sequence recurs in 12.15. These are the three things he is sure of, because Truth himself tells him: (a) God is eternal and immutable, so there is no succession in him, and therefore no change in his will regarding creatures; (b) everything that exists comes from God, who supremely is; and (c) there is a sublime creature, not co-eternal with God, but also not temporal. Finally, he says, (d) there was also formless matter, which was created by God and also was not temporal. At each of these points he imagines asking his objectors, "Is this true?" and they invariably reply, "We do not deny it."

But if the objectors concede all these points – which together constitute almost the whole of Augustine's exegesis – what is their objection? Simply that when Moses wrote of "heaven," he was not thinking of the "heaven of heaven," and when he wrote of "earth," he was not thinking of the whole material creation. So Augustine goes on to consider several rival interpretations of these expressions. What is important for our purposes is not specifically what the different accounts say, but the fact that Augustine maintains that all the accounts are true. He insists that what he says is true, and the objectors should not deny it. But what they say is also true, and he will not deny that either.

This extraordinary generosity towards other interpretations makes perfect sense in light of Augustine's epistemology and philosophy of language. Written words are signs of spoken words, and spoken words in turn are signs of the speaker's thoughts. If all goes well, the written words will exactly capture the spoken words, and the spoken words will perfectly convey the speaker's thoughts; one who reads those words will in turn understand exactly what they mean, and thus the contents of the reader's mind will exactly match the contents of the author's mind. But Augustine is always keen to draw our attention to the many ways in which things might not go so well. A speaker may be lying or self-deceived about what he thinks. The author's thoughts might surpass his skill – perhaps any human skill – to signify them by words. The reader might be too dull or too distracted to make use of the words properly so that they carry his mind to just those realities which they were meant to signify, or the words themselves might be ambiguous. Augustine is, moreover, at least intermittently mindful that he is reading the scriptures in Latin translation,[5] and translation complicates the story even further.

The words of Genesis are ambiguous, at least in the sense that as they stand they do not rule out a variety of rival interpretations, all of them plausible. Now what Moses wrote signifies what Moses would have said, so we could reduce the ambiguity if we could get Moses to speak to us – which, of course, we cannot do:

> I want to hear and to understand how in the beginning you made heaven and earth. Moses wrote this. He wrote it and went away; he passed over from here, from you to you, and he is not now in front of me. For if he were, I would get hold of him and ask him and plead with him for your sake to explain these things to me, and I would open the ears of my body to the sounds emanating from his mouth. And if he spoke in Hebrew, he would knock on my senses in vain, and none of what he said would strike my mind; but if he spoke in Latin, I would know what he was saying. (*Conf.* 11.3.5)

Ordinarily even this would hardly be satisfactory, for we cannot generally know that a speaker even believes what he is saying; "Who knows the thoughts of a man but the spirit of the man within him?" Moreover, it is normally of no great moment to find out what someone is thinking: "Surely teachers do not profess to offer their own thoughts for their students to learn and memorize, rather than the actual subject-matter that they take themselves to be propounding when they speak. For who would be so foolishly curious as to send his child to school in order to find out what the teacher thinks?" (*De mag.* 14).

With Moses matters are somewhat different, since we can assume that Moses knew his own mind and intended to communicate his thoughts faithfully, and since we have a prior commitment to believing that whatever Moses thought and said under divine inspiration was true. Even so, would an interview with Moses be all we needed to overcome the deficiencies of signs? It would not. If he spoke in Latin, Augustine says,

> I would know what he was saying. But from what source would I know whether what he was saying was true? And if I were to know that, I wouldn't know it from him, would I? No indeed: the inward Truth, within me in the dwelling-place of my thought, would say to me – not in Hebrew or Greek or Latin or any barbarous language, without any organ of mouth or tongue, without the rattling of syllables – "What he says is true." And I with certainty and confidence would immediately say to him, "What you say is true." (*Conf.* 11.3.5)

The argument thus far offers two reasons why biblical exegesis is not, after all, concerned with figuring out the author's intention. The first is that our ability to get at the author's intention is limited. Moses is not around for us to ask him questions, and any difficult text might bear more than one plausible and defensible interpretation. The second, and deeper, reason is that what guarantees the veracity of the author, and thus the text, is the divine truth; and that same divine truth is available to us even apart from our interpretation of the text.

Suppose, then, that Augustine says Genesis 1:1 means *x*, and I say it means *y*; suppose further that upon consulting Christ as Inner Teacher we find that both *x* and *y* are true. The only question is, which did Moses *mean*, *x* or *y*? Augustine asks, why not both?

> So when one person says "He meant what I say," and another says "No, he meant what I say," I think it would be more pious to say "Why not both, if both are true?" And if someone should see in his words a third truth, or a fourth, or indeed any other truth, why not believe that Moses saw all these truths? (*Conf.* 12.31.42)

Somewhat surprisingly, it is not pride but just good Augustinian theology (and epistemology) to suspect that we might find truths in Moses' writings that had never crossed his mind:

> Finally, Lord, you who are God and not flesh and blood, even if one who was merely a man did not see all there was to be seen, did not your good Spirit, who will lead me into the land of uprightness, know everything that you would reveal through these words to later readers, even if the one who uttered them was perhaps thinking of only one of the many true meanings? If so, let us suppose he was thinking of whichever meaning is most exalted. O Lord, show us that meaning; or if you please, show us some other true meaning. In this way, whether you show us just what you showed your servant, or something else that emerges from the same words, we will in any event be fed by you, not mocked by error. (*Conf.* 12.32.43)[6]

By now it would seem that scripture is entirely unnecessary: if we have independent access to the truth, what need do we have of a written revelation? Augustine's answer is twofold. First, the written words of scripture are signs, and they help direct our mind's eye to the realities they signify. Suppose I want to draw your attention to something, so I point to it and say, "Look over there." You see it, and thereby come to know it. I begin to congratulate myself on my success as a teacher, but you retort, "My vision was working perfectly well, thank you. I am the one who looked, and I am the one who saw for myself. So what I know, I know from myself, not from you." "True enough," I reply, "but would you ever have looked if I had not pointed?" Scripture is such a pointer. We do not learn intelligible things from Moses or Paul or the Evangelists; we learn them by seeing them for ourselves in the eternal Truth. But the words of scripture are signs that direct our attention to what we could, but rarely ever would, see without them.

Secondly, notice that I have been speaking thus far only of intelligible realities, since those are the timeless and unchanging realities of which Truth speaks to us in our inward ear. There are also truths that belong to the realm of time and change, and our only independent access to those truths is through our senses. I do not consult Christ the Inner Teacher in order to find out whether my office door is open; I just look. The senses can tell me only about the present; sense memory also tells me about the past – only my own past, though, and not even all of that. This means that most of the past is not merely unknown but unknowable: I cannot know it through the Inner Truth, because it is not a timeless intelligible reality, and I cannot know it through sense or sense memory, because it is not now and never was present to my senses. In that unknowable past are truths that, Augustine believes, I desperately need to be aware of; the most important, of course, is that "the Word became flesh and dwelt among us." The words of scripture make us aware of such truths in the unknowable past; if we did not believe them on the authority of scripture, we could not have any beliefs about them at all. Thus, scripture is indispensable not only because it directs our reason to see what we might otherwise miss, but because it informs us of things that neither reason nor sense can now reveal to us.

Exegetical theory: moral dimensions

The pursuit of knowledge for its own sake is bankrupt, as far as Augustine is concerned. Such a pursuit springs from curiosity, which for him is no admirable trait but a vice; he identifies it with that "lust of the eyes" of which John wrote, "For all that is in the world – the lust of the eyes, the lust of the flesh, and the pride of life – is not of the Father but is of the world" (1 John 2:16). So it is not surprising that when Augustine discusses the legitimacy of rival interpretations of scripture, he reveals a deep concern with the morality of exegetical disputes. Undue attachment to one's own exegesis manifests a sort of pride, the love of one's own opinion simply because it is one's own opinion. In *Confessions* 10 Augustine describes this as a form of the "pride of life," the third of the unholy trinity of sins from 1 John 2:16. It is more grievous still when the exegete is driven by the desire for a reputation as a brilliant scholar: "this is a miserable life and revolting ostentation" (*Conf.* 10.36.59). Moreover, since truth is common property, one's own opinion is not really one's own at all if it is true; it is the common property of all right-thinking people, and no one has any individual stake in it: "No one should regard anything as his own, except perhaps a lie, since all truth is from him who says, 'I am the truth'" (*De doct. christ.* Prologue, 8). Also, only temerity and insolence could justify such confidence in something we cannot actually know. We can know what Truth itself says, but we cannot know with any degree of certainty what Moses or Paul was thinking when he wrote the biblical text we are expounding. Most important of all, charity demands that we abstain from all such "pernicious disputes."

For charity is the ultimate aim of all worthy exegesis. "Whoever thinks he has understood the divine scriptures or any part of them in such a way that his understanding does not build up the twin love of God and neighbor has not yet understood them at all" (*De doct. christ.* 1.36.40). Charity is, moreover, the unifying and animating theme of Augustine's treatise on biblical interpretation, *De doctrina christiana* ("On Christian Teaching"). Its message is this: Be always mindful of the end, and be on your guard against the pernicious tendency of means to encroach upon the ends. The end of all things, Augustine insists, is God. He alone is to be loved for his own sake – "enjoyed," in Augustine's terminology. Whatever else is to be loved should be "used," that is, loved for the sake of God. Even human beings, including ourselves, should be "used" in this sense – which does not mean "exploited." But Augustine cannot quite bring himself to talk consistently of "using" ourselves and our fellow human beings, and he defines charity as "the motion of the soul toward enjoying God for his own sake and oneself and one's neighbor for God's sake" (*De doct. christ.* 3.10.16). Its opposite, cupidity, is "the motion of the soul toward enjoying oneself, one's neighbor, or any bodily thing for the sake of something other than God" (ibid.). Scripture, Augustine says, "commands nothing but charity and condemns nothing but cupidity" (*De doct. christ.* 3.10.15).

Interest in biblical interpretation for its own sake is one such form of cupidity; exegesis is to be used for the sake of charity, not enjoyed for its own sake. In Augustine's metaphor, it is not the distant land where we will be happy, but merely a vehicle by which we may be conveyed there:

> The fulfillment and end of the Law and of all divine scripture is the love of a being that is to be enjoyed [i.e. God], and of a being that can share that enjoyment with us [i.e. our neighbor] . . . That we might know this and be able to achieve it, the whole temporal dispensation was made by divine providence for our salvation. We should use it not with an abiding but with a transitory love and delight like that in

a road or conveyances or any other means . . . We should love those things by which
we are carried for the sake of that towards which we are carried. (*De doct. christ.*
1.35.39; see also 1.4.4)

So overriding is this end that even misreadings of scripture are scarcely objectionable if they build up charity. Someone guilty of such a misreading is to be
corrected only on pragmatic grounds, not in the interest of scholarly correctness
(an ideal to which Augustine shows not the slightest allegiance):

> He is deceived in the same way as someone who leaves a road by mistake but none-
> theless goes on through a field to the same place to which the road leads. Still, he
> should be corrected and shown how much more useful it is not to leave the road,
> lest his habit of wandering off should force him to take the long way around, or
> the wrong way altogether. (*De doct. christ.* 1.36.41)

Exegetical theory: practical dimensions

As we have seen, Book 1 of *De doctrina christiana* concerns things; it explains
which things are to be enjoyed and which are to be used. Books 2 and 3 discuss
signs, and in particular the conventional signs or words found in the biblical
writings. (Note again Augustine's concern that means should not encroach upon
ends. Signs exist for the sake of things, and not the other way around, so he must
first explain the nature of things before he can sensibly discuss the signs that
point us toward those things.) Augustine's aim is to provide practical precepts for
interpreters of the Bible to aid them in understanding both unknown signs (Book
2) and ambiguous signs (Book 3).[7]

The most important tool for understanding unknown literal signs is a thorough knowledge of Hebrew and Greek, so that the interpreter can resolve any
doubts that arise from conflicting translations.[8] To understand unknown figurative signs the interpreter needs a wide grounding in the nature of the plants,
animals, and other things that scripture uses in its figures; otherwise we will not
know (for example) why the dove brought an olive branch back to the ark or why
the Psalmist says, "You shall sprinkle me with hyssop." Interpreters must also
understand the figurative significance of numbers and should know something
of secular history. They should be acquainted with music, the arts, various trades
and professions, and sports – not as practitioners, but in order to understand the
scriptures when they use figurative expressions drawn from these areas.
Astronomy is only tangentially useful and is too closely allied with the pernicious superstitions of the astrologers to be quite safe. "The science of disputa-
tion is of great value for understanding and solving all sorts of questions that
arise in the sacred writings" (*De doct. christ.* 2.31.48), although interpreters
must be on their guard against the love of controversy and "childish showing off
in deceiving an adversary" (ibid.). Moreover, a clever person will recognize

fallacious arguments even without studying the rules of inference, and a stupid person will find it too hard to learn the rules. If you can recognize a bad argument when you see it, you do not need to know the technical name for the fallacy it exhibits; and such specialized knowledge is always a temptation to pride in oneself and disdain for others.

In acquiring the knowledge that will permit an intelligent reading of the scriptures, the Christian exegete is free to draw upon pagan wisdom, even pagan philosophy – especially the Platonists. When the Israelites fled from Egypt, they left behind the idols but took with them the gold and silver, treasures of Egypt that the Israelites could put to better use. So also the Christian must repudiate the "fraudulent and superstitious imaginings" of the pagans but appropriate whatever truths they might have found, the gold and silver that the pagans "extracted from the mines of divine providence" (*De doct. christ.* 2.40.60). After all, "every good and true Christian should understand that wherever he may find truth, it is his Lord's" (ibid. 2.18.28). Still, just as the treasures of Israel under Solomon surpassed the Egyptian gold, so also the truths to be found only in scripture are far more precious than any that can be appropriated from the pagans.

Having discussed the interpretation of unknown signs in Book 2, Augustine proceeds to consider ambiguous signs in Book 3. Ambiguities of punctuation and construction are to be corrected according to the "rule of faith" as it is found in unambiguous passages of scripture and the teaching of the Church, and by attention to the context, since any good interpretation must preserve internal consistency.[9] More difficult are the ambiguities of figurative words. We need some principle for determining whether a locution or a story is literal or figurative, and here Augustine returns to the theme of charity. "For figurative expressions a rule like this will be observed: What is read should be given careful consideration until an interpretation is produced that contributes to the reign of charity. If such a reading is already evident in the text taken literally, the expression should not be considered figurative" (*De doct. christ.* 3.15.23). For example, when scripture says "If your enemy is hungry, give him to eat; if he is thirsty, give him to drink," we should take the admonition literally. But when it goes on to say, "For in so doing you shall heap coals of fire on his head" (Proverbs 25.21–22, Romans 12.20), we must take this figuratively. A literal heaping of coals of fire would, after all, harm our enemy. We cannot even take the expression figuratively – but uncharitably – as meaning that our act of kindness will shame and confound our enemy; rather, "charity should call you to beneficence, so that you understand the coals of fire to be burning sighs of penitence that heal the pride of one who grieves that he was an enemy of a man who relieved his suffering" (*De doct. christ.* 3.16.24).

By the same principle, even stories of the evil deeds of great men and women of the faith can be taken literally, since they stand as a warning against pride in our own goodness. (The stories can be taken figuratively as well, but such readings do not take the place of a literal reading.) On the other hand, "no one would seriously believe that the Lord's feet were anointed with precious ointment by a woman, as is the custom among extravagant and worthless men whose entertainments we abhor" (*De doct. christ.* 3.12.18). The only reading conducive to charity is a figurative one: "the good odor is the good fame that anyone leading a good life will have through his deeds, when he follows in the footsteps of Christ, as if anointing his feet with a most precious odor" (ibid.).

NOTES

1 O'Donnell 1992, I:xlii-xliv discusses how "one literary project after another fell to pieces in [Augustine's] hands" in the period between his ordination and the writing of the *Confessions.*

2 John 8.25 in Augustine's version reads, "So they said to him, 'Who are you?' Jesus said to them, 'The beginning, because I also am speaking to you.'" Notice again a familiar pattern: by purely philosophical argumentation Augustine shows us what the creative word could not have been, and then through scripture he shows us what it was.

3 For Augustine's view of eternity and time, see chapter 8 of this volume.

4 The classic discussion of this mysterious creature (or possibly creatures) is Jean Pépin, "Recherches sur le sense et les origines de l'expression *caelum caeli* dans le livre XII des *Confessions* de S. Augustin," *Archivum Latinitatis Medii Aevi* 23 (1953): 185–274.

5 See, for example, *De doct. christ.* 2.11.16–2.15.22.

6 Augustine makes a similar argument at *De doct. christ.* 3.27.38.

7 Book 4 discusses rhetorical strategies for teaching and preaching and therefore falls outside our concern in this essay.

8 Augustine's precept is better than his practice: his Greek was mediocre, and he had no Hebrew at all. Consequently, he knew scripture chiefly in Latin translation. For an overview of what we know about Augustine's version of the Bible, see O'Donnell 1992, I:lxix-lxxi.

9 Augustine emphasizes this requirement in a number of places. See, for example, *Conf.* 12.29 and *De doct. christ.* 1.36.41, 3.2.2, and 3.3.6.

6

SCOTT MACDONALD

The divine nature

In 386, at the age of 32, Augustine converted to Christianity. As he tells the story in the *Confessions*, the complex and dramatic events that constituted his conversion brought to successful conclusion a search he had begun as a teenager at Carthage with his reading of Cicero's *Hortensius*. Cicero had inspired in him a passionate yearning for the sort of immortality that comes with wisdom.[1] After more than a decade of fruitless searching, Augustine finally discovered that the wisdom he had longed for was to be found with the God of Christianity. The discovery came in a moment of intellectual vision in which Augustine glimpsed and thereby came at last to understand the divine nature. "At that moment," he tells us, "I saw [God's] 'invisible nature understood through the things that are made' [Romans 1.20]" (*Conf.* 7.17.23).[2]

As Augustine quickly learned, however, discovering where wisdom is to be found is not the same as attaining it, and so his intellectual vision of God did not by itself bring his search to an end. In order to be able to cleave to God in love he needed moral healing of a kind that no merely intellectual enlightenment could provide. But whatever else might have been necessary to complete his conversion to Christianity, Augustine is clear that the understanding provided by his intellectual vision of God was pivotal for it.[3] He could not be a Christian unless and until he had become convinced that the Christian conception of the divine nature provides knowledge of the true God. Moreover, he is clear that his intellectual vision of God satisfied that purely cognitive condition. Immediately following the vision he reports: "I was now loving *you* [God], not some sensory image instead of you" and "I had no doubt of any kind to whom I should cleave" (ibid.).

The intellectual vision of God

In Book 7 of the *Confessions* Augustine recounts his vision of God more than once. Here is the main part of the first of the accounts (henceforth the *first vision passage* [FVP]):[4]

[FVP] 1 Having been admonished by the Platonists' books to return into myself, I entered
       2 into my innermost self, with you [God] as my guide. And I was able to do it
       3 because you had become my helper. I entered and with whatever sort of eye it is
       4 that my soul possesses, I saw above that same eye of my soul an immutable light
       5 higher than my mind . . . It transcended my mind, not in the way that oil floats on
       6 water, nor in the way heaven is above the earth. It was higher than I because it
       7 made me, and I was lower than it because I was made by it. The person who
       8 knows truth knows it, and one who knows it knows eternity. Love knows it.
       9 Eternal truth, true love, beloved eternity: you are my God. To you I sigh day and
      10 night. When I first came to know you, you raised me up so that I might see that
      11 what I was seeing is Being, and that I who was seeing it am not yet Being. And
      12 shining intensely on me you shocked the weakness of my sight, and I trembled
      13 with love and awe . . . I said: "Is truth nothing just because it is not diffused
      14 through space, either finite or infinite?" And you cried from far away: "No, indeed,
      15 for I am who am" [Exodus 3.14]. I heard in the way one hears in the heart, and
      16 there was absolutely no room left for doubt. (*Conf.* 7.10.16)

Taken in isolation, this first report of Augustine's intellectual vision is bound to appear cryptic. But it is nevertheless a good place to begin an investigation of his mature thinking about the divine nature, because it gives us a kind of introduction to the main elements and structural principles of Augustine's new-found conception of God. Moreover, viewed in its context in the *Confessions*, the account highlights the sorts of philosophical concerns that were particularly important to Augustine, the concerns he thought an adequate conception of God must address. We will need to look beyond *Confessions* 7 to fill out what he says here about his intellectual vision, but his account of the vision can function for us as a useful guide.

The vision passage quoted above clearly identifies two of the three most important influences shaping Augustine's mature understanding of the divine nature. First, Augustine makes it clear that the God he has encountered is the God of the Christian scriptures. Of course the whole of the *Confessions* is addressed to the God of Christianity, and so it is the Christian God whom Augustine addresses directly here. He now sees that that same God has become his intimate guide and helper (FVP lines 2–3), and he attributes the final achievement of his vision to God's activity on his behalf: "you raised me up so that I might see" (FVP 10). Moreover, and most strikingly, the God of Augustine's vision identifies himself as the God of Moses, the God whose most intimate name is "I am who am" (FVP 15). From this point on, Augustine never doubted that the Christian scriptures, properly explicated and understood, present the truth about the divine nature.

The second influence evident in the vision passage is Platonism. Augustine considered his encounter with certain Platonist books a crucial turning point in his path to Christianity. As the vision passage suggests, those books provided him with important strategic and methodological principles for his thinking about the divine: they admonished him to look within his own soul rather than to the external material world, and to look with the eye of the mind rather than with the bodily senses (FVP 1–5). Indeed Platonism provided Augustine with a rich repertoire of ideas and arguments that he would use to articulate the Christian conception of God. In this passage the allusions to and echoes of Plotinus are as prominent as the scriptural themes: the God of Moses is the immutable light that transcends the mind, eternal truth, and being itself. The mature Augustine's certainty of the truth of the Christian conception of God was matched by his conviction that the Christian scriptures require careful theoretical investigation and explication if the truth about God that they express is to be understood. The tools he found most useful in this task were primarily those of Platonist philosophy.[5]

The third important influence shaping Augustine's mature thinking about God is not explicit in the vision passage we are examining. But if we read the passage in the larger context provided by the narrative of the *Confessions*, we can see the clear role that Manichaeanism plays in shaping the conception of God that Augustine begins to articulate here. Augustine's first intellectually serious commitments were to Manichaean theology. As a result, Manichaeanism remained throughout his life a fixed point of reference and a kind of foil for many of his mature views. While a Manichee Augustine believed God to be a luminous mass extended infinitely through space; he now sees that the true God is incorporeal and infinite without extension (FVP 13–16). While a Manichee Augustine imagined God subject to attack, corruption, and violation at the hands of a rival power; he now sees that the true God is immutable and incorruptible (FVP 4–5). While a Manichee Augustine believed that there were two independent divine substances in conflict with one another; his vision now allows him to see that the true God is being itself, the one source of everything else that exists (FVP 11). Thus, Augustine's mature understanding of the divine nature was not merely incompatible with the Manichaeanism of his youth but a pointed rejection of it.

Augustine tells us that his intellectual vision of God occurred in the twinkling of an eye. But the *Confessions* makes clear that the journey leading him to that crucial point is a long one. To understand what it is Augustine saw in his intellectual vision, and what the significance was of his seeing it, we need to follow the course of his intellectual journey from Manichaeanism by way of Platonism to an understanding of the God of Christianity.

Sojourn with the Manichees

According to the *Confessions*, when Cicero had inspired him to search for wisdom, Augustine turned first to the religious tradition of his upbringing, Christianity. But he quickly lost patience with the Christian scriptures: they

THE CAMBRIDGE COMPANION TO AUGUSTINE

seemed to him, as he says, "unworthy in comparison with Cicero's dignity" (*Conf.* 3.5.9). He straightaway fell in with the Manichees, whose verbal slickness and self-confident rationalism contrasted vividly for him with Catholic Christianity.[6] They attracted the philosophically minded young Augustine, who spent the next decade of his life associated in one way or another with them.

Augustine explains his susceptibility to Manichaean persuasions by reference to his intellectual condition at the time:

> I was unaware of the existence of another reality that truly is (*aliud vere quod est*), and when they asked me: [1] "Where does evil come from?" and [2] "Is God bounded by a corporeal form, does he have hair and nails?" . . . it was as if I were being cleverly goaded into throwing in my lot with those foolish deceivers. (*Conf.* 3.7.12)[7]

He thinks of these two questions as Manichaean challenges to orthodox Christianity, intended to expose what the Manichees perceived as the absurdity of Catholic Christian belief. Christianity holds that there is one supremely good God, the creator and source of all existing things. But then, granted that evil exists, Christianity appears incoherent: either evil comes from the supremely good God (which is absurd) or it does not (in which case God is not the creator of all that exists).[8] By contrast, as Augustine understood it, Manichaeanism had a ready answer to the first question. There are two ultimate sources of things, a good God and a hostile power independent of the good God. Evil derives not from the former but from the latter, and is a consequence of the evil power's success in its cosmic struggle against the good God.[9]

The Manichees' second question ridicules the Christian belief that God created human beings in God's own image (Genesis 1.26). Since human beings have finite bodies with heads and hands, it would seem that the God in whose image they are made must have features of the same sort. The Manichees saw themselves as holding a more sophisticated conception of the divine nature: the good God is a kind of light extended infinitely through space.

Augustine's reconciliation with Christianity depended on his discovering or developing satisfactory replies to these Manichaean challenges. But at the beginning of his search for wisdom, his youthful ignorance left him defenseless against them:

> [1*] I did not know that evil exists only as a privation of good . . . How could I see it when my seeing with my eyes went only as far as the body, and with my mind only as far as sensory images? [2*] Moreover, I did not know that God is Spirit [John 4.24], not something whose limbs have length and breadth and who has a mass. (*Conf.* 3.7.12)

He gestures here toward the full-fledged replies he will eventually make on Christianity's behalf. But those replies would become possible for him only after the intellectual vision recounted in Book 7.[10]

Augustine saw that at bottom each of these two Manichaean questions raised the issue of how to think adequately about the divine nature, and from this point in the narrative that issue drives the *Confessions* forward. Augustine regularly diagnoses the fruitlessness of his search for wisdom and his own intellectual follies and frustrations as being the result of ignorance or error regarding God's nature. He sometimes puts the point in general terms: "I did not know what to think about your substance or what way would lead me, or lead me back, to you" (*Conf.* 6.5.8). More often he gives more specific diagnoses: "I thought that you, Lord God and Truth, were a luminous and immense body, and that I was a bit of that body" (ibid. 4.16.31); and "When I wanted to think of my God, I knew of no way of doing so except as a corporeal mass, for it seemed to me that anything that was not of that sort did not exist" (ibid. 5.10.19). Looking back on this Manichaean period of his life, Augustine saw himself as unable to conceive of any sort of non-corporeal reality and, consequently, unable to conceive of God in anything but corporeal terms. The importance he assigns to these conceptual mistakes and limitations is striking: "That was the *most important* and virtually the *only* cause of my inevitable error" (ibid.).[11]

As these descriptions of Augustine's conceptual difficulties suggest, freeing himself entirely from the errors he had inherited from the Manichees would crucially depend on his learning to conceive of incorporeal reality. We are now in position to appreciate the transformative effect of Augustine's encounter with Platonism.

Intellectual ascent: approaching God from below

During his Manichaean period Augustine's attention had been focused on the external corporeal world. His thinking had consequently been bound by sensory experience: he could conceive only what he could form a sensory image of. Platonism, however, admonished him to abandon the corporeal world and turn inward, using the eye of his own rational soul. When he did so, he discovered an astonishing new realm. The incorporeality, immutability, and eternity that characterize purely intellectual thought are the clues that led Augustine, by stages, to the divine nature itself.

The vision passage with which we began provides the barest sketch of the Platonist-inspired inward turn and upward movement that culminated in Augustine's vision of God. In other places he tells us more about the philosophical structure of this redirection of his thinking. His most detailed discussion of it occurs in Book 2 of *De libero arbitrio*, where he transforms his intellectual ascent into an elaborate argument for the existence of God.[12]

Augustine begins by establishing a hierarchy that sorts into general categories and ranks the natures that comprise the universe: existence, life, and understanding:

> Therefore the nature that merely exists (and neither lives nor understands) ranks below the nature that not only exists but also lives (but does not understand) – the soul of the non-human animals is of this sort. This nature in turn ranks below the nature that at once exists, lives, and understands – for example, the rational mind of the human being. (*De lib. arb.* 2.6.13)

Augustine's strategy will be to argue that there is a nature that ranks above the rational mind of the human being, a nature that he will identify as divine.[13] In order to discover it, he ascends the hierarchy of natures, turning his attention first from bodies (the first and lowest-ranking category in the hierarchy) to the soul (the nature constitutive of both the second and third categories), and then within his own soul from the sensory part (a part found in both human beings and the non-human animals) to reason: "a kind of head or eye of our soul . . . which does not belong to the nature of non-human animals" (ibid. 2.6.13).[14]

Having ascended as far as reason – that which is highest in us – he focuses on reason's distinctive perceptual capacities and the distinctive sorts of objects they put us in contact with, the objects of pure thought. By way of example, Evodius, Augustine's interlocutor in the dialogue, first suggests that they consider "the structure and truth of number," by which he means arithmetical facts and relationships of the sort expressed by such truths as "seven plus three equals ten" (ibid. 2.8.20–21). Augustine himself adds the example of the indivisible mathematical unit that is the foundation of all number.[15] He later introduces into the discussion a collection of *a priori* evaluative and normative truths such as "wisdom should be diligently sought after," "inferior things should be subjected to superior things," and "what is eternal is better than what is temporal" (ibid. 2.10.28).[16] He thinks of these truths as constitutive of wisdom itself and therefore normative for anyone who would possess it – they are "rules" of wisdom and "lights" of virtue. Moreover, anyone who is able to contemplate them will recognize their truth. Examination of these various examples leads Augustine to three conclusions: intelligible objects of these sorts are independent of our minds, incorporeal, and higher than reason. Put briefly, the main lines of his reasoning are as follows:[17]

1. Intelligible objects must be independent of particular minds because they are common to all who think. In coming to grasp them, an individual mind does not alter them in any way; it cannot convert them into its exclusive possessions or transform them into parts of itself. Moreover, the mind discovers them rather than forming or constructing them, and its grasp of them can be more or less adequate. Augustine concludes from these observations that intelligible objects cannot be part of reason's own nature or be produced by reason out of itself. They must exist independently of individual human minds.

2. Intelligible objects must be incorporeal because they are eternal and immutable. By contrast, all corporeal objects, which we perceive by means of the
bodily senses, are contingent and mutable. Moreover, certain intelligible
objects – for example, the indivisible mathematical unit – clearly cannot be
found in the corporeal world (since all bodies are extended, and hence divisible). These intelligible objects cannot therefore be perceived by means of the
senses; they must be incorporeal and perceptible by reason alone.

3. Intelligible objects must be higher than reason because they judge reason.
Augustine means by this that these intelligible objects constitute a normative
standard against which our minds are measured.[18] We refer to mathematical
objects and truths to judge whether or not and to what extent our minds
understand mathematics. We consult the rules of wisdom to judge whether
or not and to what extent a person is wise. In light of these standards we can
judge whether our minds are as they should be. It makes no sense, however,
to ask whether these normative intelligible objects are as they should be: they
simply are and are normative for other things. In virtue of their normative
relation to reason, Augustine argues that these intelligible objects must be
higher than it, as a judge is higher than what it judges. Moreover, he believes
that apart from the special sort of relation they bear to reason, the intrinsic
nature of these objects shows them to be higher than it. These sorts of intelligible objects are eternal and immutable; by contrast, the human mind is
clearly mutable. Augustine holds that since it is evident to all who consider it
that the immutable is superior to the mutable (it is among the rules of wisdom
he identifies), it follows that these objects are higher than reason.

Augustine develops the first two of these conclusions in support of the third,
which in turn directly advances the proof's strategy. But if we recall his account
of the difficulties in which his pre-Christian thinking about the divine nature was
mired, we can see independent significance to the second conclusion – that intelligible objects must be incorporeal. In the *Confessions* Augustine reports that his
inability to conceive of anything incorporeal was the "most important and virtually the only cause" of his errors. The argument from *De libero arbitrio* shows
how Augustine managed, with the aid of Platonist direction and argument, to
overcome this cognitive limitation. By focusing on objects perceptible by the
mind alone and by observing their nature, in particular their eternity and immutability, Augustine came to see that certain things that clearly exist, namely, the
objects of the intelligible realm, cannot be corporeal. When he cries out in the
midst of his vision of the divine nature, "Is truth nothing just because it is not
diffused through space, either finite or infinite?" (FVP 13–14), he is acknowledging that it was the discovery of intelligible truth that first freed him to comprehend incorporeal reality.[19]

Augustine has made his case thus far by calling our attention to the characteristics of intelligible objects of various kinds. But the conclusion he wants to draw in the end is not that there are many things higher than reason (including the infinitely many numerical truths and the so-called rules of wisdom), but that there is one such thing, Christianity's one God. He needs therefore to argue that the many intelligible objects are in a certain way a single thing. This part of his argument is less than fully explicit, and Augustine himself acknowledges the difficulty in making it clear.[20] But we can see him making the crucial transition in the following passage: "[I]t is certainly clear that [wisdom and number] are both true, indeed immutably true. For that reason, [one] cannot deny that there is an immutable truth containing (*continentem*) all these things that are immutably true" (*De lib. arb.* 2.11.32–12.33). It is difficult to know precisely what to make of the metaphor of containment in this last passage, and so to know precisely how to conceive the one immutable truth itself. But Augustine seems to want to move our attention beyond the distinct intelligible truths themselves – the distinct facts or propositions, as it were – and to direct us toward what they have in common, their truth. We recognize that each of them is true, indeed immutably true. Immutable truth, then, is a single thing shared in common by all the different intelligible truths. It is the one over the many, or the one in which the many are contained.

In other passages Augustine prefers the analogy of light to that of containment. When Evodius resists Augustine's claim that wisdom is a single thing common to all who think, on the grounds that different people seek wisdom in different things, Augustine replies with an analogy: just as the sun is a single thing despite the fact that we see many things in its light, so wisdom can be a single thing despite the fact that different people perceive and pursue different goods in its light. Similarly, Augustine supposes that the eye of the soul is able to see various immutable truths because of the light shed on them by immutable truth itself.[21] In *De libero arbitrio* the metaphor of light remains largely in the background, but in the vision passages in the *Confessions*, it comes to the fore: "I entered into my innermost self . . . and with whatever sort of eye it is that my soul possesses, I saw . . . an immutable light higher than my mind" (FVP 1–5).

Whatever the obscurities in this crucial step in Augustine's argument, it is clear nevertheless that he supposes that this inference completes the strategy he has been pursuing in the proof. "I had promised, if you recall, that I would prove that there is something more sublime than our mind, that is, than reason. Here it is: truth itself" (*De lib. arb.* 2.13.35).

Divine supremacy: conceiving God in the highest possible way

Augustine's strategy in *De libero arbitrio* 2 – to prove that God exists by proving that there is something higher than reason – appears to rely on the assumption that what is higher than reason must be God. Evodius, however, spots the unargued assumption and objects to it: "If I could find something higher (*melius*) than that which is highest (*optimum*) in me, I would *not* go on straightaway to claim that it is God" (*De lib. arb.* 2.6.14). He insists that Augustine prove not merely that there is something higher than reason but that there is something than which nothing is higher (*quo est nullus superior*). Evodius' objection causes Augustine some embarrassment in the dialogue.[22] And he is right to be troubled because Evodius is pressing a point to which Augustine himself is firmly committed. Augustine takes it as a kind of governing principle of his thinking about the divine nature that God must be supreme, that is, that than which nothing is higher or better. In Book 1 of the dialogue Augustine had exhorted Evodius to adhere to just this principle, telling him that "the most genuine root of piety consists in thinking about God in the highest possible way (*optime de deo existimare*)" (ibid. 1.2.5). In Book 2, when Evodius protests Augustine's proposed strategy for the proof, he is merely insisting on that pious principle.

In *De doctrina christiana* Augustine suggests that the notion of supremacy is part of the very concept of the divine. He tells us that despite the obvious fact that the mere word "God" (*deus*) conveys no knowledge of God, nevertheless:

> when the sound of the word *deus* strikes the ears of anyone who knows Latin, that person is prompted to think of a kind of nature that is utterly surpassing (*excellentissimam*) and immortal. For when someone thinks of that one God of gods . . . one thinks in such a way that one's thought strains to reach something than which there is nothing higher (*aliquid quo nihil melius sit*) or more sublime. (*De doct. christ.* 1.6.6–7.7)

Augustine allows that people can be confused or ignorant about what sort of thing really is that than which there is nothing higher. Hence, there are religions of various kinds. Nevertheless "all agree that God is what they place above (*anteponunt*) all other things" (ibid. 1.7. 7).[23]

Augustine takes the notions of being supreme (*summe, optime*), being that than which nothing is higher or better (*aliquid quo nihil melius sit*), and being the highest good (*summum bonum*) to be equivalent. Hence, he takes it to be a sort of conceptual truth not only that God is supreme but that God is the highest good. Ontological ranking and value ranking therefore coincide: the highest being is the highest good. Moreover, just as all agree that God is that which they place above all other things, so everyone seeks happiness in the highest good. Not everyone understands, however, what sort of thing really is the highest good.[24]

Augustine's own pre-Christian thinking about the divine nature exemplifies these points. Along with the Manichees, he rejected Christianity in part because of its putative belief that God has a corporeal form like that of a human body. Augustine preferred the Manichaean understanding of God, which he thought to be higher. But this same episode from his past reveals the limitations of the principle that God is supreme. During his years with the Manichees Augustine was straining to think of God as highly as possible. But since his thinking was bound by sensory images, his highest thoughts had fallen disastrously short of their mark. If the principle of the divine supremacy was to be of any use in his thinking about God, it had to be supplemented by other principles providing substantive direction in filling out the content of the concept of the supreme being. What sort of nature is in fact supreme? What specific attributes must characterize something than which nothing is higher? Platonism provided Augustine with important supplementary principles of the required sort.

As Augustine reports events in *Confessions* 7, it appears that Platonism began affecting his thinking about the divine nature even before the dramatic events described in the vision passages. At the beginning of Book 7 he reports a positive preliminary development:

> I was trying to think of you . . . the supreme, sole, and true God. With all my heart I believed you to be incorruptible, inviolable, and immutable, although I did not know why and how. Nevertheless I saw plainly and was certain that what is corruptible is inferior to that which cannot be corrupted; what is inviolable I unhesitatingly put above that which is violable; what undergoes no change is better than that which can change. (*Conf.* 7.1.1)

Augustine's new beliefs here were that God is incorruptible, inviolable, and immutable. But what is interesting for our purposes is the kind of reasoning he identifies as grounding them: God is supreme, and since incorruptibility (for example) is better than corruptibility, God must therefore be incorruptible. The same pattern of reasoning, *mutatis mutandis*, yields the divine inviolability and immutability. Indeed, given appropriate ranking principles the same schema can function as a constructive tool, specifying, attribute by attribute, a determinate conception of the divine nature. (We might call the general pattern *the argument from the divine supremacy*.)[25]

Augustine does not tell us here how he acquired certainty about these particular ranking principles. But it is clear that his progress with Platonism brought him to it. Even if he has not yet ascended to the point of seeing the truth itself that transcends his mind (that comes later in Book 7), he seems to have reached the point of recognizing certain *a priori* immutable rules of wisdom, of which the ranking principles driving these particular inferences are examples.[26]

In Augustine's construction of the hierarchy of natures, comparative ranking principles of the sort required by the argument from the divine supremacy function independently of the principle that God is supreme: existence that is characterized by life is better than existence that lacks it, hence living things rank above inanimate bodies; life that is characterized by understanding is better than life that lacks it, hence human beings rank above the non-human animals. The construction of the hierarchy can proceed without any knowledge of God's existence or nature. But the same comparative ranking principles can also be used in the argument from the divine supremacy. Since life is better than inanimate existence, God must be characterized by life; since a life characterized by wisdom is better than a life lacking it, God must be characterized by wisdom; and since a life characterized by immutable wisdom is better than a life whose wisdom is mutable, God must be characterized by immutable wisdom.[27]

In Augustine's hands the argument from the divine supremacy yields an impressive list of divine attributes: incorporeality, eternality, immutability, incorruptibility, inviolability, life, and wisdom, among others. His intellectual ascent toward the immutable truth that transcends the human mind identifies many of the same attributes. Augustine naturally supposes that both these approaches converge on one and the same being, that is, that the transcendent truth itself is the supreme God, the topmost being on the hierarchy of natures and the highest good. It remains, however, that the proof in *De libero arbitrio* 2 never establishes that identity. The argument from the divine supremacy can guarantee that the divine nature will include incorporeality, eternity, and immutability. But the argument in *De libero arbitrio* 2 seems to give us no firm assurance that the incorporeal, eternal, and immutable truth that is higher than our minds will also be the one true God than whom nothing is higher.

Being: God's inmost nature

The argument from the divine supremacy allowed Augustine to discover some of the particular attributes constitutive of the divine nature. But he believed that the sort of piecemeal progress the argument makes possible is in a certain way superficial. What he wanted, and what his intellectual vision of God finally gave him, is a glimpse of God's inmost nature, an understanding of the divine that is unifying and deeply explanatory of both the manifold divine attributes and the universe in which God ranks supreme.

We can see the sort of understanding Augustine was after if we look again at the passage from the beginning of *Confessions* 7: "With all my heart I believed you to be incorruptible, inviolable, and immutable, although I did not know why and how" (*Conf.* 7.1.1). Augustine here reports progress but also admits to an accompanying lack of understanding. What he means is that he does not yet see how to fit these new beliefs, together with his other beliefs, into a coherent view of God and God's place in the world. The argument from the divine supremacy shows that the true God is incorruptible. In Augustine's mind, that result exposed the incoherence of the Manichaean theodicy, which takes the supreme God to have been attacked and partly captured, subdued, and corrupted by a hostile power.[28] But the argument from the divine supremacy did not by itself provide Augustine with an alternative to the Manichaean theodicy. "But I still . . . did not have a clear and explicit grasp of the cause of evil. Nevertheless, whatever it might be, I saw it had to be investigated, if I were to avoid being forced by this problem to believe the immutable God to be mutable" (*Conf.* 7.3.4). At this point in the *Confessions* Augustine needs still to discover two things: that there are existing things that are not corporeal and that God is true being.

We have already seen how Augustine's intellectual ascent led him to the discovery of something that is both incorporeal and clearly existent, namely, immutable truth itself.[29] The vision passages from the *Confessions* also clearly display Augustine's discovery of the fact that God is being itself, that which truly and supremely *is*. Indeed Augustine presents that discovery as occurring at the pinnacle of his intellectual ascent and as giving him his deepest insight into the divine nature. We can see the paramount importance of his recognition that God is Being by paying attention both to the rhetorical features of the vision passage we have been examining and to the place the passage occupies in the larger context of the *Confessions*.

First, Augustine's recounting of his intellectual ascent toward God reaches its dramatic height with these lines: "When I first came to know you, you raised me up so that I might see that what I was seeing is Being, and that I who was seeing it am not yet Being. And shining intensely on me you shocked the weakness of my sight, and I trembled with love and awe" (FVP 10–13). As Augustine understands it, God had lifted him up with the purpose of showing him that the object of his vision is Being. The vision is in fact a mere glimpse – he could not sustain it and immediately fell away. But he takes himself nevertheless to have seen God's true nature and to have seen that it is Being.[30] Augustine makes this point clear by connecting his vision of God as true being with the scriptural divine name. God not only raised Augustine up so that he might see that God is Being (*esse*) but also spoke to him, as God spoke to Moses from the burning bush, so that he might know that God's name is "I am who am" (*ego sum qui sum*). Augustine naturally supposed that the most intimate divine name expresses God's inmost nature. His own characterization of God as Being, as that which truly *is*, is his attempt to give philosophical expression to this fundamental biblical idea.[31]

Secondly, that Augustine understood the vision of God as Being to be the climax of his intellectual ascent is confirmed by the structure the *Confessions* gives to the long search that the vision (in part) concludes. As we have seen, Augustine blamed his ignorance for the misguided intellectual commitments that characterized his sojourn with the Manichees: "I was unaware of the existence of another reality that truly *is* (*aliud vere quod est*)" (*Conf.* 3.7.12).[32] This forward-directed confession in Book 3 finds its target in Augustine's vision of the divine nature in Book 7, and specifically in his vision of God as Being, as that which truly *is*. He tells us: "So in the flash of a trembling glance [my mind] attained to that which *is* (*id quod est*)" and "I was certain that you *are* (*certus esse te*) . . . I was sure that you truly *are* (*vere te esse*)" (*Conf.* 7.17.23 and 7.20.26). Augustine's fundamental ignorance that God is the reality that truly *is* crippled his search for wisdom; his vision of God dispels that ignorance.

So Augustine presents his discovery that God is that which truly *is* as the climax of his intellectual ascent to God, as the philosophical articulation of the scriptural divine name, and as the final remedy to the long-standing ignorance that plagued his search for wisdom. For these reasons we should expect the conception of God as true being to be fundamental to Augustine's mature thinking about God. Of all the philosophically charged epithets Augustine uses to characterize the divine nature, we should expect that expressions such as "being" (*esse*), "true being" (*vere esse*), "that which *is*" (*id quod est*), and "what truly *is*" (*id quod vere est*) will take us deeper into Augustine's mature understanding of God's nature than any of the others, deeper even than "light," "truth," or "wisdom." What, then, does Augustine mean when he identifies God as what truly *is*?

Ontological independence and necessity

In the vision passages in *Confessions* 7, the recognition that God is true being is accompanied by the awareness that beings other than God are distinct from God and depend on God for their being. That which truly *is* possesses its being in its own right and independently of other things. It therefore cannot fail to be. Other existing things have being in a way, as is shown by the fact that they exist, but in a way they lack being: their existence is contingent and dependent.[33]

Cosmological monism

Augustine holds that the universe is comprised fundamentally only of existing realities, that is, of natures or substances that have being.[34] Moreover, that which truly *is* is the source of all being: every existing nature must be either that which truly *is* or the sort of thing that depends for its being on what truly *is*. Hence, insofar as a nature exists, it has being to some extent; and if it is not that which truly *is*, it must depend for its being on what truly *is*.[35] There can be no existing nature that is distinct from and utterly independent of God. As Augustine puts it: "If you look for something strictly contrary to God, you will find absolutely nothing, for only non-being is contrary to being. Therefore there is no nature contrary to God" (*De moribus Manichaeorum* (2).1.1).[36]

Augustine draws important anti-Manichaean conclusions from this cosmological monism.[37] Since God is what truly *is*, Manichaean theological dualism must be false. There cannot be two independent divine principles. Moreover, evil cannot be a nature or substance of any kind, corporeal or incorporeal. If it were, it would depend on God for its existence; but only good things come from the supremely good God. Hence, evil must be not a nature but a privation in or corruption of an existing nature.[38] Manichaean cosmological dualism must therefore be false: the universe cannot be comprised of fundamentally opposed natures – goods and evils. In the *Confessions* Augustine develops his analysis of the nature of evil immediately after his vision of the divine nature. Having discovered that God is true being, he was able to see that cosmological monism must be true and that evil, therefore, cannot be an existing nature or substance, cannot have been created by God, and cannot originate from a divine power independent of God.[39]

Creation

Augustine develops his version of cosmological monism into a philosophical account of the Christian doctrine of creation. All existing things other than God depend on God for their being. To say that they depend on God for their being is to say that God makes them, that is, causes them both to exist and to be the kinds of things they are. In making things, God requires no aid from any other independent being and uses no pre-existing, independent matter or stuff: both possibilities are ruled out by cosmological monism. Moreover, God does not make things out of God's own substance, that is, the things that God makes are not in any way parts of the divine substance – that possibility would require either that God be corrupted or that mutable, contingent creatures be equal to God. God makes things out of nothing (*ex nihilo*).[40] The fact that things are created by God *ex nihilo* explains their contingency, mutability, and corruptibility. God gives them being, but because they are made and made from nothing, they are not true being. They are tinged with non-being, as that which truly *is* is not.

Augustine sees that the doctrine of creation, like the cosmological monism on which he grounds it, is incompatible with Manichaeanism. According to the doctrine of creation, the human soul is one of God's creatures, not a part of the divine substance trapped in matter. Matter, too, is created by God; it is not the tool or vehicle of a hostile divine power. Indeed everything that exists (other than God) is created by God, and is therefore good insofar as it has being.[41]

Immutability

The attribute that Augustine links most closely to true being is immutability. He very often discusses them together, and he takes them to be mutually entailing.[42]

His understanding of the nature of change provides the conceptual link between them. Augustine conceives of change as consisting in the loss and acquisition of being.[43] That which changes ceases to be what it was and comes to be what it was not. But what truly *is* cannot lose or acquire being. Hence, what truly *is* must be immutable. Conversely, for something to be immutable is for it to be such that it cannot lose or acquire being. But only what truly *is* can be of that sort. So what is immutable must also be what truly *is*.

The divine immutability and God's true being are thus mutually entailing, but it is clear that Augustine views the conception of God as what truly *is* as the theoretically more fundamental of these two central components of his understanding of the divine nature. The best evidence of this is the fact that the conception of God as what truly *is* unifies Augustine's account of the divine nature and explains its other main components. That God is what truly *is* explains not only the divine immutability but also, as we have seen, the divine independence and necessity, the fact that God is the sole source and creator of all other existing things, and the compatibility of the existence of evil with divine incorruptibility and goodness. That is why his discovery that God is true being brought Augustine unprecedented certainty and understanding: it showed him the single conceptual source out of which the other divine attributes flow and by virtue of which they can be explained and fitted together into a coherent Christian conception of reality. The closely connected concept of immutability does not have the same theoretical fecundity for Augustine's thinking about the divine nature.[44]

Eternity and simplicity

Augustine's conception of change as consisting in the acquisition and loss of being also grounds his understanding of both the divine eternality and the divine simplicity. Augustine supposes that a being that experiences time necessarily changes, for its cognition will be (successively) affected by the temporal modalities of future, present, and past: what one anticipates as future, one will come to experience as present, and then as past. By contrast, the divine being, that which truly *is*, cannot change in this way, and so must comprehend all things in the eternal present.[45] "In the eternal, nothing passes, but the whole is present" (*Conf.* 11.11.13).[46] Augustine argues that time itself is among God's creatures and comes into existence with the creation of the universe.[47] Time's transience is itself a mark of its status as a creature – it exists but is tinged with non-being.

For similar reasons Augustine holds that what truly *is* must be metaphysically simple. "That nature is called simple which does not possess anything that it can lose and for which the possessor and what it possesses are not distinct in the way a vessel and the liquid it contains, a body and its color, the air and its light or heat, or a soul and its wisdom are" (*De civ. Dei* 11.10). Augustine argues that in cases in which a thing's substance and its attributes – what it *is* and what it *has* – are not the same, it is possible for the thing to persist through the acquisition and loss of attributes. But that which truly *is* can neither lose nor acquire being. Hence, God's substance and God's attributes must be identical.[48] "Things are said to be simple which are principally and truly divine because in things of that sort, substance and quality are the same" (*De civ. Dei* 11.10).

Supremacy

Finally, Augustine argues that what truly *is* is what exists or has being in the highest possible way. And since to be in the highest possible way is to be supreme, that which truly *is* must be supreme: "Once one has understood [that than which there is nothing higher] . . . one sees at once that what exists in the highest and primary way is what is said most truly to be" (*De moribus Manichaeorum* (2) 1.1). At this point, Augustine's approach to God through the notion of the divine supremacy and his approach by means of intellectual ascent through the realm of intelligible truth to the vision of God come together. His intellectual vision of that which truly *is* finally identifies determinately the nature toward which the principle that God is supreme points.

As these considerations show, when God raised Augustine up "so that he might see that what he was seeing is Being," God allowed him a glimpse of God's own inmost nature. Augustine harbored no illusions that he had thereby acquired complete and perfect knowledge of the infinite and ineffable God. But he also never doubted that, in that momentary vision, he had acquired a depth of understanding sufficient for this life – sufficient, that is, for grounding a unified, coherent, and philosophically rich account of the divine nature, its place in reality, and its relation to his own soul.[49]

NOTES

1 *Conf.* 3.4.7–8.
2 All translations are my own. For the *Confessions*, however, I have consulted and sometimes relied extensively on Chadwick 1991. For *De libero arbitrio* I have consulted T. Williams 1993.
3 The events described in *Conf.* 8, culminating in the celebrated crisis in the garden (8.12.28–29), provide the account of what more is needed.
4 There is controversy about the vision passages in *Confessions* 7. My own view is that (1) there are three main accounts, at *Conf.* 7.10.16 (quoted here), 17.23, and 20.26; (2) all three are accounts of the same events (and not of distinct visions); and (3) all report a successful vision of God (and not a mere attempt). In what follows, especially on pp. 81–86, I present evidence that the first account reports a successful vision of God. For dissenting views, see P. Courcelle 1968: IV.III and O'Donnell 1992b,

434–446. The question whether the vision reported in Book 7 is an ecstatic (or mystical) experience is more difficult to answer. The language of visual experience that Augustine uses need not be taken to suggest mystical ecstasy, since he takes that sort of language to be appropriate for describing all intellectual knowing and understanding. I use the term "intellectual vision" intending thereby to emphasize the vision's intellectual content (which Augustine is clearly interested in) and leave open questions about mystical ecstasy.

5 See Augustine's reflective assessment of Platonism at *De civ. Dei* 8.3–11. There is a significant body of scholarship exploring the precise nature of Augustine's indebtedness to Platonism. For useful discussion focusing on the *Confessions* (and general bibliographical guidance), see Menn 1998, Part One.

6 *Conf.* 3.6.10.

7 The passage goes on to mention a third question, about the apparent immorality of the biblical patriarchs, which I leave aside. Augustine sees a close connection between the first two questions and often treats them together; see *Conf.* 4.15.24; 5.10.19; and 7.1.1.

8 See *De lib. arb.* 1.2.4.

9 *De moribus ecclesiae catholicae* (1).10.16; *De moribus Manichaeorum* (2).3.5; *De nat. boni c. Man* 41–44.

10 The first issue is explicitly settled at 7.12.18–16.22, in the immediate aftermath of Augustine's vision. The second issue is resolved by the vision itself. See pp. 81–83 below.

11 Augustine's difficulty conceiving of God in non-corporeal terms persists even after he has begun to withdraw from the Manichees; see *Conf.* 5.14.24–25 and 7.1.1.

12 The second vision passage in *Conf.* 7 (17.23) provides a kind of précis of the argument in *De libero arbitrio* 2. Compare also Augustine's extended reflection on the process of ascent, at *Conf.* 10.6.9–24.35.

13 *De lib. arb.* 2.6.14; 2.15.39.

14 Ibid. 2.3.8–6.13.

15 Elsewhere he appeals to geometrical entities – for example, the geometrical straight line (*Conf.* 10.12.19).

16 Augustine has at least two reasons for shifting the discussion from number to wisdom. First, he is following the Platonist regimen, which takes mathematics as providing a kind of introduction to the intelligible realm and a first step toward vision of the Good. Second, he sees that the final step of his proof – identifying that which is higher than reason with God – will be more plausible if what is higher than reason is thought of primarily as wisdom rather than as number. He can, for example, cite biblical passages in support of that identity and argue for the close connection between wisdom and the highest good (wisdom being the truth in which the highest good is discerned and acquired [*De lib. arb.* 2.9.27]).

17 Ibid. 2.8.20–12.34. I use 'intelligible object' to cover all the sorts of examples Augustine appeals to. They include at least abstract entities (the mathematical unit) and the facts into which they enter (that seven plus three equals ten).

18 Ibid. 2.5.12 and 12.34.

19 Compare Augustine's reports of seeing God's *invisible* nature (*Conf.* 7.17.23 and 7.20.26) and discovering that God is infinite without being infinitely extended (ibid. 7.14.20 and 7.20.26). Compare also the argument at *Sol.* 2.2.2 that truth exists eternally.

20 *De lib. arb.* 2.11.30–32.

21 Ibid. 2.9.27.

22 Ibid. 2.6.14. Evodius' objection forces Augustine to try to negotiate terms. Augustine first proposes to prove that (a) there is something higher than reason. Evodius objects. Augustine next proposes to prove that (a) and (b) what is higher than reason is eternal and immutable. Evodius repeats his objection. Augustine's third proposal is to prove that (a), (b), and (c) if there is anything higher than it, that thing will be God. Recognizing that Augustine is not going to give him what he wants, Evodius finally tables his objection.

23 Augustine sometimes makes his point about the divine supremacy in what appears to be the modality of actuality – God must be that than which nothing *is* higher. But he clearly intends the stronger claim that God is that than which nothing higher *can be thought*. See, e. g., *Conf.* 7.4.6; *De moribus Manichaeorum* (2).11.24.

24 *De lib. arb.* 2.9.27; *De moribus ecclesiae catholicae* (1).3.5.

25 (1) Necessarily, God is supreme; (2) Necessarily, a nature characterized by attribute X is better than a nature characterized by *not-X*; [therefore (3) Necessarily, what is supreme is characterized by X]; therefore (4) Necessarily, God is characterized by X. Augustine uses a kind of contrapositive transform of this schema as a *critical* tool. In the contrapositive transform the two conclusions (corresponding to [3] and [4]) are contrapositives of the originals: therefore (3*) Necessarily, a nature characterized by *not-X* is not supreme; therefore (4*) Necessarily, something whose nature is characterized by *not-X* is not God. The most dramatic example is Augustine's argument (at *Conf.* 7.2.3) that if the Manichaean God is corruptible, it cannot be supreme and, hence, cannot be the true God. See also *De moribus ecclesiae catholicae* (1).10.17; *De moribus Manichaeorum* (2).3.5; 11.20–21; 11.12.25; *De civ. Dei* 8.6.

26 See *Conf.* 7.17.23; *De lib. arb.* 2.10.28; and *De doct. christ.* 1.8.8. Augustine credits the Platonists with the historical discovery of these sorts of principles (*De civ. Dei* 8.6).

27 *De doct. christ.* 1.8.8.

28 *Conf.* 7.2.3.

29 See pp. 73–75 above.

30 The crucial lines of the vision passage that I am discussing here *tu adsumpsisti me ut viderem esse quod viderem, et nondum me esse qui viderem* [FVP 10–11]), admit of an alternative reading. Pine-Coffin, e.g., renders them "you raised me up so that I could see that there was something to be seen, but also that I was not yet able to see it" (Pine-Coffin 1961, 147.) But the alternative reading fits badly with Augustine's own understanding of his experience. He describes this event as the moment when "I first came to *know* you (*et cum te primum cognovi* [7.10.16]),'' and he goes on to report that, on the basis of this experience, "I was now loving you (*iam te amabam*)" and "a memory of you remained with me" (*Conf.* 7.17.23). The alternative reading makes these claims unwarranted. If Augustine has come to know and love the true God as a result of this event, he must have seen more than merely that there was *something* to be seen – he must have seen *what* it was he was seeing. Moreover, the alternative reading fails to make an important philosophical point that Augustine intends. He intends these lines to draw a crucial contrast between God's nature (which is Being [*esse*]) and Augustine's own (which is not yet Being [*nondum esse*]). This secures the idea (which Augustine had introduced a few lines earlier – FVP 6–7) that God is the source of being, Augustine himself the recipient

of it. That Augustine intends this contrast is confirmed, too, by the way in which he continues in the paragraph immediately following: he turns his gaze from God and his own soul to other things below God (*inspexi cetera infra te*) and sees that they are neither entirely being nor entirely non-being (*nec omnino esse nec omnino non esse* [7.11.17]). Augustine is here applying to the rest of God's creation the point that his vision of God's being has just brought home to him for his own case, namely, that in comparison with God he himself is not yet, or not entirely, being. (See the striking parallel at *Conf.* 13.31.46: "God has given us [the Holy Spirit] through whom we see that anything that exists in any way is good, for it is from him who is not [merely] *in some way* but [simply] *is*" (*qui datus est nobis, per quem videmus quia bonum est, quidquid aliquo modo est: ab illo enim est qui non aliquo modo est, sed est est*).

31 Exodus 3.14 is especially important for Augustine. See, for example, *De doct. christ.* 1.32.35 (quoted at note 33 below), *De nat. boni c. Man.* 19 and *De civ. Dei* 12.2 (note 42), and ibid. 8.11.

32 See pp. 73–75 above. Recall that Augustine uses this general diagnosis to introduce the specific Manichaean challenges to Christianity he wants to consider. The suggestion is that his ignorance of a reality that truly *is* is the root of his other difficulties.

33 See *De doct. christ.* 1.32.35: "For the one who supremely (*summe*) and primordially (*primitus*) *is* is one who is absolutely immutable and who can say in the fullest possible sense, 'I am who am' and 'You will say, the one who *is* has sent me to you.' Hence, other things that exist, but could not exist if they were not from him, are good to the extent that they receive their being." See also *Conf.* 11.4.6.

34 Ibid. 7.15.21.

35 Ibid. 12.7.7; *De moribus Manichaeorum* (2).9.14; *De ver. relig.* 18.35–36; *De nat. boni c. Man.* 1 and 10; *De civ. Dei* 8.6.

36 See also *Conf.* 12.11.11; *De nat. bon. c. Man.* 19.

37 *Conf.* 13.30.45.

38 See William Mann's chapter in this volume.

39 *Conf.* 7.12.18–7.13.19. Moreover, having acquired the ability to conceive of incorporeal things, he is in a position to think of evil as existing but as a privation (a lack of being) rather than as a nature or substance.

40 Ibid. 11.5.7; 12.7.7; 13.13.48; *De vera relig.* 18.35–36; *De nat. boni c. Man.* 1 and 24–27; *De civ. Dei* 7.29–30.

41 *Conf.* 7.12.18; 13.31.46.

42 For example, *De nat. boni c. Man.* 19: "Therefore our God said to his servant in a magnificent and divine way, 'I am who am' and 'Tell the children of Israel, "The one who *is* sent me to you."'" For he truly *is* since he is immutable; for every change causes something that was, not to be. Therefore he who is immutable truly *is*"; and *De civ. Dei* 12.2: "God said, 'I am who am.' For God is existence in a supreme degree – he supremely *is* – and is therefore immutable."

43 See also *De Trin.* 5.2.3 and 7.5.10; *Conf.* 7.10.16; 11.17; 11.4.6 and 11.7.9; *De moribus Manichaeorum* (2).1.1; and *De civ. Dei* 12.2.

44 As we have seen, in the *Confessions*, Augustine's coming to conceive of God as immutable (reported at 7.1.1) leaves his understanding of the divine nature still crucially inadequate.

45 *De civ. Dei* 11.21. Augustine distinguishes between God's incorporeal vision, which must be eternal, and its objects, which can nevertheless be temporal. Similarly, he dis-

tinguishes between God's action, which must be eternal and changeless, and the things God moves, which can nevertheless be temporal.

46 See also *Conf.* 9.10.24 and the extended discussion of the divine eternality, ibid. 11.4.6–14.17.

47 Ibid. 11.13.16–14.17.

48 See also *De Trin.* 7.1.1–3.9 and *De civ. Dei* 8.6.

49 I presented versions of this chapter at a conference at Cornell University and at the University of Toronto. I am grateful to audiences on those occasions for helpful discussion. I am also grateful to Robert Pasnau and Eleonore Stump for comments on an earlier draft.

7

MARY T. CLARK

De Trinitate

Augustine's purposes

In writing *De Trinitate* Augustine had three main objectives. He wished to demonstrate to critics of the Nicene[1] creed that the divinity and co-equality of Father, Son, and Holy Spirit are rooted in scripture. He intended to tell pagan philosophers the need for faith in a divine mediator so that divine self-revelation and redemption can occur. Finally, he wanted to convince his readers that salvation and spiritual growth are connected with knowing themselves as images of the Triune God, from whom they came and toward whom they go, with a dynamic tendency to union realized by likeness to God who is Love.

Augustine's approach was that of faith seeking understanding of the mystery of one God as Father, Son, and Spirit. He held that one can know God's existence and attributes by human reason (Rom. 1.20) but not God as Trinity. The New Testament tells of the Persons and of their oneness. As a divine mystery, this is humanly incomprehensible. Some understanding, however, is possible by reflection on what Revelation implies. Augustine inferred that the one God is three Persons in such a way that they are one divine Being, yet distinct from one another and dynamically within one another (*circumincessio, perichoresis*).[2]

There is no evidence in *De Trinitate* that Augustine asserted divine unity to be prior to Trinity, nor Trinity to unity. He states that there is no divinity apart from the three divine Persons.[3] But since anti-Nicene critics cited scriptural texts to deduce that neither Christ nor the Word of God is God, his first effort was to defend the divine unity by scriptural exegesis. Reason was used, however, to promote understanding of the Trinity by the faithful and to convince philosophers and theologians that the oneness and threeness of God is philosophically and logically defensible.

Setting

It is necessary to read *De Trinitate* within its historical setting. The 350s to the 380s was a period of response and reaction to the Nicene Creed. Pro-Nicene and anti-Nicene theologians used technical expressions for the Son as equal to the Father or similar to the Father, or of one will with the Father.[4]

The Nicene theology of the 380s emphasized the traditional teaching that the nature of the Trinity had the result that its operations outside the godhead are inseparable. In 389 Nebridius, Augustine's student friend, wrote to ask him: How is it that, if the Trinity does all things together in unity, the Son alone is said to be incarnated and not the Father and Holy Spirit as well? This marked the beginning of Augustine's theology being structured around the inseparable activities of the Trinity, with the Son as revealer of God the Trinity.[5] His Trinitarian theology and christology are not separated.[6]

In Augustine's Letter 11 can be found an early answer to this question. He continues to answer it in the De Trinitate, which was begun in 399 and finished possibly before 421. Book 12 was incomplete when the manuscript was circulated among admirers. Considering this piracy an impediment to revising earlier books, he reluctantly finished it at the request of Aurelius, bishop of Carthage, and for friends.

All fifteen books of De Trinitate follow the method of faith seeking understanding (Isaiah 7.9). Augustine cites scriptural bases for the doctrine of the Trinity and its image in man and woman.[7] The first seven books focus on the doctrine of the Trinity established from scripture and the philosophical concepts used to prevent misunderstanding. The last eight books deal with an investigation of what the image of God in human persons can reveal of God's inner life and the human vocation to likeness to the Trinity.

The historical context of De Trinitate makes it an exegetical, theological, philosophical, and polemical work. Its systematic and pastoral character is also discernible.

Biblical exegesis and theology: Books 1–4

Augustine was not the first theologian to write extensively on the Trinity. He knew of the Trinity not only from the Nicene Creed and from scripture but also from Catholic commentators[8] on scriptural texts. The one commentator he names is Hilary of Poitiers.

Scriptural evidence for God as Trinity includes Christ's telling the apostles to baptize in the name of the Father, and of the Son, and of the Holy Spirit (Matthew 28.19).[9] The Trinity is also manifested at the baptism of Christ.[10] Only the Son became man; only the Father declared: "You are my Son" (Mark 1:10); only the Spirit appeared in the form of a dove and later at Pentecost in strong winds and tongues of fire. These manifestations, Augustine wrote, worry some who, having heard that the Trinity acts inseparably in whatever each Person does outside the godhead, want to understand how the Son's incarnation, the Father's declaration, and the Spirit's appearances were all accomplished by the one Trinity. In Book 15.11.20 Augustine answers the question why only the Son became man. Only the Word of God was made flesh, although the Trinity brought it about, in order that by the inner understanding of truth human beings might live according to truth, following and imitating Christ. Just as in human communication the spoken word follows the mental word conceived by thinking, so Christ as the Word of God took flesh to communicate with human persons. He is the exemplary cause of creation and salvation.

Scripture frequently refers to the Son as having been "sent" by the Father and to the Holy Spirit as "sent" by Father and Son. Theologians spoke of these sendings as "missions." Augustine explained them as the Father's self-communication, intended to make known God's love for humankind (the "economy" of salvation) and to give some clue to the mutual relations within the godhead. But before dwelling on these important matters, he first had to respond to past and current objections to the divinity of the Son. Two texts fully quoted by Augustine are from the Prologue to St. John's Gospel and St. Paul's epistle to the Philippians: "In the beginning was the Word, and the Word was with God, and the Word was God . . . all things were made through him (John 1.1) . . . and the Word became flesh" (John 1.14). "Jesus Christ, who being in the form of God did not think it robbery to be equal to God" (Phil. 2.6).

As evidence for the divinity of the Spirit he cites an epistle of St. Paul (1 Cor. 6.15–20) which calls the bodies of Christians members of Christ and the temple of the Holy Spirit. The Holy Spirit cannot therefore be inferior to Christ.[11]

Certain texts taken by Homoeans to mean that Christ, or even the Word of God, is subordinate to the Father Augustine interpreted by the traditional exegetical rule: the scriptural texts referring to the Son as less than the Father, in the form of a servant, are referring to the Son's humanity; scriptural texts referring to the Son as equal to the Father are referring to the Son's divinity (1 Cor. 14.28). In the form of a servant, Augustine noted, recalling Phil. 2.6, Christ said, "The Father is greater than I" (John 14.28). In the form of God, Christ said, "As the Father has life in himself, so he also gave the Son to have life in himself" (John 5.26), "I and the Father are one" (John 10.30). And when of the Holy Spirit it is said that "he will teach you all truth," this teaching is done in virtue of his divinity (John 16.13).[12]

Scriptural texts referring to the sending of the Son and Spirit into the world were interpreted by some anti-Nicene theologians and formerly by the "economic" theologians[13] to argue that the one sent is less than the sender, and therefore only the Father is God. They even held that the Old Testament recorded certain "missions" of the divine Persons. Augustine argued that the "missions" began in the New Testament. The Father had been signified by certain bodily manifestations of angels in the Old Testament but was never said to have been sent. In the Old Testament God unfolded the plan of salvation through visible symbolic phenomena and verbal utterances.[14]

A mission includes not only the state of being sent but also the purpose for which one is sent. "When the fullness of time had come, God sent his son, made of woman, made under law, to redeem those who were under law" (Gal. 4.4). Christ was sent to overcome despair and, as mediator, to unify people by incorporating them in himself. He came to give through his death and resurrection access to eternal life, "and this is eternal life, that they may know you and Jesus Christ whom you have sent" (John 17.3). Being sent, Augustine argued, means not being less than God but rather being from the Father as principle of origin, God from God, light from light.[15] The Son was made flesh, beginning a unique relationship with human persons. The Spirit was sent to unite human persons with one another, originating a unique relationship as the animating Spirit of the Christian community.

Augustine used this discussion of being sent to point out that the scriptures demonstrate that the Spirit proceeds from both Father and Son and is, therefore, not begotten. He specifies that this dual procession of the Spirit (*filioque*)[16] does not eliminate the Father's being the *principium*, or source of all deity.

Augustine wrote at length and movingly of the Son and Spirit entering human history on behalf of human persons (1 John 3.7–9). Faith, he taught, brings participation in their Trinitarian life of love through grace. Thus, for Augustine, the doctrine of the Trinity was the center of Christian spirituality, intended to affect one's way of life. He found the divine missions manifesting a Trinitarian "God for us . . . and for our salvation." In their divinity the Persons remain always transcendent, but their missions reveal the eternal generation of the Son, the procession of the Holy Spirit, and their love for humankind.

While the various semi-Arian theologians to whom Augustine responded did not deny that the names of Father, Son and Spirit are in the New Testament, they nevertheless interpreted them as descending forms of divinity, with the Father only as true God, quite like Plotinus' triad of the One, the *Nous*, and the All-Soul. It was an Arian and Neoplatonic triad that Augustine refused to accept as the true Christian Trinity. Instead, he produced scriptural evidence for the co-equality of the Three Persons as God while each is distinct from the other by a dissimilar relationship.

Not only is his response to Arians non-Neoplatonist: he directly engages in an anti-pagan philosophical discussion in chapters 3 and 4 of Book 4 over the question of mediation,[17] and argues against materialistic philosophies[18] in Book 10. Both Plotinus and Porphyry held that the human intellect could know God without a mediator or faith; Porphyry also considered it beneath human dignity to have faith in a God made flesh and crucified. Citing this as a sin of pride, Augustine declared that to know the existence of God and something about him is not union with him. Porphyry himself realized that many were unable to make the Plotinian intellectual ascent to the One. For them he advocated a purification of the imagination by theurgic rites in which demons were invoked to bring about a vision of the gods. Augustine called such theurgy a satanic deception.[19] Augustine argued that the sacrifice of Christ defeated the Devil so that people now have access to eternal life through the death and resurrection of Christ. Real purification is through faith and trust in Christ, preceded by faith in the historical actions and words of Jesus. The relation of Christian faith to history[20] and to the divine Word of God made flesh is a significant departure from Neoplatonic philosophy. The Word of God entered human history, Augustine explains, to incorporate human individuals into his body. Christ will lead them back to the Father who created them, where they will be in eternal life, "the glory of God." This is Augustine's interpretation of 1 Cor. 15.28 which had been used by anti-Nicene theologians to assert the subordination of the Son's being.[21]

Trinity language: Books 5–7

For Augustine, one can know by reason more what God is not than what God is This is called negative or *apophatic* theology. But there is some positive theology, and theologians use philosophical terms to clarify what Scripture asserts. In the Nicene creed the term "consubstantial" (*homoousion*)[22] denoted the common being of the three Persons. The Son was said to be of one "substance" with the Father.

Arians[23] had argued against the consubstantial being of the Persons. Since Aristotelian accidents modify changeable substances, the Arians asserted that God's simplicity does not allow accidents to be attributed to him. Augustine agreed.[24] But the Arians inferred from this claim that to call the Father "Unbegotten" and the Son "Begotten" meant that these terms referred to the divine Substance, and they therefore concluded that the Son differs in substance from the Father. To this Augustine responded that between substantial predication and accidental predication there is "relative" predication.[25] Since the Son is always Son and the Father is always Father, relationship in the unchangeable divine sphere is perpetual relationship. Father and Son, Augustine pointed out, are words indicating relationship and they refer to another (*ad aliquid*). "Unbegotten" merely means that the Father is not from another. Begotten and Unbegotten as predicates of relationship are not predicated of the divine Substance, but of the second and first divine persons.

Augustine criticized, as improperly applied to God, the term "substance,"[26] etymologically understood as standing under accidents. He advised that what the Greeks call *ousia* should be translated into Latin as *essentia*, i.e. being. As we have the word knowledge from "to know," so we have being from "to be" ("ita ab eo quod est esse dicta est essentia"). "And who *is* more than he who said to his servant: 'I am who am,' and 'Tell the sons of Israel: He who *is* sent me to you'?" (Exodus 3.14). That which cannot change deserves really and truly to "BE."[27]

Augustine criticized the ambiguity resulting from the Latin translation of *hypostasis* by *substantia*. The Greeks called the Trinity one *ousia* and three *hypostaseis*. He commented: "I do not know what difference they wish to make between *ousia* and *hypostasis*."[28] When the Latins translate *hypostasis* by *substantia*, this Greek statement becomes one *essentiam* or *substantiam* and three *substantias* (one being or substance and three substances!) Because of this resulting contradiction, the Latins called the Trinity one Substance (Being) and three Persons.

The term "person" is useful, but can mislead, Augustine believed. Interpreted as a theatrical mask or role, it might imply a Sabellian[29] view of Son and Spirit. By this time also the term "person" referred to individual human beings, and Augustine apparently feared it might indicate the separability of the divine Persons. He held that the Trinity's inseparable activity entails its inseparable being. Moreover, "person" was viewed by him as an absolute term predicable of each and all of the divine persons. He used it to answer the question: Three what?[30]

Augustine also wondered about the proper name for the Holy Spirit. Holy, Spirit, and Love are common to all three Persons. However, in proceeding from the Father and Son, the Holy Spirit is given all that is God. So the Spirit is from them as Gift, eternally giveable. Because the Holy Spirit's proper name is the relational one of Gift of Father and Son who are holy and spirit, the Gift's distinctive name is Holy Spirit.[31]

The Search for the image of the Trinity: Books 8–15

These books are also a search for an understanding of the belief that human persons are created to the image of the Trinity (Genesis 1.26). Since God cannot be seen directly, an indirect approach is to study human images of God. Not merely an introspective, psychological search, it is guided by the divine missions and the desire to know the value of realizing that one is an image of God. Augustine began looking within human persons to "show that there are three somethings which can both be separately presented and also operate inseparably."[32]

Book 8 is described by a recent commentator as an ontological link between the divine mystery of the Trinity and the more accessible mystery of the human self.[33] Identifying truth and goodness with God, a Christianization of Platonism,[34] Augustine links human knowing and understanding, willing and loving, to God. This is a first link between God and the human image. Augustine also explores what the word "God" means. Faith is the response to God's self-revelation and the only access to God as Trinity. By faith persons communicate with God, who communicated with them by creation and by sending the Son and Spirit. Just as some general knowledge is involved in loving what one does not know, so some knowledge is involved in loving by believing. The historical knowledge of Christ's life is prologue to loving Christ. Augustine praises *caritas* or *dilectio*, two special kinds of *amor* (love). *Amor* is both affective and volitional; the term refers to both desire and enjoyment. Going beyond the pagan appreciation of goodness to which love is directed, he declares the absolute value of love itself. He repeats St. John, who said not only that God is love, but that love is God (1 John 4.7–21).[35]

Investigating the love of self, understood as lover, object loved, and love itself, he admits that when one loves oneself, only two are present: the lover and love. "But supposing I only love myself, are there now not two merely, what I love and love? Lover and what is being loved are the same thing when one loves oneself."[36] Augustine was searching for triadic human activities that were distinct and yet somehow one.[37]

Although Augustine seeks the image of God in the human person as an analogy of the divine processions, he cannot forget what scripture has revealed of the historical course of the human image from its beauty and defacement in Adam to its renovation through the grace of Christ. These discussions are not digressions. His Trinitarian theology is not separated from soteriology.[38]

In Books 9 and 10, there is psychology without the full nature of the human soul being studied. Augustine refers not to soul-powers[39] but to the functioning of the mind, the apex or highest level of the soul. He defines the terms to be used as *animus*, *mens*, *anima*. *Animus* refers to rational soul; *mens* to its highest level; these together are the "inner man." *Anima* refers to soul but not necessarily to human soul only. It is the subject of the lower sense-functioning of the "outer man." These terms – outer and inner – are from St. Paul (2 Cor. 4.16).

Mens (mind), as spiritual, is where God is imaged, but it is not mind in the modern sense. It includes volitional, affective, and cognitive activities. In Book 9 the first mental image of the Trinity is analyzed: the mind knowing and loving itself so that, all equal but distinct, mutually related and co-inherent, consubstantial and one substance, this image is an analogue of the Trinity. Human knowledge is discussed as participation in the *rationes aeternae*[40] and as divine illumination. The latter pertains to the truth of judgments and standards by which one lives, not to concept-formation. Augustine distinguishes judgments of truth from the fabrication of images, which promotes falsehood. When in Book 10 he confronts the Delphic Oracle's command to "know thyself," he declares that the mind cannot but know itself as immediately present to itself. Why then the command? Because the mind can be unconscious of itself. "I believe that it should think about itself and live according to its nature . . . under him [God] it should be subject to and over all that it should govern . . . Indeed it does many things it does through perverse desires as if it had forgotten itself."[41] Self-presence is not enough; to know oneself one must think of oneself (*se cogitare*); only then comes understanding (*scire, intellegere*).[42] The command to know oneself is to return from overabsorption in sense images which cause forgetfulness of self. Here Augustine enumerates erroneous views of mind as material; and the certainties available to the mind are specified.[43]

The first trinity of mind knowing and loving itself, and the next two mental trinities, were inspired by the Prologue to St. John's Gospel where the Word of God is uttered by the Father. Augustine looks within the mind and says that there is nothing that humans think, say, or do that is not preceded by a mental word brought forth within us.[44] This word is conceived in love, and love joins the word with the mind from which it is born. The word is equal to the mind because what is begotten is equal to its begetter. The love or desire by which knowledge is conceived is not an offspring of the mind; but what is known, considered as known, is an offspring, and this is loved in the sense that it is enjoyed. "And so there is a certain image of the Trinity: the mind itself, its knowledge, which is its offspring, and love as a third; these three are one and one substance."[45] This mental trinity which begins with mind is superseded by two later ones beginning with memory, but the structure of the "begotten word" remains central to the later trinities.

Augustine moves to intellectual remembering and offers a second mental trinity of remembering, understanding, and loving self. He sees this triad as the human person's natural capacity for uniting with God; this capacity remains even when impaired by loss of union with God.[46] "When memory is called life, and mind, and substance, it is so called with reference to itself, but when it is called memory, it is so called with reference to another."[47] The same is true of understanding and will. Therefore the three are one and have a oneness as mind. They are three with reference to each other, co-equal, and each equal to the three because they contain each other, and are all contained by each.[48] Augustine intimates that in creating human persons to the image of God, God wished them always to be mindful of the divine presence. Only when the mind comes to the perfect vision of God will this image be God's perfect likeness (1 Cor. 13.12).

Before taking up the final mental trinity, Augustine in Book 11 offers two triads of sense perception and imagination to enable readers to recognize more easily the three members of each triad as really distinct because material. Being on the sense level, perception and imagination are not presented as images of God.[49] In this same Book two functions of the mind are distinguished: contemplating truth as the source of true judgments (*sapientia*) and the rational activity of knowing and managing temporal affairs (*scientia*). One might interpret this as the current distinction between the theoretical and the practical intellect. God's image is in the contemplative mind, for only this, as wisdom, lasts forever. The act of faith belongs to the rational (practical) mind, which focuses on the temporal Christ, his life, words, death, and resurrection. Human beings ascend from knowledge (*scientia*) in this temporal life to wisdom (*sapientia*) in eternal life where God is contemplated. Augustine's analysis of faith, which he describes as far more than an act of will, is presented in Book 13.[50]

While the mental trinity of remembering, understanding, and loving self described in Book 10 is a natural image of God as co-eternal with himself, the true image of God, thoroughly explained in Book 14, is that of remembering, understanding, and loving God. This is awakened by grace and renewed throughout one's lifetime.

In Book 15 Augustine acknowledges that even the best image is inadequate to represent a triune God who is both simple and eternal.[51] His search for such an image has at least shown that three things can be one, and has been beneficial. It gave awareness of spirit life as utterly different from material life. The dismissal of a triune God often occurs because people try to think of it imaginatively or materially. Moreover, memory as source of understanding and will makes one conscious of the Father; understanding reminds one of the Son as the self-communication of the Father; in will one recognizes the Spirit, who is love.[52]

But the dissimilarity between temporal being and eternal Being, between changeable and unchangeable Being, is greater than the similarity. The divine Trinity is one with God; the human image is not identical with the human being. Remembering, understanding, and loving are functions of a human subject, whereas the Trinitarian Persons are not functions of a divine subject. There is no substitute for faith in Christ and what he reveals of Father and Spirit.[53]

Conclusion

The originality of Augustine is mainly found in his doctrine of the Holy Spirit and in the centrality he gave to love in Trinitarian life, and to love as renewing human likeness to the Trinity. That human beings were created images not of the Son alone but of the whole Trinity, according to Genesis 1:26, was a departure from the teaching of some predecessors.[54] The likeness to the Trinity occurs because "the love of God has been poured into our hearts through the Holy Spirit who has been given to us" (Rom. 5.5). Referring to the mutual love in the Trinity, Augustine wrote: "We are commanded to imitate this mutuality by grace, both with reference to God and to each other, in the two precepts on which the whole law and the Prophets depend" (Matthew 22:40).[55] Thus Christian Trinitarian spirituality is a continual rhythm of receiving love and giving love. Moreover, Augustine advanced Trinitarian theology by his use of relative predication to show that the unity and trinity of Father, Son, and Holy Spirit are not impossible. Augustine admitted the incompletion and limitation of his theological findings and looked to others to continue the search for more understanding. He never aimed to eliminate the mystery of the Trinity, revealed in scripture and calling for faith.

Augustine ends with a prayer: "Let me remember you, let me understand you, let me love you. Increase these things in me until you reform me completely."[56] He reminds his readers that to be mindful of God in this way and to image the Trinity who is Love is a lifelong process and the dynamic vocation of every human creature. The image will be perfected in the future, transformed through the Spirit. "When this image therefore has been renewed by this transformation, and thus made perfect, then we shall be like to God, since we shall see him not through a mirror, but just as he is, which the Apostle calls face to face"(1 Cor. 13.12).[57]

NOTES

1 The first Ecumenical Council's confession of faith, a creed composed at Nicaea in 325 to defend the equality of the Son with the Father against Arius and Arians; with additions at Constantinople, 381.

2 *De Trin.* 9.5,8. For the dynamic co-inherence or being-in-one-another of the divine Persons see John 10.38; 14.10; 17.21; 1 Cor. 2.10.

3 *Ep.* 120.13–20.

4 Homoeans were an anti-Nicene group formed in 359 who defined the Son of God as similar to God (*homoios*) without mentioning substance (*ousia*). Anomeans were an anti-Nicene group who taught that Father and Son are one in will but unlike in essence; homoiousians held similarity in substance between Father and Son. Homoousians were pro-Nicene and held identity of substance.

5 See Barnes 1999. He refers to *Ep.* 11 and 14, *De diversis quaestionibus octoginta tribus* 69, *In Johannis epistulam ad Parthos tractatus* 20, *Contra sermonem Arianorum*, and *De symbolo ad catechumenos*.

6 On Christ and Trinity, see Clark 1994, 58–72.

7 *De Trin.* 12.7.12–8.13.

8 Hill 1991, 38, #65 lists Tertullian, Novatian, Hilary, Victorinus; almost certainly Justin and Irenaeus; and Gregory Nazianzen, Didymus the Blind; possibly Basil the Great and Epiphanius of Salamis. See *De Trin.* 1.2.7 and 6.2.11.

9 Ibid. 15.28.51.

10 Ibid. 1.2.7.

11 Ibid. 1.6.13.

12 Ibid. 2.3.5.

13 The technical term "economic" theologians refers to certain second- and third-century theologians (among them Novatian and Tertullian) who identified the "economy" (*oeconomia*) or missions of Son and Spirit with subordinationism.

14 *De Trin.* Books 2 and 3.

15 Ibid. 4.19.25–21.32.

16 *Filioque* ("and the Son"), added to the Nicene–Constantinople creed in the West to express the "procession" of the Holy Spirit as distinguished from the generation of the Son from the Father. See Principe 1997.

17 De Régnon, 1892–1898 is responsible for the impression that Augustine's Trinitarian theology is Neoplatonic with undue priority to divine unity. See Barnes 1995b.

18 He calls "materialistic" those philosophies which identify the mind with air, fire, atoms, or brain, confusing their sense images with themselves. Others consider the mind to be merely an organization of the body, thinking as they do only of bodily things (*De Trin.* 10.7.9).

19 *De civ. Dei* 10.9–10.

20 See Studer 1997.

21 *De Trin.* 1.8.15–16.

22 This word is not discussed by Augustine although it is the main focus in Marius Victorinus' *Theological Treatises on the Trinity*, written in AD 351+ (Clark 1981).

23 Although Arius subordinated the Son to the Father, Augustine is responding here to late fourth-century Arians and, according to Barnes (1993), not the followers of Eunomius.

24 *De Trin.* 5.5.6.

25 Ibid. 5.11.12–13.14. Suggested by Gregory Nazianzen, *Orationes* 29.16 and Didymus the Blind, *De Trinitate* 1.11. But it entered into common theological language through Augustine.

26 *De Trin.* 7.5.10.

27 Ibid. 5.2.3.

28 Ibid. 5.8.10.

29 Sabellius, a third-century theologian, taught that the distinctions in the godhead were only transitory modes of God's operation.

30 *De Trin.* 7.4.7–9. See Hill 1991, 234 n. 36, quoting Aquinas, *Summa theologiae* I.29: "the name person was adapted to stand for relationship owing to the suitability of its meaning, i.e. it can stand for relationship not just because of usage, as the first opinion would have it, but because of what it really means." (Person signifies relationship indirectly).

31 *De Trin.* 5.11.12.

32 *Sermons* 52.17–18. I owe this quotation to Barnes 1999, note 27.

33 Hill 1991, 25.

34 Plato's Forms were not in a mind; Plotinus' Forms were in a mind (*Nous*), a lower being than the One; for Augustine the Logos or Word of God is the Wisdom, source of all forms, one with the divine Being.

35 *De Trin.* 8.2.3–9.13.

36 Ibid. 9.1.2.

37 Ibid. 8.10.14.

38 According to Hill 1991, 19, Aquinas improved the technical expression of Augustine's theology in *Summa theologiae* Ia, qq.27–43, but began with the divine processions in the godhead and ended with the missions of the divine persons, whereas Augustine took the historical approach by beginning with the missions. Aquinas also separated his treatment of the Trinity from that of the divine image in man (*Summa theologiae* Ia, q.93), missing the point of "coordinating them in one work." Hill adds that the subsequent tradition of Catholic theology missed it too.

39 See Hill 1991, 25 for Peter Lombard's erroneous placing of the divine image in "faculties" (*Sentences* I.3.2.). A misunderstanding of Augustine corrected by Aquinas in *Summa theologiae* Ia, 7, ad 2.

40 Augustine, *De diversis quaestionibus octoginta tribus* 46. Ideas in the Logos,

impressed upon the soul; ideas directly experienced by the mind such as happiness, truth, goodness, God, just law, numbers, by which judgments are made concerning particular events. See *De Trin.* 8.3.4, 14.15.21, 4.2.4, 9.2.9. Illumination is participation in the Word, namely, of that life which is the Light of men. Christ is the interior teacher. See *De magistro.*

41 *De Trin.* 10.5.7.

42 Ibid. 14.6.8.

43 For Descartes the act of doubting leads to a certainty. Augustine says that there is no doubt that he lives, remembers, understands, wills, thinks, knows, and judges (*De Trin.* 10.10.13). He thus establishes the certain reality of the human image of God.

44 Ibid. 9.7.12.

45 Ibid. 9.12.18.

46 Ibid. 14.8.11.

47 Ibid. 10.11.18.

48 Ibid.

49 *De Trin.* 12.5.5–6.8 where Augustine rejects the "family" as an image of the Trinity because it too is a "sensible" reality. Victorinus (Clark 1981, 193) included the body in the divine image since he held that human beings are created to the image of the Image, Christ (IB64.3).

50 See Studer 1997, 7–50: faith is a kind of historical knowledge, and based on the apostolic community's experience of the Paschal mystery.

51 *De Trin.* 15.27.50.

52 Ibid. 15.23.43.

53 Ibid. 15.22.42–23.44.

54 Ibid. 7.6.12.

55 Ibid. 6.5.7.

56 Ibid. 15.28.51

57 Ibid. 15.11.21 I thank Michel Barnes, Joseph Lienhard, S.J., and Eleonore Stump for their helpful comments on a draft of this chapter.

8

SIMO KNUUTTILA

Time and creation in Augustine

Augustine's most extensive discussions of philosophical and theological cosmology are found in his commentaries on Genesis (*De Genesi contra Manichaeos, De Genesi ad litteram imperfectus liber, De Genesi ad litteram libri duodecim*), in the last three books of the *Confessions,* and in Books 11 and 12 of the *De civitate Dei.*[1] The main lines of his view of the creation are as follows. God created both the spiritual realm of angels and the visible world, including the incarnated souls, out of nothing (*ex nihilo*), without any pre-existing matter or other things outside God, so that ontologically new beings came into existence.[2] The creation was based on an eternal free act of God's perfectly good will.[3] It took place through God's omnipotence without toil, effort, or industry.[4] God created simultaneously all first actualized things and, through "seminal reasons" inherent in them, the conditions of all those things which were to come up to the end of the world.[5] God is the only creator. Created beings cannot bring things into existence out of nothing.[6] God created time in creating movement in the universe.[7] The story of the six days of creation is a metaphor which helps human imagination.[8] Augustine sometimes interprets the "beginning"' (*in principio*) of Gen. 1.1 as a temporal beginning, but following an established tradition, he also takes it to refer to the Word or the Son of God (John 1.1–3): "In this beginning, God, you made heaven and earth, in your Word, in your Son, in your power, in your wisdom, in your truth" (*Conf.* 11.9.11).[9]

There was nothing radically new in Augustine's conception of the creation. Late second- and early third-century theologians began to stress the idea of creation out of nothing, and it became a standard doctrine of the Church. Some second-century Christian apologists could still accept a literal Platonic interpretation of the *Timaeus* to the effect that the universe had a temporal beginning and was built out of pre-cosmic matter.[10] Plato's story of the divine world-maker remained a popular theme in Patristic thought even later, but the assumption about pre-cosmic matter was rejected as a restriction of divine omnipotence and sovereignty. While the doctrine of independent matter was also given up by Neoplatonic thinkers, they did believe that the world emanated from the highest principle without a temporal beginning.[11] Augustine stated that the Christians should not understand the universe's being created as its being dependent upon God without a temporal beginning (*De civ. Dei* 11.4). He regarded it as a revealed truth that fewer than 6000 years have passed since the creation (ibid. 12.11).

Augustine was very fond of associating the conception of simultaneous creation with the doctrine of seminal reasons (*rationes seminales* or *rationes causales*) which was found in slightly different forms in Stoic and Platonic philosophy. He was not the first to regard this as a theologically significant conception, but he systematized it more than his predecessors.[12] According to Augustine, the members of the natural kinds which unfolded later on their own were created in seminal form at the beginning, but the seminal reasons also involved the seeds of all miraculous deviations from the common course of nature. In this way God remained the ultimate creator of every new being (*De Gen. ad litt.* 6.10.17–11.19, 6.14.25–15.26; *De Trin.* 3.8.13–9.16). Augustine held that all human beings were seminally in Adam, though their individual forms were not yet existent (*De civ. Dei* 13.14, 22.24). He did not accept the view that immortal human souls were created in the beginning to wait for later incarnation, but it remained unclear whether they were embedded in the seminal reasons.[13] Augustine distinguished between God's instantaneous creative act and God's conservational and providential activity. The existence of the created order is continuously dependent on God (*De Gen. ad litt.* 4.12.22; *De civ. Dei* 12.26).

Before discussing some philosophical themes associated with Augustine's conceptions of time and creation, let us have a closer look at the structure of the created world. According to Augustine's Trinitarian view, the Son is a perfect image and resemblance of the Father and, as the Word of God, the seat of the models of all finite beings which could serve as partial imitations of the highest being. The models of the minor resemblances are called the ideas.[14] They exist as divine thoughts and their contents refer to possible actualization in the domain of mutability.[15] God is absolutely immutable. Created things are mutable because of their compositional structure, which involves form and spiritual or corporeal matter. God simultaneously created the forms of things and the matter as the possibility of their being formed (*De Gen. ad litt.* 1.15.29; *De fide et symbolo* 2.2; *Conf.* 12.9.9). In his later works, Augustine takes "heaven"' and "earth" in Genesis 1.1 to refer to spiritual matter and corporeal matter respectively. Spiritual matter is the substrate of angels which were created when God said "Let there be light." It was formed into angelic spirits through turning into a vision of divine intelligibility (*De civ. Dei* 11.9).[16] This account of the creation of spiritual beings is strongly influenced by Plotinus' theory of the first emanation, though angels are created by choice, according to Augustine, and are not a result of a Plotinian emanation which actualizes all possible things at all possible levels of being. The lower part of the universe in which material things represent their ideas is also created directly by God; it is not an emanated imitation of the higher sphere as in Plotinus. (I shall return to this question in the next section.)

According to Augustine, time requires change and it is obvious that things in the changing corporeal part of the world are temporal. In *Confessions* 12.9.9 Augustine states that the heaven of heaven does not change, though it is capable of change. In later works he assumes that there is some kind of motion among the angels, which are the highest creatures. They may see things as they exist in divine art, or as created. This change of the scope of attention was meant to explain the expressions "Morning came" and "Evening came" in the creation story. The angels came to know the simultaneously created universe in this manner (*De civ. Dei* 11.7, 9, 29).[17]

Augustine regarded God as being itself (*ipsum esse*) and anything less than God as less existent.[18] The scale of the degrees of existence overlaps the scale of the degrees of goodness. God is perfectly good (*De civ. Dei* 12.1–2). The created beings are more or less good but they are all good because otherwise they would not exist. When God saw on the seventh day of creation that the created order was very good (Gen. 3.1), it was good in the sense that all singular beings were good and the whole formed a good and beautiful order (*Enchiridion de fide, spe et caritate* 3.9–10). Augustine admits that there are created things which most people do not consider good at all, such as poisonous animals, but he says that they are useful for some purpose and add to the beauty of the whole. Furthermore, many things cause distress to human beings only because of the corruption of the original human condition. Augustine also registers some structural weaknesses and the potential for suffering among animals, but he says that some things are less perfect than others and, depending on the place which a creature occupies in the great chain of being, its life is better or worse in a relative sense. This is the price for there being a harmonious whole with a great variety of things. "They are unequal in order that all of them can exist" (*De civ. Dei* 11.22, 12.4).[19]

What was God doing before he created the world?

In many places Augustine discusses the questions of what God was doing before he made heaven and earth and why the world was created at that moment when it began to be – why not earlier or later?[20] Putting forward queries of these kinds was part of popular criticism of the ideas of temporal beginning of the universe and God as a world-maker.[21] It was assumed in these questions, contrary to the general opinion, that there was time before the universe, but this was not the point of criticism. In his *Timaeus* Plato states that time came into existence together with the universe, but he also speaks about motion before the creation of time. This was taken to mean that one can make a distinction between orderly time, which began together with the ordered cosmos, and disorderly time associated with disorderly matter and motion.[22] Velleius, the spokesman for the Epicureanism in Cicero's *De natura deorum,* refers to this distinction while asking "why the world-builders suddenly awake into activity, after sleeping for countless ages" (1.21–22).

The "why not sooner?" argument against the temporal beginning of the universe had already been formulated by Parmenides, and Aristotle applied it in his *Physics* (8.1.252a11–19): if the world begins to exist at a certain moment without any other change, there is no reason why this should take place at that particular time.[23] If this beginning was based on a divine decision, there seems to be no reason why the decision should have been made at that time. Augustine says that some Platonists argued for the eternity of the world in order to avoid the criticism that divine acts are fortuitous and that new ideas come into God's allegedly unchanging mind (*De civ. Dei* 11.4). If the decision was not a sudden whim, but God wanted to launch something good, why not earlier? Why was God idle before? If creating the world was taken to add something to God's happiness, how could such a change take place in divinity?[24] Augustine states that some Platonic proponents of God's unchanging goodness thought that it required an everlasting series of identical or almost identical world cycles: God is never idle, and the cycles, being finite and uniform as distinct from an infinitely varying series, are accessible to divine knowledge (*De civ. Dei* 12.18; cf. 11.4–5).[25]

In addition to these theological remarks there was a well-known group of conceptual arguments against an absolute beginning. According to Aristotle, when a being begins to be, that is the first moment of its existence, before which it was not existent. Time cannot have a beginning, because there would then be time before time (*Physics* 8.1, 251b10–13, *Metaphysics* 12.6, 1071b8). Similarly, everything which begins to move is moved by something (*Physics* 8.1, 251a8–b10) and everything which begins to exist receives its constituents from already existing things (ibid. 1.9, 192a27–32; *Metaphysics* 7.7, 1032b30–7.8, 1033b19).

Augustine's answer to the arguments against the temporal beginning of the world is based on a sharp distinction between time and timelessness. Time depends on movement, and since God is unmoving, there is no time before creation (*Conf.* 11.13.15; *De civ. Dei* 11.6). The creation is an actualization of God's eternal and immutable decision: to will a change does not imply a change of will. There is no sudden new decision in God's mind (*Conf.* 11.10.12; *De civ. Dei* 11.4, 12.15, 12.18, 22.2). Similarly the questions "Why not sooner?" or "Was God idle before?" make no sense when God does not precede the created world in any temporal sense. The Aristotelian analysis of the beginning applies only to things having a temporal beginning, not to the beginning of time (*Conf.* 11.12.14–14.17, 11.30.40; *De civ. Dei* 11.5, 12.16). Its remarks on the coming-to-be from pre-existing matter apply to the generation of natural beings and artifacts but not to the creation (see *Conf.* 11.5.7, 12.8.8).

Augustine's solution was very influential in medieval times. A well-known later application is Leibniz's criticism of Newton's absolutist view of time. Leibniz said that the conception of time which goes on independently of whether anything else exists makes God create without sufficient reason at a certain moment. Leibniz's view was that the existence of time requires that of change.[26] Many contemporary philosophers of religion have dealt with the question of whether the Augustinian conception of God's timelessness is compatible with the doctrines of divine omniscience and voluntary action.[27]

Did God create everything he could create?

In *De spiritu et littera* Augustine gives an answer to Marcellinus, who was concerned, among other things, about how Augustine could say that something is possible even though there is no example of it in the world. In Marcellinus' opinion, to call such things possible was not comprehensible (*De spir. et litt.* 1–2). The question was raised in accordance with the view that all generic possibilities prove their genuineness through actualization. This principle was generally included in the paradigms which shaped the ancient philosophical theories of modality. Whether there are genuine individual possibilities which remain unrealized was somewhat more controversial.[28] Elsewhere Augustine mentions other objections to Christian doctrines, based on the view that the ordinary course of nature defines what is possible or impossible (*De civ. Dei* 21.7–10, 22.4, 11). Augustine's answer in each case is that things which may seem impossible from the point of view of natural powers are often possible, because God can do them. He also mentions the idea that miraculous events are not unnatural. Our concept of nature is based on observational regularities, but the ultimate nature is God's will or providential design, which provides natural history with all kinds of exceptional events. They are incomprehensible to men and function to demonstrate God's sovereignty to believers (*De civ. Dei* 21.8).

Augustine stresses that even though God's immense power is not comprehensible to human minds, God's works are not irrational (ibid. 21.5). Augustine asserts an eternal system of mathematical, dialectical, and metaphysical principles based on "the archetypal forms or stable and unchangeable reasons of things, which are not themselves formed but are contained in the divine mind eternally and are always the same" (*De diversis quaestionibus octoginta tribus* 46). A rational will cannot wish anything unrealizable (e.g. to change unchangeable truths), and it is clear that the power of realization, conceptually distinct from the will, is efficient only as far as the will to which it is attached is rational. When Augustine defined omnipotence as the power to do what one wills (see e.g.,

Enchiridion de fide, spe et caritate 96; *De civ. Dei* 21.7), he took it for granted that God's will cannot be directed to anything which is contradictory, for such volitions would prove that God is not omnipotent.

According to Plato, the domain of the forms exhausts the possibilities of the types of beings and there are no forms without a sometime imitation in the empirical world. Plotinus' version of this view is that the power of being proceeding from the One does not leave any part of the maximal universe unrealized. At each level the generic forms are instantiated by particular beings as numerously as possible (*Enneades* 4.8.6). In this sense Plotinus asserted an equation between possibilities and their realizations, i.e. he accepted in one form the idea A. O. Lovejoy dubbed "the principle of plenitude" in his famous book *The Great Chain of Being*. According to Lovejoy the same applies to Augustine, but this is not true. As for the possible individuals, this is clearly false, and as for the types of being, the example mentioned by Lovejoy can be understood in different ways.[29] Lovejoy and those following him think that Augustine had in mind all possible types of being when he argued that degrees of perfection are required because otherwise not all kinds could be actual. But this can be understood as a remark about the actual world and its kinds.[30] It is not quite clear whether or not Augustine assumed that there are empty generic forms, but he thought that the number of merely possible individuals was much larger than that of the individuals which occur in the world history. In *De civitate Dei* 12.19 Augustine criticizes the ancient doctrines which claimed that the only permissible notion of infinity is that of potential infinity. According to him, an infinite series of numbers actually exists in God's thought, and God could create an infinite number of individuals and know each of them simultaneously: "If he wished that there will always be new things of all kinds unlike their predecessors, none of them could be for him undesigned or unforeseen, nor would he see each just before it comes into being, but it would be contained in his eternal prescience."

Augustine qualified the notion of God's power by relating it to other divine attributes, e.g. "God could do it according to his power, but not according to his justice" (*Contra Gaudentium Donatistarum episcopum* 1.30).[31] In dealing with divine providence, Augustine referred to unrealized possibilities using the slogan "Potuit sed noluit" ("He could, but he did not want to"; see *C. Faust.* 29.4; *De nat. et gratia* 7.) The phrase became well known in early medieval times. It was not introduced by Augustine, but was used by other theologians before him.[32] When Augustine used this conception in analyzing the freedom of human will, he had in mind an intuitive model of diachronic possibilities. Before a choice is made, it is possible that the act of choice will be this or that. According to Augustine, divine foreknowledge about free choices does not influence them, and God's knowledge about them could be other than it is: "A man does not sin unless he wills to sin, and if he had willed not to sin, then God would have foreseen that refusal" (*De civ. Dei* 5.10). The view that real alternatives are open to the will before it makes a choice qualifies the concept of freedom of will. Freedom is not mere absence of external constraint.[33] This is also true of God's will. Augustine regarded God's omnipotence as an executive power between alternatives which is factually limited by God's actual choice. God's free choice of the universe is conceptually preceded by knowledge about alternative possibilities. Plotinus sometimes applies the notion of will to the One, but because the One is essentially good, it will realize all possibilities.[34] This is how Plato also characterized the generous divine goodness in *Timaeus* 29d-e. Augustine appreciated the Platonic view (*De civ. Dei* 11.21), but his conception of divine possibilities contained an intuitive idea of alternative worlds of which only one is actualized. He thought that God could have made various worlds, and hence he saw God's eternal decision as free and voluntary in a manner which was beyond the purview of the Platonic tradition. According to Augustine, God has created the world, because he is good and the world is good, but his goodness could have taken other forms. The world exists because God has willed it, but there is no ultimate answer to the question of why God has willed it (*De Gen. c. Man.* 1.2.4).[35]

Even though Augustine's remarks on the divine will remained sketchy, they gave rise to the conception of God as acting by choice between alternative universes. It played an important role in the emergence of the intuitive idea of modality as referential multiplicity with respect to synchronic alternatives. This modal paradigm hardly occurred at all among ancient thinkers. It was introduced in early medieval discussions which were strongly influenced by Augustine's philosophical theology.[36]

Time and eternity

Augustine's meditations on time in Book 11 of the *Confessions* belong among the most discussed philosophical parts of his works. The general remark about time in the *Confessions* is often quoted: "I know what it is, provided that nobody asks me; but if I want to explain it to an enquirer, I do not know" (11.14.17). Augustine is mainly interested in a psychological account of time, but he also takes some basic ideas formulated in ancient natural philosophy for granted. Since many of them owe their origin to Aristotle, let us have a brief look at Aristotle's treatment of time in the closing chapters of the fourth book of the *Physics*.

After having formulated some paradoxes of time in chapter 10, Aristotle begins his systematic discussion in chapter 11 with some remarks on the experience of the present time (now) and on the corresponding concept of the present based on an immediate awareness of actuality. When the content of the present now changes we say that there is a new "now." Without a change we could be aware neither of distinct moments nor of time, because time is some kind of distance between different "nows." Looking at things from the point of view of the actual present time was natural for Aristotle, as can be seen from the above terminology and from his habit of considering temporally indeterminate sentences as paradigms of informative statements in general. Such sentences contain an explicit or implicit reference to their moment of utterance, e.g. "Socrates is sitting (now)," and the same sentence can sometimes be true and sometimes false, depending on how things are at the moment of their utterance. If a sentence is always true, it is necessarily true, and if it is never true, it is impossible. If it is possibly true, it is at least sometimes true. If statements with existential import are true whenever they are uttered, they refer to things which are actual at any moment of time and hence necessary (*Metaphysics* 9.10, 1051b9–17). Necessary beings are omnitemporal, but if there were only such beings without motion, they would not be called "omnitemporal" because there would be no time in a world without motion.

In natural philosophy the present "now" must be understood as a durationless boundary between the past and the future. Such "nows" or "instants" with unchanging content are the limits between which the processes with definite temporal length take place. (In Book 6 of the *Physics* Aristotle developed detailed rules of how to set the boundaries of processes and moments of change in a physical theory operating with the doctrines of the categories and continuous time, space, and motion.) Aristotle's conception of the temporal length or quantity (number) of a motion can be described as follows. Let us assume that an object X moves continuously from place A to place B, so that there is a last instant M at which it is at A and a first instant N at which it is at B. The instants ("nows") differ from each other because of the position of X in them. There is a spatial length between these positions and there is a temporal length between X's being in these positions. The temporal length is the quantity of the motion "in respect of before and later"(*Physics* 4.11.219a11–220a27). To measure is to apply a unit to a whole and to count how many units it involves. A convenient temporal measuring unit is the orbit of something moving uniformly in a circle which can be easily divided into equal parts. The length of a motion or anything in time is measured by comparing it with a regularly divisible simultaneous motion. Celestial motion is the universal clock, but time is not this motion any more than any other motion (*Physics* 4.12.220b18–24; 14, 223b13–20).

Aristotle found the question of the reality of time cumbersome. The parts of time are the past and the future and neither of them exists. They are divided by the present, which is the boundary between the past and the future (like a point which divides a line) and no part of time. As time is never actual as time, does it exist at all? The same question could be asked about motion, the reality of which Aristotle regarded as a basic fact. Time is not the same as motion, but is real as a countable aspect of motion which expresses itself to human minds (4.14, 223a22–29). It does not exist outside the soul, but has some kind of objective reality. Motion can be slower or faster, but this is not true of time. Time also has a fixed direction. The future changes into the past but not vice versa. The past and the present are necessary; the future is partially contingent (4.10, 218b13–15; 12, 220a32–b5; 13, 222a10–11, b1–2, *De int.* 9).[37]

Insofar as Augustine deals with time as a topic of natural philosophy, his views show similarities to those of Aristotle and his Stoic followers.[38] Like Aristotle and the Stoics, Augustine assumed that time is an infinitely divisible continuum (*Conf.* 11.15.20); that there would be no time if there were no motion and no souls (*De Gen. ad litt.* 5.5.12; *De civ. Dei* 11.6, 12.16); and that time and motion are distinct even though time is not independent of motion (*Conf.* 11.24.31, 12.11.14). In criticizing the view that time is the motion of a celestial body, Augustine states that time would still pass if the sun stood still, and it would not be affected if the heavenly bodies were accelerated. Time as duration is not dependent on any specific motion, but if nothing passed or arrived or existed, there would be no past, future or present times (11.23.30–24.31; cf. 11.14.17). Augustine also thought that we measure the temporal length of something by comparing it to something, basically to the number of fixed parts of a regular motion serving as measurement units (*Conf.* 11.16.21, 11.24.31).

There are some peculiarities in Augustine's physical conception of time. One of them is that he called the present "a part of time" though he assumed that it was without duration (*Conf.* 11.15.20).[39] This notion was probably influenced by Augustine's stance in the controversy about the moment of instantaneous change. Aristotle's theory of the limits of changes is based on the assumption of a continuous structure of time, place, quantity, and motion. There are no contiguous instants in a continuous time, and therefore the main purpose of the theory is to justify assigning the moment of beginning or cessation of a permanent being, or of a temporal process, either to the last instant of actuality of the preceding state or to the first instant of actuality of the following state. Aristotle's physical model did not include an element which would function as a transformer between the contradictory states associated with beginning and ceasing. In the Platonic tradition going back to the *Parmenides* (156c–157a) it was thought that generations and corruptions, or beginnings and cessations, take place at an instant of change at which neither of the contradictory statements describing the terms of change is true. This theory, which involves truth-value gaps and dismisses the law of the excluded middle, is presented in a popular form by Aulus Gellius in his *Attic Nights* (7.13). The author tells how his teacher Calvenus Taurus applied it in answering the question of when a person, strictly speaking, is dying. This passage was probably known to Augustine when he discussed the same question in *De civ. Dei* 13.9–11.[40]

Augustine found the question confusing, for before death comes, one is not dying but alive, because the soul is still in the body and has not yet departed; and when death has come and the soul has departed, one is dead and not dying. Augustine says that the time at which one is dying seems to disappear, and the same seems to happen when the future changes into the past without interval. Like Aulus Gellius, Augustine excludes the possibility that the moment of death could be an intrinsic limit of the period when the soul has not yet departed or of the period when it has departed. He also regards it as absurd that contradictory statements could be true at the same time. What remains is that the instant of death is the Platonic "suddenly" at which the law of the excluded middle is not in force. Augustine does not explicitly state this, but says that it is not possible to give any rational account of the moment of dying.

In Book 11 of the *Confessions* Augustine first deals with God's atemporal eternity, the temporality of the created beings, and the beginning of time and the world at the creation. From 11.14.17 the theme of the book is the measurement of time. Augustine is particularly puzzled by the question of how a measured time exists. We speak of "a long time" and "a short time," but the future is not yet actual and the past is no longer actual. How can something which does not exist be long or short? The present, which is actual, is without duration. It is not long or short (*Conf.* 11.15.18–20). Even though time moves backwards so that the present continuously ceases to be present and becomes a part of the past, there is no store out of which the future is issuing to become the present and then be stored again in the past (11.17.22–18.23). Nevertheless, we are conscious of intervals of time and measure them. Augustine argues that the practice of the measurement of time is based on the fact that human consciousness functions by anticipating the future, remembering the past, and being aware of the present through perception. Through this distension of the soul (*distentio animi*) we have in our memory images of things which were present and which we expect to be present. Therefore we have in the soul a present of past which is memory and a present of future which is anticipation or expectation (11.20.26, 11.26.33). In this sense time exists as a distension of the soul.[41] To measure time is to measure temporal extensions between impressions which passing events have made upon the soul and which abide when they have gone. Past events do not exist. When the duration between them is measured, the present consciousness of past events is associated with a consciousness of past measuring motion. The same is applied to evaluating the duration of future events (11.27.35–36).

That time has some kind of existence in the soul had already been suggested by Aristotle, who thought that it was a special aspect of the motion of which human intellect becomes aware in remarking the distance between the presents with different contents. Like Aristotle, Augustine thought that these distances had an objective aspect:

From the moment we begin to exist in this body which is destined to die we are involved all the time in a process whose end is death . . . All are driven on at the same speed and with a similar movement. The man whose life was shorter passed his days no more swiftly than the long-lived. Moments of equal length rushed by for both of them at equal speed . . . If a man passes through a more extended period of time on this road to death, he does not proceed more slowly; he merely has a longer journey. (*De civ. Dei* 13.10)

Even though Augustine's psychological theory of time is not a novelty in ancient philosophy, there is something new in his attempt to illustrate the time sense through the concepts of memory and anticipation. Augustine's terminology is close to Husserl's account of phenomenological time, which is based on a distinction between primal impression, retention, and protention which is associated with the temporal determination of now, past, and future.[42] Augustine assumed that one can imagine a certain duration by using one's memory and evaluate the time of future processes in this way:

Suppose someone wished to utter a sound lasting a long time, and decided in advance how long it was going to be. He would have planned that space of time in silence and then, committing it to memory, he would begin to utter the sound which goes on until it has reached the set end. (*Conf.* 11.27.36)

Our ability to measure times and evaluate temporal lengths is based on our ability to memorize experienced durations. We become aware of time through experiencing temporal extension. Contrary to what has often been maintained, Augustine does not offer any philosophical or theological definition of time in Book 11 of the *Confessions*. He tries to explain how we are aware of time and how its existence could be explained from the psychological point of view.[43]

NOTES

1 Solignac 1973; for a concise summary with textual references and bibliography, see Mayer 1996.
2 *De Gen. c. Man.* 1.6.10; *Conf.* 11.5.7, 12.7.7, 12.8.8; *De Gen. ad litt.* 1.14.28–15.29; *De civ. Dei* 12.1.
3 *De Gen. c. Man.* 1.2.4; *De Gen. ad litt.* 1.5.11, 2.6.14; *De civ. Dei* 11.21, 24.
4 *De diversis quaestionibus octoginta tribus* 78; *De Gen. ad litt.* 9.17.32; *De civ. Dei* 12.18.
5 For the simultaneous creation, see *De Genesi ad litteram imperfectus liber* 7.28; *De Gen. ad litt.* 1.15.29, 4.33.52. For the seminal reasons see e.g. *De Gen. ad litt.* 6.10.17–6.11.19.
6 *De civ. Dei* 12.26.
7 *De Gen. ad litt.* 5.5.12; *De civ. Dei* 11.6.
8 *Conf.* 13.29.44; *De Gen. ad litt.* 4.33.52.
9 See also *De civ. Dei* 11.33. For the history of the latter interpretation before Augustine, see Nautin 1973.

10 May 1978, 120–182. Plato's immediate followers in the Academy thought that the universe was without beginning. Plutarch and Atticus are usually mentioned as the Middle Platonic representatives of the literal interpretation, but according to Proclus, there were many others. Dillon 1977, 33, 42, 207–208, 252–254, Sorabji 1983, 268–272, Meijering 1979, 40.

11 See also Sorabji 1983, 313–315.

12 Mayer 1996, 86–91.

13 Augustine often discussed the question whether both the material bodies and the immaterial souls are handed down from parents (the traducianist view of the soul's origin) or whether individual souls are constantly created by God (the creationist view). His theological convictions suggested the traducianist view, but he preferred to suspend judgment on this matter. The main reason for bothering about these and some related themes was the doctrine of Adam's original sin and its consequences. See O'Connell 1987; O'Daly 1987, 15–20; Rist 1994, 317–320.

14 *De Genesi ad litteram imperfectus liber* 16.57–58; Gilson 1960, 210–212. The idea of the Word which contains within himself the ideas of possible things was accepted by practically all the medieval theologians. In Augustine's approach the ideas represented the finite modes of imitating the infinite divine being. The possibilities had an ontological foundation in God's essence. This was the dominating view of the metaphysics of modalities in the thirteenth century. Duns Scotus gave up this habit of thought by introducing the concept of logical possibility and maintaining that God knows the possibilities as such before comparing them with his essence from the point of view of imitation. See Knuuttila 1996.

15 Rist states (1994, 256) that the ideas are in the Word as the Neoplatonic forms are in the Nous, the first sphere of emanation; but the Word is not subordinate and the forms are not equal to the Word.

16 In *Conf.* 12 "heaven" usually refers to the "heaven of heaven" which unchangingly contemplates God and "earth" is the formless matter, but Augustine also mentions as a possible interpretation of Genesis 1.1 that "heaven" refers to the formless spiritual realm and "earth" means formless physical matter (12.17.26). When Augustine speaks about the "heaven of heaven" as an intellectual entity, it is not quite clear whether the distinction between matter and form can be applied to it. He later preferred to speak about angels as the highest created beings.

17 Sorabji 1983, 31–32.

18 *In Johannis evangelium tractatus* 38.8–10; *De civ. Dei* 12.2; Gilson 1960, 210–211.

19 According to Plotinus, badness is the price of variety; it is a privation of the good without an independent ontological status (*Enneades* 1.8.3; 3.2.11); for the notion of *privatio boni* in Augustine, see *Enchiridion de fide, spe et caritate* 3.11. The fallen world has become a place of suffering through the moral evils which people bring about and through the natural evils which befall us apart from human agency. The fragility of the mental and physical dispositions of fallen men is penal. See Kirwan 1989, 80–81; Rist 1994, 256–289.

20 *De Gen. c. Man.* 1.2.3–4; *Conf.* 11.10.12, 11.12.14, 11.30.40; *De civ. Dei* 11.4–5. See also Peters 1984, 3.

21 For a detailed historical discussion, see Sorabji 1983, 232–252, 268–283.

22 Dillon 1977, 253–254.

23 Sorabji 1983, 232–238.

24 These points are repeated in the Epicurean criticism in Cicero, *De natura deorum*

1.9.21–22; Lucretius, *De rerum natura*, 5.156–180; and Aetius, *Placita* (Diels 300a18–301a7). Effe (1970, 23–31) tries to show that they derive from Aristotle's *De philosophia*; see also Sorabji 1983, 281–282. The Epicureans believed that the present world order had a beginning and that gods had no influence on it.

25 Chadwick (1991, 226–227) remarks that Origen argued against the eternity of the world with the argument that the infinite cannot be known (*De principiis* 2.9.1, 3.5.2, 4.4.8; *Commentarii in Matthaeum* 13.1) and that Porphyry may have answered this criticism with the hypothesis of world cycles. This approach was then used by the pagan antagonists of Christianity mentioned by Augustine. Plotinus argued for the recurrence by referring to the finite number of seminal reasons (*Enneades* 5.7.1–3) and the Stoic doctrine may have been based on a similar view. See also Sorabji 1983, 182–188.

26 See the discussions in Kirwan 1989, 162, and Sorabji 1983, 79–80, 256–258.

27 A work often quoted in this connection is Pike 1970.

28 Knuuttila 1993, 1–38.

29 Lovejoy 1936, 67.

30 Lovejoy quotes, without giving the reference, *De civ. Dei* 11.22. For similar formulations, see 12.4 and 12.27.

31 Cf. Origen, *Commentariorum series in Matthaem* 95.

32 See Tertullian, *De cultu feminarum* 1.8.2.

33 I do not discuss the problems associated with Augustine's attempt to combine human freedom and theological determinism.

34 Sorabji 1983, 316–318; Rist 1994, 265.

35 Augustine did not defend the thesis that the created world is the best possible. He thought that it was "very good" and that there was no cause for complaint. See also Kirwan 1989, 67.

36 Knuuttila 1993, 62–98.

37 For Aristotle's view of time, see Conen 1964.

38 O'Daly 1981; 1987, 152–161. For a more general comparison of Augustine's account with ancient philosophical views, see Callahan 1948, 1967.

39 See also O'Daly 1987, 155–156.

40 See Strobach 1998, 41–45.

41 Augustine's characterization of time as a distension of the soul shows certain similarities to Plotinus' description of the world-soul whose spreading out of life (*diastasis*) involves time (*Enneades* 3.7.11.41). Teske (1983a) has suggested that time is the extension of the world-soul for Augustine too, but the traditional view is that Augustine is talking of the human soul in this connection. See O'Daly 1989, 154; Rist 1994, 83. Augustine's other views about time were also influenced by Plotinus' treatise on eternity and time (*Enneades* 3.7).

42 Husserl 1966; see also Ricœur 1988, 12–59.

43 For a concise classification of historical interpretations, see Ross 1991, 191–192.

9

ROLAND TESKE

Augustine's theory of soul

Knowledge of the soul is central to Augustine's search for wisdom, as is seen in his claim that he desires "to know God and the soul" (*Sol.* 1.2.7). And when Reason, with whom he converses in the *Soliloquia*, presses him as to whether he does not desire to know anything more, he answers, "Absolutely nothing." Later he expresses the same desire in his prayer, "God ever the same, may I know you, and may I know myself" (*Sol.* 2.1.1). Though all living beings have souls, Augustine's principal interest is the human or rational soul. He uses the Latin *anima* for soul in general, while reserving *animus* or *mens* for the rational soul. In his earlier writings he defines the human soul in Platonic fashion as "a certain substance partaking in reason and suited to rule the body" (*De quant. anim.* 13.22) and says that "a human being, as seen by a human being, is a rational soul using a mortal and earthly body" (*De moribus ecclesiae catholicae* 1.27.52). In later writings he places more emphasis upon the unity of the human being. Though Augustine says that a human being is "a rational soul which has a body," he also says that "the soul which has a body does not make two persons, but one human being" (*In Johannis evangelium tractatus* 19.15). A human being can be defined as a single substance with a body and a soul: "If we should define a human being such that a human being is a rational substance consisting of soul and body, there is no doubt that a human being has a soul which is not the body and has a body which is not the soul" (*De Trin.* 15.7.11).[1]

Augustine's doctrine on the soul as an incorporeal, immortal substance is Platonic in origin; it was initially derived from his contact with the "books of the Platonists" (*Conf.* 7.9.13) in the summer of 386 and was developed in reaction to his previous Stoic and Manichaean views.[2] Biblical language, however, in which "soul" often stands for the whole person, reinforced the Platonic tendency to identify the person with the mind or soul.

The soul's mid-rank position

In an early letter to his friend Celestine, Augustine locates the soul in his scheme of reality beneath God and above bodies. God is absolutely unchangeable, while bodies are changeable in both place and time and souls are changeable only in time. Everything changeable is, Augustine adds, a creature, while that which is unchangeable is the Creator. The soul as changeable in time, but not in place, holds the mid-rank position below the highest and above the lowest. "By turning down toward the lowest the soul lives unhappily, but by turning back toward the highest it lives blessedly." One who believes in Christ, Augustine immediately adds, "does not love the lowest, is not proud over the intermediate, and thus becomes fit to cling to the highest. This is the whole of what we are commanded, admonished, and set afire to do" (*Ep.* 18.2).

In his hierarchy of being the human soul is more excellent than all things known by the senses, and among the things more noble than sensible things which God created, "there is something inferior and something equal: something inferior such as the soul of an animal, and something equal such as that of an angel, but there is nothing better" (*De quant. anim.* 34.78). There is nothing closer to God than the rational soul (*De civ. Dei* 11.26), and if they are compared to "the holy and sublime creatures of the celestial or supercelestial powers," Augustine holds that "rational souls are unequal in function, but equal in nature" (*De lib. arb.* 3.11.32).

The soul's status as a creature

Augustine clearly recognized the soul's status as a creature, at least soon after baptism, but during his earlier Manichaean years he had held, as he phrased it years later, that he had

> two souls or spirits or minds, one soul proper to the flesh and this same soul co-eternal with God and evil, not because of a defect befalling it, but by its nature, and the other soul good by its nature, as a particle of God, but stained by mixture with that evil soul. (*Contra Julianum opus imperfectum* 6.6)

Because he identified his real self with the good soul, Augustine thought that he himself did not sin, but "that some other nature sinned in us, and it delighted my pride to be without guilt and, when I had done something evil, not to confess that I had done it" (*Conf.* 5.10.18). Thus, in the garden scene before his conversion, he described his inner struggle in Manichaean terms as a conflict between two minds or wills, a struggle which he came to understand "did not reveal the nature of an alien mind within me, but rather the punishment of my own," a punishment stemming from "a sin which was more free, for I was Adam's son" (*Conf.* 8.10.12).

In his earliest writings, under the influence of the books of the Platonists, Augustine still seems to have entertained the idea that the soul was divine. In *Contra Academicos* 1.1.1, he speaks of "the divine soul," and he later describes a life devoted to reason as "living in accord with that divine part of the soul" (*C. Acad*. 1.4.11). Very soon, however, Augustine came to the conviction that the soul is not what God is, but a creature made by God, made not out of God, but out of nothing.[3] His standard argument against any view that the soul is divine or a part of God rests upon his insight that God alone is absolutely immutable, while the soul is clearly subject to change.[4] He writes to Jerome that the soul "is not a part of God. For if it were this, it would be utterly immutable and incorruptible. If it were such, it would not become worse and make progress for the better, nor would it, in terms of its dispositions, begin to have in itself what it did not have or cease to have what it had" (*Ep*. 166.2.3). Though the human soul is immortal because it does not cease to live, it is in some sense mortal. "For in every changeable nature the change itself is a death, because it causes something which was in it to exist no more" (*C. Max*. 2.12.2).

Incorporeality of the soul

During his early years Augustine shared the common Stoic corporealism of the Western empire and was convinced that whatever is real is bodily.[5] His nine years as a "hearer" in the Manichaean sect did nothing to disabuse him of the conviction "that anything not a body was nothing at all" (*Conf*. 5.10.20). In fact, he complains that his inability to conceive of a spiritual substance was almost the sole cause of his errors (*Conf*. 5.4.25, 10.20). After all, if evil was something real, it too had to be a body and a body which placed a limit on the good God who was infinitely extended except where evil limited him. From his encounter with the books of the Platonists in 386 and later, Augustine learned to conceive of God and the soul as non-bodily.[6] In the Latin West, before the time of Augustine, there was no clearly articulated concept of non-bodily or spiritual beings – except in the "Milanese circle" of Christian Neoplatonists, including Ambrose, within which Augustine came into contact with the spiritualist metaphysics of Plotinus.[7] In writing to Theodorus, another member of the Milanese circle, Augustine remarks with amazement how he

> noticed often in the words of our priest and at times in yours that, when one thinks of God, one should not think of anything bodily at all, and the same thing holds with regard to the soul, for among all things it is the one closest to God. (*De beata vita* 1.4)

Writing to Jerome in 415 with a plea for his help about the origin of the soul, Augustine tells him that he is convinced that the soul is incorporeal and articulates the concept of an incorporeal soul. To avoid a merely verbal dispute, he admits that, if one holds that every substance or essence is a body or that only an unchangeable substance is non-bodily, then the soul is a body

But if only that is a body which is either at rest or in motion through a stretch of place with some length, breadth, and height so that it occupies a larger place with a larger part of itself and a smaller place with a smaller part of itself, the soul is not a body.

The soul, by contrast,

is stretched out through the whole body which it animates, not by a local diffusion, but by a vital intention, for through all the parts of the body it is simultaneously present as a whole and is not smaller in smaller parts nor larger in larger parts. (*Ep.* 166.2.4)

That the whole soul is present simultaneously in all parts of the body is shown by the whole soul's ability to be simultaneously aware of what occurs in distinct parts of the body.[8] Augustine also argues that the mental power by which he forms images of bodily things cannot itself be a corporeal substance (*Conf.* 7.1.2), and argues for the incorporeality of the soul from its ability to form images of bodies (*De nat. et orig. anim.* 4.17.25).

The number of souls

In *De quantitate animae* Augustine tells Evodius that his mind "must first be trained to gaze upon and distinguish these realities so that you can understand most clearly whether the statement of certain very learned men is true that soul can be in no way divided by itself, but can, nonetheless, be divided by the body" (*De quant. anim.* 32.68). These learned men were, it would seem, the Platonists whose books had recently permitted Augustine to conceive of an incorporeal substance.[9] And the issue in question was what later philosophers called the individuation of souls, especially of souls separated from their bodies. Augustine raises the question of the number of souls only to postpone dealing with the problem, but not without making some revealing comments to his interlocutor in which he clearly rejects the idea that soul is merely one. After all, soul "is happy in one person and unhappy in another, and one and the same being cannot be happy and unhappy at the same time" (ibid. 32.69). He also rejects the idea that soul is simply many, perhaps because he has in mind the Plotinian hypostasis "soul," in which individual souls partake and which makes them somehow one despite their diversity. In any case he finds less objectionable the idea that soul is both one and many – precisely the view, however strange it may seem to those outside the Neoplatonic tradition, which he could have found in *Ennead* 4.9.

The world-soul

In his early works Augustine seems to have accepted the idea of a universal or world-soul.[10] In *De immortalitate animae* he says that "Form is given to body by the highest essence through soul. Body subsists, therefore, through soul, and is by the very fact that it is animated, whether universally, as the world, or particularly, as each living being within the world" (*De immor. anim.* 15.24).[11] In *De ordine* he tells his young friends:

> Reason is that movement of the mind capable of distinguishing and connecting what we learn, and only the most exceptional kind of person is able to use it as a guide to understand God or that soul which is either in us or everywhere, precisely because it is difficult for one who has entered into the concerns of these senses to return to himself. (*De ord.* 2.11.30)

So too, *De musica* 6.14.44 seems to imply that the world is a living being, and in *Retractationes* 1.9.4 Augustine states that he was unable to settle this question by argument or by the authority of scripture. He does not, however, say that his previous statement is false, but simply that he does not see that it is true. Hence, though he was aware that "Plato and very many other philosophers" (*Retract.* 1.9.4) thought that the world had a soul, he maintained an agnostic stance on that point. The doctrine of a universal soul with which individual human souls are somehow one may underlie the definition of time in *Confessiones* 10.26.33 as the distension of the mind, for it would allow Augustine to avoid viewing time as the distension of individual souls with the loss of a public or objective time which that view entails.[12]

The origin of the souls

In the first paragraph of his first extant work, while asking Theodorus' help in attaining wisdom, Augustine mentions that we souls have arrived here because "God or nature or necessity or our will or some combination of these has cast us into this world" (*De beata vita* 1.1), and a few paragraphs later he expresses his doubt about his ability to make progress "while the question about the soul" remains in doubt (ibid. 1.5). The soul of Adam was clearly created by God, but the origin of the souls of subsequent human beings posed a considerable problem. Approximately ten years later, Augustine listed four hypotheses concerning the origin of these souls with a view to defending the justice of God, no matter which hypothesis might be the correct one. The first hypothesis is that one soul was created and from it the souls of those who are now born are drawn; the second that souls are individually created in each child who is born (*De lib. arb.* 3.20.56). The third hypothesis is that souls already existing in some secret place are sent by God to animate and rule the bodies of individuals who are born (ibid. 3.20.57), and the fourth hypothesis is that souls existing elsewhere are not sent by God, but "come of their own accord to inhabit bodies" (ibid. 3.20.58). Augustine sums up these four views about the soul: They come from propagation; they are created new in each individual; they exist elsewhere and are sent into the bodies of the newborn; or they exist elsewhere and fall of their own accord in these bodies (ibid. 3.21.59). Though Augustine's language here is less than precise, it seems fair to say that the first hypothesis closely resembles traducianism, while the second resembles creationism, and that the last two both presuppose that souls exist before their embodiment and are either sent by God or fall of their own accord into bodies.[13] Even so careful a historian as Gilson acknowledged that Augustine assumed the soul's pre-existence in his early writings.[14] Augustine claimed in *Retractationes* (1.1.3) that he did not know then (that is, in the Cassiciacum period) and that he does not know now (that is, in the last years of his life) whether souls come to be in the body from the one soul of Adam or are individually created. It is, nonetheless, quite possible that he once thought that he knew the answer to the question about the soul, namely that souls existed before their embodiment and fell through sin into bodies or at least into these mortal bodies.[15] As we shall see from his account of memory, Augustine favored in some of his early writings the Platonic doctrine that learning is remembering, together with its implication of the soul's pre-existence. Even as late as the *Confessiones*, there is language which implies the fall of the soul.[16] Toward the beginning of the Pelagian controversy, Augustine realized that Paul's statement in Romans 9.11 that Jacob and Esau had not sinned before they were born ruled out the view that individual souls sinned before they were embodied. Augustine also learned of and rejected the Origenist view that the sensible world was created as a place of punishment for sinful souls and argued that God made all things good by his goodness (*C. Prisc. et Orig.* 8.9). In 415, while writing to Jerome, Augustine claimed to know that the soul is created and immortal, but admitted his ignorance about its origin and begged for help from Bethlehem (*Ep.* 166.3.6). In 419 in replying to the accusations of the young convert, Vincent Victor, Augustine wrote the four books of *De natura et origine animae*, in which he defended his agnosticism about the creationist position which his young opponent – like many Pelagians – considered to be Catholic doctrine.

The problem of the origin of human souls other than Adam's is discussed at length in *De Genesi ad litteram libri duodecim*.[17] The question is first raised in reference to the soul of Eve (*De Gen. ad litt.* 10.1.1). Here only three hypotheses regarding the origin of souls subsequent to Adam are present: One, that all souls were created in the soul of Adam on the first day; two, that all subsequent souls come from the soul of Adam by propagation (traducianism); and three, that new individual souls are created in the course of time (ibid. 10.3.4). The first two theories fit best with Genesis 2.2, which teaches that creation was completed on the sixth day, and with Sirach 18.1 which affirms that everything was created simultaneously. While traducianism seems most easily to explain the common inherited guilt of original sin and the need for infant baptism, it seems to endanger the incorporeality of the soul insofar as it thinks of souls as propagated in a bodily fashion, as Tertullian had done. While creationism is thoroughly compatible with the incorporeality of the soul made to the image of God, it makes it more difficult to understand how a soul could be created by God with the guilt of Adam's sin. Hence, the first hypothesis seems least problematic as representing Augustine's view at this point.

The destiny of the soul

Augustine firmly rejected the doctrine of the transmigration or reincarnation of souls because such a view implied that the happiness of the blessed could never be assured if the soul were either ignorant of the truth about its future unhappiness or wretched in fear of it (*De civ. Dei* 12.14, 12.21). In *Soliloquia* and *De immortalitate animae* Augustine tried to prove the immortality of the human soul. Soon, however, Augustine's concern shifted from the immortality of the soul to the resurrection of the body.[18] The latter doctrine, one so at odds with his early Platonism, is not even mentioned until *De quantitate animae* 33.76. Later he commented that, while many pagan philosophers have argued extensively in favor of the immortality of the soul, they rejected the resurrection of the flesh, contradicting that teaching without hesitation, "and their contradiction was such that they said that it was not possible that this earthly flesh could ascend to heaven" (*Enarr. in Ps.* 2.88.5). Apart from his early dialogues Augustine hardly mentions the immortality of the soul except within the context of the resurrection of the body. After death souls are in a state of rest, or possibly of purification, until the resurrection, when the good will rise to beatitude and the evil to everlasting punishment.[19]

NOTES

1 For general treatments of Augustine's doctrine of the soul, the following studies remain valuable: Gilson 1960; O'Daly 1986, 1987.

2 See Gilson 1960, 44–55; Courcelle 1968; and Masai 1961, 1–40.

3 See *De Gen. ad litt.* 7.28.43, where Augustine sums up what he knows with certitude about the soul.

4 See *Conf.* 7.1.1, where Augustine recounts how he saw in an insight which is the prime analogate of divine illumination that the corruptible is inferior to the incorruptible, the violable to the inviolable, the mutable to the immutable.

5 Tertullian, the principal theologian of Africa prior to Augustine, held that both God and the soul were bodies; see *Adversus Praxeam* 7 and *De anima* 7.

6 Masai (1961, 16–17), reverses the conclusion of Verbeke 1945, and argues that the concept of spiritual or incorporeal being is due to Platonism, while the term "spirit" is due to the scriptures.

7 See Courcelle 1968, 93–174, for the existence of a group of Christian Neoplatonists in Milan. Courcelle's study undercut the presuppositions of Alfaric (1918), and others that in 386 Augustine was converted to Neoplatonism rather than to Christianity.

8 See Teske 1983b.

9 Augustine may refer to Plotinus, *Ennead* 4.1, or perhaps *Ennead* 4.3, which scholars are more confident he read.

10 See Bourke 1954.

11 In *Retract.* 1.5.3 Augustine admits that he said this with utter rashness, but this admission came roughly a half-century later.

12 See Flasch 1993; Teske 1983a, 1996.

13 O'Daly (1986, 320) holds that the fourth hypothesis of *De lib. arb.* 3.20.58 is morally neutral. Though Augustine does use morally neutral language ("they come of their own accord to inhabit bodies"), the fact that he says that "whatever ignorance and difficulty followed upon their own will, the creator is in no way to be blamed for this" indicates that their coming into bodies was blameworthy, and in *De lib. arb.* 3.21.59 Augustine uses the verb "labantur," which more clearly indicates a fall.

14 See Gilson 1960, 71–72.

15 See O'Connell 1968, 150.

16 See *Conf.* 12.10.10, 13.8.1.

17 See the note on the origin of individual souls in relation to the doctrine of original sin in Agaësse and Solignac 1972, 530–541. Also see O'Connell 1987, 201–245; Mendelson 1998.

18 See Mourant 1969, which charts Augustine's move from a Platonic to a fully Christian view.

19 On the interim state between death and resurrection, see *Ep.* 7.55.13: "The souls of all the saints, of course, are at rest before the resurrection of the body." Augustine has some vague references to a purification of souls by fire which may anticipate the later doctrine of purgatory.

10

ELEONORE STUMP

Augustine on free will

Introduction

There is an enormous scholarly literature on Augustine's account of free will, and it is remarkable for the range of views it contains. Historians of philosophy read Augustine on free will so variously that it is sometimes difficult to believe they are reading the same texts. John Rist says:

> There is still no consensus of opinion on Augustine's view of each man's responsibility for his moral behaviour . . . There are those who attribute to Augustine the full-blown Calvinist position that each man has no say in his ultimate destiny . . . Other interpreters reject this view in varying degrees. They will not hold that for Augustine man's will is enslaved, or they would dispute about the sense in which it is enslaved and the sense in which it is free.[1]

Rist is surely right here.

One might suppose that this divergence of views is less a difference of historical opinion about Augustine's account of the will and more a difference of philosophical opinion about the nature of free will. Some scholars, one might think, are bringing to bear on Augustine's texts a libertarian view of free will, and some a compatibilist view; and that is why some scholars think Augustine takes human beings to be free and others disagree. But this sensible explanation of diversity of scholarly interpretation of Augustine is mistaken. Even scholars who are careful to make explicit what they mean by "free will" still don't agree about the nature of Augustine's theory of free will.[2]

In my view, the confusing difference of interpretation in the literature arises at least in part because presenting Augustine's theory of free will adequately requires more philosophical complexity and nuance than scholars have generally brought to bear on his texts.

For this reason, I think it is important to look carefully, even if only briefly, at certain issues involving free will before turning to Augustine's texts themselves.

Compatibilism and libertarianism

Scholars examining Augustine's work often take their view of the possible philosophical positions as regards freedom of the will from contemporary philosophy, which typically recognizes only two major positions available to those who think human beings have free will and are at least sometimes responsible for their actions. The first is compatibilism, which supposes that the world can be causally determined and yet also contain free acts and acts for which an agent is morally responsible. The second is libertarianism. Libertarianism is usually taken to include at least these two claims:

(L1) an agent acts with free will, or is morally responsible for an act,[3] only if the act is not causally determined by anything outside the agent;

and

(L2) an agent acts with free will, or is morally responsible for an act, only if he could have done otherwise.

Historical scholars familiar with contemporary philosophical discussions of free will thus tend to ask whether Augustine is a compatibilist or a libertarian.

In fact, however, these two positions don't exhaust the possibilities. That is because it is possible that an agent's free or morally responsible act A be indeterministic and yet that the agent have no alternative to doing A. (L1) doesn't entail (L2), because there are more ways to restrict an agent's alternatives for action than by something's causally determining the agent to do a particular action.[4]

So, in order to reject compatibilism and yet maintain that human beings have free will and are at least sometimes morally responsible for what they do, it isn't necessary to maintain both (L1) and (L2). A defender of human free will can reject both compatibilism and (L2). It isn't clear what to call such a position. It seems to me to be a species of libertarianism, although some philosophers may want to save the name "libertarianism" for the position which includes both (L1) and (L2). Because some short designation is helpful, I will call the position which accepts both (L1) and (L2) "common libertarianism," and I will call the other position, which rejects (L2) and compatibilism, "modified libertarianism." For present purposes, the salient point is just that there are three, and not only two, major positions available for defenders of human freedom and moral responsibility.

It is important to see this point, because it means that not everyone who denies that the ability to do otherwise is necessary for free will is thereby shown to be a compatibilist. It is possible to maintain that there can be no free act, no act for which an agent is morally responsible, in a world which is completely causally determined, without also holding that any agent who does a free or morally responsible act could have done otherwise than he did. Someone who rejects compatibilism can maintain that it is possible for an agent to act with free will, indeterministically, when he could not have done otherwise. In order to know whether Augustine is a compatibilist, then, it is not enough to consider whether he rejects (L2). We need also to know whether he accepts or rejects (L1).

Finally, I have characterized the two species of libertarianism by some of their necessary conditions, but these are not also sufficient conditions. For my purposes here, it is not essential to characterize either species of libertarianism completely, but it will be helpful to specify one more condition for modified libertarianism. Modified libertarianism is at least similar to what is sometimes called "liberty of spontaneity," the liberty an agent has when she acts spontaneously or on her own. For an agent to act on her own, however, she herself needs to be in control of her action; her act has to be produced only by her own intellect and will. So we can add this necessary condition for modified libertarianism:

(L3) an agent acts with free will, or is morally responsible for an act, only if her own intellect and will[5] are the sole ultimate source or first cause[6] of her act.[7]

Hierarchical accounts of the will and freedom

Harry Frankfurt has been influential in focusing contemporary philosophical attention on the distinction between what he calls "second-order volitions" or "second-order desires" and "first-order volitions" or "first-order desires."[8] A volition is an effective desire, that is, a desire which is translated into action if nothing external to the will impedes it.[9] A first-order volition is the will's directing some faculty or bodily power to do something. A second-order volition, by contrast, is a will to will something. So, for example, a person determined to become a vegetarian may form a volition to will not to eat meat.[10]

Although the terminology here is new, the idea is old. It is a commonplace of medieval philosophy that the higher faculties of human beings are characterized by reflexivity. The intellect can understand itself; the memory can remember itself and its acts; and the will can command itself, as well as other parts of the willer. When the will commands itself, its act is second-order. Augustine is keenly aware of the fact that the will can command itself,[11] and he puzzles over the fact that the command is not always successful, that (to use the contemporary idiom) some second-order motions of the will remain at the level of desires rather than volitions.[12]

The fact that the will can command itself and resist its own commands means that the will can be divided against itself in various ways. The will can, of course, have conflicts on the first-order level, but there can also be conflicts between the second-order and the first-order level. For example, one can have a first-order volition to eat veal now which is in conflict with one's second-order desire for a will that doesn't will to eat veal. People who violate the rules they have set for themselves or the reforms of their habits which they have resolved to undertake are commonly in such a condition.

Freedom and divisions in the will

The possibility of division in the will raises various issues as regards freedom of the will. For our purposes here, the most important is this. In cases where there is a conflict between first-order and second-order desires or volitions, does it matter to determinations of the willer's freedom how the conflict is resolved? Suppose, for example, that Smith wants very badly to reform and quit smoking; he wants to have a will that wills not to smoke. But this second-order desire on his part is in conflict with a very powerful first-order desire to smoke, and the conflict is often won by that first-order desire. So Smith wants to quit smoking, but he finds to his distress that he isn't giving up smoking altogether; on occasion, he still smokes. Now suppose that there is some science-fiction device that operates on the will and that can be employed to make the will will not to smoke. For the sake of simplicity, suppose too that the device is such that Smith can put it on or take it off any time he wants to do so. The device operates on the will with causal efficacy but only as long as it is, as it were, plugged in to the willer; and at any given time it is up to the willer whether or not the device is plugged in. Let it also be the case for purposes of the example that the world is not causally determined and that Smith's acts of will are indeterministic in ordinary circumstances. Now if Smith avails himself of that device and the device acts on him to bring it about that he wills not to smoke, does Smith act freely when he wills not to smoke?

Contrary to first appearances, the answer to this question is "yes" for either species of libertarianism.

Consider, to begin with, the condition in (L2). The device operates only because Smith has willed to use it. If Smith had wanted not to use it, the device would not have operated; and if Smith ceases to want to use it, he can unplug it from himself. Whether or not the device operates is thus solely up to Smith. So although Smith cannot do otherwise than will not to smoke when the device operates, it is also true that Smith could have done otherwise than will not to smoke. He could have willed not to employ the device, and then he could have willed to smoke, just as he did before he employed the device. So Smith does have alternative possibilities, to will to smoke or to will not to smoke, and it is up to Smith which of the possibilities is actualized.

Similarly, the condition in (L3) is not violated. It is true that Smith's will is caused to be in a certain state by the device when it operates. But the device is caused to operate by certain acts of Smith's, and those acts have as their ultimate cause Smith's own intellect and will. So even though the device causes certain states in Smith's will, the *ultimate* cause of what Smith wills remains Smith's own intellect and will.

As I have formulated (L1), that condition is violated, however; and since (L1) is shared by both common and modified libertarianism, it seems as if Smith's act of will not to smoke should still count as unfree for libertarians of both sorts. But this is a counter-intuitive conclusion.

To see why, consider the cartoon character Popeye.[13] Popeye is a lightweight without much bodily power; but if he eats spinach, he becomes possessed of superhuman strength. Suppose that Popeye's girlfriend Olive Oyl is chained to the tracks in the path of an oncoming train and that Popeye is unable to rescue her because he lacks the muscle power needed to break the chains. Popeye's inability to break the chains is causally determined by the state of his muscles; not breaking the chains is thus the only alternative open to Popeye in his light-weight state. Nonetheless, we think that Popeye's breaking the chains is in Popeye's control if Popeye has access to spinach. That is because it is up to Popeye whether or not he eats the spinach, and he *can* break the chains if he eats the spinach. Consequently, even when he is causally determined by the condition of his muscles not to break the chains, he is still free to break the chains because the condition of his muscles is in his control;[14] and for this reason, he is morally responsible if he does not break the chains, provided that he has access to spinach.[15]

The case of Smith the smoker is analogous. For Smith, the device operates on the will and not on the muscles; and the inability in question for Smith – the inability to will to smoke – is one that Smith has *with* the use of the device. But the conclusion remains the same, namely that an agent who in one condition is causally determined to do what he does nonetheless is responsible for his act and has the ability to do otherwise because of his control over a device which alters his condition.[16] And so it seems that if the case of Smith the smoker violates the condition in (L1), the condition ought to be reformulated, rather than letting the condition alter our intuitions about the case.

We can reformulate (L1) this way:

(L1') an agent acts with free will, or is morally responsible for an act, only if the act is not *ultimately* causally determined by anything outside the agent.

If we recast (L1) as (L1'), then nothing about the case involving Smith requires the violation of any condition for either species of libertarianism. Although when it operates, the device determines Smith's will to be in a certain state, the ultimate cause of the state of his will is not the device but only his own intellect and will, so that his act isn't ultimately causally determined by anything outside himself. Furthermore, even though the device determines his act of will, Smith could have willed otherwise than he did and he is responsible for his causally determined act of will, because it is up to Smith whether or not the device determines his will.

It is also worth noting that if the original point of (L1) was the rejection of compatibilism, the compatibility of causal determinism and free will or moral responsibility is as effectively rejected by (L1') as by (L1). As far as the dispute with compatibilism goes, then, libertarianism has no reason to insist on (L1) instead of (L1').

Further complications

Now suppose that we add to the case of Smith the smoker the stipulation that, unless he employs the device, Smith is unable to form the first-order volition not to smoke. That is, suppose that Smith has a second-order desire for a will that wills not to smoke, but that *without the device* Smith's craving for cigarettes is irresistible, so that in the conflict between his second-order desire and the first-order desire for smoking, the first-order desire inevitably wins, and he forms a volition to smoke. When he forms a first-order volition to smoke, then, that volition is compelled or determined by the irresistible craving to smoke. In this condition, does Smith have libertarian freedom when he wills to smoke?

Here, as before, the answer is "yes." Although Smith's will is determined by his craving, he does have the device available to him, and he can use it if he wills to do so.[17] He can act on his second-order desire for a will that wills not to smoke by availing himself of the device, which causes him to will not to smoke. In this sense, then, it is open to Smith not to smoke even if he has an otherwise irresistible craving to smoke. Consequently, although Smith's craving to smoke causes him to will to smoke, Smith can will otherwise than he does, and so he satisfies the condition in (L2). Because of the device, he can will to smoke or will not to smoke, and which will he forms is up to him. Whether he wills to smoke or wills not to smoke, Smith also meets the condition in (L1'). As I have presented the case, if Smith wills to smoke, it is because he has willed not to employ the device and to let his craving have its way; if he wills not to smoke, it is because he has willed to employ the device. Either way, the state of his will is ultimately determined by his own intellect and will, and consequently it isn't *ultimately* determined by anything outside Smith. So Smith meets the conditions for common and modified libertarianism whether he wills to smoke or wills to refrain.

It is important to see that this is the case even though Smith's first-order will is causally determined either way, either by the craving or by the device. Since the craving is under his control by virtue of the fact that the device is under his control, his will can be caused by the device or by the craving, and it will none-theless be true both that Smith can do otherwise than he does and that his own intellect and will are the ultimate causes of what he does.

Would it make any difference if we substituted a clever neuroscientist instead of a device in this case? That is, suppose that Smith is in control of his craving and his first-order volitions because there is a neuroscientist who, for one reason or another, can and will make Smith's first-order volitions what Smith wants them to be just when Smith wants him to do so. Would the results of the preced-ing discussion be any different with this substitution?[18] I don't see any good reason for thinking so, as long as it remains true that it is ultimately up to Smith what the state of his will is.[19]

The results in this and the preceding sections make a significant difference to some of the main scholarly controversies over Augustine's account of free will, as I will show in what follows. In the end, however, one problem remains which these results alone are insufficient to solve. I will address that problem at the end of this essay and suggest one way to deal with it.

De libero arbitrio

It is a common scholarly opinion that Augustine's views on the nature of free will, and particularly on the relation of free will and grace, developed over the course of his writings, especially in consequence of his controversy with the Pelagians. Augustine's early views on the will's freedom are laid out in his trea-tise *De libero arbitrio*, and some scholars go so far as to suppose that Augustine later repudiated his views in that treatise.[20]

It is certainly true that over the course of time Augustine developed his views on the relation of free will and grace, as he himself makes clear in some of his late writings. In *De dono perseverantiae,* for example, Augustine complains that he has as much right as anyone to grow and develop in his views and that he should not now be held to defending views he presented so much earlier in *De libero arbitrio*.[21] But here the issue is not the nature of free will itself; the issue is the state and condition of infants. In *De praedestinatione sanctorum*, he confesses to an error about the will and grace in an earlier treatise,[22] but what concerns him in this case is his exposition of a passage in Romans, and the error in question has to do with whether faith is a gift of God. As far as his account of free will in *De libero arbitrio* is concerned, what Augustine himself says in the *Retractationes* is just that his views of grace were undeveloped, not that his views of free will were wrong. On the contrary, in the *Retractationes* he asserts vigorously that the Pelagians are mistaken to think he ever held a view of free will like theirs, that is, a view of free will which makes the freedom of the will independent of divine grace.[23] On his own account, then, Augustine does not repudiate his *basic* view of the freedom of the will in *De libero arbitrio* even during the Pelagian controversy. It is therefore worthwhile to look carefully at his theory of free will in that early treatise.

As Augustine reminds his readers in the *Retractationes*,[24] he claims in *De libero arbitrio* that anything good in a human person, including any goodness in the will, is a gift of God.[25] On his view in the *De libero arbitrio*, then, human beings are unable to form a good volition unless God produces it in them or co-operates in producing it.[26] Nonetheless, when they will to sin, according to Augustine they are culpable. It apparently follows that a person can be morally responsible for a sinful act of will even when it was not possible for her not to will to sin. It seems, then, that for Augustine in *De libero arbitrio* it is not requisite for moral responsibility that an agent have the ability to do otherwise.[27] I have put this conclusion in a hedged way, because some reasons will emerge for reconsidering it; but even with that reconsideration, this much remains true: for Augustine, a person who is unaided by grace cannot do otherwise than sin, and yet she is morally responsible for the sin she does.

On the other hand, in *De libero arbitrio* Augustine does apparently accept some version of the condition in (L1), so that he rejects compatibilism. For example, he insists that human beings would not be culpable if their will were constrained by any necessity or by their nature.[28] So Augustine rejects as unfree a causally determined will.

If (L1) entailed (L2), then it would be perplexing or worse to find Augustine rejecting (L2) and accepting (L1), but, as I explained above, (L1) doesn't entail (L2). It is possible for an agent to act indeterministically and yet not have alternative possibilities for action. There are more ways of limiting the alternatives for action to only one besides having something act on the will with causal necessity. Augustine's explanation of why a post-Fall human will cannot will the good without grace is not very developed, but all his attempts at explanation are in terms of what the will itself wants. So, for example, he says, "the mind becomes a slave of sinful desire only by its own will";[29] and elsewhere he says, "What remains is [the conclusion] that . . . nothing else makes the mind the ally of evil desire except its own will and free choice."[30] For a post-Fall human being, on Augustine's view, the alternatives for willing are limited not by causal necessity but by what the agent himself fervently wants.

Finally, Augustine's insistence that a will determined by nature or causal necessity is not a free will (in fact, is not a will at all, properly speaking), and certain other things he says about the nature of the will, strongly suggest that he accepts the condition in (L3). So, for example, he says, "There are two sources of sins, one from our own thought and one from the persuasion of someone else . . . and each is voluntary. For just as no one sins unwillingly by his own thought, so when he consents to someone persuading him to evil, he consents just by [his own] will."[31]

Elsewhere, when Augustine is trying to explain why post-Fall human beings do not will the good, his explanation is couched in terms of intellect and will as well. Post-Fall human beings are unable to do what is good, he says, either because they are ignorant of what the good is in a given case or because although they see the good and want to have a will that wills it, they find doing it too difficult.[32] Augustine's main explanation for the culpable evil that post-Fall human beings will is both their ignorance and their difficulty in governing their own wills (that is, in making first-order volitions conform to good second-order desires). Here, too, then, intellect and will are picked out as the ultimate causes of acts for which agents are morally responsible.

In addition, when Augustine explains his view of the way in which the will functions, he ties it closely to the mind. A person who wills has to will something, he says, and unless this something were suggested by the bodily senses or arose in some way in the mind, the will wouldn't will it.[33]

It looks, then, as if Augustine's position in *De libero arbitrio* is a modified libertarianism.

There is, however, a certain additional complexity to his position in this early treatise which is crucial to see, because it challenges this classification of his position.

In explaining the culpability of post-Fall human evil, Augustine takes a somewhat surprising stand. According to Augustine, neither ignorance of the good nor weakness of will is itself culpable. What post-Fall human beings are culpable for is not the corruption of their post-Fall nature but something very different:

> There is everywhere present someone who in many ways, by means of creatures who serve him as lord, calls the man who is turned away [from him], teaches the man who believes, consoles the man who hopes, exhorts the man who loves, helps the man who strives, [and] hears the man who prays. And so it is not attributed to you as a fault that you lack knowledge unwillingly, but that you fail to seek the knowledge you do not have. And it is not attributed to you as a fault that you fail to bind up the parts [of yourself] which are wounded, but that you disdain him who is willing to heal them. These are your own sins. For no man has taken away from him the knowledge that it is beneficial to seek what it is not beneficial to lack knowledge of or [the knowledge] that [his] weakness should be confessed with humility. And so a man, seeking and confessing, will be aided by [God], who neither toils nor errs when he gives aid.[34]

And elsewhere in the same treatise he says,

> The soul is charged with guilt, not because by nature it lacks knowledge or is incapable, but because it did not make an effort to know and because it did not work adequately at acquiring the capability of doing well.[35]

> [The soul] does not know what it should do because it has not yet received [this knowledge]; but it will receive this too if it uses well what it has received. What it

has received is [the ability] to seek carefully and devotedly if it is willing [to do so]. [The soul] has also not yet received [the ability] to carry out immediately what it knows that it should do . . . so from this very difficulty the soul is prompted to plead with him who helps it to perfection.[36]

Here Augustine is apparently thinking of God as always willing to give grace to any person who wants God to give it to him, either in the form of knowledge about what is to be done, or in the form of grace which strengthens the will in the good. For Augustine, therefore, it seems that God plays a role analogous to that of the device or the friendly neurosurgeon in the example involving Smith the smoker. I argued that Smith meets the conditions for both common and modified libertarianism given above by virtue of the fact that Smith's own (second-order) will is the ultimate cause of what Smith wills and that, even if Smith's will is causally determined, it remains true that Smith could have done otherwise than he does. Augustine's idea here looks very similar, except that God plays the role of the device or the neurosurgeon. A person who sins in ignorance is nonetheless culpable – not for the ignorance in which he sins but because the ignorance that results in his sin is his own fault. He didn't seek the knowledge he needed when he could have done so; if he had sought it, God would have given it to him. Similarly, a person who is unable to will the good on his own is nonetheless culpable for the evil he does, because he could have asked God to help his will; and if he had done so, God would have given him the help he needs to do the good.

So although for Augustine in *De libero arbitrio* it is true in one sense that a post-Fall human being is unable to will not to sin, in another sense it is false. A post-Fall human being is not able to bring his first-order volitions under the control of his good second-order desires, and in this sense he is unable to will not to sin. But his good second-order desire is enough to enable him to form the first-order volition to ask God to strengthen his will in good; and when he does, God gives him the strength of will he wants and needs. In this sense, even a post-Fall human being *is* able to will not to sin.

Since this is Augustine's position, it is not as clear as it first seemed that in *De libero arbitrio* Augustine rejects the condition in (L2). Consequently, it is possible to argue that his account of post-Fall free will in this treatise should be grouped with common, not modified, libertarianism. A further and much more important issue, which threatens the classification of Augustine's position as libertarian of any sort, depends on what Augustine has to say about good second-order desires, a matter which will be addressed below.

Augustine's theory of free will in his later works

Even in his later treatises, Augustine is insistent that post-Fall human beings have free will. Among other reasons for thinking so, he maintains that the exhortations of scripture would be pointless unless human beings have free will.[37] So, for example, he says,

> One must not think that free choice has been removed because [the Apostle] said, "It is God who works in you both to will and to do, of [his] good will." Because if this were so, he would not have said above, "Work out your own salvation in fear and trembling." For when it is commanded that they work, their free will is invoked.[38]

In his controversy with the Pelagians, he emphasizes the point he made even in *De libero arbitrio*, that post-Fall human beings are unable to will not to sin unless their will is aided by grace; but he argues that God gives grace to the intellect and will of a person who desires it. By his grace God gave the law, so that people might know what they should do, and that, knowing it, they might ask God for help in doing it.[39]

He also continues to maintain his earlier explanation of the post-Fall inability to will the good. It stems from ignorance and difficulty, but the remedy for ignorance and difficulty is readily available. In *De natura et gratia*, for example, he quotes *De libero arbitrio* and re-emphasizes the point he made there: ignorance and difficulty aren't themselves culpable; what is culpable is just the failure to seek God's help with them.[40]

Many of the places scholars point to in support of their claim that Augustine is a compatibilist are in fact places where what is at issue is the governance of first-order volitions by good second-order desires. So, for example, Gerard O'Daly maintains that the "concept of a will that is morally determined represents Augustine's mature thought on the subject";[41] and he cites *De gratia Christi et de peccato originali* 18.19–20.21 as a text in which Augustine maintains that the "causes of good and evil actions are twofold good and evil wills, determined in turn by grace or sin."[42] But in the immediately preceding text, when Augustine is explaining the difference between law and grace, he says that grace produces sweetness rather than fear, and that is why we pray to God "in your sweetness teach me your righteousness . . . so that I am not forced to be under the law as a slave out of fear of punishment but might have delight with a free love in the law."[43] Here the person praying has a second-order desire that God might strengthen his first-order will in goodness; the determination of the will by grace works together with the human second-order desire for that grace. That is why Augustine goes on to say that in such a case the will is *helped* by grace.[44]

Passages such as the one cited by O'Daly are thus not enough to show whether Augustine rejects even the condition in (L2), let alone whether he rejects the condition in (L1'). Augustine himself makes this point clearly in one of his rejoinders to the Pelagians. He cites a passage from Pelagius in which Pelagius accuses

Augustine of inconsistency. Certain words of Augustine's in *De libero arbitrio* commit him to accepting that human free will has the ability to do otherwise, Pelagius says, whereas now (Pelagius claims) Augustine is trying to argue against the Pelagians that human free will is unable not to will to sin. In response Augustine says:

> I acknowledge it, these are my words [in *De libero arbitrio*]; but [Pelagius] might also find it appropriate to acknowledge all that was said previously [in *De libero arbitrio*]. In fact, the subject [there] is the grace of God, which aids us as a medicine through the mediator, and not the impossibility of righteousness. Whatever, then, may be the cause [of the state of the will], [unrighteousness] can be resisted. Plainly it can. For this is why we ask for help, when we say, "Do not bring us into temptation," and we would not plead for help if we believed that there was no way to resist it. It is possible to ward off sin, but by the aid of him who cannot be deceived.[45]

Here Augustine agrees with Pelagius at least so far as to accept the claim that post-Fall human beings have the ability to will not to sin and so the ability to do otherwise – provided that we understand this ability in the right way, as analogous to the ability Smith the smoker has to will not to smoke when he has an irresistible craving to smoke and a device which will override that craving if Smith wills to employ it.

Whether Augustine would go so far as to suppose that the ability to do otherwise is essential to free will is not made clear by this passage. There are certainly passages in various treatises which imply that he would not. So, for example, in *De natura et gratia* he says that if we accepted this condition on free will, which he takes to be absurd, we would have to suppose that God is good of necessity since it is not open to him to will to sin.[46] And in *Contra Julianum opus imperfectum*, he says to his opponent, "if, as you say, only the possibility of willed good and willed evil is freedom, then God does not have freedom, since there is no possibility of sinning in him."[47]

Whether Augustine's view of free will in *De libero arbitrio* constitutes common or modified libertarianism is open to question; but these passages indicate that at least in his later treatises he rejects the condition in (L2). Furthermore, since he is willing to allow a free will to be determined by God at the first-order level in response to a second-order desire for God's doing so, he clearly accepts the condition in (L1) only in the form it takes in (L1'), if he continues to accept it at all in his treatises on the Pelagian controversy. Finally, he thinks that a person's intellect and will must be the source of what she does, as the remarks about the remedy for post-Fall evil make clear. So if Augustine in his later treatises does in fact accept (L1'), his view of free will in his later period constitutes modified libertarianism.

Grace and faith

There is a real question whether Augustine accepts (L1') in his anti-Pelagian treatises; and if he doesn't, then since (L3) entails (L1'), he must reject (L3) also. In
that case, his account of free will is not libertarianism of any sort. The question
arises because of what Augustine says about the second-order volition which is
a crucial component of justifying faith. He describes this second-order volition
variously as an acceptance of grace, a desire for a righteous will, a desire that
God make the will good, a will to believe, or even just as faith.[48] For the sake of
brevity, I will refer to it as the will of faith, where "will" is to be understood as a
second-order act of will or a second-order volition.

The particular nature of this act of will is not nearly as important for my purposes here as its origin. Where does this second-order volition come from? Is it
also a gift of God's and caused only by divine grace? If it is, then the argument
that Augustine's account of free will is libertarian appears to collapse like a
house of cards. One can argue that the smoker Smith has libertarian free will
even when his first-order will is causally determined either by an irresistible
craving or by some device, as long as we can tell a story that makes it entirely up
to Smith which of these determines his will. We can even attribute to Smith the
ability to do otherwise when his first-order volition is causally determined – but
only if control of the causal determination operating on his will is ultimately up
to Smith. We would evaluate the case very differently if the story were that a
paternalistic neurosurgeon took it on himself, without consultation with Smith,
to cause Smith to have the second-order desire to quit smoking, so that the neurosurgeon and not Smith is responsible for Smith's decision to employ the device.
In that case, control over Smith's will with regard to smoking would be vested in
the neurosurgeon and not in Smith, and Smith's volitions to smoke or not to
smoke wouldn't meet the conditions for being free and responsible on either
modified or common libertarianism.

For theological as well as philosophical reasons, it certainly seems as if
Augustine ought to deny that the will of faith is caused only by divine grace. If
God causes this act of will, too, then a person's second-order volition for a
good will is in God's control, not in the control of the willer. Furthermore, if
God then responds to the second-order volition he has caused in a person and
strengthens her first-order will in the good, the responsibility for this good also
lies with God and not with her. And if God thus determines her will at the
second-order as well as the first-order level, it is hard to see why her will should
be thought of as free in any sense.[49] It is also difficult to ward off the conclusion that in this case God is responsible when a human will doesn't will the
good since even the volition for a good will is in his control. Finally, on this position, it is hard to see why a good God wouldn't cause the will of faith in

everyone, so that everyone is saved. As Augustine himself says regarding the second-order will of faith, "this is the question: where does [the will of faith] come from? . . . If it comes to us as a gift of God's, then why doesn't it come to everyone, since God wills all men to be saved and to come to the knowledge of the truth?"[50]

So there seems to be every reason for Augustine to reject the claim that the will of faith is a gift of God and caused by grace. There can be no doubt, however, that Augustine did in fact accept it. As he puts it in one place, "without grace men can do no good, in thought, will and love, or action."[51]

Nonetheless, Augustine also wants to maintain that human beings have free will and are solely responsible for their sins and that God wills all human beings to be saved, even the sinful who are in fact not saved. His attitude is summed up well in *De spiritu et littera* where he argues at length that the will of faith is caused by grace. "Are we then doing away with free choice through grace?" he asks; and he answers with vehemence, "God forbid!" ("absit").[52]

There are texts where Augustine is plainly trying to make human beings at least a partial source of the will of faith. So, for example, in a famous passage in his sermons, cited later by Aquinas,[53] Augustine says, "He who made you without you does not justify you without you. And so he made you when you were unknowing; he justifies you when you are willing."[54] As his views on grace develop, however, Augustine becomes increasingly insistent that the will of faith is a gift of God in the sense that God alone is the cause of it. So, for example, in *De gratia et libero arbitrio* he says, "When he begins, God operates [in us] that we might will, and he co-operates with those who are willing when he perfects [us] . . . And so he operates without us that we might will; but when we will, and will in such a way that we act, he co-operates with us."[55]

Augustine wants this theological position to be – somehow – compatible with the theory of free will he presented in his *De libero arbitrio*. In the *Retractationes*, when he is willing enough to retract earlier views of his and when his view of grace and faith has matured, he stands by his theory of free will in the early treatise. Rather than retracting his earlier theory of free will when he emphasizes the view that the will of faith comes from God, he struggles instead to find some way of reconciling the two. The main question for any evaluation of Augustine's account of free will is, then, whether he can have both these positions. Is there after all some way in which even the will of faith can be caused by grace and yet ultimate control of the state of a human being's will can be vested in that human being, rather than in God?

One attempt Augustine makes in some treatises to show that this is possible is to suggest that God offers this grace to everyone, but that it is open to human beings whether to reject it or accept it. So, for example, he says presciently:

> [An objector] might reply that we have to be careful lest someone suppose that the sin which is committed by free choice is to be attributed to God, if in [the passage] where it is said, "What do you have which you did not receive?" the will by which we believe is taken to be a gift of God's . . . But to consent to the calling of God or to dissent from it belongs to the will itself . . . And this not only does not invalidate the saying, "For what do you have which you have not received?," it in fact confirms it. For the soul cannot receive and have these gifts . . . except by consenting. And so whatever it has and whatever it receives comes from God, but to receive and to have comes from the one receiving and having.[56]

But Augustine doesn't develop this line, and in the end he appears to have dropped it, as he had to do. If there is nothing good in a human being which she has not received, and if the consent to receive God's grace is itself a good act of will, then that very consent also has to be a gift of God. And so sometimes Augustine takes the will of faith to be just the assent to grace itself. He says, "And so this grace, which is secretly given to human hearts by God's generosity, is rejected by no hard heart. On the contrary, it is given just in order first to take away the hardness of the heart."[57]

Augustine also seems to try and then give up on a line which makes God's grace a matter of God's making the Gospel available, presenting people with good preachers, or even introducing thoughts into their minds so that they may come to hold certain beliefs, which will in turn prompt them to certain desires and volitions.[58] In this case, although God does all the work of bringing a person to belief, the human willer responds by believing, and the belief stimulates certain acts of will. The problem here is that Augustine himself takes believing to be thinking with assent.[59] And so the same problem as before arises: the assent to a belief, which is itself an act of will, must also be a gift of God if it is good.

In other places, Augustine espouses the somewhat different idea that God arranges the circumstances of our lives in such a way that we freely will to believe.[60] Here the idea seems to be that God knows what we would freely will in any given circumstances, that there are circumstances in which everyone (or at any rate many people who in the actual world die faithless) would freely accept faith, and that God is able to bring about those circumstances. So, for example, Augustine says, "For if he had willed to teach even those for whom the word of the Cross is foolishness so that they might come to Christ, without doubt even they would have come."[61]

The problem with this idea is that it makes it up to God entirely whether or not a person forms the will of faith. Although in such a case a human being forms this volition without being caused by God to form it, it remains true that ultimate control over that person's will is vested not in the human person herself but in God. Although God doesn't act on the will with causal determination, God ultimately controls what that human being wills because God knows what free volitions will be produced in any given circumstances and he controls the circumstances. So here it is arguable both that the will of faith is a gift of God and that human beings have libertarian free will, but this position nonetheless constitutes a Pyrrhic victory for Augustine because it simply raises all the hard questions again in a different form. For example, if this view of God's relations to the will is right, then why doesn't God arrange the circumstances in such a way that everyone wills to believe? And why shouldn't we think God responsible for any human failure to will the good since God puts sinners in circumstances in which he knows they are not going to will the good?

In one treatise after another, Augustine grapples with the problem of making God the sole source of all goodness in the post-Fall human will without taking away from human beings control over their wills, so that God becomes responsible for the evil of the human will. In the end, Augustine makes it clear that he cannot solve this problem and that he knows it. For example, in one of his latest works, *De dono perseverantiae*, after he has argued hard that any good in a human will is God's gift, Augustine imagines an objector who wants to know why God saves those who have the will of faith and punishes the others, if it is only God's grace that causes anyone to have the will of faith. This is a question Augustine will not answer; "and if you ask me why [not]," he says, "I confess that it is because I haven't discovered what I should say."[62]

It does not follow either that the problem of grace and faith is insoluble or that Augustine thought it was. On the contrary, even in the face of his own inability to find a solution, Augustine refused to give up either his conviction that grace is the sole source for the will of faith or his insistence that human beings have real free will – and there is no indication that he felt he had to abandon anything in his earlier exposition of freedom of the will to maintain this position. In *De dono perseverantiae*, for example, Augustine discusses his *De libero arbitrio* and his reflections on it in his *Retractationes,* and he takes back nothing of his early view. Instead, he concludes the Pelagians are wrong to think that if the will of faith comes from God alone, God would be unjust to punish those who don't have it. As for the question *why* God wouldn't be unjust and *why* God gives this grace to some and not to others, Augustine takes refuge in the claim that God's judgments are inscrutable to us.[63] Clearly, this is less than an optimally satisfactory conclusion.

A friendly suggestion

Augustine's difficulties would be solved if he could find a way to hold that human beings are able, on their own, to reject grace, without God's being ultimately responsible for their doing so. Suppose that God offers to every person the grace that produces the will of faith, but that it is open to a person to refuse that grace.

Then the will of faith would be a gift of God, but it would be up to a human person whether he had such a will or not. Augustine is kept from such a solution by his conviction that he would then also have to say that human persons have it in their own power to accept grace. His attitude, and his problem, are brought out well in his consideration of Jacob and Esau. Jacob was saved because God's grace produced the will of faith in him. But, then, what about Esau? Augustine says:

> why was this mercy [of God's] withheld from Esau, so that he was not called in such a way that faith was inspired in him when called and, believing, he became merciful so that he might do good works? Was it perhaps because Esau was unwilling? But then Jacob believed because he willed it and God didn't give him faith, but Jacob prepared it for himself by willing and he had something [good] which he had not received.[64]

In my view, the problem is insoluble for Augustine because he assumes, in the way illustrated by his treatment of the example of Jacob and Esau, that the will has only two positions available to it as regards volitions: assenting or rejecting. On this view, a person who does not assent to grace rejects it, and a person who does not reject grace assents to it. Therefore, if God is solely responsible for the good will of faith which assents to grace, then God is also solely responsible for those acts of will which reject grace; those are just the wills in which God has not produced assent to grace.

At least some thinkers in the later Middle Ages, however, supposed that there are more than two positions for the will as regards volitions. So, for example, Aquinas holds that the will can assent to something or reject it, but it can also simply do nothing at all. It can just be turned off.[65] Sometimes the will is determined to want some thing by the nature of the will's object, Aquinas says, but the exercise of the will – whether the will is turned off or not – is always in the power of the will itself.[66] Furthermore, in principle, the will can move directly from any one of these positions to another. That is, it can move from rejecting to quiescence, from quiescence to assenting, from assenting to rejecting, and so on.

If this view of the will is right, then there are at least three possibilities for the will as regards grace, and not just two: the will can assent to grace; it can refuse grace; or it can be quiescent. When it is quiescent, it doesn't refuse grace, but it doesn't accept it either. It is thus possible to hold that a human person has it in her power to refuse grace or to fail to refuse grace without also holding that she has it in her power to form the good act of will which is the assent to grace.

This view of the will allows us to tell a theological story that attributes any good human will to God's action on the will and yet permits human beings to be the ultimate source of their own volitions. I am not now claiming that this theology story is true, that it is a story Augustine believed, or even that it is a story he ought to have believed. My point in presenting the theology story is only to show that Augustine's position as regards grace and free will is not hopeless; there is at least one way in which he can have all the things he wants to hold as regards grace and the will.

So suppose the following theology story to be the case. (1) God is constantly offering grace to every human being in such a way that if a person doesn't refuse that grace, she receives it and it produces in her the will of faith. (2) Normal adult human beings[67] in a post-Fall condition who are not converted or in the process of being converted refuse grace continually, even if they are not aware of doing so. (3) Ceasing to refuse grace is accompanied by an understanding that grace will follow and that grace would not follow if the refusal of grace were continued. (4) It is solely up to a human person whether or not she refuses grace.[68] A person who ceases to refuse grace in these circumstances is thus in some respects analogous to a person suffering an allergic reaction who actively refuses an injection of an antidote to the allergen, perhaps out of a hysterical fear of needles. Such a person might not be able to bring himself to will that the doctor give him the injection. If the doctor were asking him whether he would accept the injection, he might not be able to bring himself to say "yes," for example. But he might nonetheless be able to stop actively refusing the injection, knowing that if he ceases to refuse it, the doctor will press it on him. In this case, whether or not he receives the injection is in his control, even if it is also true that he cannot bring himself to answer "yes" to the doctor's request to give him the injection.

We can take claims (1)–(4) to be true, without having the dilemma Augustine thought he had in the case of Esau and Jacob, if we suppose that there are three, rather than two, positions available to the will as regards volitions. We can postulate that it was in Esau's power to reject grace without thereby being committed to supposing that Jacob had it in his power to accept grace. It can be the case that God alone causes in Jacob the acceptance of grace but that he causes it in Jacob because Jacob, unlike Esau, ceases to refuse grace. If the will can move directly from rejecting to quiescence, without first moving to acceptance, then Jacob has two alternatives for his will as regards grace, even if it is also true that it is not possible for his will on its own to accept grace.

On the theology story I have told, then, God gives grace to anyone who ceases actively refusing it, but these are not people who already assent to grace. They don't accept grace or reject it. Their wills were actively refusing grace, but then cease doing so, without moving all the way to accepting grace. Once their wills are quiescent, God acts on their wills in such a way as to move them to the acceptance of grace, which is the will of faith.

Consequently, on this theology story, the will of faith is a gift of God, but a human person's will is still ultimately in the control of that person, because it is up to her either to refuse grace or to fail to refuse grace, and God's giving of grace depends on what the will of a human person does.[69]

Conclusion

If there are three possibilities for the will as regards volition and if Augustine had been willing to accept this view of the will as well as the theology story I told above, or any theology story like it which makes God's giving of grace responsive to a human person's will, he could maintain his opposition to the Pelagians and still hold that human beings have free will in one or another variety of libertarian free will. The will's simply failing to refuse grace is not yet a good state of will. Since the will of faith is a will for righteousness, a will which doesn't refuse grace but hasn't yet accepted it is a will which doesn't so much as will to will the good; and it seems reasonable to deny that any will in this condition is in a good state.[70] On the other hand, if God gives grace only in response to a human willer's failing to refuse grace, then whether God gives grace or not will be up to the human willer alone.

Consequently, it is possible for Augustine to have his anti-Pelagian thesis and still maintain (L1') and (L3) even with regard to the second-order will of faith. It is also possible for him to hold (L2), provided the ability to do otherwise is understood in the latitudinarian way discussed above. Since a human willer can refuse grace or fail to refuse grace, a human willer has alternative possibilities available to her, even if God alone produces any good in her will. Furthermore, as I argued above, what Augustine says about the determination of a person's first-order will is compatible with the will's having libertarian freedom if the second-order will is within that person's control. On the theological story I have told here, then, a person can have libertarian freedom even if God determines her will at both the first- and the second-order level, provided only that it is up to her whether or not God acts on her will, so that her own intellect and will are the first and ultimate determiner of the final state of her will.

I think, then, that there is a stronger line of defense available to Augustine than he recognized. Whether he would have been happy to take it or not is not clear. If he is really wedded to the claims he sometimes makes, that God knows what a human being would freely will in any circumstances and that it is within God's power to produce or not produce those circumstances, then God is the ultimate controller (whether or not he is the ultimate cause) of the human will, and his giving of grace is not responsive to anything in the human will. In that case, I don't see how Augustine can suppose that his view of the will in the Pelagian controversy is already contained in his *De libero arbitrio*. On the contrary, unless Augustine is willing to accept that God's giving of grace is responsive to something in human beings, even if that something is not good or worthy of merit, I don't see how he can be saved from the imputation of theological determinism with all its infelicitous consequences.[71]

NOTES

1 Rist 1969a, 420. For representatives of different positions, see not only Rist's own interpretation in the paper cited, but also Clark 1958; Kirwan 1989. See also note 2.

2 For some idea of the diversity of views, see e.g. Craig 1984, 49; Chadwick 1983; O'Daly, 1989; Incandela 1994.

3 "Act" here, as well as in (L2) and (L3), is meant to refer to mental as well as bodily acts.

4 The quickest way to see that this is so is by considering what has come to be called "a Frankfurt-style counter-example" or "a Frankfurt story," after Harry Frankfurt, whose work (Frankfurt 1969) has called the importance of these cases to the attention of contemporary philosophers. David Widerker (1995a and b) has argued that in Frankfurt stories the victim must be causally determined, so that Frankfurt stories beg the question against libertarians. I argued against Widerker's position in Stump 1996a. There is also dispute in the literature over whether or not the victim in a Frankfurt story does after all have some sort of ability to do otherwise. John Martin Fischer has dubbed the ability to do otherwise at issue in this literature "a flicker of freedom." Fischer 1994, 134–140, discusses the controversy surrounding the flicker of freedom and supports the conclusion of Frankfurt stories. In Stump 1999 I argue that it is possible to construct a Frankfurt story in which there is no flicker of freedom.

5 Some philosophers are uncomfortable with the terms "intellect" and "will" because they suppose them to be part of some outmoded faculty psychology. But this unease is misplaced in my view. By talk of intellect and will here, I don't mean to suggest that there is a cognitive or conative faculty which is correlated with a single neurobiological structure or even a single neurobiological system. Whatever exactly a human intellect or a human will is, it is undoubtedly correlated with many subsystems which have to work together to yield the faculty or capacity in question. Vision seems to be like this. It is entirely appropriate to speak of the faculty of vision, but many different neural subsystems have to work together properly in order for a person to have the capacity to see. It may also be the case that some of the subsystems which constitute a faculty have multiple uses and function to constitute more than one faculty. This seems to be the case in vision, too.

6 By saying that the first cause of a person's act is her own intellect and will, I mean to leave open whether the cause is an act of intellect and will or just the faculties of intellect and will themselves, as seems to be the case in certain theories of agent causation.

7 In order to avoid having to employ the clumsy locution "ultimate source or first cause" throughout, in what follows I will speak just of first or ultimate causes in describing the condition in (L3), but that locution should be understood as a shorthand for the disjunctive phrase spelled out here. Furthermore, there is a complication which I am leaving to one side here. Insofar as God is the creator of every created thing and insofar as any created cause is always dependent on the operation of divine causality, no created thing can ever be the sole cause of anything or the ultimate first cause of anything. What is at issue for Augustine on free will and grace, however, is whether God is also the cause of the will in some stronger sense than this. And so for the sake of simplicity in this paper, I am simply bracketing the operations of God as first cause and creator. I am grateful to Claudia Murphy for calling to my attention the need to spell out this point.

8 Frankfurt 1971.

9 For the sake of simplicity, in this paper I will treat "an act of will" as generally equivalent to "a volition," "a will to O" as generally equivalent to "a volition to O," and forms of the verb "to will to O" as generally equivalent to forms of the verb "to have (or, to form) a volition to O."

10 Elsewhere I have discussed whether it is possible to have desires and volitions which are of a higher order (Stump 1988, 1996b).

11 James Wetzel (1992) has also called attention to the usefulness of Frankfurt's thought for interpretations of Augustine's account of free will.

12 Cf. e.g. *Confessions* 8.9. On this subject, see also Stark 1990.

13 I am grateful to three of the members of the St. Louis Autonomy Reading Group – Joel Anderson, Sigidur Krisstenson, and Thad Metz – for coming up with this example, which is philosophically useful even if it isn't drawn from the classic works of literature.

14 What would have to be the case in order for it to be true that the condition of Popeye's muscles was under his control is a question that is outside the scope of this paper. But perhaps this much can be said here. If Popeye can transform the condition of his muscles instantly by the consumption of a small amount of spinach, to which he has ready access, the condition of his muscles is under his control. On the other hand, if Popeye could transform the condition of his muscles by several years of training and weightlifting, for purposes of the rescue of Olive Oyl he does not have the condition of his muscles under his control.

15 Augustine uses an example involving vision which is similar to this one and designed to support the same conclusion; see *De nat. et gratia* 47.55.

16 For a point which is at least very similar, see Kane 1996, 60–78.

17 Someone might suppose that if the craving is genuinely irresistible, then Smith cannot will to use the device; but this supposition is mistaken. In the case of Smith the smoker, a second-order desire not to will to smoke is in conflict with a first-order desire to smoke. Now to say that the first-order desire is irresistible is just to say that the first-order desire always wins and is efficacious in producing action when it is pitted directly against the second-order desire. But it is not to say that the first-order desire wins no matter what, or that there is nothing at all that the agent can do to contravene it. The second-order desire may be efficacious in doing something *else* other than controlling the first-order desire; and that something else might be efficacious at least in preventing the first-order desire from being translated into action. A person who cannot control obsessive first-order desires, but who has a second-order desire for a different set of first-order desires, may avail herself of drugs or other help on the part of psychiatrists or counselors, and that help might be efficacious in bringing the obsessive desires under the control of the patient's second-order desire even though the patient's unaided second-order desire would not have been able to do so.

18 This is a question only about the conclusion of the discussion of the preceding case, namely, that Smith has libertarian freedom when he wills not to smoke. There are, of course, other, important differences between the case involving the device and the case involving the neurosurgeon. Perhaps the most important is that when it is the device, rather than the neurosurgeon, that acts on Smith's will, Smith's own intellect and will are the first cause in a straightforwardly causal chain that eventuates in Smith's will not to smoke. But when the neurosurgeon acts on Smith's will in response to Smith's desire that he do so, things are more complicated. Smith's own

intellect and will are the ultimate source of the chain of events resulting in Smith's will not to smoke. But the chain of events isn't straightforwardly causal. Smith's wanting the neurosurgeon to act on his will isn't itself a cause which determines the neurosurgeon to do so. Someone might worry that the neurosurgeon might exercise his own libertarian freedom and fail to respond to Smith's request for help, but we need not entertain this complication. We can build into the case that the neurosurgeon is constrained by something compatible with his acting freely to grant Smith the help he wants. As the Frankfurt stories show, it isn't hard to come up with such a constraint.

19 For a different evaluation of somewhat similar cases, see Kirwan 1989, 109–111. My reasons for disagreeing with Kirwan are implicit in the discussion of the case of Smith the smoker.

20 See e.g. Babcock 1988.

21 *De dono persev.* 12.30.

22 *De praed. sanct.* 3.7.

23 *Retract.* 1.9.

24 Ibid.

25 *De lib. arb.* 2.19.50.

26 Augustine makes this point explicitly and at length, ibid. 3.18.51.

27 In other treatises, it is clearer that Augustine rejects (L2), as I will explain below.

28 *De lib. arb.* 3.1.1. Elsewhere in the treatise, he argues that a free will's turning from a greater good to a lesser good is not done out of any necessity but of its own accord and voluntarily (ibid. 2.19.53). At 3.3.8, in response to an imaginary objector who thinks he can be caused to will something, Augustine argues that a caused will is no will at all. At 3.17.48–9, Augustine maintains that a sinful will wouldn't be the root of all evil if there were something else which was the cause of the will; he also argues there that no cause operates on the will to determine its states and that Evodius is therefore asking a confused question when he asks what the cause of an evil will is.

29 Ibid. 3.1.2.

30 Ibid. 1.11.21.

31 Ibid. 3.10.29. According to this passage, when someone does a morally culpable act, the ultimate cause of the act is the agent's own intellect and will, whether he has been persuaded by another or not. And even if he was persuaded by someone else, his own intellect and will remain the ultimate cause of his act. The attempts of A to persuade B to do something will have any force with B only if B accepts A's persuasions.

32 *De lib. arb.* 3.18.30–32.

33 Ibid. 3.25.75.

34 Ibid. 3.19.53.

35 Ibid. 3.22.64.

36 Ibid. 3.22.65.

37 *De gratia et libero arbitrio* 2.2.

38 Ibid. 9.21.

39 See e.g. *De nat. et gratia* 12.13. There are even places where Augustine applies this point to pre-Fall human beings: "Even if [Pelagius] were speaking about a whole and healthy human nature . . . what he says would not be correct, [namely], that not sinning depends only on us, as sinning depends on us. For even then there would be the help of God . . . which is prepared for those who are willing [to receive it]" (*De nat. et gratia* 48.56).

40 Ibid. 47.81.
41 O'Daly 1989, 88. For another example of the same sort of position, see Djuth 1990.
42 O'Daly 1989, 89.
43 *De gratia Christi et de peccato originali* 13.14.
44 Ibid. 14.15.
45 *De nat. et gratia* 67.80. See also *De gratia et libero arbitrio* 16.32, where he makes a similar point.
46 *De nat. et gratia* 46.54.
47 *Contra Julianum opus imperfectum* 6.11.
48 For some discussion of the connection among these and other ways of describing the will of faith, see *De spir. et litt.* 32.56.
49 Even compatibilists, who maintain that an agent can be morally responsible for a causally determined act, generally hold that an agent is not morally responsible for an act if he is caused to do that act by another person.
50 *De spir. et litt.* 32.57.
51 *De corrept. et gratia* 2.3.
52 *De spir. et litt.* 30.52.
53 See e.g. *Summa theologiae* IaIIae q.111 a.2 obj.2 and ad 2.
54 *Sermo* 169.11.13.
55 *De gratia et libero arbitrio* 17.33.
56 *De spir. et litt.* 34.60.
57 *De praed. sanct.* 8.13.
58 See e.g. *De spir. et litt.* 34.60; cf. also *De diversis quaestionibus ad Simplicianum* 1.2.7.
59 See e.g. *De spir. et litt.* 30.54 and *De praed. sanct.* 2.5.
60 See e.g. *De diversis quaestionibus ad Simplicianum* 1.2.13.
61 *De praed. sanct.* 8.14.
62 *De dono persev.* 8.18.
63 Ibid. 11.26–27; see also *De dono persev.* 8.16, where he takes the same line.
64 *De diversis quaestionibus ad Simplicianum* 1.2.10. Elsewhere Augustine takes a different line. For example, in *De correptione et gratia* he says, "If a person who is already regenerate and justified relapses by his will into an evil life, he is certainly not able to say, 'I have not received [the gift of perseverance],'" because in his free choice for evil he let go of the grace of God which he had received" (*De corrept. et gratia* 6.9; cf. 7.11).

Here Augustine is apparently willing to entertain the possibility that the will's perseverance in good is produced in the will by God alone but that the will's failure to persevere can be attributed to the willer. But he doesn't explain how these claims can be compatible, and he doesn't develop this line as a solution to the problem of grace and free will.

65 See e.g. *Summa theologiae* IaIIae q.9 a.1.
66 See e.g. ibid. IaIIae q.10 a.2.
67 Children and adult human beings in non-normal conditions pose special problems which complicate the case, and so I am simply leaving those cases to one side here.
68 By saying that it is solely up to her, I do not mean to rule out all the influences for good which Augustine sometimes also describes as grace, such as the influence of good preaching or good friends; I mean only that it is up to the human willer alone whether such good influences are persuasive with her, so that rejecting the influence of graces of this sort is possible for her.

69 I am presenting this position as one which allows Augustine to have both the apparently incompatible claims he wants, but I am not proposing this position as problem-free. For a more detailed discussion of the position, see Stump 1989.

70 It is true that a will which ceases to refuse grace is better than one that refuses grace, but comparatives don't presuppose positives; Smith can be taller than Jones without being tall.

71 I am grateful to William Alston, Joel Anderson, John Heil, Sigidur Krisstenson, Scott MacDonald, Colleen McCluskey, Al Mele, Thad Metz, Claudia Eisen Murphy, David Robb, Nicholas Wolterstorff, and audiences at Cornell University, Georgetown University, Davidson College, Wheaton College, and the University of Pennsylvania for helpful comments on an earlier draft.

II

ROLAND TESKE

Augustine's philosophy of memory

The topic of memory in Augustine's thought includes much of his philosophy of mind, for memory is not a distinct power or faculty of the soul, but the mind itself, from which memory, understanding, or will are distinguished only in terms of their different activities.[1] Memory for Augustine has not merely the rather straightforward role of retaining recollections of past experiences, but also the much more problematic tasks of holding in mind present realities and even of anticipating the future.[2] Augustine's account of memory shows a marked development from his early writings, in which he accepted a Platonic doctrine of reminiscence, up to the works of his maturity, in which he clearly rejects almost all, if not all, traces of such a teaching. In the *Confessions*, Augustine devotes the first half of Book 10 to a description of the contents of his memory as he searches for God, and in Book 11 memory plays a key role in the perception of time. In *De Trinitate*, Augustine finds in the memory, understanding, and will of the human soul a series of psychological analogies or images of the three persons in one God.

Platonic reminiscence

In his early writings there are a number of indications that Augustine held that the soul existed prior to its embodiment and brought with it into this life a knowledge of all the arts.[3] For example, he says of those trained in the liberal arts that "in the process of learning they bring to light knowledge which is undoubtedly buried in oblivion within them and in a sense disinter it" (*Sol.* 2.20.25). In another dialogue, Augustine tells his interlocutor, Evodius, that the two of them are "holding opinions so diametrically opposed that you think that soul has brought no art with it, while in my view it has brought all of them with it, and what is called learning is nothing other than remembering and recalling" (*De quant. anim.* 20.34). And in *De libero arbitrio*, Augustine says to Evodius

You say that we have never been wise, as if it were clearly true; you are only thinking of the time since we were born into this life. But since wisdom is in the soul,
whether the soul lived in another life before it was joined to the body and whether
at one time it lived in a state of wisdom is a great question, a great mystery to be
considered in its proper place. (De lib. arb. 1.12.24).

In writing in 389 to his friend Nebridius, who thought that memory required
images or phantasms, Augustine disagrees, but first takes up the question of
whether memory is only of things whose existence is past or also of things which
continue to exist in the present. Memory, he explains, clearly retains past things,
whether those which leave us (as Augustine's father has through death left him)
or those which we leave (as Augustine has left Carthage). Both of these require
images, and Augustine notes that it is enough for the present that he has shown
that memory can be of things which continue to exist, such as Carthage. He
adds, "There are some who falsely attack the most noble Socratic discovery
which claims that the things which we learn are not presented to us as something
new, but are recalled to mind by recollection." The critics of Platonic reminiscence claim that "memory is of past events, while the things we learn by intellectual knowledge, on the authority of Plato himself, remain always, cannot be
destroyed, and cannot therefore become past." Then comes the crucial sentence:
"They do not notice that that vision is past because we formerly saw these things
by the mind and that, because we have flowed down from them and began to see
other things in another way, we see them again by remembering, that is, through
memory." Hence, Augustine concludes that, if "eternity itself always remains
and does not require some figments of the imagination by which, as if by its vehi-
cles, it may enter the mind, and if it cannot come unless we remember it, there
can be the memory of some things without any use of images" (Ep. 7.1.2).
Hence, as early as Epistula 7, Augustine holds that the things which memory
remembers can be entirely in the past or still existing in the present; that the
memory of those things which always exist, such as eternity itself, requires no
imagery; and that, though such things which always exist are present, the intellectual vision of them is past – a vision from which we have flowed down so that
we have begun to see other things – that is, sensible things – in another way: that
is, through the senses.[4]

In his later writings Augustine clearly rejected the doctrine that we have recollection of the intellectual disciplines from a previous existence. He argued that
an illumination of the mind by God provides a better explanation of such
knowledge:

For if even untrained persons give true replies concerning certain disciplines when
they are properly questioned, it is more credible that there is present in them, to the
extent that they can receive it, the light of eternal reason where they see these

immutable truths, and not that they knew them once and have forgotten them, as Plato and people like him thought. (*Retract.* 1.4.4)

In *De Trinitate* Augustine explicitly rejects the sort of recollection Plato proposed in the *Meno* and argues that, if the slave boy's correct answers were the recollection of things he had learned in a previous life, then "surely all or almost all people would be unable to do this when they are questioned in that way. After all, not all persons were geometers in their previous life, since geometers are quite rare in the human race" (*De Trin.* 12.15.24). He claims that it is more believable that "the nature of the intellectual mind was created so that, subject to intelligible realities by a natural order as the creator arranged, it sees these things in a certain incorporeal light of a special kind, just as the eye of the flesh sees those things which lie before it in this corporeal light" (ibid.). Augustine also points out that Platonic reminiscence had at most claimed that we recall intelligible things, and he insists that no one recalls sensible things without having seen them in this present life. Accordingly, he rejects as illusory the Pythagorean claim to recall sensory experiences from a previous earthly life, along with its implication of the transmigration of souls. "For one should not believe those who report that Pythagoras of Samos recalled certain things of this sort which he had experienced when he had previously lived here in another body" (ibid.).

Though in his later writings Augustine rejected the Platonic view that learning is recollection, he does not necessarily abandon all thought of the preexistence of the soul. He speaks of a person who remembers his Lord and adds, "He surely does not recall his own happiness; that, of course, was and is no more, and it has been completely blotted out and, for this reason, cannot be recalled" (*De Trin.* 14.15.21). But if all memory of one's previous happiness has been forgotten so that it cannot be recalled, that happiness must have existed, or its memory could not have been blotted out.[5] In fact, Augustine adds that with regard to that happiness such a person believes the scriptures, "which tell of the happiness of paradise and reveal in their historical account that first good of man and his first evil" (ibid.). For, though none of us had as yet begun to live our own proper lives in which we could commit personal sin, we were all present in that one man, Adam, and we all sinned in him.[6]

Memory in the *Confessions*

Though Augustine clearly held the Platonic doctrine of reminiscence in his early writings and clearly abandoned it in his later writings, there is considerable disagreement among scholars about his position at the time of the *Confessions*. In the subtitle of his book on the *Confessions*, namely, "The Odyssey of Soul," Robert O'Connell suggested as the unifying theme of the work the soul's fall into these mortal bodies from a state of happiness; its wandering in this life away from its fatherland, but not without a memory of its former happiness; and its gradual return to God and its heavenly home.[7] Other scholars do not find in the *Confessions* such a view of the soul's fall along with its memory of a previous happiness.[8] In any case the topic of memory plays an extensive role in the *Confessions*, a work which Jean-Marie Le Blond has described as "a work of memory, of Augustinian memory" ("une œuvre de mémoire, de mémoire augustinienne"),[9] by which he means a memory that is not restricted to the past, but includes the present and anticipates the future. Le Blond sees the unifying theme of the work as lying in the threefold function: memory of the past (Books 1 through 9), intuition of the present (Book 10), and expectation of the future (Books 11–13),[10] each of which is in a sense a function of memory.

In *Confessions* 10, Augustine develops a long *exercitatio animi* – an exercise to train the mind – as he engages in a search for God which follows the typical Augustinian move from the exterior to the interior and from the inferior to the superior.[11] After failing to find his God in the external world, in the power of the soul by which it vivifies and governs the body, or in the power of the soul by which it gives sensation to the body, he turns to "the fields and spacious palaces of my memory" which contain "countless images of all sorts of things brought there from objects perceived by the senses" (*Conf.* 10.8.12).[12] Also contained in that place is whatever the mind thinks about, and among these objects of thought some are readily recalled, while others are buried more deeply. This level of memory keeps distinct from one another various images admitted through the different senses, and contains only the images of things, not the things themselves.

In memory Augustine also encounters himself and recalls himself, his past actions, and the images of everything which he has perceived and not completely forgotten and upon which he thinks as he plans his future actions (*Conf.* 10.8.15). Memory is "a vast and unlimited inner chamber," at which Augustine marvels, for he claims that he could not speak of the mountains, seas, rivers, ocean, and stars, "unless I saw within, in my memory, in such vast spaces as if I saw them outside, the mountains, waves, rivers, and stars which I have seen and that ocean which I believe to exist" (*Conf.* 20.8.15).

Memory also contains everything which was learned in the study of the liberal arts and has not been forgotten; at this level the things themselves, and not merely images of them, are put into "an interior place, yet not a place" (ibid. 10.9.16). When Augustine hears a set of questions from logic, such as: Does it exist? What is it? What properties does it have? he retains in memory the images of the sounds of the words, but also what they signify. He notes that he did not attain the things which the words signify by any bodily sense, and yet he finds them in his mind or memory, where he has stored away the things themselves and not merely images of the words. He suggests that such things were in his memory before he learned them, but "removed and shoved back, as if in more hidden caves, so that, unless they were unearthed by someone's admonition, I would perhaps have been unable to think of them" (ibid. 10.10.17). He explains that to learn things of this sort is simply to gather together by thinking "things which memory contained scattered about and without any order," and by attending to them, to place them near at hand in memory. Accordingly, he interprets the verb *cogito* ("I think") as simply the iterative form of *cogo* ("I gather") (ibid. 10.11.18). This level of memory also contains the principles and laws of mathematics, geometrical lines and figures, and the numbers by which we count – none of which are perceived by the bodily senses (ibid. 10.12.19).

Memory also contains the affections of the mind, such as joy, sorrow, desire, and fear not in the way in which the mind has them when it experiences them, but far differently, more in the way the power of memory retains memory itself. For we remember joy without being joyful, and we remember fear without being fearful. We remember bodily pain without feeling pain, and this is not surprising, since mind is one thing and the body another. When, however, we remember joy, why, Augustine wonders, do we not feel joy, since the mind is memory itself? He suggests that the memory of these affections is like the mind's stomach, where joy and sorrow can be stored away without being tasted and later brought back for rumination in further thought. Yet, with the affections we do not keep in memory merely the sounds of their names, nor do we have the affections themselves; rather, we have what he calls "notions" of them (ibid. 10.14.21–22).

We remember memory so that memory itself is present to itself, but we also remember forgetfulness, which is merely a privation of memory. As Augustine probes further into memory, the *exercitatio animi* becomes laborious, and yet he is not calculating such abstruse things as the distances of the stars or the weight of the earth. Rather, he says, "It is I who remember, I the mind . . . What is nearer to me than I myself?" (ibid. 10.16.25). The memory of forgetfulness presents a particular conundrum: If forgetfulness is retained in memory through its image, it must itself have been once present for us to acquire its image; yet, how could it inscribe its image on memory when by its presence forgetfulness wipes away whatever it finds there? Augustine is, nonetheless, certain "that I have remembered forgetfulness itself, whereby what we remember is destroyed" (ibid.). Hence, he marvels at the power of memory, which contains some things through their images – such as bodily things – other things through their very presence – such as the arts – and still other things through certain notions, such as the affections of the mind. Augustine attempts to move beyond his memory in his search for God, though he is faced with the paradox that, if he finds God apart from memory, he is unmindful of him. Hence, he asks, "How then shall I find you, if I do not remember you?" (ibid. 10.17.26).

Reflection on the parable of the lost coin in Luke 15.8 brings out the fact that, in order to find some physical object we have lost, we must retain an image of it by which we can recognize the thing found as the one we have lost. But when memory itself loses something, such as a name, we have to look for what we lost in memory itself, and we cannot recognize the name unless we have retained something of it in memory. What we have completely forgotten, we cannot even look for (ibid. 10.18.27).

The stage is at last set for the central question: "How then do I seek you, O Lord? For when I seek you, my God, I seek the happy life" (ibid. 10.20.29). Augustine asks whether he seeks the happy life through remembrance, as if he had forgotten it but still held onto the fact that he had forgotten it, or whether he desires to come to know something unknown, either something he never knew or something he has completely forgotten. All human beings desire the happy life – as Augustine read in Cicero's now lost work, the *Hortensius*, a work which led to his first conversion, a conversion to philosophy.[13] Where have human beings known the happy life so that they love it? In this life human beings are not now happy in fact, but only in hope or not at all. Yet all would not desire to be happy unless they had known happiness somehow. Augustine says

> Concerning this knowledge I am hard pressed as to whether it is in memory, for if
> it is there, then all of us were already happy at some time, either all of us as indi-
> viduals or in that man who first sinned, in whom we all died and from whom we
> are all born in misery. (*Conf.* 10.20.29)

He shelves the question of where all of us have been happy, and turns to whether the happy life is in our memory, and his answer is an emphatic "yes." "For we would not love it if we did not know it" (ibid.). But all do know it; for, if we could ask various peoples in their own language whether they want to be happy, they would undoubtedly answer that they do. This could not be so unless the reality itself signified by the word "happiness" were "contained in their memory" (ibid.).

How then is the happy life contained in memory? It is not there like Carthage, which Augustine saw with his eyes, for it is not a body. It is not in memory like numbers, for one who knows the numbers does not still seek to know them, whereas we are still seeking the happy life. It is not in memory like the arts of oratory, for even unskilled speakers recall the thing itself when they hear the word, and many desire to speak eloquently because they have heard other pol ished speakers. Augustine suggests that the happy life may be in memory in the way we remember joy, which we can remember when we are unhappy and which we have never experienced by a bodily sense (ibid. 10.21.30). Hence, he asks where and when he had experience of his happy life so that he remembers it, loves it, and longs for it. Not just Augustine alone, "but all of us want to be happy.

Unless we knew this with sure knowledge, we would not want it with so sure a will" (ibid. 10.21.31).

People may differ about the choice of a particular way to become happy, but all agree about desiring the happy life, which, Augustine says, is to rejoice over God, for God, and because of God (ibid. 10.22.32); and since God is the truth, "joy in the truth is the happy life" (ibid. 10.22.33). Hence, all human beings have known the happy life and have known it where they knew the truth, for they would not love it if there were not some knowledge of it in their memory. In tantalizing ambiguity Augustine exclaims, "See how far within my memory I have traveled in search of you, Lord, and beyond it I have not found you! Nor have I found anything about you except what I have kept in memory since I first learned of you" (ibid. 10.24.35). The ambiguity is tantalizing because it is not at all clear when Augustine "first learned" of his God, whether as a youngster from Monica's lips or at some later point in his life or when all of us were once happy, either individually or all together in Adam. I suggest that the latter alternative makes best sense of the long exercise on memory: We were all once happy either as individuals or in Adam.[14]

In what part of the memory, Augustine asks, has God made his abode? In one sense God is not in memory, since he is not an image, nor an affection of the mind, nor the mind itself, but the Lord of the mind who remains unchangeable above the mind. And yet, Augustine tells us, God has deigned to dwell in his memory. Again, in language which is ambiguous, he says:

> I have remembered you from the time I learned of you, and I find you there when I call you to mind. Where then did I find you so that I might learn to know you? You were not in my memory before I learned to know you. Where then have I found you, if not in yourself and above me? There is no place; both backward do we go and forward, and there is no place. (*Conf.* 10.25.36–10.26.37)

Memory and time

The role of memory in the *Confessions* is not limited to Book 10, for the long discussion of time in Book 11 also involves a role for memory. In commenting on the first verse of Genesis, Augustine contrasts the timeless eternity of God with the temporal being of creatures. In struggling with the question "What is time?" which seems to call for a definition of time, Augustine notes that past time no longer exists and future time does not yet exist, so that there is only the present moment of time – which has no extent. He comes to see that the three times, past, present, and future, exist only in the mind's present memory of the past, present intuition of the present, and present expectation of the future (*Conf.* 11.20.26). Augustine defines time as a distension of the mind, a distension which is produced by the mind's holding on to the past while attending to the present in anticipation of the future. Augustine's life, as he recites a psalm, "is distended into memory on account of what I have spoken, and into expectation on account of what I am about to say; yet my attention remains present, through which what was future is carried along into past" (*Conf.* 11.28.38). Augustine is claiming that the present attention of the mind must be stretched out or distended as a condition of our being able to recite a psalm or to perceive anything temporal.[15] In an earlier work Augustine had pointed out that we cannot hear even a single syllable "unless memory helps us so that, at the moment when not the beginning but the end of the syllable sounds, that motion remains in the mind which was produced when the beginning sounded" (*De musica* 6.5.10). Hence, Mourant claims that "for Saint Augustine memory is essentially duration and a spiritual power that both transcends and spiritualizes space and time."[16]

Memory and the Trinity

From the time of his baptism, Augustine was convinced that the image of God in which human beings were made according to Genesis 1.26 was to be found in the incorporeal soul, a position which allowed him to escape the Manichaean inference that the God of the Catholic Church must be bounded by the shape of a human being, if human beings are made in the image of God.[17] He also soon came to the conviction that the image of God was an image of the Trinity, not merely of the one God.[18] Hence, when in *De Trinitate* Augustine seeks the image of God, he is seeking an image in the human soul of the three Persons in the one God. In Book 10 Augustine singles out three aspects of the mind, namely memory, understanding, and will. "These three are not three lives, but one, nor are they three minds, but one mind. When we say that memory is life, mind, and substance, we speak of it in relation to itself, but when we call it memory, we speak of it in relation to something else" (*De Trin.* 10.11.18). Like the Persons of the Trinity who are one God, memory, understanding, and will are one mind, and whatever is said of each of them is said of the three together in the singular, just as the three Persons are not three gods, but one God. Moreover, memory, understanding, and will are three as related to one another, just as the Persons of the Trinity are distinguished by their mutual relations.[19]

After finding a trinity of "the outer man," which consists of the external object we see, the actual vision, and the mind's attention linking our vision to the object seen (*De Trin.* 11.2.2), Augustine points to a more interior trinity, though still a trinity of the outer man, which consists of a memory of the external object once seen, an internal vision of its likeness, and the will directing our internal vision to the memory of the object seen. "When these three are gathered (*coguntur*) into one, it is called thought (*cogitatio*) from this being gathered together (*coactu*)" (ibid. 11.3.6). Augustine notes that there can be no will to remember unless we hold in memory (at least partially) the thing we want to remember, for what we have completely forgotten we cannot even will to recall. Each act of recollection involves a trinity: "that which is hidden in memory even before it is thought of, that which results in thought when it is seen, and the will which forms a link between the two of these" (ibid. 11.7.12). As the will applies the senses to an external body, so the will applies memory to the senses and the mind's attention to memory, but the will also at times turns the senses away from a sensible object, turns memory away from the senses, or turns the mind's attention away from memory. The will turns the senses away from a sensible object by the movement of the body. The will turns memory away from the senses in cases where the will fixes our attention elsewhere so that we seem not to have heard words spoken to us. Finally, the will turns the attention of the mind away from what is in memory, for this "is nothing else than not to think of it" (ibid. 11.8.15). There are also false memories, such as Pythagoras' alleged recollections of events from a previous existence or our experiences in dreams when we seem to remember seeing or doing things (ibid. 13.5.24).

Memory allows us to make conjectures about the future from the past. In reciting a poem, we foresee by thought what follows, and yet "it is not foresight, but memory that instructs us so that we foresee it" (ibid. 15.7.13). So, too, we say that we sing a song from memory, not from foresight, and yet, until we finish the song, there is nothing of it we do not foresee.

Memory plays a role in relation to the Christian faith. The trinity of faith does not consist in commending to memory merely the sounds of the words of the Creed without understanding them; rather, a believer not only commends to memory the events which these words signify and recalls them, but also loves what these words proclaim, command, and promise. For one can hold in memory the events of Christ's life and think of them, while regarding them as false or trying to refute them. "But when we believe to be true what we hold in thought and love what we ought to love, we then live in accord with the trinity of the inner man" (ibid. 13.20.26).

In the present life of faith "we see through a glass in an enigma," as Paul said in 1 Cor. 13.12. Augustine explains that an enigma is an obscure allegory and that an allegory is simply a trope in which one thing is understood from another (De Trin. 15.9.15). The enigma or obscure image of the Trinity in the human mind includes the mental word which is brought forth from memory. Augustine's account of the mental word provided him and later Trinitarian theology with a means of coming to some understanding of the generation of the eternal Word from the Father. "Whoever, then, can understand the word, not only before it is sounded externally, but even before the images of its sounds are present in thought . . . can already see through this glass and in this enigma some likeness of that Word" (ibid. 15.10.19), of which Saint John wrote in the Prologue of his Gospel.

When we speak something true, that is, something we know, [Augustine adds] it is necessary that from the knowledge which we hold in memory there be born a word which is absolutely of the same sort as the knowledge from which it is born. The thought formed by that which we know is a word which we speak in our heart. (ibid.)

Such a word does not belong to any of the languages spoken by various peoples; rather, words we speak aloud are signs of our inner words.[20]

All the knowledge the mind acquires, whether from the senses or through itself or through the testimony of others, it holds stored away in "the storehouse of memory from which is born a true word when we speak what we know, but before every sound, before every thought of a sound" (ibid. 15.12.22). Hence, in the human mind, memory is analogous to the Father, and a mental word is analogous to the Word of the Father; as a mental word is born of or proceeds from memory, so the Son is born of or proceeds from the Father. An inner word which we speak in the heart, when we know the truth, is

knowledge born from knowledge, vision from vision, and the understanding which is found in thought from the understanding which had been in memory, but was hidden. And yet, unless thought had a certain memory of it, thought would not return to those things which it had left in memory when it thinks of other things. (ibid. 15.21.40)

In the enigma which is the human mind, Augustine finds a likeness of the Holy Spirit in love. Love is present in understanding along with memory, "for without memory the gaze of our thought has no object to return to, and without love it has no reason to return to it" (ibid. 15.21.41). Hence, memory, understanding, and love provide an obscure understanding of the triune God. The primacy of memory for Augustine's account of human cognition is seen from its analogy with the Father who is first in the Trinity.

NOTES

1 See *Conf.* 10.14.21: "In this case the mind is memory itself, for when we command that something be held by memory, we say, 'See that you have that in mind,' and when we forget something, we say, 'That was not in mind,' and 'It has slipped from mind,' calling the memory itself the mind." Though Augustine does not explicitly discuss the issue, he clearly presupposes, as the later Franciscan tradition did, that various powers of the soul, such as memory and will, are really identical with the essence of the soul.

2 Gilson (1961, 102) points to the puzzling character of Augustinian memory when he says, "Since the soul remembers everything present to it even though unaware of it, we can say that there is a memory of the present which is even far more vast than the memory of the past." So too Mourant: "although we obviously cannot have a memory of the future as we do of the past and the present, memory is basic to any anticipation we make of the future" (Mourant 1980, 24). See also *De Trin.* 14.11.14 for memory of the present and 15.7.13 for memory's role with respect to the future.

3 Gilson concedes that it is "possible that during the early days of his conversion Augustine combined the theory of the soul's pre-existence with its natural complement, the doctrine of Platonic reminiscence" (Gilson 1961, 71–72). O'Daly finds no evidence for such a conclusion; see O'Daly 1987, 199–204 for an interpretation of these texts as metaphorical and/or inconclusive.

4 O'Daly (1974) interprets *Ep.* 7.11.3 as simply figurative language. The strongest arguments against a literal interpretation of the reminiscence passages is the simultaneous presence of the doctrine of divine illumination, even in the early works, such as *Sol.* 1.13, 15 and 2.33.

5 See Teske 1984.

6 See O'Connell 1987, especially pp. 300–310. In his anti-Pelagian works Augustine often insists that we all were in Adam, quoting Ambrose's words from his *Commentary on the Gospel of Luke* 7, 234: "Adam existed, and we all existed in him; Adam perished, and all perished in him."

7 See O'Connell 1968, 1969. O'Connell points to two previous studies (O'Meara 1954 and Knauer 1957) which in different ways anticipated his conclusion.

8 See O'Daly 1987, 202–4 and O'Donnell 1992a, 2.34.

9 Le Blond 1950, 6.

10 Ibid. 17; Mourant 1980, 66–67.

11 See *Enarr. in Ps.* 145.5 as well as *De Trin.* 14.3.5.

12 Bourke 1992 provides a valuable commentary on the first half of Book 10, along with the Latin text and translation.

13 See *De Trin.* 13.4.7; for Augustine's initial contact with the *Hortensius*, see *Conf.* 4.4.7.

14 O'Donnell (1992a, 3.195) takes this line to refer to Augustine's infancy (*Conf.* 1.11.17) or to his finding God in Milan (ibid. 8.12.29) or at Ostia (ibid. 9.10.24–25).

15 See Teske 1996; Flasch 1993, especially 388–389.

16 Mourant 1969, 23. See also Moreau 1955.

17 See *Conf.* 3.7.12 and 5.10.19–20.

18 See *De Genesi ad litteram imperfectus liber* 16.61, where Augustine changes his earlier interpretation of Genesis 1.26 and interprets the image as Trinitarian.

19 There has been little explicit discussion of the role of memory in *De Trinitate*; the notes to *La Trinité (Livres VIII-XV)* (Agaësse 1955) are helpful, though they are concerned more with the image of Trinity than with the role of memory in human cognition.

20 See *De Trin.* 15.11.20.

12

GERARD O'DALY

The response to skepticism and the
mechanisms of cognition

Skepticism

Augustine, like Newman, was not by temperament inclined to acquiesce in prolonged or systematic doubt.[1] Yet his growing dissatisfaction with Manichaeism, whose dogmatic dualism he had embraced as an eighteen-year-old in 372, made him a temporary skeptic in about 383 or 384, at a particularly insecure and unstable period of his life.[2] A year or two later he encountered Platonism in Milan, and gradually laid the foundations of the theory of cognitive certainty that characterizes his earliest extant writings.[3] He was subsequently to argue polemically that skepticism is a form of despair of finding truth.[4] Yet he considered the refutation of skepticism to be of primary importance. He devoted the first of the programmatic series of philosophical writings of 386–387, *Contra Academicos*, written in the aftermath of his conversion, to criticism of skeptical positions and defense of the attainability of knowledge. He continued, moreover, to use skeptical arguments and method in his writings: they are found, for example, in his anti-Manichaean polemic from 388 onwards, and some survived in his later, mature thought.[5]

Augustine's knowledge of skepticism is knowledge of the form it took in the Platonic "New" Academy from the middle of the third to the middle of the first century BC (the key figures are Arcesilaus in the earliest stage of this development, and Carneades in the middle of the second century).[6] His chief source of information is Cicero's *Academica*.[7] But Cicero's *Hortensius*, which played a decisive role in awakening Augustine's early interest in philosophy, is also used.[8] There were undoubtedly other sources, even if they cannot be identified with certainty.[9] We can exclude any direct use of Sextus Empiricus, the most important Pyrrhonist Skeptic, who wrote at the end of the second century AD, or of other Greek writers, given Augustine's slight knowledge of Greek.[10] Plotinus was one Greek philosopher whom Augustine knew in Latin translation; but Plotinus' arguments against skepticism appear not to have influenced him.[11]

Given his identification of skepticism with that of the New Academy,

Augustine will, from the start, have seen it as a form of critique of Stoic dogmatism. He also came to believe – something that he did not find in Cicero's account – that the arguments of the New Academy were a device of Arcesilaus to protect genuine Platonic doctrine, to which Academic skeptics continued to subscribe esoterically.[12]

The version of skepticism that Augustine takes from Cicero's Academic books is that adopted by Cicero himself. Despite Cicero's evidence, Augustine attributes it to Carneades. Augustine does not exploit the clues that Cicero provides concerning the nature of "classical" skepticism (the position of Arcesilaus, Carneades, and the Pyrrhonists), which did not argue that nothing can be known or that one should always withhold assent. Classical skeptics criticized such views as being no less dogmatic than the dogmatism against which they were directed. Dogmatic skepticism of the kind espoused by Cicero, and accepted by Augustine as the only kind of skeptical position, appears to have been a development of later Academics, at some time prior to Cicero's day.[13]

The *Contra Academicos* is Augustine's principal and only sustained response to skeptical arguments which he found in Cicero's books. It is written, like Cicero's Academic books, in dialogue form. In Book 1, starting from the premiss that the wise man alone is happy, Augustine asks whether wisdom consists in finding truth or in seeking it. Book 2 expounds the dogmatic Academic view that knowledge is impossible and that the sage will assent to nothing. Augustine develops his objections to the Academic view in Books 2 and 3.[14]

There is one puzzling detail of Augustine's presentation of Carneades, not found in Cicero or any other source: "The Academics . . . insisted . . . that man could not have knowledge of the things which concerned philosophy, and as for other things, Carneades said that he did not bother about them."[15] Augustine understands the "things which concern philosophy" to be questions subsumed under its traditional parts, physics, ethics, and dialectic.[16] In that case, the "other things" are the "probable" or "likely" perceptions of our everyday lives. Carneades' restriction, in Kirwan's words, "may have been dialectical, for the sake of argument," in which case Augustine does not make much positive use of it. Augustine may, however, have misunderstood Carneades' argument.[17]

Augustine's arguments against skeptics seek to expose inconsistencies and inadequacies in Academic positions, such as the claim that there can be an Academic sage, and the concept of the "persuasive" or "probable."[18] We must consider these two positions in turn.

Augustine is not persuasive in his arguments against the "wisdom" claimed by the skeptic (or at least by Carneades).[19] Being "wise," or being a sage, entails for the skeptic not possessing incontrovertible knowledge of any kind, but so acting that one does not assent to what is not the case, to that for which there is insufficient evidence.[20] Academic "wisdom" is a skeptical strategy, and does not entail knowledge of something called "wisdom," in the sense of an idea or Platonic Form of wisdom, as Augustine's critique seems to imply.[21]

Augustine subscribes to the Stoic view that the sage alone has secure knowledge of truths, and that, in consequence, the sage alone is happy. Hence, his principal objection to the Academics is directed at the claim attributed to them that one may be wise and attain happiness in the quest for truth, even if there is no possibility of its attainment.[22] Augustine counters by arguing that nobody can be happy if he cannot attain something that he desires greatly, such as the truth.[23] But this argument presupposes that happiness entails accomplishment of desired goals rather than the conviction that the pursuit of a worthwhile desire, even if unfulfilled, is satisfying.[24] In fact, it is not clear that Augustine ever repudiates the premiss that the unremitting search for truth may in itself be a worthy activity.[25] Yet we would expect him to repudiate it, for it seems to run counter to his views on happiness and wisdom.

against Augustine

Augustine exploits the fact that Cicero translates *pithanon* ("persuasive"/"credible") or *eikos* ("likely") by *veri simile* ("like truth") or *probabile* ("probable").[26] Augustine argues that it is absurd to claim that something is like the truth when one purports not to know what the truth is: he is applying a version of Plato's thesis that comparing x with y entails prior knowledge of y.[27] But I can say that x is like y if I know how y would seem if it existed. For the Academic claim to stand, he merely, in Kirwan's words, "needs to know how a truth would seem if there were any," which he could do without having knowledge of truth.[28] Augustine's argument thus fails.

against Augustine

Augustine's critique of skeptical *epochē* or suspension of judgment (itself an intended safeguard against the risk of error) concentrates on the inevitability of risking error, in the sense of committing error sooner or later, if one habitually assents to what he does not know: "for he will of necessity err, if he assents to uncertain things."[29] This is neat. The Academic concedes that action and the forming of judgments cannot be avoided: how then can he claim that suspension of judgment is either possible or brings with it avoidance of error?[30] Augustine (1) prefers the view that error can be avoided by assuming that in all perceptive acts something "appears to be," whether it is objectively the case or not, i.e. it is a matter of subjective opinion, and that if we assent to no more than the proposition that the appearance is such-and-such, we cannot be deceived.[31] Propositions relating to recognized optical illusions are true, as in the case of the school example of the oar that appears bent in the water:

> against Augustine

> Is what they say regarding the oar in the water therefore true? Of course it is true. For, given that the cause of its appearing so is present, if the oar submerged in water should appear straight, I should have greater reason to accuse my eyes of a false report. For they would not have seen what should have been seen, given the existence of such causes.[32]

Augustine does not specify what these "causes" are, but we can assume that they are simply the conditions under which the particular perception occurs.[33]

Cicero translates the Stoic term *phantasia* ("impression" or "presentation") by *visum* ("appearance," usually in the plural form *visa*). He understands these *visa* to be the objects of perception, to which we may or may not assent, rather than arguing, with Arcesilaus, that assent can be given only to propositions and not to impressions.[34] Following Cicero, Augustine's attack on skepticism takes the form of a qualified defense of the Stoic criterion of truth.[35] Cicero's version of the criterion, with its insistence on the role of the cognitive impression (*phantasia katalēptikē*), is also the source of Augustine's formulations.[36]

> As for their [the Academics'] opinion that truth could not be perceived, they apparently took this from the famous definition of the cognitive impression given by the Stoic Zeno, that that truth could be perceived, which was so impressed on the mind from the source of its origin that it could not originate from whence it did not originate.[37]

By this account, truth "was so manifestly true that it could be distinguished from what was not true through a dissimilarity in indications (*notae*)," i.e. it is based on unambiguous appearances.[38] Thus "truth can be perceived by those signs (*signa*) which cannot be present in what is not true."[39] Augustine subsequently modifies this, asserting that the truth of propositions is such that "no one can confuse them with any likeness to the false."[40] Augustine believes that the evidence of sense perception cannot, strictly speaking, satisfy the conditions of the criterion. There are no characteristics of our sense perceptions that enable us infallibly to distinguish "true from false."[41] By this, Augustine does not mean to say that no perceptual beliefs are true. He regularly uses the term "true" (*verum*) to denote "really existent," as opposed to "illusory."[42] Thus he uses the phrase "like what is false" (*simile falso*) when talking about sensible objects, i.e they are as likely to be deceptive as not. Proteus is a metaphor for the elusiveness of truth in our present condition.[43]

There seems, therefore, to be an affinity between Augustine's position and the Academic one, even if Augustine does not exploit this. He searches, rather, for propositions which satisfy the conditions of the Stoic cognitive impression, as he understands it. They would be propositions of such a kind that they cannot be taken for false. Augustine argues that mathematical equations satisfy the conditions.[44] Equations such as $1 + 2 + 3 + 4 = 10$ and $3 \times 3 = 9$ "must be true even though the human race were snoring."[45] The conditions of the criterion are also satisfied, Augustine argues elsewhere, by such propositions as "I exist," "I am alive," or even "If I am deceived, I exist."[46] It is arguable that propositions of this last kind are intended to demonstrate the impossibility of thinking of any kind without existence, and that Augustine is inferring the certainty of our existence from the fact of consciousness. But it may be that he is arguing that he cannot mistakenly believe that he exists, or is alive, etc.[47] That the argument takes the form it does, with the concession that either we know that we are or are mistaken in thinking that we are, does not call into question our direct knowledge of our existence, but rather takes on the skeptic by defeating a challenge to the claim to know that we exist: it is a tactical argument.[48]

Augustine also maintains that the necessary truth of logical principles, such as the law of contradiction or the law of excluded middle, grounds an array of the things that we know with certainty ("I am certain . . . that there is one world or not one," etc.; "If there are four elements in the world, there are not five. If there is one sun, there are not two. The same soul cannot both die and be immortal," etc.).[49] But what is the substance of his claim about such propositions? What is their truth value? Carneades would have accepted the logical necessity of such propositions, while denying that they tell us anything about states of affairs or events.[50] Moreover, Augustine avoids the more tricky Academic arguments, such as their use of the Sorites and the Lying arguments, although he would have found them both in Cicero.[51] Yet Augustine himself later distinguishes between the truth of propositions and the validity of deductions. Valid deductions may be made from false premises, just as invalid deductions may be made using true statements.[52]

Augustine presents a version of the skeptical "how do I know that I am not dreaming?" argument.[53] Against the skeptics, he argues that some knowledge claims are not affected by the assumption that I am (now) dreaming.[54] In fact, as we have seen, Augustine allows, against skeptical argument, that subjective states give certain knowledge about a "world" that may simply be tantamount to whatever "appears" to us.[55]

Does Augustine anticipate Descartes's Cogito? When Descartes's correspondents and "objectors" (Mersenne, Arnauld, Colvius, Mesland) suggested to him that this was so, Descartes replied that, although each had proved the indubitability of his own existence, there was a difference between Augustine's use of the argument and his own: "I do indeed find that he [Augustine] does use it to prove the certainty of our existence . . . I, on the other hand, use the argument to show that this I which is thinking is *an immaterial substance* with no bodily element."[56] But Augustine also wants to demonstrate that there is a range of propositions that can be known to be true. And elsewhere he concludes, from the fact of the mind being certain about its own substance, that its substance is not material.[57]

Some texts dispute that perception gives us any knowledge of the external world, suggesting that there are no characteristics of our sense perceptions that enable us infallibly to distinguish between true and false.[58] But many other texts make claims for our ability to know the external world, the kind of knowledge that Augustine often calls *scientia*, contrasting it with *sapientia*, the knowledge of eternal and immutable truths.[59] Even optical illusions have a kind of consistency.[60] Augustine maintains that if our perception of an object is comprehensive and our faculties are functioning normally, reliable information may be acquired about the external world.[61]

Augustine argues that belief, if properly founded, is a kind of "knowledge." Belief, which is "thinking with assent," may be rational. The validity of our beliefs depends upon the authority by which they are held, the evidence or testimony that commands assent.[62] Historical evidence and the truths of religion are different kinds of authority: yet it is the same type of mental activity that engages in belief in each case. Yet historical evidence can only be believed: it can never be knowledge in the strict sense.[63] But religious truths may be understood one day, and so known by believers, if only in the afterlife.[64] Belief is inferior to knowledge. Augustine, in rhetorical mode, distinguishes sharply between the certainty of knowledge and the insubstantial nature of belief.[65] Despite his claims for belief as something rational, justified, and trustworthy, he argues that it lacks the first-hand justification of knowledge, and the comprehensive synoptic overview of a complex field achieved by understanding.[66] It also lacks the first-hand justification of sense perception: properly authenticated sense perception is a form of knowledge, in a sense that historical testimony never can be.[67] It is only when Augustine is arguing against skeptics that he talks of our "knowing" historical facts.[68]

Despite what he says about the nature of belief as a kind of knowledge, Augustine is none the less worried by any attempt to question what he takes to be our certain knowledge of ethical principles. He could have maintained that believing the claims of these principles would be sufficient to maintain morality. Instead, he argues unpersuasively that anything that falls short of ethical dogmatism undermines the basis of moral behaviour.[69] He may be influenced by Stoic views on the links between epistemic certainty and morality.[70]

dogmatism

Mechanisms of cognition

Augustine's theory of sense perception has a physiological bias. Like Plotinus, he exploits the discovery of the nervous system by the Alexandrian physician Herophilus (c. 330–260 BC), and the complex physiology, uniting respiration, the nervous system, and other phenomena like the vascular system, of Herophilus' contemporary, Erasistratus of Ceos.[71] In Augustine's account, the fine, pipe-like passages of the sensory nerves transmit stimuli to the brain (to which they are attached) from the various sense organs. Augustine identifies with precision the part of the brain that is the source and the terminus of sensation, namely, the foremost of the three ventricles in the cerebrum. The other two are the seat of memory and the source of the motor nerves respectively.[72]

Like Erasistratus, Augustine believes that the nerves contain soul "breath" (*pneuma*) as a means of communication between brain and senses.[73] Augustine co-ordinates this belief with other traditional philosophical accounts of perceptive processes, such as the ray theory of vision. In Augustine's version of the theory, rays emanate from the pupil of the eye to impinge upon objects, so that seeing becomes a kind of visual touching. Seeing presupposes a space between eye and object: the eyes cannot see themselves, nor can they see a body directly superimposed on their surface.[74] But the ray theory none the less maintains the principle that bodies are physically contiguous with what they feel, and Augustine adopts the Stoic metaphor of the rod held in the hand to touch an object, in order to illustrate the quasi-tactile extension of sight beyond the eye to the seen object.[75]

The senses are not reflexive, and our awareness of their activity is a perception of the so-called internal sense, which controls and judges our sensations. It corresponds to Aristotle's distinction between the special and the common sensibles, and there are some similarities between Augustine's account and Aristotle's *koinē aisthēsis*. But the Stoic concept of the role of the intellect or "commanding faculty" (*hegemonikon*) in recognizing, co-ordinating, and judging sense-impressions is also likely to have influenced him.[76]

Augustine's account of sensation considers it as a form of motion or change. He believes that it is a motion running counter to that set up in the body by sensory stimuli.[77] Sentience is the product of the interaction of these two movements of qualitative change. Augustine demonstrates this by considering the counter-case, that we do not feel certain things done to our bodies:

> the reason why we do not feel anything when bones, nails, and hair are cut is not because these parts of us are utterly lacking in life . . . but because they are not sufficiently permeated by . . . air, that is to say, an active element, to allow the soul to effect a motion as rapid as the counter-motion which occurs when it is said to "feel."[78]

But what changes when this sensory motion occurs? Most likely it is the soul "breath" (*pneuma*) that is set in motion in this process. Because of the presence of *pneuma* in the sensory nerves, they are themselves sentient. The perceiving subject, soul, is entirely present in them, and is not merely located in a central receptive organ with which they communicate in a non-sentient way.[79]

Sensation may have a physiological mechanism, but perception is none the less a psychological process. The body–soul interaction in perception is a kind of blending or mixing (*contemperatio*): sometimes this blending is described in the Pythagorean terms of Plato's *Phaedo*, as a tempering or attuning of body by soul.[80] The mental counterpart of this process is called concentration (*intentio*, *attentio*). In vision, for example, the visual ray is the necessary physical counterpart of mental concentration. This concentration is an activity, a dynamic concentration of soul power. Perception is exercised upon the sensory stimulus, and is not a passive reception of the latter: "perception is something directly undergone by the body of which the soul is aware."[81] Augustine extends the notions of concentration and counter-motion to his accounts of feelings such as pleasure and pain. In the case of the latter the soul "becomes more concentrated because of the trouble which it has in functioning. This trouble is called 'perceiving,' since soul is aware of its concentration (*attentio*), and this [perception] is called 'pain' or 'distress.'"[82] Augustine is not thereby equating perceiving with being in pain: rather he is using the vivid example of perception of pain to make a point about the role of concentration in the mechanism of perception.

The awareness implicit in any perceptive process is underpinned by the instantaneous operation of memory. A series of memory impressions is stored in the mind in the course of even the shortest perception. This is so, because all mental concentration persists of necessity over a time-span: to hear even the briefest sound memory is needed, for the beginning of a sound does not coincide temporally with its end, and cannot be perceived simultaneously in its entirety. Augustine argues implausibly that it is the same with visual perception of an extended body. He maintains that we cannot perceive even the smallest body simultaneously in its entirety. This mental registering of a series of memory impressions is essential to the very process of perception.[83]

Sense perception is perception of images of objects, not of the objects themselves.[84] These images are not corporeal: Augustine describes them as a kind of "spiritual matter," but the analogy is confusing, for, like Aristotle, Augustine argues that perception is the ability to receive forms without matter.[85] Moreover, perception is the perception of like by like. There is an affinity between the percipient's reason and the image or form of the object perceived, which is described by Augustine in rational, numerical terms or in the language of proportion and measure. It is this affinity which makes perception possible in the first place, as well as guaranteeing its reliability.[86]

The mechanism of cognition is underwritten by Augustine's metaphysics. The objects of perception are themselves formed by the Forms (or Reasons or Ideas) in the mind of God, to which they owe their existence.[87] In sense perception these Forms function as criteria (*regulae*) accessible to our minds, enabling us, through the divine illumination of our minds, to distinguish between the "truth" and "falsity" of what is conveyed by perception.[88] When the mind errs in its evaluation of perceptions, it does so because it applies itself to the phenomena in question in some defective way: "The mind is . . . deceived by the likenesses of things, not through any defect in the latter, but because of a faulty opinion, when, lacking in understanding, it assents to that which resembles something rather than to the thing which it resembles."[89] Access to the Forms is no guarantee of infallibility in perception. Assembling of evidence and common sense will prevent mistakes being made. Augustine believes that we are capable of establishing working distinctions between reliable and illusory perceptions: "in all perceptions both the testimony of the other senses, and especially that of the mind itself and reason, is adduced, that the truth appropriate to this class of things may be found, to the extent that it can be found."[90] Strictly speaking, perception does not convey the certainty that we associate with knowledge.[91] But empirical sciences like zoology and history nevertheless operate on the basis of a distinction between reliable and unreliable evidence. Knowledge of the Forms underpins the reality of the objects of these sciences. Thus it somehow guarantees the knowledge that we associate with zoology and history, even if it does not actually generate this knowledge in zoologists and historians.[92]

NOTES

1 Newman 1.1.3, 6.1.2–3 (= Ker, pp. 11–12, 114–119). Newman, ibid. 6.2.2, discussing the "pleasures of Doubt," reduces acquiescence in doubt to an act of assent or conviction (= Ker, p. 137).

2 *Conf.* 5.10.19, 5.14.25, *De util. cred.* 8.20.

3 *Conf.* 6.11.18.

4 *Ep.* 1.3; *Retract.* 1.1.1. On this "emotional" element in Augustine's attitude to skepticism see Alfaric 1918, 356–358; cf. Hume 1896, 1.4.7 (= Selby-Bigge, 267–271), on the despair of skeptical doubt.

5 See Alfaric 1918, 270–320 on skeptical arguments in Augustine's anti-Manichaean polemic; ibid. 321–350 on Academic positions in Augustine's later thought.

6 For the arguments of the skeptical New Academy see Long 1974, 75–106; translations of texts with commentary in Long and Sedley 1987, 438–467.

7 Cicero wrote two versions of the *Academica*. Of the earlier version, the second book (of two) survives. This early version is often referred to as *Academica priora*: in this chapter the surviving book is given its authentic title *Lucullus*. Of the later version in four books only part of the first book survives. It is commonly referred to as *Academica posteriora*: in this chapter it is referred to as *Academica 1*. For the foregoing cf. Powell 1995, xiv-xvi. Recent studies of Cicero's *Academica*, apart from several chapters of Powell 1995, are Lévy 1992 and Inwood and Mansfeld 1997. We cannot be certain which edition of the *Academica* Augustine knew: the latest discussion, Fuhrer 1997, 37–40, is agnostic.

8 Augustine on the influence of Cicero's *Hortensius*: *Conf.* 3.4.7. It is used in *Contra Academicos*, as *C. Acad.* 1.3.7 (= *Hortensius*, fr. 101 Mueller) and 3.14.31 (= fr. 100 M.) testify.

9 Fuhrer 1997, 40 and 407–408 suggests Cicero, *De re publica* 1.10.16, as well as a further source with Neopythagorean elements, for the history of Platonism in *C. Acad.* 3.17.37–19.42.

10 Even if Sextus Empiricus was not used by Augustine, some of the views which he reports are also found in *C. Acad.*: see further n. 12 below.

11 Plotinus' anti-skeptical arguments are discussed, with illuminating comparisons with Descartes, by Rappe 1996, developing ideas in Wallis 1987.

12 *C. Acad.* 3.17.37–9; cf. Fuhrer (1997, 418–424), who cites Sextus Empiricus and Numenius as partial antecedents. The influence of Porphyry is argued by Glucker (1978, pp. 311–322), unconvincingly. The secret doctrine theory is related by Augustine in *C. Acad.* 3.17.37–20.43 (cf. *Ep.* 1; 118.3.16–20; 118.5.33) to the thesis of a continuity in Platonist doctrine from Plato to Plotinus. Some modern scholars link this thesis in turn to the tradition of the unity of Platonist and Aristotelian doctrine, on which Porphyry wrote a (lost) work, but which is already found in Cicero, *Academica* 1.4.17–18, as well as being controversial in Middle Platonism (Dillon 1988, pp. 114–119). Augustine himself (*C. Acad.* 3.20.43) gives Cicero as his authority: *Lucullus* 18.60 is the probable Ciceronian passage, but scholars have been tempted (references in Fuhrer 1997, p. 468) to construct from the Augustine allusion elements of the lost parts of Cicero's Academic writings.

13 Cicero, *Lucullus* 48.148 hints at dogmatic developments. On the two kinds of assent in skepticism and the differences between classical and dogmatic skepticism see Frede 1997, 140–147.

14 O'Meara 1951 provides a translation of *C. Acad.* with valuable introduction and notes; Fuhrer 1997 is an extensive commentary on Books 2 and 3.

15 *C. Acad.* 2.5.11, tr. O'Meara 1951, p. 76; cf. ibid. 3.10.22.

16 *C. Acad.* 3.10.23–13.29.

17 Kirwan 1989, 28, suggests that Carneades' restriction is dialectical. Fuhrer 1997, pp. 145–146, 323–325, believes that Augustine may have misunderstood the argument.

18 *C. Acad.* 2.5.12; 2.7.19, 3.14.30–32.

19 See Cicero, *Lucullus* 21.67; 24.78.

20 Ibid. 20.66–21.67; Striker 1980, 74, 77.

21 *C. Acad.* 3.4.9–10.

22 This argument is attributed to Cicero in *C. Acad.* 1.3.7, probably from the *Hortensius* (see n. 8 above).

23 *C. Acad.* 1.3.9.

24 Kirwan 1989, 17–20.

25 *C. Acad.* 1.5.13–14.

26 Cicero, *Lucullus* 10.32; 31.99; Augustine, *C. Acad.* 2.5.12; 2.7.16; 2.7.19, 2.12.27–28. On Cicero's translation of *pithanon*, *eikos*, and related terms see Glucker 1995.

27 Plato, *Phaedo* 74d–e; cf. Plato, *Phaedrus* 259e–260c. A similar argument is found in Cicero, *Lucullus* 11.33–5. See Fuhrer 1997, 174 n. 1.

28 Kirwan 1989, 22.

29 *C. Acad.* 2.5.11.

30 Ibid. 3.15.33–16.36; see Kirwan 1989, 22–3.

31 Ibid. 3.11.24–26.

32 Ibid. 3.11.26. Stock school example: Fuhrer 1997, 353 (it is cited by Cicero at *Lucullus* 7.19 and 25.79).

33 For the Epicurean background of the argument about optical illusions and truth see Long and Sedley 1987, 86.

34 Translation of *phantasia*: Cicero, *Academica* 1.11.40; *Lucullus* 6.18. Arcesilaus' argument: Sextus Empiricus, *Adversus mathematicos* 7.154; see Kirwan 1989, 25.

35 *C. Acad.* 2.5.11; 3.9.18; 3.9.21.

36 Cicero, *Lucullus* 6.18; 35.113; Rist 1969, 133–151.

37 *C. Acad.* 2.5.11, tr. O'Meara 1951, 76.

38 Ibid. 2.6.14, tr. O'Meara 1951, 80.

39 Ibid. 2.5.11, tr. O'Meara 1951, 77.

40 Ibid. 3.10.23, tr. Kirwan 1989, 28–29.

41 C. Acad. 2.5.11, 3.9.18, 3.9.21, 3.17.39.

42 See e.g. Sol. 1.15.28–9, 2.4.6–5.8; cf. O'Daly 1987, 186.

43 "Like what is false": De diversis quaestionibus octoginta tribus 9. Proteus metaphor:
C. Acad. 3.6.13.

44 C. Acad. 2.3.9, 3.9.21, 3.10.23, 3.11.25, 3.13.29. cf. De doctrina christiana
2.31.49 35.53.

45 C. Acad. 3.11.25, tr. O'Meara 1951, 127.

46 De beata vita 2.7; Sol. 2.1.1; De lib. arb. 2.3.7; De vera relig. 39.73; De Trin. 10.10.14;
De civ. Dei 11.26. Kirwan 1989, 30 claims that such instances of indubitable knowl-
edge are absent from C. Acad.: but Fuhrer 1997, 309–311, 323, draws attention to C.
Acad. 3.9.19 and 3.10.22.

47 Matthews 1972; Kirwan 1989, 30–34; Rist 1994, 63–67.

48 De civ. Dei 11.26; cf. De lib. arb. 2.3.7, where the strategy is not anti-skeptical argument, but rather part of the construction of a demonstration of God's existence: Rist
1994, 67. Matthews (1992, 32–34), stresses the tactical nature of the argument.

49 C. Acad. 3.10.23, 3.13.29.

50 Long 1974, 102–103.

51 The Sorites or "Heaper" argument was so called because it used the example of a
heap of wheat ("how many grains are a heap?") to exploit, on a "little-by-little"
basis, the absence of clear boundaries between contraries like "few" and "many."
The "Lying" argument took the form "If you say you are lying, and you say so truly,
are you lying or telling the truth?" (Cicero, Lucullus 29.95) to argue against the Stoic
position that every proposition is either true or false. For discussion of both arguments see Cicero, Lucullus 28.91–30.96; cf. Long and Sedley 1987, 229 (texts: ibid.
221–224); Burnyeat 1982, 33.

52 De doct. christ. 2.31.49–35.53.

53 C. Acad. 3.11.25–26; De Trin. 15.12.21; cf. Plato, Theaetetus 158b–c; Cicero,
Lucullus 27.88–28.90.

54 Matthews 1992, 54–55.

55 C. Acad. 3.11.24–26. See Burnyeat 1982, 28–29.

56 Letter of 14 Nov. 1640 to Colvius, in The Philosophical Writings of Descartes, vol.
3: The Correspondence, tr. J. Cottingham, R. Stoothoff, D. Murdoch, and A. Kenny
(Cambridge: Cambridge University Press, 1991), p. 159 (3.247–8 Adam-Tannery);
Matthews 1992, 11–38; Rist 1994, 88.

57 De Trin. 10.10.16; cf. Matthews 1992, 15. The Descartes texts are discussed by Menn
1998, 66–67 n. 42. For Descartes's uses of skepticism in his Meditations see Menn
1998, 220–244.

58 C. Acad. 3.17.39; De diversis quaestionibus octoginta tribus 9.

59 De Trin. 12.11.16–12.17; 12.13.21; 15.11.21.

60 C. Acad. 3.11.26.

61 Ep. 147.9.21; De civ. Dei 19.18.

62 De praed. sanct. 2.5; C. Acad. 3.19.42–20.43; De ordine 2.9.26–7; De lib. arb. 2.2.5;
De util. cred. Kretzmann 1990 analyzes the philosophical implications of faith in
Augustine.

63 De mag. 11.37; De diversis quaestionibus octoginta tribus 48.

64 De Trin. 9.1.1; Sermons 43; Enarr. in Ps. 118 (here Sermon 18.3).

65 *C. Acad.* 3.17.37; 3.20.43; *De diversis quaestionibus octoginta tribus* 9 and 48; *Ep.* 147.2.7; 147.4.10.

66 *De mag.* 10.31; 12.39–40; 14.46; *Ep.* 147.9.21; Burnyeat 1987.

67 *Ep.* 147.16.38; *De Trin.* 12.3.3; *Retract.* 1.14.3.

68 *De Trin.* 4.16.21; 15.11.21.

69 *C. Acad.* 3.16.35–6; 2.9.22.

70 See Long and Sedley 1987, 256–259.

71 Plotinus 4.3.23; *Oxford Classical Dictionary*, 3rd edn., s.v. Erasistratus, Herophilus. Verbeke 1945, 175–220 discusses Augustine's *pneuma* doctrine. For the following see O'Daly 1987, 80–84.

72 *De Gen. ad litt.* 7.13.20, 7.18.24.

73 Ibid. 7.13.20, 7.19.25.

74 *De Trin.* 9.3.3; *Sermons* 277.10.10, 277.14.14.

75 *De quant. anim.* 23.43.

76 *De lib. arb.* 2.3.8–5.12; cf. Aristotle, *De anima* 418a7–25, 424b22–427a16; O'Daly 1987, 90–92, 102–105. Stoic *hēgemonikon*: see Long and Sedley 1987, 315 (text 53G = SVF 2.879).

77 *De musica* 6.5.10–11, 6.5.15.

78 Ibid. 6.5.15.

79 *De immor. anim.* 16.25; *C. ep. fund.* 16.20.

80 Plato, *Phaedo* 85e–86d; cf. *De quant. anim.* 30.59; *De musica* 6.5.10. See O'Daly 1987, 84–87.

81 *De quant. anim.* 25.48. For these views on perception see ibid. 23.41–25.49; *De musica* 6.4.7–5.11; *De Trin.* 11.2.2; *De Gen. ad litt.* 7.20.26, 12.12.25, 12.20.42.

82 *De musica* 6.5.9; cf. ibid. 6.4.5, 6.9.23, 6.10.26, 6.12.34–17.58.

83 *De musica* 6.8.21; *De Gen. ad litt.* 12.11.22, 12.16.33. Augustine's claim that memory is essential to the performance of all serial operations is unconvincing in, at the very least, the instances of visual perception and time-awareness. Although not directed specifically against Augustine, the arguments of Ryle 1949, ch. 6. sect. 4 (= Ryle 1963, pp. 160–173), against the application of the concept of memory in such activities hold good here.

84 *De quant. anim.* 13.22–14.24, 23.41–30.61; *De Trin.* 9.6.10; *De Gen. ad litt.* 12.16.32–33, 12.24.50–1.

85 Spiritual matter: *De anima et eius origine* 4.17.25. Forms without matter: *De quant. anim.* 5.8–9; cf. Aristotle, *De anima* 424a17ff.

86 *De musica* 6.2.2–3; *De ordine* 2.11.32–3; *De Trin.* 11.2.2; 11.2.4; 11.9.16.

87 *De diversis quaestionibus octoginta tribus* 23 and 46. Dillon 1977, 91–96, 254–256, discusses the Middle Platonist evidence for the Forms as thoughts of God.

88 *Sol.* 1.15.27; *De vera relig.* 31.58; *De Trin.* 9.6.9–11. Augustine is again using "true" and "false" in the sense of "really existent" and "illusory": see p. 162 above. The concept of a *regula* or criterion of truth and falsity occurs in Cicero, *Lucullus* 11.33; 18.58.

89 *De Gen. ad litt.* 12.25.52.

90 Ibid.

91 *Retract.* 1.14.3.

92 *De Trin.* 4.16.21.

13

GARETH B. MATTHEWS

Knowledge and illumination

Skepticism

In Rome at the beginning of his stay in Italy, Augustine became disenchanted with the Manichaeism he had provisionally embraced in Carthage. He found himself increasingly attracted to the skeptical position taken by the Academics, the followers of Arcesilaus and the New Academy, who, as he writes in his *Confessions*, "held that everything is a matter of doubt and asserted that we can know nothing for certain" (5.10.19). What Augustine knew of ancient skepticism, including the debate between Arcesilaus and the Stoic Zeno of Citium, he seems to have learned from Cicero's *Academica*.

If Augustine ever considered becoming a skeptic himself, the thought can only have been short-lived. Soon after this period in which, as he reports, he took skepticism seriously, he became interested in Neoplatonism; he then converted to Christianity. Yet, even though he seems never to have become a skeptic himself, skepticism remained for much of his life a threat he felt he needed to respond to. Most of his responses take the form of relatively short passages in works taken up principally with other matters. But he did devote one complete dialogue to this subject: it is the earliest of his surviving works, *Contra Academicos*, a work which was written at a villa in Cassiciacum near Milan, to which he, two pupils, and a friend had retreated for philosophical discussion, enquiry, and reflection.

According to Augustine, the Academics base their skeptical claim that nothing can be known on the application of a strict criterion for knowledge that had been put forward by Zeno. Augustine formulates Zeno's criterion in several different ways. The point common to the several different formulations seems to be this: Something can be known just in case it cannot even seem to be false. Accepting this criterion, Augustine poses a dilemma for the skeptics. Either Zeno's criterion itself is known to be true, or it is not. If it is known to be true, then the skeptics are wrong, since something is known. If it is not known to be true, then the skeptics have given us no adequate basis for justifying their skepticism (3.9.18).

Augustine is not, however, content to show a pragmatic contradiction in the Academic position. His chief response to Academic skepticism is something positive; it is to offer sample knowledge claims that he dares the skeptic to discredit. These sample knowledge claims fall naturally into three groups: *logical truths* (for example, "There is one world or there is not"), *mathematical truths* ("Three times three is nine"), and *reports of immediate experience* ("This tastes pleasant to me") (3.10.23–11.26). In response to the skeptic's taunt that one might be asleep and dreaming, Augustine claims that truths in each of these three groups are unassailable, whether one is awake or dreaming.

Of special interest in this discussion is the response Augustine gives to skepticism directed at apparently tautological claims about the world. "How do you know that this world [even] exists, if the senses are mistaken?" (3.11.24). Augustine replies: "I say I call 'the world' this whole thing, whatever it is, which encloses us and nourishes us, this thing which appears to my eyes and seems to me to make up earth and heaven, or ostensible earth and ostensible heaven" (3.11.24). He adds that, even if he is asleep and dreaming, he can refer to *the world*, so understood, and say, without chance of error, that either it is one or it is not.

Augustine's strategy here is especially interesting, since, to a modern reader, it raises the Cartesian "problem of the external world." Thus, even if, like Augustine, I can be certain that my phenomenal world exists, how do I know that there exists a physical world, independent of me and my phenomenal world? In fact, Augustine does not go on to pose the problem of the external world, either in *Contra Academicos* or in any later work. But it is noteworthy that he does come close to doing so in this passage. And certainly he goes on to develop a very Cartesian concept of the mind.

In his later writings Augustine's most striking response to skepticism is one which finds an echo many centuries later in Descartes's *cogito ergo sum*:

> In respect of these truths I fear no arguments from the Academics. They say, "What if you are mistaken?" If I am mistaken, I am [*si fallor, sum*]. Whoever does not exist cannot be mistaken; and thus I exist, if I am mistaken. Because, therefore, I exist if I am mistaken, how am I mistaken about my existence, when it is certain that I exist if I am mistaken? (*De civ. Dei* 11.26)

Similar reasoning is to be found in the *De Trinitate* at 15.12.21, except that in the latter passage Augustine defends the claim that we each know, in our own case, not that we exist, but that we are alive. One is, no doubt, to understand "alive" here not in a specifically biological sense, but in the Platonic sense in which the soul is essentially alive even when it animates no body, and in the sense in which we ask if there is life after death, without, of course, requiring that an afterlife be a biological one.

Although Augustine does not use this *cogito*-like reasoning to establish a foundation for the rational reconstruction of knowledge, in the fashion of Descartes, there are two respects in which his appeal at *De Trinitate* 15.12.12 to what he calls "inner knowledge" comes to more than merely a rejection of the global skepticism of the Academics.[1] First, it is important to him to add that knowledge of such truths is, as one might want to say, "iterative." That is, not only do I know that I live, I know that I know that I live, and I know that I know that I know that I live, etc. And even though I cannot fully comprehend an infinite number, I can, Augustine says, comprehend the fact that the list of such items of knowledge goes on without limit (ibid.). Second, a criterion of indubitability figures in the way Augustine characterizes the nature of mind (see below).

Learning

A good way to approach Augustine's positive views on knowledge and illumination is to consider what he has to say about language acquisition. Some of his positive views can be found in his early dialogue *De magistro*, most of which is devoted to the topic of language and learning.

The dialogue begins with an engaging discussion of why we use language. This discussion is remarkable for its sensitivity to the variety of things we do with words, a sensitivity quite like that of the twentieth-century philosophers Ludwig Wittgenstein and John Austin. On the side, it also raises (at 1.2) a significant puzzle about why we speak in prayer, when we hardly believe that we can teach or remind God of anything.

The dialogue soon moves on to a consideration of the meanings of words. Words, Augustine says, are signs, and a sign cannot be a sign, he insists, unless it signifies something. Yet it is not easy to say what, for example, the conjunction "if" (*si*) signifies, let alone what the pronoun "nothing" (*nihil*) signifies. Faced with the conviction that "nothing" is certainly a sign, and therefore signifies something, not nothing, Augustine suggests that what "nothing" signifies is an unsuccessful search (2.3). (See chapter 18 in this volume.)

The discussion then turns to questions about whether what a word signifies can be shown by pointing. It is well to realize that Augustine's interest in whether what a sign signifies can be pointed to, or somehow demonstrated, is a question about what has come to be called "ostensive learning." It is thus a question about how we can make the right connections between language and the world. Thus when Augustine asks Adeodatus, his son and interlocutor, whether one can show another person what the word "*paries*" ("wall") signifies by pointing one's finger at a wall, his question concerns the problem of connecting "*paries*" to the walls in the world.

Ostensive learning, as Augustine discusses it with Adeodatus, not only includes pointing with a finger to the object signified, or at least to an example of the object signified, with the finger: It also includes demonstrating or showing without a sign. Here Augustine's example is "walking." Augustine wants to know from Adeodatus whether one who is already engaged in walking can, while walking, show another what "walking" signifies. Adeodatus replies that one could walk a little faster (3.5). Probingly, Augustine asks Adeodatus if he does not realize that hurrying is something different from walking.

This and other examples in the *De magistro* show that ostensive learning is chronically and unavoidably plagued with ambiguity. Whether we are pointing to something to show what "blue" means, or showing someone a blue color sample to illustrate what the word signifies, any given effort at ostensive teaching is open to misunderstanding. How can one know whether what is being pointed out is the color blue, a particular shade of blue, a hue, a colored object, its shape, or something quite different? In the walking case, is what is being demonstrated walking, hurrying, running away, taking so and so many steps, or what? (10.29).

Augustine's response to the problem of ambiguity in ostension is to say that a person who is intelligent enough will eventually catch on (10.32). But that response needs to be filled out. In any case, there seems to be no way the teacher can limit the multiple possibilities of ambiguity in each ostension to assure in advance that the learner will be able to latch onto the right object of signification.

This radical conclusion needs to be put together with something even more radical that comes at the end of the dialogue. There Augustine focuses on an Aramaic word of uncertain meaning, *sarabarae*, in its Latinized form, which is used in the biblical book of Daniel. In the verse in which this word appears the author of the book writes of the three men in the fiery furnace that their "*sarabarae* were unchanged" (Daniel 3.27). Augustine himself takes the word *sarabarae* to mean "head coverings." He imagines someone explaining that this is its meaning. But then he asks rhetorically if, upon being told this meaning, I have learned either what a head is or what a covering is? (*De mag.* 10.33).

One might think that Augustine is here making only the boringly obvious point that a dictionary definition is of no help to someone who is ignorant of the meanings of the terms used in the word's definition. But that is not right. Suppose *sarabarae* does indeed mean "head coverings." Then what the word signifies is head coverings. Knowing what the word is, Augustine tells us, includes knowing what it signifies, which, he supposes, includes being familiar with the things themselves. So being able to give synonyms for *sarabarae* will be insufficient to show that one knows what the word signifies and hence, according to Augustine, what it is. Moreover, only someone who is familiar with the things signified, the *sarabarae* themselves, can be said to know what the word is.

Augustine makes clear that he supposes we can't come to know what head coverings are without "consulting our senses." One who has taken to heart the point about the ambiguity of ostension will be dissatisfied. If there is no way, in principle, to eliminate ambiguity about what, say, "walking" signifies, there is also no way in principle to eliminate ambiguity in the attempt to get help in grasping mentally what a head covering is. So how does the person who succeeds in coming to understand what a head covering is manage that feat? Augustine's answer is the doctrine of illumination (see below). With respect to all of the things we understand (including what head coverings are), Augustine says we consult "not the speaker who makes a noise outside us, but the Truth that presides over the mind within" (11.38). The Truth is then identified as Christ, the Teacher. "The sun . . . the moon and the other stars, the lands and the seas, and all things which are generated in them without number," Augustine writes, "are all exhibited and shown through themselves by God and nature to those who perceive them" (10.32).

How can Christ, the Teacher within, succeed in helping us pick out what is exhibited and shown through itself – say, what walking is, or what a head covering is – when no outside teacher can eliminate the possibility of ambiguity in teaching? We shall re-examine this question when we take up Augustinian illumination more generally below.

Sense perception

Augustine is said to have an "active" theory of sense perception. The term "active" in this context includes the idea that in vision the eyes emit rays that touch the object of vision. This idea is to be found, for example, in Plato's *Timaeus* at 45b–46a. More generally, it is Augustine's view that, although bodily sense organs undergo change during perception, perception is not something undergone by the soul. "Perception," he writes in a famous and somewhat enigmatic passage in the early work *De quantitate animae*, "is something undergone by the body *per se* that is not hidden from the soul [*non latens animam*]" (48). His idea is that in perception the soul takes note of what the body undergoes. "For it is not the body that perceives," he writes in Book 12 of *De Genesi ad litteram libri duodecim*, "but the soul through the body, which messenger, as it were, the soul uses to form in itself the very thing which is announced from the outside" (12.24.51).

Book 12 of *De Genesi ad litteram libri duodecim* has, in fact, very little to do with Genesis; it is, rather, an independent treatise on what Augustine calls "three kinds of vision." Although what Augustine has to say about the first of those three kinds of vision, "bodily vision," is indeed focused, as one might assume, on visual perception, he also includes perception through the other sense modalities under the heading "bodily vision." The discussion includes perhaps his most serious attempt to account for error in sense perception (12.25.52).

Although commentators have sometimes suggested otherwise, Augustine's theory of sense perception is not representational, if one understands by "a representational theory of sense perception" one according to which an image or sense-datum is the direct object of perception. In his discussion of vision in *De Trinitate*, and elsewhere, he claims that in seeing a body, we immediately form an image of the form of the body seen (11.3.6.) But he thinks this fact is not at all obvious. Thus he offers analogies and arguments to convince his readers that there is an image of the body seen as soon and as long as that body itself is seen. If he had supposed that the image were the direct object of sense perception in the first place, he would have felt no obligation to prove to the reader that an image is formed as soon as the body is seen. Thus he can say that just as images are the objects of the vision of imagination (what he sometimes calls "spiritual vision") so the bodies themselves ("ipsa corpora") are what we see in bodily vision (*De Gen. ad litt.* 12.6.15).

Self-knowledge

At the beginning of Augustine's *Soliloquies* we get this exchange between Augustine and his interlocutor, Reason:

> Reason: What then do you want to know?
> Augustine: All these things I have prayed for.
> Reason: Summarize them briefly.
> Augustine: I wish to know God and the soul.
> Reason: Nothing more?
> Augustine: Nothing at all. (*Sol.* 1.2.7)

By the time we get to Book 2 of the *Soliloquies,* the soul that Augustine says he wants to know is simply his own soul.

Augustine's search for self-knowledge continues through many of his other writings. But perhaps the most extensive and most philosophically interesting of these discussions is Book 10 of his *De Trinitate*. That book starts off with a puzzle that is closely related to Plato's "paradox of enquiry" (*Meno* 80d–e). Augustine does not, like Plato, focus on the question of how one can succeed in directing an enquiry specifically at something one is ignorant about. Nor does he emphasize Plato's puzzle about how one could even recognize the as yet unknown object of the enquiry, if one were simply to stumble on it. Instead, he brings up a related problem about what could motivate an enquiry into something unknown. He supposes that an enquiry would have to be motivated by a love of the thing being enquired into. But how can one love something, and so be motivated to enquire into it, when it is unknown?

Perhaps the enquirer already knows what he is enquiring into according to its genus, Augustine suggests at one point. Perhaps he loves the genus

> and is now eager to know it [instantiated] in some particular thing or particular things which he does not yet know, but whose praises he has happened to hear, and therefore represents in his mind by an imaginary picture by which he is aroused to love . . . Yet perhaps he will not love the form that was praised when he finds out how different it is from the one which he pictured in his mind . . . (*De Trin.* 10.2.4)

Yet this is not the resolution Augustine accepts to the puzzle about how he could be motivated to enquire into himself. The classic admonition, "Know thyself!" Augustine interprets as an admonition to the mind to know itself. But instead of puzzling over what could motivate such an enquiry, he asks how the mind could fail to know itself. And he decides that, in an important way, the mind cannot fail to know itself. Nothing is so present to the mind as itself (10.7.10).

Why, then, Augustine asks in exasperation, was the mind commanded to know itself? He decides that the admonition to "know thyself" is to be understood as an admonition not to turn away from oneself but to live according to one's nature under God (10.5.7).

What then is the nature of a mind? "The nature of the mind," he writes, "is to be a substance and not to be a corporeal one, that is, it does not occupy a smaller extension of place with a smaller part of itself, and a larger with a larger part"(10.7.10). Indeed, the mind is, he concludes, something that lives, remembers, understands, wills, thinks, knows, and judges. These essential activities of the mind, he argues in an interesting passage, are self-certifying in an interlocking way. For who would doubt, Augustine asks rhetorically,

> that he lives, remembers, understands, wills, thinks, knows, and judges? For even if he doubts, he lives; if he doubts, he remembers why he doubts; if he doubts, he understands that he doubts; if he doubts, he wants to be certain; if he doubts, he knows that he does not know; if he doubts, he judges that he ought not to consent rashly. Whoever then doubts about anything else ought never to doubt about all of these; for if they were not, he would be unable to doubt about anything at all. (10.10.14)

Augustine's argument for the incorporeality of the mind builds on his demonstration that the mind is so present to itself that its essence (*substantia*)[2] is known to itself. Yet all the suggestions of the materialists that the mind is fire, or air, or this kind of body or that, yield no similarly indubitable claims. What the mind indubitably knows is that it lives, thinks, understands, etc. If it were some body or other, it would not be able to doubt that it is that body. But it can. So it is no body. Therefore, it is an incorporeal substance (10.10.16).

All this talk of what we might call the "self-transparency" of the mind should not be taken to imply that Augustine finds nothing puzzling or problematic about his mind. That is far from the case. Among the puzzles about his mind that Augustine discusses, one of the most philosophically interesting is a puzzle about how the "affections of the mind" (*affectiones animi*) can be in one's memory. Augustine begins with a worry about how one can remember what gladness is without being glad (*Conf.* 10.14.21). He goes on to puzzle over how one can succeed in remembering forgetfulness. It seems to him that the forgetfulness remembered would obliterate the memory.

Perhaps the most interesting example in the series of puzzles Augustine brings up in this part of Book 10 of the *Confessions* is pain (*Conf.* 10.15.23). How can one think about what a pain is, or what the word "pain" means, without being in pain?

A pain has, Augustine supposes, a perceptible quality. Pains will, doubtless, be qualitatively distinct from one another as well as being qualitatively distinct from other sensations and feelings. Like many philosophers, Augustine supposes that we must have an image before the mind for us to be able to think of such phenomenally differentiated entities as pains, aches, and the like. But what would an image of pain be like? To count as an image of pain, he reasons, the image would have to resemble pain. But there is nothing about pain for the image to resemble except for its painfulness. But that means that an image of pain would have to be painful. And that, in turn, seems to mean that we could not think about what pain is, or about what the word "pain" means, without being in pain. And that, Augustine thinks, quite rightly, is absurd (*Conf.* 10.15.23).

Knowledge of other minds

If nothing is so present to the mind as the mind itself, as Augustine supposes, then we certainly have knowledge, each of us, of our own mind. But what about *other* minds? How do I know that there is a mind to go with this or that other human body?

Augustine addresses this problem in Book 8 of his *De Trinitate*. In what is perhaps the first statement of what has come to be called "the Argument from Analogy for Other Minds," Augustine has this to say:

> For we also recognize, from a likeness to us, the motions of bodies by which we perceive that others besides us live. Just as we move [our] body in living, so, we notice, those bodies are moved. For when a living body is moved there is no way open to our eyes to see the mind [*animus*], a thing which cannot be seen by the eyes. But we perceive something present in that mass such as is present in us to move our mass in a similar way; it is life and soul [*anima*]. Nor is such perception something peculiar to, as it were, human prudence and reason. For indeed beasts perceive as living,

not only themselves, but also each other and one another, and us as well. Nor do they see our soul [*anima*], except from the motions of the body, and they do that immediately and very simply by a sort of natural agreement. Therefore we know the mind [*animum*] of anyone at all from our own; and from our own case we believe in that mind which we do not know [*ex nostro credimus quem non novimus*]. For not only do we perceive a mind, but we even know what a mind is, by considering our own; for we have a mind. (8.6.9)

It is striking that Augustine here attributes what we might call the "functional equivalent" of the argument from analogy for other minds to non-human animals. He doesn't, of course, suppose that such animals go through a reasoning process that leads them to the conclusion, "There are other minds." But he does suppose that they have an ability to perceive our souls and those of other animals by a certain natural harmony or agreement ("quadam conspiratione naturali"), an agreement between their souls and the other souls they recognize in this way.

Although Augustine presents the argument from analogy for the existence of other minds and even supposes that beasts can deploy the functional equivalent of this argument to recognize minds and souls in us and other beasts, he is characteristically diffident about knowing what is in other minds. In going behind the words others utter, he says, we must employ a principle of charity to determine their thoughts. In fact, he adds, his readers cannot know whether what he has written in his *Confessions* is a true account of what he is "inside." It is only their charity, he says, that leads them to believe him (*Conf.* 10.3.4).

Knowledge of eternal truths

Already in his early dialogue *De magistro*, Augustine claims that our minds have direct access to the eternal truths of reason. "Indeed when things are discussed which we perceive with the mind," he writes, "that is, by means of intellect and reason, they are said to be things which we see immediately in that inner light of truth by which he himself who is called the inner man is illuminated, and from which he takes pleasure" (12.40).

Augustine expresses a similar idea in other works. Here, for example, is what he says in his *Confessions*, where his way of talking about the mind is to discuss "memory" (*memoria*): "Memory also contains innumerable principles and laws of numbers and dimensions. None of these can have been impressed on it by the bodily senses, because they are not colored, nor do they sound or smell or have any taste or feel" (10.12.19).

Augustine was aware, through Cicero, of Plato's "theory of recollection," according to which we have knowledge of the Forms from a direct communion with them before our birth, and what we call learning is just the process of making manifest to ourselves this latent knowledge. Alluding to Plato's dialogue *Meno*, in which the slave boy, under Socratic questioning, is able to figure out for himself how to construct a square with an area twice that of a given square, Augustine says this:

> But if this were a recollection of things previously known, then certainly everyone, or almost everyone, would be unable to do the same thing if questioned in that way. For not all have been geometricians in their previous life, since there are so few of them in the human race that one can hardly be found. (*De Trin.* 12.15.24)

Rather than accept the Platonic idea that we can recollect knowledge the soul acquired before this present incarnation, Augustine counsels us that

> we should rather believe that the nature of the intellectual mind is so formed as to see those things which, according to the disposition of the creator, are brought under intelligible things in the natural order, in a sort of incorporeal light of its own kind, as the eye of the flesh sees the things that lie about it in this corporeal light, which light it is able to accept and to which it is suited. (12.15.24)

Illumination

What, exactly, is Augustine's so-called doctrine of divine illumination? As we have seen, the doctrine is found already in Augustine's early dialogue *De magistro*. It is appealed to many times in the Augustinian corpus. Yet the exact significance of the doctrine is elusive.

To begin with, the doctrine is appropriately called a doctrine of *divine* illumination because Augustine tells us that it is the light of Christ, or the light of God, by which the mind is said to be able to discern the objects of intellectual vision. Thus near the end of *De Genesi ad litteram libri duodecim* Augustine writes:

> For that light is already God Himself; the soul, on the other hand, is a creature, although in reason and intellect it is made in his image. And when the soul tries to fix its gaze upon that light, it quivers in its weakness and is not quite able to do so. Yet it is from this light that the soul understands whatever it is able to understand. (12.31.59)

Some readers have supposed that it is only *a priori* truths that Augustine thinks are made intellectually visible by divine illumination. But this seems not to be correct. There are good reasons for thinking that, according to Augustine, all human understanding arises from this source. The quotation immediately above suggests the much broader view. In fact, as early as *De magistro* Augustine suggests that view. "Concerning everything we understand," he writes in that dialogue, "we consult, not the speaker who makes noises outside us, but the Truth that presides over the mind within" (11.38). As we noted above, to learn the truth about what a head covering is, Augustine supposes we must make use of the bodily senses. In fact, he thinks we must be able to perceive, with the bodily senses, an actual head covering. But the ambiguity of ostension means that no amount of seeing head coverings or pointing to them or having them displayed will make unambiguously clear what "head covering" signifies and hence what a head covering is. If we manage to grasp what a head covering is, it must be through the inner illumination of the divine light.

One might note here that the chief ancient rival to the doctrine of illumination is the Aristotelian idea of abstraction. According to that idea, when we come to know what, say, blue is, our passive intellect takes on, without the matter, the form of the object known. This idea of abstraction does not, of course, address the question of ambiguity in ostensive teaching. Thus the blue dress will have not only the form blue, but also the more specific form powder blue and the more general form color, as well as the form dress, and so on.

Perhaps Augustine's idea of *divine* illumination is meant to invoke supernatural aid in dealing with the problem of ambiguity. Thus perhaps Christ, the Teacher, can, through special powers, illuminate blue without illuminating anything more general, such as color, or anything more specific, such as powder blue. Again, Christ, the Inner Teacher, can perhaps, non-naturally, point to walking without pointing to hurrying, or to taking so and so many steps. If that is right, the learner who is intelligent enough will be precisely the one who is able to profit from this ambiguity-free inner ostension that only Christ, the Teacher, can perform.

A more obvious function of the doctrine of divine illumination is to account for our access to realities that can in no way be directly sensed. Question 46, "Concerning Ideas" (*De ideis*), of Augustine's *De diversis quaestionibus octoginta tribus* is clearly an attempt to offer a christianized interpretation of Plato's Theory of Forms. Augustine says there that these Forms may be referred to indifferently in Latin as *formae* ("forms"), *species* ("species"), or *rationes* ("reasons"). He then adds that they can be thought to exist nowhere but in the mind of the Creator. It would be sacrilegious, he adds, invoking the picture of creation from Plato's *Timaeus*, to think that God was looking at something outside himself when he created in accordance with it what he created.

Question 46 draws to a close with this peroration:

> But among the things which have been created by God, the rational soul, when it is pure, surpasses all [other things] and is closest to God. And in the measure in which it has clung to him in love, in that measure, imbued in some way and illuminated by him with intelligible light, the soul sees, not with physical eyes, but with its own highest part in which lies its excellence, i.e. with its intelligence, those reasons by the vision of which it becomes supremely blessed.

Knowledge of God

As mentioned above, Augustine begins his *Soliloquies* with the confession that the two things he wants to know are his soul and God. In Book 2 of *De libero arbitrio*, Augustine says to his interlocutor, Evodius: "At any rate you are quite certain that God exists." Evodius replies, "I firmly believe it, but I do not know it." There follows a discussion of "belief in search of understanding," a characteristic Augustinian idea, which is later picked up by St. Anselm. This section ends with Evodius' saying, "But we want to know and understand what we believe" (2.2.5).

The proof that Augustine later offers goes like this. First, Augustine gets Evodius to agree that

1. x is God if and only if x is more excellent than our minds and nothing is more excellent than x.

He then tries to establish that

2. Truth exists and it is more excellent than our minds.

From these two premises he concludes:

3. Something is God (i.e. God exists).

Augustine's idea is that either nothing is more excellent than truth, so that, since truth is more excellent than our minds, truth itself is God; or else something is more excellent even than truth, in which case it (or, we must add, something even more excellent than it) is God.

Augustine does not return to the project of offering an argument to prove the existence of God. About his own book *De vera religione*, written a year or so before the *Confessions*, he writes almost two decades later to his friend Evodius: "If you would review [that work] and look into it, it would never seem to you that reason can prove the necessity of God's existence, or that by reasoning it can be established that God must exist" (*Ep.* 162.2).

Augustine does, however, offer descriptions of mystical experiences that may be assumed to be autobiographical, and to have therefore revealed to him, as he supposes, some sort of direct knowledge of God. According to the account in Book 9 of the *Confessions*, he made the mystical ascent with his mother, Monica. The following description, like his other reports, echoes motifs common in the "ascent" tradition, which goes back to Plato's *Symposium;* yet even the familiar motifs are transformed with striking eloquence:

> If one is somehow snatched far away from his bodily senses, so that he is among those likenesses of bodies which are seen by the spirit, and then in the same way is snatched away from those so as to be carried into that, as it were, intellectual or

intelligible region where, without any bodily likeness, the clear truth is perceived, unobscured by any clouds of false opinion, there the virtues of the soul are not laborious and wearisome. For there desire is not bridled by the work of temperance, or adversities borne by the work of fortitude, or iniquities punished by the work of justice, or evils shunned by the work of prudence. There the one virtue and the whole of virtue is to love what you see and the greatest happiness is to have what you love. For there the heavenly life is drunk at its source, from which a little is splashed over onto this human life so that it is lived among the temptations of this world with temperance, with fortitude, with justice and with prudence . . . There the splendor of the Lord is seen, not through a symbolical or a bodily vision, as it was seen on Mt. Sinai, not through spiritual vision, as Isaiah saw it or John in the Book of Revelation, but through sight rather than through figures (*per speciem non per aenigmata*), as much as, by the additional grace of God, the human mind can grasp it, so that mouth speaks to mouth, God to him whom he has made worthy of such a dialogue, not the bodily mouth but that of the mind, as I think what is written of Moses is to be understood. (*De Gen. ad litt.* 12.26.54)

For Augustine, knowing God includes knowing that God exceeds our powers of comprehension, as well as our powers of description. As he puts the point in a sermon, "If you have been able to comprehend it, then it is God you contemplate" (*Sermons* 113.3.5). Sometimes, as in the very next section from *De Genesi ad litteram libri duodecim*, Augustine combines the idea of God as the source of epistemic illumination with the idea of God as a blinding light which, even as it enables us to bring other things into focus, cannot be brought into focus itself:

For the Light is God himself, whereas the soul is a creature . . . And when [the soul] tries to behold the Light, it trembles in its weakness and finds itself unable to do so. Yet from this source comes all the understanding [the soul] is able to entertain. (12.31.59)

Knowledge and philosophical understanding

In some of his early writings Augustine gives the impression that he thinks philosophical investigation may by itself yield the knowledge of important truths. But already in his *Confessions*, he admits that "we are too weak to discover the truth by reason alone and for this reason need the authority of the sacred books" (6.5.8). In his *De civitate Dei* he tries to scale back expectations we might have had for using philosophy to add to the store of our knowledge. "It is a great thing," he writes, "and quite exquisite, by sheer effort of mind to go beyond the created universe, both corporeal and incorporeal, and, having examined it and found it mutable, to arrive at the immutable being of God" (11.2). But now the liklihood of success in such an intense and ambitious philosophical undertaking is thought to be small, given the limitations of the human mind:

But because this very mind, in which reason and understanding are naturally present, is itself enfeebled by long-standing faults which darken it, it is too weak to cleave to that changeless light and to enjoy it; it is even too weak to endure it, until it has been renewed and healed day after day so as to become capable of such happiness. [And so the mind] had first to be imbued and purged by faith. (Ibid.)

Such devaluation of unaided reason and systematic philosophy is hardly unusual in Augustine's mature writing. So what is the importance for Augustine of philosophical investigation, if he considers its fruits are so meager and its results so unreliable?

We get a clue from Augustine's discussion of time in Book 11 of the *Confessions*. When Augustine there asks, "What then is time?" he comments, in a deservedly famous line, "If nobody asks me, I know; if I should want to explain [it] to a questioner, I don't know" (11.14.17). He then launches into what is perhaps the most famous of his philosophical excursions; the passage is also a classic text in the philosophy of time.

Perhaps the central puzzle that motivates Augustine's discussion of the nature of time is a perplexity about how time can be measured. Quite plausibly, Augustine takes it to be a basic datum that some times are short and some are long (10.15.18). Thus time can be measured. Yet, he supposes, in order to measure something one must have the object to be measured present for measurement. Yet of time, he reasons, not a century, not a year, not a month, nor a day, nor an hour, nor a minute is, strictly speaking, present. For any *period* of time that we call, loosely speaking, "present," some segment may be yet future and the remainder yet past, but no duration will actually be present. All that is present, he concludes, is a durationless divider between the future and the past. But that, being durationless, is certainly not long; strictly speaking, it is not a short time either.

The puzzle that motivates this discussion of time belongs to a family of philosophical perplexities that can be cast in the schematic form "How is it possible that *p*?" Here the puzzle is "How is it possible that some times are long and others short?" or, more succinctly, "How is it possible that we measure time?" Even philosophers who do not accept the conclusion that Augustine himself reaches in this passage – that time is the measure of something mental – may applaud the open and provocative way in which Augustine pursues his investigation.

Asking questions of the form "How is it possible that *p*?" is one of Augustine's persistent preoccupations. To be sure, such questions may be asked skeptically, in an effort to discredit the assumption that *p*, even to prove that *not p*. Thus when Zeno of Elea asked how it is possible that Achilles can catch up with the tortoise, he meant to show that Achilles can't really catch up, and more generally, that motion and change are illusory.

But questions of this form need not be asked skeptically. Thus when Kant asked how synthetic *a priori* knowledge is possible, he thought it certain that we have such knowledge, and therefore that having such knowledge is possible. He still wanted to know *how* it is possible. Augustine's interest in such questions is similar. He thinks he knows many things, perhaps not fully or adequately or satisfactorily, but nevertheless he knows them. Some things he knows are truths of common sense (for example, that some times are short, or that we can think about what pain is without being pained). Some things are truths of faith (for example, that God foreknew Adam would sin of his own free will). But even a truth that *p* about which Augustine harbors no doubt whatsoever may be to him profoundly perplexing. When Augustine finds such a truth perplexing he asks the philosopher's question, 'How is it possible that *p*?" And sometimes, though not always, reflection leads him to a philosophical understanding of how what he knows, or firmly believes, to be the case, can in fact be the case.

NOTES

1 I am here amending the position I took in Matthews 1972.
2 Earlier on in this work, at *De Trin.* 5.9.10, Augustine makes clear that he understands the philosophical meaning of *substantia* to be indifferent between "essence" and "substance." It seems clear that what Augustine needs for this argument for the incorporeality of the soul is the meaning "essence."

14

CHRISTOPHER KIRWAN

Augustine's philosophy of language

The "Augustinian picture"

Philosophers have come to speak of an Augustinian picture of language. The picture is not really Augustine's, as we shall see, but it makes a good starting point for exploring what his views actually were. Those views, though not as crude as the "Augustinian picture," will turn out to be mainly unoriginal, following a tradition that was already several hundred years old in his day, and helping to sustain that tradition for a further millennium and more. We know better now, thanks mainly to the fundamental insights of Frege and Wittgenstein.

It is, of course, Wittgenstein himself who presents us with the Augustinian picture. The *Brown Book* starts:

> Augustine, in describing his learning of language, says that he was taught to speak by learning the names of things. It is clear that whoever says this has in mind the way in which a child learns such words as "man", "sugar", "table", etc. He does not primarily think of such words as "today", "not", "but", "perhaps".
> (Wittgenstein 1958, 77)

When Wittgenstein later set out to put together the *Philosophical Investigations*, he promised himself that he should start "with a description of a situation from which the material for all that follows can be obtained" (paraphrase of MS vol. VI 243, Baker and Hacker 1980, 64). The situation he chose was suggested to him by the same passage from Augustine's *Confessions*, which he now quoted, translated and commented on as follows (I give Anscombe's English throughout, with a few of the original words):

> "When they (my elders) named [*appellabant*] some object, and accordingly moved towards something, I saw this and I grasped that the thing [*rem illam*] was called by the sound they uttered when they meant [*vellent*] to point it out. Their intention was shewn by their bodily movements, as it were the natural language [*verbis naturalibus*] of all peoples: the expression of the face, the play of the eyes, the movement of other parts of the body, and the tone of voice which expresses [*indicante*] our state of mind in seeking, having, rejecting or avoiding something. Thus, as I

heard words repeatedly used in their proper places in various sentences, I gradually learnt to understand what objects they signified [*quarum rerum signa essent*]; and after I had trained my mouth to form these signs, I used them to express [*enuntiabam*] my own desires." (Augustine, *Confessions* I 8 [13])

These words, it seems to me, give us a particular picture of the essence of human language. It is this: the individual words in language name objects – sentences are combinations of such names. – In this picture of language we find the roots of the following idea: Every word has a meaning [Bedeutung]. This meaning is correlated with the word. It is the object for which the word stands.

Augustine does not speak of there being any difference between kinds of word. If you describe the learning of language in this way you are, I believe, thinking primarily of nouns like "table", "chair", "bread", and of people's names, and only secondarily of the names of certain actions and properties; and of the remaining kinds of word as something that will take care of itself. (Wittgenstein 1953, 1.1)

What Wittgenstein misses in his comments on this little passage is that the early stages of language learning are of interest to Augustine in the *Confessions* not for what Augustine thinks he learnt, but for how he thinks he learnt it. Language is not just picked up; much of it is taught, by parents and others. But how does that succeed with infants, when the teachers cannot use language as their medium of instruction? Augustine's answer is complicated by doubts (aired, as we shall see, even in the *Confessions* passage itself) about the propriety of applying the word "teach" to any merely human informant. We shall have to come back to the doubts. Ignoring them for the moment, the answer to the "how?" question seems to be: teacher and infant communicate wordlessly, by the "natural language" of facial expression, tone of voice, and bodily movement. One of the many ways in which we can see such pre-linguistic communication at work, Augustine suggests, is in the business of teaching language itself, which can be illustrated from pointing and naming.

Wittgenstein's procedure is to fasten on the illustration; and what he says about it is beyond reproach. He is right, first, to point out that it would be a woeful mistake to infer from the illustration that learning the names for things is all that is necessary for mastery of a language. For one thing, as Wittgenstein immediately hints, not all words are names. But even if they were, they might be used for other purposes than naming – e.g. for giving instructions, as happens in the primitive "slab" language which Wittgenstein goes on to describe in *Philosophical Investigations* 1.2, and which he there says fits the "description given by Augustine."

Wittgenstein is also right in stating that Augustine does not guard against this mistake, for he "does not speak of there being any difference between kinds of word"; and we might add that Augustine's own example of a use of language, to express (state, *enuntiare*) his own desires, is so simple as not to be far away from mere naming. Finally, and crucially, there is plenty of reason to think that Wittgenstein is right in his implicit castigation of philosophers, and other theorists, for falling into the same mistake when they start to think about language. Many there have surely been who have been tempted to adopt as their "picture of the essence of human language" the picture of a system of names.

But Augustine was not one of them. He knew better, because he knew his grammar. He actually wrote a book about grammar. As he tells us in *Retractationes*, the review or 're-treatment' of 93 of his works which he composed near the end of his life in 426 or 427,

> At the time I was about to receive baptism in Milan [spring 387], I also set out to write textbooks [*disciplinarum libros*], questioning those who were with me and who were not averse to that kind of study. My ambition was to advance, and lead others, from the corporeal to the incorporeal by, as it were, sure footsteps. But the only ones I managed to finish were a book on grammar [*De grammatica*] which later I lost from our library, and six volumes on music which cover the part of the subject called rhythm; and I wrote those six books only after I had been baptized and had returned from Italy to Africa [388], having no more than begun work on the subject at Milan. The other five textbooks, on dialectic, rhetoric, geometry, arithmetic, and philosophy, were similarly begun there; but only their first parts remained, and I lost even those, though I believe that some people have them. (*Retract.* 1.5)

These books could have survived elsewhere than in Augustine's library at Hippo; as we shall see, one of them, on dialectic, probably did and does. But the one on grammar probably does not. There is a sketch *De grammatica* copied in various medieval MSS and printed in various early modern editions under Augustine's name: it is no more than a scrap, examining, without preamble, the accidence (terminations, genders, inflections, tenses, moods, etc.) of words which it groups under eight different headings: nouns, pronouns, verbs, adverbs, participles, conjunctions, prepositions, interjections. These are the eight parts of Latin speech, "partes orationis," that had become standard in later Roman antiquity and are familiar to us through the tradition of Priscian's sixth-century *Institutiones grammaticae* ("noun" translates *nomen*, the ordinary word for "name," and *verbum* does double duty, both for "verb" and in its ordinary sense of "word"). But this *De grammatica* – which is extremely dull – seems unlikely to be Augustine's, a small indication being that it prescribes a construction (*libet mihi*) without permitting the unusual variant (*libet me*) which according to the Maurist editors Augustine invariably preferred. We cannot even be sure that parts of speech were covered in Augustine's book, because in his day the word "grammar" could still refer to literary as well as linguistic studies – meter, for example, though Augustine dealt with that in his *De musica*. Nevertheless there can be little doubt that Augustine knew about the parts of speech: he mentions them in *De dialectica* (e.g. 5.8, see below), if that work is authentic; and in *De magistro*, an early work (389) which does survive – we shall return to it – and which is cast as a dialogue between himself and his bright young son Adeodatus, he makes Adeodatus say that "*si*" ("if") and "*ex*" ("from") are "words [*verba*], yet not nouns [or names, *nomina*]; and many such are found" (*De mag.* 4.9). Thus Augustine repudiated the view that it is of the essence of human language that "the individual words in language name objects."[1]

The purpose of language

This first result rescues Augustine from being an oger in the history of the philosophy of language. But we must be cautious about jumping to the conclusion that he is a paragon. The rescue has appealed to his knowledge of (what we call) grammar; and although grammar's successes during ancient times in the area we are considering (the first of them coming, so far as we know, with a distinction by Plato which is like ours between nouns and verbs; Plato, *Sophist* 262a) were hard won and ought to command admiration, Augustine himself had no role in those successes; on the contrary, his son's comment in *De magistro*, "And many such are found," applies what was, by the fourth century, a mere commonplace of the schoolroom. We have yet to see whether Augustine made contributions of his own.

In order to do so it is necessary now to look further than the *Confessions*. There, Augustine had used language acquisition to test ideas about human teaching, or what passes for human teaching. The motivation is characteristic. Although circumstances were to compel him to give most of his life to the activities of a pastor and a controversialist, Augustine's natural aptitudes had a somewhat different, but also double, focus: teaching and philosophy. It is therefore not surprising that the intersection of these two, namely philosophizing about teaching, should often have occupied his mind, especially while his professional teaching career (roughly to 376 to 386) was still fresh in view (the *Confessions* were completed about 400). One result of this fascination is *De magistro* itself, "On the Teacher," written before his ordination (and shortly before his son's early death), which leads from a discussion whether teaching is effected through signs (*signa*) to the conclusion that is it not a route to knowledge at all, unless God is the teacher. Another work, *De doctrina christiana*, started before 400 but completed a quarter-century or more later, is also set in the frame of a general discussion of teaching (*docere*, cognate with *doctrina*), which Augustine now divides between the teaching of things, *res*, and of signs, *signa*.

But is human teaching possible at all? This postponed question now needs to be faced. According to Wittgenstein, Augustine said in the *Confessions* that he was "taught to speak" (Wittgenstein 1958, 77). Burnyeat has pointed out

(Burnyeat 1987, 2–4) that, on the contrary, the sentence preceding Wittgenstein's quotation from *Conf.* 1.8.13 contains Augustine's statement that "It wasn't that my elders had been teaching me," and goes on to imply that he had been finding out for himself, using God's gift to him of a mind.[2] Burnyeat refers to *Retractationes*, where Augustine comments on *De magistro* (which had been composed some ten years before the *Confessions*):

> At the same time I wrote a book entitled *De magistro*, in which after discussion and investigation it is discovered that there is no teacher who teaches men knowledge (*scientia*) except God, as is in fact written in the Gospel: "One is your teacher, Christ" [Matthew 23.10]. (*Retract.* 1.11)

The argument in *De magistro* for this conclusion need not concern us here; but the conclusion presents a problem, for it seems to banish all human teaching. The solution of the problem can be put briefly: the conclusion at least does not banish the transmission of information from one human being to another, which is all that matters for our purposes. The rest is quibbling. Augustine can – and often does – call such transmission teaching, either because (as Burnyeat suggests) he understands *De magistro*, as the *Retractationes* carefully reports, to ban only human teaching "of knowledge (*scientia*)," *scientia* being (as Burnyeat documents) for Augustine a Platonistically austere conception; or because he permits an "improper" usage of "teach" to match the improper usage of "know" that (as Burnyeat points out) is sanctioned by *Retract.* 1.13.3.

In either case human teaching is after all possible, and *De magistro* and *De doctrina christiana* share an interest in finding out how it happens – how the contents of one mind can be conveyed to another. It was obvious to Augustine, of course, that among humans the chief instrument of this conveyance is language. The role is so important that Augustine does not hesitate to describe it as the purpose of language:

> And undoubtedly, words were instituted among men not so that men should deceive one another by means of them but so that anyone might bring his thoughts (*cogitationes*) to another's notice by means of them. (*Enchiridion de fide, spe et caritate* 22.7, composed in 423)

> I posit two reasons for speaking: either to teach, or to remind others or ourselves. (*De mag.* 1.1)

In addition to *De magistro* and *De doctrina christiana* there is one other work to be added, if it is authentic, to the list of sources for Augustine's philosophy of language: *De dialectica*. This comes down to us in a number of MSS, in some of which it is anonymous while others attribute it variously to Augustine or, for almost certainly negligible reasons, to a barely identifiable contemporary of his called Fortunatianus. The work is incomplete, exactly fitting the description in

Retractationes, "Only its first part remains." At one point in it the author identifies himself as "Augustinus" (*De dialectica* 7.13). After long doubts, modern
scholarship comes down in favour of identifying this work with the textbook on
dialectic referred to at *Retract.* 1.6.[3]

Signs

From these three works we get a clear view of how Augustine supposes that language fulfils its purpose of conveying information. It does so by *signifying*:

> All teaching (*doctrina*) is of things (*res*) or signs (*signa*), but things are learnt
> through signs. . . . There are . . . signs, such as words (*verba*), whose sole use is in
> signifying (*significando*). For no one uses words except for the purpose of signify-
> ing something. (*De doct. christ.* 1.2.2)

Words as well as speakers can be said to signify, and each word is a separate sign:

> AUGUSTINE. Are we agreed then that words are signs?
> ADEODATUS. We are.
> AUG. How can a sign be a sign unless it signifies something?
> AD. It cannot.
> AUG. How many words are there in this verse?
> 　　Si nihil ex tanta superis placet urbe relinqui
> 　　[If it please the gods that nothing should be left from this great city: Virgil, *Aeneid*
> 　　2.659]
> AD. Eight.
> AUG. Then there are eight signs.
> AD. Yes. (*De mag.* 2.3)

De doctrina christiana expatiates on signs. They are of two kinds, natural (*nat-
uralia*) and given (*data*):

> The natural ones are those which, without a will (*voluntas*) or any kind of urge to
> signify, cause something else beyond themselves to be recognized from them. An
> example is smoke signifying fire, which it does without willing to signify; rather by
> observation of and attention to familiar phenomena it is recognized that there is
> fire lurking, even if only smoke is apparent. The track of a passing animal belongs
> to this kind; and a face will signify the state of mind of someone who is angry or
> sad, even without any will on the part of the angry or sad person. . . . Given signs
> are those which living things give among themselves for demonstrating, so far as
> they are able, the impulses of their mind (*motus animi sui*), or whatever it may be
> that they have sensed or understood. There is no reason for our signifying – that is,
> giving a sign – except to express and transmit (*depromendum et traiciendum*) to
> someone else's mind what is going on in the mind of him who gives the sign. (*De
> doct. christ.* 2.1.2–2.2.3)

Given signs need not be verbal, or even human. But

> Words have acquired complete dominance among men for signifying anything conceived in the mind that anyone may wish to communicate (*prodere*). (*De doct. christ.* 2.3.4)

Words are signs, then, given for the purpose of conveying information. But what are they signs *of*? On this crucial question Augustine's answers are neither clear nor clearly consistent; and we shall be led by the evidence to conclude that what mainly is to be learnt from his engagement with the philosophy of language is the inadequacy of theories such as his. For this we need not seriously blame him. Though he wished for a scholarly or semi-scholarly life, the wish was granted to him only for the few years between conversion at Milan (386) and ordination at Hippo (391). That period – plus his earlier education – afforded him time to learn something of the tradition of ancient philosophy of language, mainly, we shall find, the Stoic tradition. But Stoicism was not, in that part of philosophy, a sufficiently firm foundation.

Signs are indications, and indications are either evidence or reminders. (The other meaning of the Latin *signum*, "representation," may also sometimes be present below the surface of Augustine's mind.) Augustine rejected the Platonic thesis that what passes for teaching is really reminding, the calling back to pupils' minds of opinions that had been "in" them since before birth (*Meno* 85b–e). So for him, if words are to be instruments of teaching, their work must include the supplying of evidence. One way they could do so is by being evidence of the truth of the lesson to be taught, the information to be conveyed. But that could happen variously. Suppose, for example, that I wished to convey to you the information that I can speak French. I could give you evidence by speaking French. The evidence would be a sign, and a verbal one, but in this case it would do its job only because of the very special nature of the information it is evidence for, namely information about my verbal competence. Evidence for information of other kinds – that Jones speaks French, that there will an eclipse tomorrow – must, if it is verbal, proceed differently. In one recurrent characterization, Augustine identifies what is signified by a speaker's utterance as the state of the speaker's mind: we signify that which is "conceived in the mind that anyone may wish to communicate" (*De doct. christ.* 2.3.4); "one who speaks gives forth a sign of his will" (*De mag.* 1.2); we "demonstrate, so far as [we] are able, the impulses of [our] mind" (*De doct. christ.* 2.1.2 above). Information is conveyed in speech by being "expressed" (*De doct. christ.* 2.2.3). According to Augustine, then, speech is a means of mind-exposure, and speakers expose their minds by giving signs of their minds' contents.

As an account of the procedure for conveying information verbally, this is fine so far as it goes. But as a general account of how language works it is not fine, for at least two reasons. In the first place, it requires verbal expressions actually to be signs, not (merely) to be intended as such; but speech which is intended as a sign of the speaker's state of mind may fall short of actually being a sign of his state of mind in Augustine's sense of "indication," for the speaker's audience may have good reason to judge – whether rightly or wrongly – that the speaker is not "teaching" but lying. (In the quotation above from *De doctrina christiana* 2.2 it is the genus *sign*, not the differentia *given for demonstrating*, which makes lying a counter-example to Augustine's thesis.) And secondly, speech need not even be intended as a sign of the speaker's state of mind, if, for example, it is uttered on the stage. Thus, even though one might say (compare the passage at *Enchiridion de fide, spe et caritate* 22.7 cited above) that the *point* of having words such as "There will be an eclipse tomorrow" is so that speakers can use them as a sign of their so believing, nevertheless one cannot say that those words *are*, always and necessarily, a sign of their so believing.

These objections might be met by giving a more complex account of the nature of linguistic signification: for example, by explicating "signifies the belief/desire that . . ." as "has the (conventional) role of giving a sign of having the belief/desire that . . ." But there is another and deeper objection to Augustine's proposal, which arises from the application of the proposal to individual words.

The unit of speech that is employed to "express and transmit to someone else's mind what is going on in the mind of him who gives the sign" (*De doct. christ.* 2.2.3) will rarely be a single word and will usually be a many-worded sentence. Yet individual words too are reckoned by Augustine to be signs. What are they signs of?

The obvious answer to this new question is not "thoughts" but "things." Here is the opening of *De dialectica*:

> A word (*verbum*) is a sign (*signum*) of any kind of thing (*res*), which can be understood by a hearer, and is uttered by a speaker. A thing is whatever is sensed or understood or is hidden. A sign is what shows both itself to the senses and something beyond itself to the mind. To speak is to give a sign by an articulate utterance. By articulate I mean one that can be comprised of letters. (*De dialectica* 5.7)

Augustine would doubtless have amplified this textbook sketch, if he had spent more time on the book. He does amplify its first sentence, with frank attention to the difficulties, in his discussion in *De magistro* of the line from Virgil already quoted:

> si nihil ex tanta superis placet urbe relinqui.

Having established that the line contains eight signs, Augustine goes on:

AUGUSTINE. I suppose you understand this verse.
ADEODATUS. Well enough, I think.
AUG. Tell me what (*quid*) its individual words signify.

AD. I'm aware what "*si*" ["if"] signifies; but I can't find any other word that I'm able to explain it by.

AUG. Can't you at least find the whereabouts of whatever is signified by this word?

AD. It looks to me as if "*si*" signifies doubt; and where is doubt if not in the mind? (*De mag.* 2.3)

"In the mind" seems to be the answer that Augustine's last question was inviting; and that suggests that he is keen to introduce the idea – not yet explicit in *De magistro* – that words signify states of mind. We can well imagine that not only propositional thoughts, such as the thought that there will be an eclipse tomorrow, but also states of mind, such as doubt, are to be counted among the *cogitationes* at *Enchiridion de fide, spe et caritate* 22.7 and the "impulses of the mind" at *De doct. christ.* 2.2.3. But if so, what of the different word "doubt" ("*dubitatio*")? Does "doubt" also signify doubt? Do "doubt" and "if" therefore signify the same thing? Must we distinguish different modes of signification, at least for words belonging to different parts of speech? The last of these questions gets an airing at *De mag.* 5.12, with the somewhat perfunctory suggestion that etymology can distinguish between adjectives ("visible" and "colored") that have the same extension. Here, meanwhile, the dialogue continues:

AUGUSTINE. I'll accept that for now. Go on.

ADEODATUS. "*Nihil*" ["nothing"]: what can that signify except what is not?

AUG. You may be right, but that cancels my assent to what I conceded earlier, that it is not a sign unless it signifies something. If a thing is not, it certainly cannot be something. (*De mag.* 2.3)

Father and son agree that this won't do, but they cannot find a solution; and the next word, "*ex*" ("from"), proceeds to baffle them in its turn.

"'Nothing' signifies nothing" suggests at least a formula, even though one that fails to work for that teasing word. One might speculate that, in general, the textbook thesis that *words* signify *things* gets its appeal from the cases in which such a formula does work. These are what modern logic calls referring expressions or subject expressions or designators, including proper names and (in Latin which has no articles) some uses of common nouns. Such words do signify things: they signify what they refer to. But this line of thought should alert us to two conclusions, which are surely among the lessons that ought to be learnt from Augustine's inspection of the Virgil line.

The first lesson is that proper names and common nouns tend to behave very differently from one another, despite their being grouped by Augustine's grammar (though not by earlier Stoics) under the same part of speech: for a central function of common nouns – as of adjectives, traditionally a third kind of "noun" – is to form part of a verb phrase ("is a soldier," "is wealthy") in which no sub-part signifies a thing (Adeodatus was not a soldier; so which soldier does "soldier" signify in the sentence "Adeodatus was a soldier"?). Augustine tackles common nouns later in *De magistro,* with the example *fluvius* ("river," 4.8): he says that *fluvius* signifies rivers, all of them. Yet that cannot be the right thing to say, since the Tiber, for instance, which is a river, is not all rivers (neither is it the class of rivers).

The second and more general lesson to be learnt from Augustine's discussion of the Virgil line is that in examining the way words work in a language it is necessary to distinguish between what to say of each word taken in abstraction (the word-type) and what to say about particular uses of the word (its tokens, or perhaps certain classes of its tokens). It might be claimed, for example, that the words "Elizabeth" and "I" both signify my sister Elizabeth, but we have to recognize that the former signifies her only when it is used of her, and the latter only when it is used by her; contrast the word "and" which, if it signifies at all, has much the same signification over most of its range in English use. The Graeco-Latin concept of signification banefully blurs that distinction (and is not alone in doing so: compare English "mean," or French "vouloir dire").

Stoic dialectic

These lessons, it must be said, were lost on Augustine. But before we write him off as a philosopher of language, we must next look at a further text which seems to tie him back into some at least of the greater sophistication that had been achieved in the centuries before him by Stoicism. The text is a short one, and its brevity cannot help leaving doubt in the reader's mind whether he understood what he was drawing on. But it provides a possible explanation of the route by which he advanced to what has the best claim to be counted as his original contribution to the philosophy of language, the concept of inner words.

Before I quote the text, it will be useful to interpose here some general remarks about Stoicism and its influence on this fourth-century Christian. There is a temptation to overestimate the influence, for the double reason that the Stoics were beyond doubt the most potent source of intellectual endeavour over a long spread of centuries during ancient times (roughly 300 BC to AD 200), and that examination of their legacy is currently fashionable. In the case of Augustine, however, no one disputes that among pagan schools it was not the Stoics who had the greatest importance for his formation, but Platonism, revived and transmuted by Plotinus (AD 204/5–270) and transmitted to Augustine through the Christians around Ambrose and Simplicianus, successively bishops of Milan, whom he had met during his years there. Yet despite Augustine's attention being directed elsewhere, Stoicism in the late fourth century remained an unavoidable influence, some of which can be traced in his writings. He must, in particular, have known something of Stoic "dialectic."

Dialectic, originally the practice of reasoning between enquirers and later also the study of that practice, had further widened its scope within the classification of sciences adopted by the Stoics. According to one of our sources, it was defined by Chrysippus (c.280 – c.206 BC), the most eminent and prolific of the school's many heads, as the science concerned with "what signifies and what is signified" (Diogenes Laertius, *Lives of the Philosophers* 7.62). Another source, Sextus Empiricus (AD c.200), elaborates the distinction:

> The Stoics said that three things are linked to one another, the thing signified, the thing that signifies, and the thing come upon [*to tunchanon*]. Of these the thing that signifies is an utterance [*phōnē*], e.g. the utterance 'Dio'; the thing signified is the very state of affairs [*pragma*] revealed by an utterance, and which we Greeks apprehend as it subsists in accordance with our thought, whereas non-Greek-speakers do not understand it although they hear the utterance; and the thing come upon is the external subject [*ektos hupokeimenon*], e.g. Dio himself. (*Adversus mathematicos* 8.12)

No work by Chrysippus or any other early Stoic survives, so that we are dependent on reports and occasional quotations by "doxographers" from later antiquity – who usually attribute what they report to "Stoics" collectively. But this passage of Sextus is well confirmed by other sources (see e.g. Long and Sedley 1987, 1.195–202).

The passage describes a theory of signification different from both those that we have offered in explanation of the texts so far examined in Augustine. Sextus does not tell us how widely its theory is meant to be generalized, but at least in the case of the word "Dio," a proper name, the theory holds that what the name signifies is neither its bearer, Dio – who occupies the third role of "what is come upon" – nor a thought in the mind of one who speaks the name. What it signifies is rather a state of affairs – its nature here unspecified – when that accords with the thought of anyone who hears the name and understands the language to which it belongs. The Stoics, who did not shy from technical vocabulary, called such items *lekta*, sayables. Unlike external objects such as Dio, and thoughts such as my or your conception of Dio, *lekta*, they held, are incorporeal.[4]

The literal Latin translation of *lekton* would be *dicibile*, a neologism from which earlier Latin commentators on the Stoics, such as Cicero and Seneca, had abstained. In Latin texts surviving from antiquity the word *dicibile* occurs in a single passage only, chapter 5 of the *De dialectica* of Augustine. We know that *De dialectica* is responsive to the Stoics, because in chapter 9 its author attributes to "the dialecticians" a view about ambiguity which is characteristically theirs. In chapter 5 he does not refer to any authority. Here is how the chapter ends (I leave the key terms in Latin):

> But sounds are not the concern of dialectic. For we concern ourselves with the sound of a *verbum* [word] when we ask or attend to the question how speech is smoothed

by spreading the vowels or split up by juxtaposing them, or again how it is shaped by setting consonants at intervals or harshened by crowding them together, or how many syllables it has and of what kind, or where there is poetic rhythm and accent. Such matters having to do with hearing alone are treated by the *grammaticus* [grammarian, or grammar teacher], although any dispute about them is not outside the concern of dialectic, since dialectic is the science of discussion.

Verba are signs of *res* [things] whenever *res* are our subject, but of *verba* when those are under discussion; for since we cannot speak about *verba* except in *verba* and we never speak without speaking about something or other, the mind recognizes that *verba* are signs of *res* without themselves ceasing to be *res*. Hence any *verbum* that issues from the mouth, if it is issued for its own sake – that is, with the purpose of asking or discussing something about the *verbum* itself – is obviously the *res* subject to discussion and question, although that *res* is called a *verbum*.

But whatever is perceived from a *verbum* by the mind, not the ears, and is kept shut up in the mind itself, is called a *dicibile* [sayable]. When a *verbum* is issued not for its own sake but for the sake of signifying something else, it is called a *dictio* [saying]. The *res* itself, which is not a *verbum* nor the conception of a *verbum* in the mind, is called merely a *res* in the proper sense of that name.

So these four must be kept distinct: *verbum, dicibile, dictio, res*. The "*verbum*" in this list [literally: "which I have just said"] both is a *verbum* and signifies a *verbum*. The *dicibile* in the list is a *verbum*; however it signifies not a *verbum* but what is understood in a *verbum* and confined in the mind. The "*dictio*" in the list is a *verbum* but signifies both together of the things signified by the first two, that is, both the *verbum* itself and what is brought about [*fit*] in the mind by means of the *verbum*. The "*res*" in the list is a *verbum* which signifies whatever remains beyond the other three in the list.

But I can see that all this needs to be illustrated by examples. So take the case of a boy being questioned by a *grammaticus* as follows: "What part of speech is 'arms' ['*arma*', the opening word of the *Aeneid*]?" "Arms," as said [literally: "which has been said"], is said for its own sake, that is, the *verbum* for the sake of the *verbum*. The remaining things that he says, "what part of speech?," are mentally perceived, or vocally uttered, not for their own sake but for the sake of the *verbum* "arms" as said. But when they are mentally perceived, before utterance they will be *dicibilia*, but for the reasons I have given they will become *dictiones* when they have escaped into utterance. "Arms" itself, which is here a *verbum*, was a *dictio* when enunciated by Virgil, because it was not uttered for its own sake but in order that the wars waged by Aeneas, or his shield, or the rest of what Vulcan forged for our hero, should be signified by it. The wars or arms themselves that were waged or worn by Aeneas, I mean the things which during the waging and during their existence were visible, and which we could point to or touch if they were present now, which even if they were not being thought [*cogitentur*] would not thereby be made not to have existed – those things of themselves are neither *verba* nor *dicibilia* nor *dictiones* but *res*, now called *res* in the proper sense of the name.

In this part of dialectic we have to treat of *verba*, of *dicibilia*, of *dictiones*, and of *res*. Among these it is sometimes *verba*, sometimes not *verba*, that are signified, but in every case the discussion is necessarily in *verba*. Accordingly, let us begin by discussing these, not denying that discussion of the others will be by means of these. (*De dialectica* 5.7–8)

The exposition is laborious, and Augustine finds it difficult, in particular, to explain the difference between using and mentioning a word. Stripping that difficulty away (which for us is eased by the convention of quotation marks, unknown to ancient scripts), we can begin by examining Augustine's distinction between *verbum* and *dictio*. (The latter may translate the Stoic "*lexis*", but, if so, departs from its standard Stoic sense.) According to Augustine, when Virgil enunciated "*arma*," "*arma*" was a *dictio*; whereas the grammar teacher, asking after its part of speech, enunciates only a *verbum*. The difference lies in what "is brought about in the mind by means of the *verbum*," that is, the presence, consequent on the *verbum*'s utterance, of a particular effect of that utterance in the mind of the audience. Normally, we must suppose, that effect is present (because normally the speaker is rational in expecting it). Augustine seeks to illustrate the contrasting abnormal case in which there is no such effect, and he hits on the example of somebody talking *about* a *verbum* – something that he must in any event explain, on the threshold of a book which will have to engage in just that activity. The grammar teacher asking about parts of speech aims to produce in his pupil's mind, and is supposed by Augustine standardly to succeed in producing, a thought not of the *res* of which "*arma*" is normally a sign, but of the *verbum* of which it is a sign during the lesson – itself.

The example calls for two comments. First, it does not work as an illustration of the contrast between *verbum* and *dictio*, because what is special to the former is supposed to be that it does not include the effects it produces, whereas what is special to the *verbum* in the grammar teacher's mouth is that the effect it produces is an abnormal one, the thought not of a *res* but of itself. Secondly, however, no other example would improve matters, because the distinction between a word, *verbum*, and a word together with its effect, *dictio*, is misconceived. Words are inert and have no effects; effects come from their use. The distinction Augustine needs is between words themselves on the one hand – the word-types – and their uses in utterance on the other – word-tokens. We shall find in the end, however, that even if we are allowed to reclothe Augustine's doctrine about *dictiones* as a doctrine about the uses of words, it still embodies a deeply erroneous theory, Speech–thought Isomorphism.

For the moment I postpone that, in order to say something about another of *De dialectica*'s categories, the *dicibile*.

According to the passage we are examining, the word *dictio* "signifies both the first two," that is, the combination of a *verbum* and a *dicibile*. Since a *dictio* is a *verbum* plus the thought caused by its utterence, it follows that a *dicibile* must be the latter, the thought caused: it is what is left over from a *dictio* when you subtract its component *verbum*. But that is not all. The passage also tells us that *dicibilia*, besides being what in the process of verbal communication end up in the hearer's mind, are also what start off – and, of course, may remain – in the speaker's mind: they are items that are "mentally perceived, before utterance," and become *dictiones* on utterance. They are thus the mental counterpart of words.

It is worth asking how the Augustinian conception of a *dicibile* compares with the Stoic conception of a *lekton*. It seems that the similarities are few. Like *lekta*, *dicibilia* are incorporeal, but that, which was a major concession by the materialist Stoics, is no big deal for Augustine, whose Platonism saw all superior entities – God, the souls of animals, the things contained in those souls – as incorporeal. On the other hand, it results from this same Platonism that Augustine has no motive for denying what the Stoics denied of *lekta*: that *dicibilia*, being among the soul's contents ("shut up in the mind," "confined in the mind"), are to be identified with thoughts or conceptions; and he does not deny it but seems – as I have taken him – to accept it. Moreover, and crucially for our major theme, *dicibilia* play no role in Augustine's account of signification in *De dialectica*: the chapter in which they turn up had begun by announcing that *verba* are signs and *res* are signified, yet *dicibilia* are neither *verba* nor *res*. We can conclude that even if Augustine learnt the terminology of *De dialectica* chapter 5 from Stoic or sub-Stoic sources, he either misunderstood the sources or deliberately adapted them to his own purposes.

Inner words

More important than the relationship with Stoics is the question whether those purposes endured in Augustine's later thought. Of course, as we have seen, he continued to be interested in signification, and was to discuss its nature, in *De magistro* and especially in *De doctrina christiana*, much more thoroughly than had been done in *De dialectica* before he lost that work or put it by. But what about *dicibilia*, the vehicle by which, according to *De dialectica*, language performs its mind-exposing and thought-transmitting function? The word *dicibile* did not survive into Augustine's later writings; but that is not surprising, given that from the time of his ordination, at latest, he always wrote for a Christian audience or (in *De civitate Dei*) as a Christian apologist. Our question, rather, is whether the conception survived. In particular, is it present in Augustine's later theory of inner words?

The investigation of this can well start from *De quantitate animae*, a work he composed in 387 or 388 before his return from Italy to Africa. This too is a dialogue, and as in *De magistro*, its author is once more a participant, now with his friend (and later fellow bishop) Evodius. Augustine is explaining how an animal body can be mutilated without thereby "cutting" the animal's soul (*anima*). He uses an analogy:

EVODIUS. All right, I accept that a signifying sound is one thing, the *res* which is signified another.

AUGUSTINE. Then tell me whether you, who are well acquainted with Latin, can in speaking name the sun, if understanding of the sun [or "sun"?] does not precede the sound?

EV. I certainly cannot.

AUG. Now, before the name itself is uttered from your mouth, suppose that, wishing to pronounce it, you hold yourself in silence for a time. Does not something stay in your thought (*cogitatio*) which someone else is about to hear vocally expressed?

EV. Obviously.

AUG. Now the sun is a great size; but can the notion of it (*notio*), which you hold in your thought in advance of speech (*ante vocem*), seem long or broad or anything of that kind?

EV. Certainly not.

AUG. Well tell me, when the name itself escapes from your mouth and I, hearing it, think of (*cogito*) the sun which you have been thinking of in advance of speech and during speech – when, as it might be, we now both think of it – does it not seem to you that the name itself received from you, so to speak, the signification it was to convey to me through my ears?

EV. It does.

AUG. So since the name itself is made up (*constet*) of sound and signification, and the sound reaches the ears but the signification reaches the mind, do you not think that the sound is in the name, in the way that the body is in a living thing, whereas the signification is, so to speak, the soul of the sound? (*De quant. anim.* 32.65–66)

How does this relate to *De dialectica* 5? It retains from that passage the doctrines that what a word signifies is a *res*, that the *res* is to be distinguished from the thought (*notio* or *cogitatio*) which has been conveyed by speaking the word, and that the thought is incorporeal (it does not "seem long or broad or anything of that kind"). It also retains the idea that thought precedes the moment when "the name itself escapes from your mouth." What is new is division of the word into two aspects, sound and signification, and identification of the thought with that signification (but not with what is signified). Words have become significant sounds, and their signification *consists* in the thought that precedes and accompanies their utterance.[5]

It is not a long step from this view to treating the thought that accompanies a sound as itself a kind of word. Augustine seems to have been led to take the step by reflection on the word of God, which cannot be a sound because God is incorporeal, and which is heard in the heart and not through the ears. He always expounds inner words in a religious context, often, interestingly, in sermons (e.g., with their dates: 288.3, 401; 225.3.3, between 400 and 405; 179.7.7, before 409; 187.3.3, before 411–412).

There are also many references to inner words in *De Trinitate* (composed over the years 399 to 419), which explores elaborate analogies between the triune deity and the human mind (e.g. 8.6.9; 9.7.12; 9.10.15; 15.10.17; 15.10.19; 15.15.25). I shall quote only one passage, from a collection of sermons on John's Gospel dating from c.407 to c.416:

> Observe your own heart. When you conceive a word to be spoken – I shall describe, if I can, what we observe in ourselves, not how we come to grasp it – when you conceive a word to be produced, there is something which you wish to say and the very conception of that in your heart is a word: not yet uttered, but already born in your heart and waiting to be uttered. You take note who it is to be uttered to, who you are talking to: if he is Latin, you search for a Latin utterance; if he is Greek, you think of Greek words; if Punic, you see whether you know any Punic. Matching the differences in your audience, you employ different languages in order to produce the word you have conceived; but what you had conceived in your heart was confined to no language. (*In Johannis evangelium tractatus* 3.14.7)

When Plato, seven and a half centuries earlier, had introduced the idea of thought as inner speech (*Theaetetus* 189e, *Sophist* 263e), he was in the midst of strenuous philosophical discussion. Augustine, on the other hand, is preaching, and knows that some of the folk in his Hipponese, or sometimes Carthaginian, congregation are "a little on the slow side" (*tardiores*, *Sermons* 52.20, cf. 247.1). Characteristically, then, he seeks to persuade by making his audience think of something utterly familiar, the rehearsal of words or "saying to yourself" that may precede utterance. He then adds, plausibly enough in a cosmopolitan maritime city, that a rehearsed speech may need different words, indeed different languages, depending on who it is addressed to. And finally he springs his surprise: before utterance the words are in *no* language (cf. *Sermons* 288.3, 225.3.3, 187.3.3; *De Trin.* 15.10.19). So they are not a rehearsal after all, and nothing remains to stop us generalizing the inner word doctrine to cover all thought whatever – as other texts do, although not this one.

I have called the *dicibilia* in Augustine's *De dialectica* the mental counterpart of words. We can now see that he continued to believe in these counterparts. He differed from the Stoics in identifying what "we . . . apprehend as it subsists in accordance with our thought" as something mental: it *is* a thought or conception or notion (though at one place Augustine says *notum*, "thing noted": *De Trin.* 11.10.15). And he also differed from the Stoics in describing the counterparts not as what words signify, but as themselves a kind of languageless word.

Isomorphism of speech and thought

These differences may be for the worse. Many philosophers have been skeptical of the inner speech theory (Wittgenstein 1953, 1.330ff.); and the notion of words in no language is surely not a starter (champions of mentalese perhaps do not mean "*language* of thought" seriously; if they do not, they will not foist mental *words* on us). But I shall pass over these doubts in order to propound a criticism of a different sort, one which does not depend on any of the conspicuous differences between Augustine and the Stoics and may in the end (although of course I shall not argue that here) apply to some Stoic ideas as well. It is a criticism of what I call Speech–thought Isomorphism, which must now be introduced.

Augustine has founded his theorizing about language on the underlying principle that its general function is to transmit thoughts from one mind to another. Words do that by signifying thoughts; and signification is not only a property of grouped words, such as sentences, but extends all the way down to the individual word itself. We are therefore to understand the thought-transmitting function as one that is performed not only sentence by sentence but word by word, each word in an utterance conveying a sort of sub-thought which the hearer reassembles into the speaker's message. It is as if in a music-broadcasting system, each note in a chord were encoded separately into a radio signal and the signals transmitted one after another, to be rejoined into the simultaneous notes of the chord by the receiving apparatus. In order for that to be a possible method of chord transmission, chords must be analysable into constituent notes, each one signified by a distinct radio signal. Just so, Augustine seems to assume, in order for language to be a possible method of thought transmission, thoughts must be analysable into constituent elements, each one signified by a distinct word. There must be a one–one correspondence between the elements of a sentence, which are words, and the elements of the thought signified by that sentence. That is Speech–thought Isomorphism.

Speech–thought Isomorphism is not stupid. It is wrong, but wrong by being a mislocation, or misdescription, of one of those truths that are so obvious as to go without saying, and that therefore risk going without accurate identification: the truth that thoughts which can express beliefs, desires, questions, and the like are structured. In *The Varieties of Reference*, Gareth Evans expounded the truth in question as follows:

> I should prefer to explain the sense in which thoughts are structured, not in terms of their being composed of several distinct *elements*, but in terms of their being a complex of the exercise of several distinct conceptual *abilities*. Thus someone who thinks that John is happy and that Harry is happy exercises on two occasions the conceptual ability which we call "possessing the concept of happiness." And similarly someone who thinks that John is happy and that John is sad exercises on two occasions a single ability, the ability to think of, or think about, John. (Evans 1982, 101)

Evans went on to derive what he called the Generality Constraint:

> If we make that claim [that the thought that *a* is F and the thought that *b* is G are structured], then we are obliged to maintain that, if a subject can entertain those

thoughts, then there is no conceptual barrier, at least, to his being able to entertain the thought that *a* is *G* or the thought that *b* is *F*. And we are committed in addition to the view that there would be a common partial explanation for a subject's having the thought that *a* is *F* and his having the thought that *a* is *G*: there is a single state whose possession is a necessary condition for the occurrence of both thoughts. (ibid. 102)

I am concerned only with the first and last of the things Evans says in these passages: that a thought's structure (a) is not to be explained as its composition from elements (sc. elements that are sharable with other thoughts), but (b) does imply necessary conditions for having it that are sharable with other thoughts. Speech–thought Isomorphism derives its appeal from denial of (a); not that denial of (a) leads one all the way to the theory (which is really rather fantastic given the divergences of syntax between different and equally expressive languages), but because the denial is liable to start one on that road, by suggesting that thoughts that have common *features* (such as each being concerned with happiness) must have common *parts* (such as each having the thought of happiness as one of its components). (b) shows another and better way: there is something about me, who think that John is happy, which I share with you, who think that Harry is happy; but that is not a common *element* of our thoughts. If it were a common element, then there would indeed be pressure to infer that the element is conveyed by the word that is (or might be) common to the expression of our thoughts in language, the word "happy." But once that pressure is removed, the objections against Speech–thought Isomorphism can have due weight.

And the objections are indeed formidable. If "happy" conveys the thought of happiness, what thoughts do "happiness" and "happily" convey? If "happiness" conveyed a thought, would that not have to be the thought of happiness? Then do "happy" and "happiness" convey thoughts of the same thing, happiness, but different kinds of thought of it? What differences of kind might be relevant? There is risk of the Isomorphist being reduced to babbling (e.g. "the thought of happiness conveyed by 'happy' is adjectival"). Non-nominal parts of speech raise difficulties of a different kind. Adeodatus rightly avoided answering his father's question about "*si*" with anything that could be translated "'*si*' is a sign of if," for such a conjunction of words makes no sense; and "'if' conveys the thought of if" is nonsense for the same syntactical reason. But "'if' conveys the thought of doubt" leads back to the problem of accounting for the difference between the word "if" and the word "doubt"; while "'if' conveys doubt" (which seems to be what Adeodatus himself intended) departs from the compositional model altogether, since doubt is not a *part* of the thought conveyed by "if it please the gods that nothing should be left from this great city." For such reasons, Speech–thought Isomorphism is demonstrably false.

I will end by going back one stage further: the result we have arrived at ought to loosen the grip on us of the doctrine that words are signs. That doctrine was not new with Augustine, of course; on the contrary it had long been commonplace. Aristotle had allowed some exceptions (*De interpretatione* 10. 20ª13; *Poetics* 20.1456ᵇ38ff.) to his general rule that "vocal sounds (*ta en tēi phōnēi*) are symbols of affections in the soul" (*De interpretatione* 16ª3–4; a "symbol" is originally a token, evidence of a treaty or contract). The other ancient schools had followed the doctrine, often without the exceptions, and Aristotle and Augustine between them were destined to ensure its survival into scholastic and early modern philosophy (and grammar). But Augustine's explorations, intellectually honest though they are, ought to lead us to conclude that this doctrine too is false, whether it is taken as meaning, for each word, that the word has the role of being used as a sign of some particular thing (or range of things), or that every use of the word is its use as a sign of that thing (or range of things). One may admit that some words, alone or in combination, have such a role, and that some uses of words, alone or in combination, are such uses: for example, the single word "courage" has the role of indicating courage, and the word-combination "courage is a virtue" is sometimes used to indicate a speaker's thought that courage is a virtue. But such facts are not enough to make it right to say in general, with Augustine, that words are sounds that signify.

Wittgenstein wrote: "When we say: 'Every word in a language signifies (*bezeichnet*) something' we have so far said *nothing whatever*; unless we have explained exactly *what* distinction [i.e. contrast with non-significance] we wish to make" (Wittgenstein 1953, 1.13). I wish to conclude that Augustine, who does say this, has not said nothing whatever, but on the contrary has explained what he means, if not exactly, at least painstakingly and sufficiently: sufficiently for us in our time, who are standing on his and so many others' tall shoulders, to be able to see that he is wrong, though not for the reason presented by Wittgenstein in *Philosophical Investigations*.

NOTES

1 I ignore here the passage, Stoic-inspired, which has all words functioning *exceptionally* as names, viz. names of themselves: see *De mag.* 5.13; Kirwan 1989, 50–52, reprinted in Everson 1994, 201–205.
2 The text is doubtful; the most recent editor (O'Donnell 1992a, 1.7, 2.57–8) differs from Burnyeat's reading and punctuation, but without disturbing this general sense.
3 See the thorough discussion in Jackson 1975.
4 On the Stoic doctrine of *lekta* see e.g. Frede in Everson 1994, 109–128.
5 Words, incidentally, are always sounds (*soni*) or utterances (*voces*) according to Augustine, not written marks. Writing consists not of words but of signs of words: *De dialectica.* 5.7; *De mag.* 4.8; *De doct. christ;* 2.4.5; cf. *De Trin.* 15.10.19; Aristotle, *De interpretatione* 1. 16ª4, Kirwan 1989, 54–55, reprinted in Everson 1994, 207–208.

15

BONNIE KENT

Augustine's ethics

Augustine regards ethics as an enquiry into the Summum Bonum: the supreme good, which provides the happiness all human beings seek. In this respect his moral thought comes closer to the eudaimonistic virtue ethics of the classical Western tradition than to the ethics of duty and law associated with Christianity in the modern period. But even though Augustine addresses many of the same problems that pagan philosophers do, he often defends very different answers. For him, happiness consists in the enjoyment of God, a reward granted in the afterlife for virtue in this life. Virtue itself is a gift of God, and founded on love, not on the wisdom prized by philosophers.

The art of living

In Book 8 of *De civitate Dei* Augustine describes "moral philosophy" (a Latin expression), or "ethics" (the Greek equivalent), as an enquiry into the supreme good and how we can attain it. The supreme good is that which we seek for its own sake, not as a means to some other end, and which makes us happy. Augustine adds, as if this were an uncontroversial point, that happiness is the aim of philosophy in general.[1] Book 19 opens with a similar discussion. In his summary of Varro's treatise *De philosophia*, Augustine reports that no school of philosophy deserves to be considered a distinct school unless it differs from others on the supreme good. For the supreme good is that which makes us happy, and the only purpose of philosophizing is the attainment of happiness.[2] Both of these discussions cast philosophy as a fundamentally practical discipline, so that ethics appears to overshadow logic, metaphysics, and other comparatively abstract areas as a philosopher's chief concern. Notice, though, that Augustine does not present this as a distinctively Christian view, much less as some innovation of his own; he reports it as an opinion common among pagans.

However odd by today's standards, Augustine's conception of both philosophy in general and ethics in particular was shared by all leading philosophers of the period. After the death of Aristotle, philosophy became more and more the "art of *living*," an expression one might run across without noticing it in Augustine's summary of Varro.[3] Ethics emerged as the dominant part of the discipline, with more speculative areas like logic and the philosophy of nature (alias "physics") gradually being downgraded to subordinate roles. As ethics gained ascendancy, so philosophy as a whole took a strongly practical turn. Hellenistic philosophers[4] saw it as their mission to reflect upon the ultimate human goal, *eudaimonia*, to share their understanding with others, and to live by it themselves. The practical, eudaimonistic framework of Greek philosophy during the Hellenistic period became even more pronounced in the heyday of the Roman empire. Augustine's focus on what true happiness amounts to, and whether our everyday conduct brings us any closer to this goal, accordingly represents the rule, not the exception, for contemporary philosophical discourse.

As philosophy was far more practical than it is now, so, too, was it much closer to what people now regard as religion. All self-respecting philosophers offered a view of God, or the gods, and the implications of their view for everyday human conduct. Small wonder, then, that pagans would regard Christian intellectuals as philosophical rivals, even as Christians would claim to offer the one true philosophy: the only one that lives up to its own promises of teaching people what genuine happiness is and how it can be attained. St. Paul's experience in Athens may serve as a reminder of the intellectual milieu. When Paul taught in the marketplace, Epicurean and Stoic philosophers came to debate with him.[5] By Augustine's time, some three centuries later, pagan philosophy had moved even closer to religion, becoming concerned with what might be called both "conversion" and "salvation," even demonstrating a growing penchant for monotheism.[6] The affinities between Neoplatonism and Christianity were especially striking, so that Augustine's praise of "the Platonists" would not have been surprising at the time.[7]

The ultimate end

To say that all human beings seek the same ultimate end, happiness, seems to be true from one standpoint and false from another. The claim is plainly false if one means to suggest that all individuals have the same conception of happiness. On the other hand, it seems to be true insofar as happiness is the final explanation that people typically give when repeatedly pressed to explain their various choices and activities. Imagine, for example, the following dialogue:

Q. Why are you studying for a bachelor's degree?
A. Because I want to become a stockbroker, and most firms require a bachelor's degree.
Q. Why do you want to be a stockbroker?
A. Because I want to get rich.
Q. Why do you want to get rich?

A. Because I want to retire by fifty and spend my time traveling.
Q. Why do you want to retire by fifty and spend your time traveling?
A. Because this would make me happy.

Up to this point the questioner might be regarded as naive, or annoying, or both, but not as entirely unreasonable. If, however, she proceeds to ask, "Why do you want to be happy?" the dialogue has taken a strange turn. Having related his various choices and activities to the ultimate end of happiness, the student has given all the explanation necessary to make sense of them. Ask him why he wants to be happy, and he might simply reply, "Doesn't everyone?"[8]

Classical philosophers took "What is *eudaimonia*?" – or the Latin equivalent, "What is *beatitudo*?" – to be the most important question of ethics, for one's answer goes a long way towards determining how virtue should be characterized and the role it should play in human life. Some scholars prefer to translate these words not as "happiness" but as "blessedness," "flourishing" or "well-being," all of which correctly suggest a stable condition open to assessment by objective standards: a condition in many respects analogous to health, not merely the ephemeral, subjective feeling that present-day English speakers often refer to as "happiness." "Blessedness," however, seems to imply the existence of some divine blesser, which neither *eudaimonia* nor *beatitudo* does (they only leave this possibility open.) "Well-being" has no convenient adjectival form, since "well-off" may mean nothing more than well-heeled, and "flourishing," unlike *eudaimōn* or *beatus*, could describe potted plants just as well as human beings and gods. Despite its drawbacks, "happiness" therefore seems the best of the available translations for the *beatitudo* so often discussed in Augustine's works. ✓

The importance of happiness in Augustine's ethics can scarcely be overestimated. Of his surviving works, the very first he completed is a dialogue entitled *De beata vita* – an early indication of issues he continued to reflect upon to the very end of his career. On at least two broad points he agrees with standard philosophical teachings. First, all human beings desire happiness. Indeed, Augustine recognizes that the skeptical Cicero himself chose "We certainly all want [or will] to be happy" when seeking an assertion that nobody doubts.[9] Second, only "people who like to argue" equate happiness with merely living as one wants. No serious philosopher would take such a view, for who could be more miserable than someone who lives as he wants but wants something inappropriate?[10] Imagine wanting to live on a diet of gin and chocolate, or any of the various self-destructive desires that people actually have. Augustine again sides with Cicero in claiming that we are often better off in failing to get something that we want than we would be in simply wanting something inappropriate, because fortune does less to make us happy than our own minds do to make us unhappy. For example, someone might buy what turns out to be a losing lottery ticket week after week, year after year, without feeling distressed at the failure to strike it rich. (There is nothing wrong with wanting to be rich, just as long as we do not pin our happiness on it.) On the other hand, somebody with an excessive desire for wealth might possess millions and still continue to labor, miserably and compulsively, at acquiring even more. A radical decline in his wealth might likewise plunge such a person into despair, as it did some of the millionaires who saw their investment portfolios devastated by the US stock market crash of 1929. In Augustine's view, wanting wealth is one thing, loving it another. We must always be on guard against falling in love with objects unworthy of love.

Epicureans and Stoics likewise argue that unhappiness arises mainly, even entirely, from the individual's own beliefs, values, and attitudes; but they argue for the correlative position as well: that happiness depends mainly, even entirely, on the same individual characteristics. While ordinary pagans continued to believe that happiness owes much to sheer luck, or the favor of the gods, or both, philosophers emphasized just how much lies within the human being's own control. These disagreements about how much depends on the individual reflect deeper disagreements about what constitutes the happy life. If it requires little or nothing in the way of wealth, or fame, or even ordinary worldly success, one can make a plausible case for a high degree of individual control. Most Hellenistic philosophers take this route, describing the happy life as a life characterized by completeness and self-sufficiency (the secure possession of everything one needs), and especially by freedom from all trouble and anxiety. The happy life, in a word, is one of *tranquillity*, a goal supposed to be best attained by the practice of philosophy, which helps people reorder their priorities and thereby avoid needless distress. Academic skeptics diverged from the intellectual mainstream in treating philosophical enquiry as an end in itself. Even skepticism, however, cannot be considered a complete hold-out. The Academics themselves came under attack by Pyrrhonian skeptics, who taught that skeptical suspension of judgment does more than to safeguard one's intellectual integrity: it leads to tranquillity.

Augustine criticizes all pagan philosophers for giving a false account of happiness, bad advice on how to attain it, or both. Again and again he argues that philosophers' teachings fail even by their own standards. The Academics become a target of such criticism in Augustine's dialogue *De beata vita*. Replying to their description of the happy life as one spent searching for the truth, Augustine observes that they must want the truth and yet have thus far failed to find it, else they would not be searching. But how can people who lack what they want be the model of happiness? Would happiness not lie in finding the truth instead of merely searching for it?[11] The skeptical rejoinder that human beings are unable to find the truth, that even the wise can know nothing at all, receives extended consideration in Augustine's dialogue *Contra Academicos*. He stands with the philosophical majority in arguing that human knowledge is indeed possible, and that the happy life is a life in accordance with what is best in us, namely, the mind or reason.

Augustine later regretted this second assertion. In the *Retractationes* he writes:

> Insofar as human nature is concerned, there is nothing better than mind and reason; and yet the person who wants to live happily should not live according to this, for then he lives as man lives, although in order to be able to attain happiness he should live as God lives. To attain this, our mind should not be self-contented but should be subjected to God.[12]

The *Retractationes* include many other passages where Augustine expresses reservations about works he wrote in the first decade following his conversion. He regrets that he gave more praise to the Platonists than any pagan philosophers deserve, that he placed too much emphasis on expertise in the liberal arts, and that he overrated the importance of knowing immutable truths, which many Christians do not learn until the afterlife, while pagans who have attained such knowledge perish.[13] He also regrets suggesting that perfect virtue can be attained in this life, instead of only in the next, and that happiness in this life depends strictly on the state of one's soul, so that a wise man is happy regardless of the condition of his body – when in fact, the only life deservedly called happy is one where the body cannot suffer or die and obeys the mind without resistance.[14]

In sum, the youthful Augustine looked to the older Augustine like something of an intellectual snob, still too much under the influence of Hellenistic philosophy. Though even his mature writings reveal such influence, some of the earlier arguments and positions drop out, and Augustine's conflicts with pagan thinkers become more clearly defined. His efforts to meet them on their own ground nonetheless continue.

Happiness, morality, and immortality

According to Augustine, immortality ranks high among the prerequisites for true happiness. Materalists like the Epicureans and the Stoics, he argues, are especially misguided on this point. On the one hand, they firmly declare that every human being wants happiness, which they interpret as freedom from all suffering and anxiety. On the other, they deny the immortality of the soul, believing that the only happiness we shall ever enjoy must come from the lives we have now: lives subject to countless troubles, all the way from the common cold and anxieties about exams to such agonies as bone cancer and grief at the death of a loved one. Noticing the tension between these two positions, they ought to reconsider whether their denial of immortality might be wrong. Instead, Augustine argues, they choose to redescribe the ideal of happiness in such a way that it becomes attainable in this life. They lower the goal all the more in an effort to place an individual's happiness within his own control, for no better reason than that they want to claim credit for making themselves happy.[15]

The Platonists, praised by Augustine as the best of the pagan philosophers, have enough wisdom to teach the immortality of the soul, but they too go awry on crucial points, especially in declaring that the human soul will be happiest when liberated from the body. Having himself believed this during his Manichaean period, Augustine argues all the more passionately later on against denigrating the body. Indeed, Christian doctrine on the resurrection of the body, a source of dismay to the Athenians who heard St. Paul preach, was one of the main issues dividing early Christianity from all contemporary pagan schools of philosophy. Far from equating the human being with the soul, Augustine insists that human beings are by nature embodied – that God created us this way, so that we should never regard our bodies as prisons or punishments. He thinks the Platonists go even more disastrously wrong in failing to acknowledge Jesus Christ, the incarnation of God, as both the teacher and redeemer without whom no human being could ever succeed in attaining happiness.[16] For all their impressive insights, even the Platonists share the fatal, blinding pride demonstrated by other pagan philosophers.

In arguing that happiness requires immortality Augustine tries to show that his opponents' own assumptions should lead them to agree with him. Consider, for example, the famous Epicurean dictum "Death is nothing to us," a position defended in the belief that there are no punishments in some imagined afterlife to be feared, nor any rewards to be hoped for. While one might reasonably fear the pain of *dying*, Epicureans argue, death itself should be no cause for concern, for when we are *dead*, we no longer exist. So what is there for any right-thinking philosopher, as opposed to some superstitious peasant, to worry about?[17] Augustine challenges the coherence of Epicurean doctrine. It claims that we all want happiness, even insists that everything we do, we do for the sake of happiness; but since we cannot be happy without being alive, why should Epicureans not agree that the ultimate in the way of happiness requires the ultimate in the way of life? When our lives are happy, or happy enough to satisfy us, we want them to continue indefinitely. When they are unhappy, perhaps we would willingly have them end, but then how, *ex hypothesi*, could this willingly lost life be described as happy?[18] Either way, Augustine thinks it strange that Epicureans could insist so strongly upon happiness as the universal human goal while denying not only immortality but even the inevitable human longing for it.

Augustine questions whether anyone, including someone who commits suicide, truly wants her life to end. When I deliberately swallow fifty sleeping pills, am I actually aiming at non-existence? Or am I rather yearning for peace, for an end to all my suffering, only too muddled at the time to recognize that the experience of peace presupposes life, just as all experience presupposes life? Do people who kill themselves really aim at non-existence, or do they aim instead, without being clear about their own goal, at a continued but pain-free existence?[19] Augustine argues that even suicides aim at the goal of the happy life, only misunderstand exactly what it is that they want.

Stoicism rates higher in Augustine's judgment than Epicureanism, for the Stoics taught that happiness comes not from the pleasure of the body but from the virtue of the mind.[20] Agreeing that the virtue of the mind is a necessary condition for happiness, Augustine concentrates on arguing that it cannot be a sufficient condition. One objection, already made by his philosophical predecessors, says that the Stoic view flies in the face of common sense. Anybody who insists that "a man can be happy on the rack" must be so much in the grip of a theory that he can no longer recognize the obvious: that human beings are not merely minds but composites of bodies and minds, so that we cannot be happy when suffering intense physical pain, regardless of how virtuous we might be. Augustine adds to this standard objection that Stoics err in the direction of arrogance, just as Epicureans err in the direction of sordidness; as Epicureans overweight pleasure, so Stoics overweight glory. In praising virtue as the highest human good, says Augustine, the Stoics try to make other people feel ashamed. They themselves should feel ashamed of whittling down the supreme good to such a point that they can claim to be the sole cause of their own happiness, instead of acknowledging that mere human beings cannot make themselves happy. Even if the Stoics were correct in teaching that a virtuous mind suffices to make a person happy, they would still be mistaken in failing to recognize that the mind's virtue is itself a gift of God, not a triumph of human achievement.[21]

Augustine's mature works initially appear inconsistent regarding our prospects for happiness in the present life. Some texts seem to suggest that at least Christians can be happy now, by living in hope of union with God after death; other texts seem to deny that even the greatest degree of hope suffices to make anyone happy in the present. When speaking with precision, Augustine says that nobody can attain happiness in the present life, and yet anyone who accepts the present life with firm hope of the afterlife "may without absurdity be *called* 'happy' even now, though rather by future hope than in present reality."[22] This carefully nuanced position reflects his concern to avoid downgrading the ideal of happiness while still providing some grounds for the use of "happiness" in everyday speech.

Despite his attacks on philosophers' pretensions that genuine happiness can be attained here and now, Augustine never reduces the present life to some miserable waystation on the train route to heaven. *De civitate Dei*'s notorious, often-reprinted catalogue of all the troubles of mortal life – a staple of late twentieth-century anthologies – comes followed by a much less noticed catalogue of all the *goods* of the present life.[23] These include not only God-given virtues, which enable us to work at attaining salvation, but also human accomplishments such as science, music, art, and literature. According to Augustine, God did not make the world strictly as a means for us to survive now and to work toward happiness in the afterlife; he made it for our aesthetic pleasure, too, sometimes even at the expense of practicality. How else can one explain why God gave men nipples, which serve no useful purpose, but did not give women beards, which would have served to protect their faces? Secularized or puritanical visions of God as some austere celestial bookkeeper, obsessed with keeping track of our moral merits and demerits, accordingly cannot claim Augustine as their authority. Augustine's God always appears more as the lover and the artist than as the bookkeeper or the judge.

Augustine's teachings on happiness nonetheless raise troubling questions, not only about the status of virtue in his ethical theory but even about the status of God. Pagan philosophers had labored for centuries to prove moral virtue a constitutive feature of the happy life. Against popular opinion, which often praised good conduct only as the means to avoid punishments and reap rewards, philosophers steadily proclaimed that virtue has intrinsic value. (Recall that Plato devotes roughly nine books of his *Republic* to arguing that virtue is desirable for its own sake, allotting scarcely more than half a book to confirming the popular opinion that virtue has beneficial consequences, too.) A quick look at Augustine's ethics might give the impression that he himself aims to revive the very opinion that high-minded philosophers had so long worked to discredit. If everything we do, we do for the sake of happiness, and happiness itself comes in the afterlife, as a reward for virtuous conduct in this life, how can virtue in this life have intrinsic value? Does it indeed have intrinsic value, or is it merely a means of attaining our ultimate, otherworldly end? Considering the doctrine of hell, one might wonder whether Christians are motivated to virtuous conduct even more by fear of eternal punishment than by hope of eternal reward.

Pause to consider the place assigned to God, and one may become all the more troubled by the eudaimonistic cast of Augustine's ethics. Today eudaimonism counts as one approach to ethical theory, deontology as another. The first takes as its starting point happiness, the ultimate end that all human beings seek; the second takes as its starting point our duty or obligation to respect the moral law, regardless of the costs to our own happiness. Although Augustine appears to favor something roughly approximating the eudaimonistic framework of ancient ethical theory, he never forgets that Christ gave us two commands: to love God above all, and to love our neighbors as ourselves. Christ did not command us to seek happiness or to love ourselves. How, then, can the Gospel be reconciled with eudaimonistic ethics? If Christians seek God as the provider of complete, everlasting happiness, do they love God for himself or merely as the source of their own satisfaction? If the latter, do they truly love God, or do they only love themselves?

Love of God and neighbor

Augustine draws an important distinction between two kinds of value.[24] One is the value that something has intrinsically, according to the natural hierarchy created by God. On this scale, living beings are always worth more than inanimate objects; among living beings, those with reason and free choice are worth more than animals; and God's worth is infinite. Augustine claims that human beings continue to have greater natural value than animals even when we abuse our God-given powers. As a runaway horse is still better than a stone, so a sinful human being is still better than a well-behaved horse.[25] The other kind of value is that which we assign to beings or things according to the utility they happen to have for us. Utility value may be so high that we even casually use the term "love" in referring to it, as, for example, when one says, "How I love lobster!" Of course, the meaning of "love" in such statements differs greatly from the meaning in such a statement as "How I love my son!" The value that lobster has for me is purely instrumental: when I profess to love lobster, what I actually mean is that I love the pleasure I myself derive from eating lobster. While I might likewise derive pleasure from reading to my son, playing with him, and many other experiences that I could not have without him, so that he does have utility value for me, surely he has intrinsic value as well, as evidenced by my willingness to promote his interests even when they conflict with my own.

Beginning with this common-sense distinction between natural, intrinsic value and utility value, Augustine proceeds to demonstrate its moral significance. First, he reminds us that we routinely judge according to the utility scale of value, despite serious conflicts with the natural scale. "Would not anyone prefer to have food in his house, rather than mice, or money rather than fleas?" he asks.[26] Readers often chuckle at this question, only to wince at Augustine's next observation: that we commonly assign less value to other human beings than we do to animals and inanimate objects, as when we pay more for a horse or a gem than we would for a servant. Pause to compare the vast sum that people willingly pay for a new car, even though their present car remains functional, with the small donation they willingly make to feed the starving or shelter the homeless, and one may begin to develop the feeling of moral discomfort that Augustine believes all reflective persons should have.

By emphasizing the difference between these two scales of value, Augustine wants to highlight the discrepancy between the value judgments we make, or would make, when judging as free, rational agents, and those we make in everyday life, when driven by our own needs and desires. Where reason can see the values that things have in their own right, our drives look always to the value that things might have in serving our own purposes. Thus "What is this worth to *me*?" tends to become the ruling standard for everyday value judgments. The standard is seriously flawed because answers to this question typically reveal more about the human subject's individual constellation of fears, ambitions, cravings, and needs than they do about the intrinsic value of the object. Virtue requires that we love others as they deserve to be loved, according to their intrinsic worth, instead of in proportion to how well they happen to serve our own interests or satisfy our own desires.[27] The virtuous person will therefore never regard others as merely the means to her own ends.

Christ's command to love our neighbors as ourselves automatically prohibits "instrumentalizing" our fellow human beings. Elaborating on this command in *De vera religione*, Augustine explains that we must love our neighbor as a human being, for his intrinsic worth, not for some pleasure or advantage that we hope to derive from him, as if he were no more than an amusing parrot or a beast of burden.[28] To put the point another way, we must love people because they belong to God, not because they belong to us. Augustine goes so far as to declare it more *inhuman* to love somebody because he is your son than because he is a human being, made in the image of and belonging to God.[29]

How could partiality for one's own family be reckoned inhuman? Aristotle regards it as thoroughly human, and most readers will agree. Augustine explains that this tendency arises from merely biological relationships contingent upon birth, that it represents the same mindless preference for kin that animals display – a classic example of what he dismisses as "carnal custom," i.e. human conduct and values produced by habituation but running counter to human nature as created by God. Partiality for kin represents one more case of judging the value of someone in relation to us, to our own private advantage, instead of considering the person's intrinsic value. (From this perspective one might question how well I actually do love my son: Do I love him in his own right and for his own sake or because he is *mine*?)

The interpretation of Augustine just presented does, however, seem contradicted by *De doctrina christiana*. There we find his pronouncement that God alone is to be loved for his own sake, i.e. to be "enjoyed," and that all human beings are to be loved for the sake of God, i.e. to be "used."[30] This notorious passage nonetheless tends to mislead, for two reasons. One is that "use" (*usus*) does not have for Augustine the inevitable connotations of manipulation and exploitation that "using" has for us now; the other is simply that his conception of "use-love" is far wider in *De doctrina christiana* than it is in *De vera religione*. In works written after *De doctrina christiana*, Augustine prudently retreats from his claim that human beings are to be "used" while God alone is to be "enjoyed," returning to something closer to the ordinary meaning of these terms. He teaches that we should love people for their own sakes as well as for the sake of God, or more briefly, that we should enjoy them as related to God. We should enjoy *ourselves* in the same way.[31] In other words, while we ought to appreciate the value that all people have in their own right, we must never forget that none of us has value independent of God. The value we have simply as human beings, as beings with a certain kind of nature, we owe to God as the creator of nature. The additional value we might have thanks to virtue we likewise owe to God, for virtue itself is a gift of God.

Now we may be in a better position to understand why Augustine does not regard virtue as merely a means to an end, but neither does he regard it as something to be desired and exercised purely for its own sake. The theoretical balancing act is difficult, with mistakes very easy to make on both sides. On the one hand, Augustine defines virtue as rightly ordered love.[32] Because all true virtues are forms of love rooted in charity, the love of God and neighbor commanded by Christ, virtues are by their very nature other-regarding. Apparently good conduct motivated mainly by the individual's fear of punishment would therefore not be virtuous; nor would conduct motivated mainly by the individual's desire for reward, whether now or in heaven. In all such cases the self-regarding overshadows the other-regarding: self-love clearly predominates over love of God and neighbor. On the other hand, virtue must never be allowed to supplant God as the supreme good, as the sole good to be loved purely for its own sake and without reference to any higher good.

Augustine attacks the Stoics for having made the second mistake. To his mind, the Stoics heap praise upon virtue, oblivious of the fact that virtue itself is God-given. Do they not teach, in effect, that a human being's state of character is the highest good in the cosmos? But how could any reflective person hold such an opinion? Augustine suggests two possibilities: either the Stoics are secretly aiming at "glory" – that is, their greatest desire is to be praised and admired by other human beings – or they actually do value their own virtue more highly than anything else – in which case they look to Augustine like nothing more than sophisticated narcissists.[33]

One might reasonably reject Augustine's bleak view of the Stoics and yet concede his basic point. Ethical theories that regard virtue as the product of natural aptitude, sound upbringing, individual human effort, and a just community (or some combination of these) do indeed differ significantly from ethical theories that regard God as the creator of nature and the giver of virtue. Once God has been recognized as the supreme good, immeasurably higher than any other good, human virtue can at best occupy second place. If the supreme good alone is to be loved purely for its own sake, without reference to any other good, then Christian ethics in general must to some degree be committed, just because it is Christian, to "instrumentalizing" virtue. Notice that Augustine shares the Stoics' conviction that we can be made happy only by that through which we are made good,[34] but disagrees, vehemently, about what this is. In Stoic ethics, that which makes us good and happy is our own character, whereas in Augustine's ethics, it is God: a divine being, not a human state of mind.

Augustine himself sees no serious conflict between declaring happiness our supreme good and declaring God our supreme good, for love itself works to overcome the distinction. Even in ordinary human love at its best, the division between self and other tends to break down, so that what might otherwise have been a self-sacrificing act, willingly but joylessly done for the sake of another, becomes instead an act done with pleasure and essential to one's own happiness. Recall the great "sacrifices" that parents will happily make for their children, or that spouses will make for each other, and we can find in our own experience something roughly approximating the kind of love that Augustine prizes so highly. An ethics that might initially appear to exclude self-love and to require self-sacrifice proves far more subtle on closer examination.

Why, for example, does Christ command us to love God and our neighbors but not to love ourselves? According to Augustine, there is no *need* for such a commandment. By our very God-given nature we love ourselves and cannot help loving ourselves, so that Christ might as well command us to breathe.[35] Augustine goes still farther in arguing that it is improper not to love oneself and not to do for oneself what one does for a neighbor. Christ's command is to love one's neighbor *as* oneself, not to love him *more than* oneself.[36] We must be especially careful not to serve the interests of another at the expense of our own ultimate good. However admirable it is to risk one's bodily life to save another's, it would be wrong to risk one's immortal soul. The individual's own soul has more value than anyone's body. Augustine would therefore be horrified by the notorious case where a woman arranged a murder in order to improve her daughter's prospects of making the cheerleading squad. Shall one commit a mortal sin and lose one's own soul merely to advance someone else's worldly ambitions? When the good that a person sacrifices has far greater intrinsic worth than the good thereby achieved, she has effectively substituted her own scale of values for God's.

For all his praise of love, Augustine never forgets the power of human love to warp the priorities that one ought to have. When speculating in the *Confessions* about his own youthful motivations for stealing a neighbor's pears, he calls attention to the pleasure that he took simply from having partners in crime.[37] As the human craving for companionship has its advantages, so it also has its dangers. In later works Augustine claims that it was this very craving that led Adam, the "father" of all future human beings, to disobey God's command. Although Eve was deceived by the serpent's false promises, Augustine argues, Adam was not deceived when Eve repeated those promises. Instead, Adam accepted Eve's invitation to eat the forbidden fruit because the two were so closely bound in partnership that he refused to be separated from her, not even when the only way he saw to preserve their bond involved sharing her sin.[38]

We need not worry that God requires us to be self-sacrificing in loving our neighbors or even in loving him, for in Augustine's view, nobody can truly love God without learning how to love herself.[39] In understanding what makes God so supremely worthy of love, one also comes to understand the elements in oneself that make one worthy of love. Exactly what is it in *yourself* that you ought to value? If you value most highly your muscle tone or your wealth, your expertise in abstraction or your flair for amusing remarks, even your loyalty to fellow human beings, regardless of what they want you to do (recall the loyalty of German soldiers to their Nazi leaders), you have gotten your priorities wrong. You ought to value most highly your patience, kindness, willingness to forgive, the courage to do the right thing despite the worldly costs, and other virtues exemplified by Christ. For this reason Augustine declares Christ's entire life on earth a splendid education in morals. Not only was God's son poor, uneducated in theoretical abstractions, and destined for the agonizing, shaming execution usually reserved for the dregs of human society – the ultimate "anti-hero" by pagan-philosophical standards – Christ also shared the normal human fear of being tortured to death, even pleaded with his father to spare him, yet ended his prayer humbly, saying, "Nevertheless, not as I will, but as thou wilt."[40] Once we do learn what we should value in ourselves, Augustine believes, we must perforce develop humility, since we shall recognize that the best elements in us we owe far more to God's generosity than to our own accomplishments, and that his will is simply better and more important than our own.

Pride and fear

Scholars sometimes suggest that Augustine developed a far more negative attitude toward self-love as he grew older.[41] In later works, such as *De civitate Dei*, he appears to draw a sharp dichotomy between self-love, on the one hand, and love of God, on the other. Indeed, the very division between the city of God and the earthly city may be thought to reflect Augustine's belief that love of God and love of self are mutually exclusive. A closer reading nonetheless reveals more a change in emphasis than a change in substance. Consider, for example, Augustine's famous description of the two cities:

> And so the two cities were created by two loves: the earthly city by self-love reaching the point of contempt for God, the heavenly city by the love of God reaching the point of contempt for self. In fact, the earthly city glories in itself, the heavenly city in the Lord. While the one looks for glory from human beings, the greatest glory for the other lies in God, the witness of conscience.[42]

Augustine begins not by denigrating self-love as such but by criticizing self-love that has grown beyond its proper bounds, warping one's priorities so badly that the individual comes to see himself as the highest being in the universe. He does not bother to repeat this qualification in the second sentence, though he alludes to it in the next, in declaring that the greatest glory for the heavenly city (as distinct from the only glory) lies in God. Later in *De civitate Dei* Augustine also says explicitly that in the two rules, love of God and love of neighbor, "a person finds three objects of love – God, himself, and neighbor – so that someone who loves God does not do wrong in loving himself."[43]

As reflection upon God's commands reveals nothing intrinsically wrong with self-love, so too does reflection upon primal sin. Augustine describes the rebellious angels who founded the earthly city as motivated not by self-love but rather by *pride*, a perverse and highly specific kind of self-love that leads one to arrogate to oneself a place that properly belongs to God alone. Cain, described by Augustine as the human founder of the earthly city, largely followed the angelic precedent. Cain was so consumed by the destructive lust of envy, so eager to glory in the exercise of his own power, that the very thought of having to share power, even with a human partner, was intolerable to him. He killed his own brother in a futile effort to establish himself as the sole ruling power.[44]

We sin, then, by loving the inferior aspects of ourselves, or by loving ourselves to excess – by claiming for ourselves God's place, and in the process grossly perverting what true love actually is. True love, as Augustine sees it, does not seek private advantages. It recognizes that the common good has greater worth than the private, merely individual good. Love heals divisions and eliminates competition. Far from being possessive, love seeks to share its happiness, thereby uniting all servants of God, both angelic and human, in peaceful association.[45] Although we find in pagan philosophers of the time a comparable view of humans as naturally social creatures who can be happy only as members of a community, Augustine diverges in two important respects. First, he argues that the only true community is a just one, but that no such community can be created by human beings on earth, so that we cannot be entirely happy until we join in the afterlife the community governed by God.[46] Second, Augustine repeatedly contrasts human nature as created by God and human nature in its present condition, crippled by original sin. In describing our present condition he emphasizes our egoism, our pride and lust for glory, our struggle to dominate others, even our tendency to feel more satisfied from the knowledge that others are worse off than ourselves.

Again and again, Augustine's observations seem to anticipate the bleak description of human nature presented over a thousand years later by Thomas Hobbes in *Leviathan*.[47] Remember, though, that what Hobbes takes to be natural Augustine himself believes contrary to human nature as created and hence as it ought to be. However universal our present condition, it remains in Augustine's view both *un*natural and morally reprehensible. That we make ourselves and each other so unhappy should therefore come as no surprise. Power and glory "addicts" are every bit as dangerous and self-destructive as drug addicts.

The tensions between loving God and fearing him are more troubling than those between loving God and loving ourselves. Of course, love can trigger fear; arguably, in normal human experience, it is only because people love that they do fear. If we did not love our own bodily lives, why should we be as frightened as we are of dying? But we usually learn the lesson long before we are driven to confront our own mortality. Only pause to consider the wrenching anxieties that parents suffer regarding a child who should have been home from school many hours earlier, or the queasiness that a child feels about misbehaving, just from fear of disappointing her parents, and the connection between love and fear in everyday life should be evident.

Fears such as these are nonetheless more admirable, reflective of a higher stage of moral growth, than the primitive, self-centered fear of punishment. When Joe refrains from tormenting his little sister because he fears disappointing his parents, he has at least advanced beyond the stage where he refrained only because he feared getting caught and being given a spanking. Ideally, Joe will one day outgrow both his fear and his penchant for sibling rivalry. He will stop regarding love as a scarce, non-renewable resource, on a par with petroleum, as if any bit of it given to his sister or to someone else inevitably endangers his own supply. Ideally, he will grow beyond mere avoidance of tormenting his sister: he will learn to help her, and to want his parents to smile upon her, simply because he loves his sister, loves his parents, and recognizes that the whole family, himself included, is happiest when each willingly seeks the good of all the others.

These prosaic observations regarding human love and moral development may shed some light on Augustine's ambivalence about the fear of hell as a motivation for obeying God's "rules." Since fear of God's punishment often leads people to conduct themselves better than they would otherwise do, it has its value as a first step in moral education and should not be considered a dead loss. On the other hand, fear of punishment is never more than a first step. If a person progresses no farther, then one of the most important messages of Christianity has been lost. Unlike Pelagius, Augustine tries to avoid preying on people's terror of the Last Judgment.[48] He even issues a solemn but tart warning against the dangers of being driven by fear:

> He, then, is an enemy to righteousness who refrains from sin only through fear of punishment; but he will become the friend of righteousness if through love of it he avoids sin, for then he will be really afraid of sin. For the person who only fears the flames of hell is afraid not of sinning but of burning . . . [49]

On the whole, Augustine prefers to highlight the difference between Christianity's vision of God as a loving father and the view of popular pagan religion, which encourages people to see the gods mainly as sources of rewards and punishments. As pagan belief in an afterlife spread, so too did belief in divine rewards and punishments in the afterlife, along with people's anxieties about how they might fare. Epicureans worked to relieve such anxieties by denying that there is an afterlife, much less one in which we experience divine rewards or punishments.[50] Augustine instead chooses to contrast the slavish motivation of fear with the liberating motivation of charity. The one true God, he reminds us, expressly asks that we call him "father" (as opposed to "master"). So if all we see in him is the same prospective source of punishments that the pagan gods are taken to be, have we not missed the very message that God steadily teaches?[51]

The divided will

Augustine writes at length in his *Confessions* of feeling two wills at war in himself. He longed to convert to Christianity, yet he continued to resist and delay: a conflict so painful, he says, that it tore his soul apart. We are all familiar with milder versions of inner conflict, as when people want to stop drinking, or smoking, or even to get out of bed when their alarm clock first buzzes, but somehow cannot seem to muster the will to do it. Augustine himself shifts in a single chapter from the dramatic image of a soul torn apart to the mundane struggle to get out of bed, thereby reminding readers that internal conflicts are the stuff of everyday life, not some special problem experienced only by the religious.[52]

In analyzing the conflict he himself experienced, Augustine distinguishes between his new will to follow God and his old will, which forged the very chains of habit (or custom: *consuetudo*) in which he had come to be trapped. Far from believing himself imprisoned by some Prince of Darkness, as Manichaean doctrine suggested, Augustine emphasizes that his bondage was *self*-created. There were not two selves in him, nor was there one true (good) self at war with some alien (evil) force. The two wills were both expressions of a single self, however sorely divided:

> When I was deliberating about serving the Lord my God, as I had long meant to do, it was I who willed to do it, I who refused. It was I. Neither did I wholly will nor did I wholly refuse. Thus I struggled with myself and was torn apart by myself, an experience I underwent although I did not want to, and which nevertheless did not reveal the nature of some alien mind, but rather the punishment of my own mind.[53]

The Latin text is more powerful than an English translation can convey, thanks to Augustine's steady repetition of *"ego"* ("I"). Latin authors need not use the pronoun "I" to say, for example, "I run" or "I exist." The first-person form of a verb, such as *sum* ("I am, I exist") suffices without the pronoun, as in Descartes's well-known pronouncement, "Cogito ergo sum." Augustine, however, repeatedly uses the emphatic *ego*. It was *I* who willed, *I* who refused, *I* who tore myself apart: it was *I*.

The centrality of the will in this analysis marks a major change from ancient moral psychology.[54] Although philosophers such as Aristotle discuss rational appetite, decision, intentional, uncoerced action, and other notions associated with the later concept of the will, they are most impressed by the division between the soul's rational and non-rational powers. Regarding intellect, the rational power *par excellence*, as the true self, they tend to treat ordinary emotions as non-rational and hence as in some sense external to the true self. In contrast, Augustine attributes three powers to the soul: reason or intellect, memory, and will. As the will comes to supplant the intellect as the true self, the morally responsible "I" becomes less the "I" who knows, believes, speculates, and reasons and more the "I" who loves, fears, struggles, and chooses. Not only does Augustine posit no basic division between will and emotion, he also suggests that different emotions might even be understood as different kinds of volition:

> The important factor is the quality of a person's will, because if the will is perverse, it will have these perverse affections, but if it is right, they will be not only blameless but even praiseworthy. The will is in all of them; indeed, they are nothing other than expressions of will. For what are desire and joy but the will in agreement with that which we want? And what are fear and grief but the will in disagreement with that which we reject?[55]

Exactly what does Augustine mean by "the will"? What is this power that human beings and angels supposedly have and animals supposedly lack? Quasi-formal definitions of the "will" prove virtually useless. To understand Augustine, one does better to ponder the theoretical work that he believes the concept of the will is needed to do.

Begin with a thought experiment that Augustine proposes: Suppose that there are twins, precisely the same in mind and body, social conditioning, personal histories, and all other respects, who find themselves in the same situation, equally attracted by the same forbidden object. One succumbs to temptation, the other does not. How can we explain this phenomenon, Augustine asks, except with reference to the will?[56] Of course, a skeptic would remain unpersuaded. The problem itself is spurious, the skeptic might retort, because two persons who are so much the same would in the same situation do precisely the same thing. The suggested thought experiment "proves" the existence of the will only by tacitly assuming it.

Augustine, however, does not believe the concept of the will necessary for descriptive psychology so much as for *moral* psychology. If human beings sin, and God justly punishes us for it – two assumptions Augustine considers indisputable – then we ourselves must be morally responsible for sinning. It is precisely to explain moral responsibility that we must posit the will. Pause to reflect upon Adam and Eve, the premier example of human sin.[57] They had no unsatisfied needs; they suffered no agitations of mind or body; and God gave them only a single command, supremely easy to obey. How can we explain why they nonetheless disobeyed? Contrary to the psychological theories of pagan philosophers, the explanation cannot lie in ignorance, faulty reasoning, or emotional disorder. Nor can it lie in some defect of nature that made it impossible for Adam and Eve to obey, since God would not have punished them for what they could not help doing. The only explanation Augustine can conceive is that their sin arose from an evil will which itself had no prior or external cause. Either the will is the first cause of sin, not merely one more link in a chain of natural efficient causes, or there is no sin.[58]

Does Augustine's argument for positing the will depend for its validity upon the assumptions that God is just and that human beings sin? It seems rather to depend on two weaker but still disputable assumptions: (1) We are justified in holding people, but not animals, morally responsible for their actions; and (2) we would not be justified in holding people morally responsible if they did not have a will which somehow transcends natural appetite and the natural order of efficient causes. Kant presents an argument along roughly similar lines, without any references to God, sin, or other theological concepts.[59] Despite their many differences, both Augustine and Kant take as a starting point the moral practices of praise and blame, reward and punishment. Both assume that these practices are justified only if people *deserve* to be praised, blamed, punished, or rewarded. It is not enough that the practices may have the beneficial consequence of modifying people's behavior and thereby producing a more peaceful community.[60] To be morally responsible, people must deserve their punishments and rewards; otherwise they do not differ significantly from dogs, whose behavior can likewise be modified by "conditioning."

Augustine and Kant further agree that moral desert or merit depends less on the ability to perform one physical action or another than on the capacity for certain kinds of motivations. Artificial intelligence, for instance, might one day be developed to the point where it could exceed human beings in all intellectual calculations and physical actions, could learn from experience, and so could be more successful than we are at ensuring its own survival. It could be supremely rational, yet if it could not act from love (in Augustine's view) or from duty (in Kant's), it would still lack the status of a moral agent. We see in Augustine, then, the beginnings of a Western tradition that treats the distinction between will and nature, which lies chiefly in motivations, as indispensable for any adequate account of moral responsibility. This distinction cuts across the ancient distinction between rational and non-rational powers rather than duplicating it.

Shared, flawed humanity

The consequences of Adam's sin prove just as important as its cause to the development of Augustine's ethics. As we share in Adam's humanity, so we share in his guilt and punishment. Even when the guilt of original sin is forgiven in baptism, the punishment remains, particularly in the form of concupiscence, a radical disorder in our desires alien to human nature in its original condition. In his early works, Augustine confesses, he underestimated the extent of the damage to human nature. His own thinking changed owing to continued reflection upon St. Paul's lament in Romans 7:

> I can will what is right, but I cannot do it. For I do not do the good I want [or will], but the evil that I do not want is what I do. Now if I do what I do not want, it is no longer I that do it, but sin which dwells within me . . . For I delight in the law of God, in my inmost self, but I see in my members another law at war with the law of my mind and making captive to the law of sin which dwells in my members. Wretched man that I am! Who will deliver me from this body of death? Thanks be to God through Jesus Christ our Lord![61]

At first Augustine believed that Paul was describing how he felt before becoming a Christian. Only gradually did he decide that Paul was speaking in his own voice, as a Christian with the gift of God's grace. Without grace, how could Paul delight in God's law? Without such delight, how could the very conflict he describes even be possible? Of course, Augustine does not think the passage should be taken to mean that Paul continued to do wrong or that he even had sinful intentions. When Paul writes of "doing" the evil that he hates, all he means, says Augustine, is that he continues to desire what he should not desire, a failing he abhors; but precisely because he does not consent to the urgings of concupiscence, Paul can justifiably say, "It is no longer I that do it."[62] Augustine's new interpretation of Romans highlights the profound damage to human nature by original sin and hence the continued, profound dependency on God's grace, even by the best of us.

The works of Pelagius and his followers declare it absurd to suggest that Adam's sin damaged anyone but himself, except in the trivial sense that Adam set a bad example. Every one of us, in their view, is born in the same condition that Adam was before his fall, with a will entirely free and no need of external aid in order to be good. This holds for pagans no less than Christians. We have as evidence the injunction of Jesus: "You, therefore, must be perfect, as your heavenly Father is perfect."[63] How could anybody have an obligation to be perfect if he lacks the ability to be? Could God justly command of us what we are unable to do? If we *ought* to be perfect, Pelagians argue, it follows that we *can* be perfect, so that we shall richly deserve the punishments of hell if we fail. As for Romans 7, Augustine's interpretation must be rejected. Writing in the voice of someone who has yet to convert, Paul laments not the damage of original sin but only the necessity arising from his own individually self-created bad habits.[64]

Most modern readers, especially Americans, find the Pelagians' teachings far more appealing than Augustine's. Not only does Pelagian doctrine give full moral credit to persons of other faiths, even of no faith at all, it also treats us all as individuals, individually responsible for our own fortunes. Each of us is free to succeed or fail, depending entirely on his own efforts – a theological doctrine later secularized and politicized by such authors as Andrew Carnegie and Horatio Alger. Indeed, the Pelagian bishop Julian of Eclanum carried the defense of human freedom so far as to pronounce us "emancipated from God."[65] In giving each of us the power of free will, God grants us our independence, so that we need worry only about using the gift well enough to "pass" when we must finally face God's judgment.

Why does Augustine argue so vehemently against the Pelagians? First and foremost, he faults them for ignoring the sheer universality of human failings. If Adam's descendants are indeed able to be perfect through their own efforts, why can we not find in the whole of human history a single one who actually was perfect, including even so great a saint as Paul?[66] Before dismissing Augustine's assessment of the human condition as excessively negative, recall that the center of the moral life is for him overwhelmingly internal to the individual's own soul. He has a sharp eye ever trained on the wide variety of wishes, fantasies, and emotional reactions that never translate into action but are nonetheless real and morally revealing.[67] The slothful yearning to offload one's own duties onto a family member or colleague, the thrill of pleasure at seeing a competitor fail, the fantasy of revenge against an enemy, the fury at being criticized, however deservedly, and so on, endlessly – our inner lives have a streak of ugliness that seems to endure no matter how well we learn to control our speech and actions. Augustine scorns the suggestion that we are born innocent and good and grow worse only as a result of social conditioning. Babies, he points out, cry, throw tantrums, and are veritable monsters of jealousy and selfishness. If we regard them as *innocentes* (in Latin, either "innocent" or "harmless"), we are thinking about the weakness of their bodies, not about any quality of their minds.[68]

To the Pelagians' complaint that Christ could not justly command us to be perfect if we were unable to be, Augustine has roughly three replies. The first challenges the Pelagians' narrow understanding of how imperatives are actually used, and hence what might justly be commanded. Christ might justly command us to be perfect in the same way that he could justly command a lame man to walk. In trying to walk, only to discover that he cannot, the man would learn first-hand his own inability, his own need for a physician to cure him, and thus his own need to be healed by Christ, the one true physician of the soul.[69] Even in everyday human discourse, commands may be given in order to teach, not merely to produce obedient performances.

Augustine's second reply challenges the Pelagians' literalist interpretation of the word "perfect." Granted, if what one means by "perfect" is a purity of soul so complete that it allows no space for vengeful fantasies, lustful cravings, and so on, no human being can be perfect in this life. But why restrict the word's meaning so drastically? If "perfect" is going to play any useful role in everyday moral language, we should apply it to those making *progress*, i.e. moving in the right direction and well advanced in their journey to God, regardless of their continuing flaws. St. Paul deserves to be called "perfect" in this sense, all the more because he attained such a degree of self-knowledge and humility that he ceased to blush at confessing his own enduring imperfections.[70]

Augustine's third reply challenges the Pelagians' interpretation of "I am able" (or "unable"), along with the excessively individualistic perspective it reflects. Is this individualistic perspective even consistent? When we inherit our parents' good looks, their physical health, their IQ, their talents for music or mathematics, and their material wealth, all without complaint – as if we somehow deserved these legacies – how can we reasonably complain if we likewise inherit their weaknesses, illnesses, and debts? In fact, no human being comes into this world as some atomic individual. Every one of us is born into a massive, massively complicated, nexus of assets we did not individually earn, though we shall benefit from them, and liabilities we did not individually incur, though we shall suffer from them. Thus we are justified in saying "I am able to do x," when what we mean, strictly speaking, is "I am able to do x with the help of others I count upon to help me." In the same way, we might reasonably say "I am able to be perfect" when what we mean, or ought to mean, is "I am able to be perfect with God's help."[71] Here again, Augustine's conception of moral progress plays a role, for he has confidence that God purifies all persons who make progress in observing his commandments and forgives their sins, just as they forgive the sins of their neighbors.[72]

As Augustine emphasizes what we are able to do with God's grace, so he emphasizes what we are unable to do on our own, thanks to the nature we share with Adam. On the one hand, the nature created in Adam, endowed with the power of free choice, makes all human beings moral agents. (To this limited extent Augustine accepts the principle that "ought" implies "can": if human nature had not been created with free choice, people would have no more moral responsibility than cats do.) On the other hand, we all sinned "in Adam," so that we now suffer the consequences: the inability to be good without God's grace.[73] Contrary to the Pelagian view that all sins are individual, and that Adam's sin damaged nobody but himself, Augustine insists strongly upon what we share. Along with our individual, personal lives we have a common, damaged nature. As a result, we are all equally in need of healing by Christ, "the second Adam." Notice that the doctrine of our oneness in Adam has as its happier correlate our oneness in Christ. While we suffer the consequences of a sin that none of us individually committed, we may also benefit from a sacrifice that none of us individually made.[74]

Augustine's reflections upon human imperfection ultimately led him to attack the inseparability of the virtues, a doctrine central to ancient and Hellenistic ethics. His arguments on this topic are all the more noteworthy because they were revived over eight centuries later by Christian theologians concerned that Aristotle's influence was inspiring a neo-pagan movement in the universities.[75]

True imperfect virtue

Despite serious disagreements on other issues, all leading ancient philosophers defend a position that most present-day readers find bizarre: that the moral virtues are inseparable. No one can truly have courage, justice, or temperance without practical wisdom (*phronēsis* or *prudentia*), nor can one truly have practical wisdom without courage and the other moral virtues. The inseparability thesis embraced in antiquity takes roughly three forms. The identity version, presented by Socrates in Plato's *Protagoras*, makes every virtue identical with the knowledge of good and bad. Thus words like "courage," "temperance," and "justice," while different in meaning, nonetheless all refer to the same single state of mind. The unity version, defended by the Stoic Chrysippus, acknowledges a plurality of virtues, each with its own chief area of concern, but claims that all virtues belong to the mind, have the same end, and share the same principles. The reciprocity version, presented in Aristotle's *Nicomachean Ethics* 6.13, both acknowledges a plurality of virtues and distinguishes the virtues of character ("moral" virtues) from those of intellect. Even though Aristotle grants that certain intellectual virtues can stand on their own – a craftsman, for instance, may have no virtue other than skill – he still argues for a reciprocal dependence between the moral virtues and the intellectual virtue of practical wisdom. Nobody can have any moral virtue in the strict sense without practical wisdom, nor can he have practical wisdom without *all* the moral virtues; so what appear to be freestanding moral virtues turn out to be merely "natural dispositions," "natural virtues," or "imperfect virtues" called "virtues" only in a loose sense.

Ancient theories about the inseparability of the virtues never enjoyed wide support among persons untrained in philosophy.[76] Philosophers' teachings suggested, contrary to common-sense intuitions about morality, (1) that perhaps no human being on the face of the earth has ever been so excellent as to meet this high standard of virtue, and (2) that any individual who did manage to become virtuous must have progressed in an instant from possessing no genuine virtue to possessing them all. Since we have already considered Augustine's thoughts about (1), we turn now to difficulties concerning (2). Whichever version of the thesis an ancient author adopts, the implication does indeed look to be the same: whoever truly has one moral virtue must have them all; whoever lacks one cannot truly have any. If, for example, a courageous soldier drinks too much while on leave, his defect in temperance shows that he lacks practical wisdom, which in turn proves that he has no true moral virtue, and, by corollary, no true courage. Of course, we might continue to describe the soldier as courageous, but we would not be speaking with the precision expected of philosophers.

Augustine attacks this all-or-nothing perspective in a letter written in 415, one of the last in his long, rather strained correspondence with Jerome.[77] His stated purpose is to make sense of James 2.10: "Whosoever shall keep the whole law but offend in one point is guilty of all." Augustine recognizes that the passage from James might easily be explained by philosophers' teachings on the inseparability of the virtues. The inseparability thesis, however, holds no attractions for him. He himself works to interpret the passage from James in a manner consistent with scripture, especially with the teachings of St. Paul, but not with the teachings of the Stoics or pagan philosophers in general. In the *Retractationes* Augustine expresses satisfaction with his letter and reports that he published it after Jerome's death.[78]

Quite early in the letter Augustine expresses distaste for the paradoxes that Stoic philosophers derive from their all-or-nothing view of moral character: a person has no wisdom at all until he has perfect wisdom; there are no degrees of virtue and vice; the transition from vice to virtue must accordingly be complete and instantaneous, as when someone drowning suddenly bursts forth into the air; and all faults (or sins: in Latin, *peccata*) must therefore be equal, for even if one person is only a hand's breadth beneath the surface while another is fathoms deep, both are equally drowning. Augustine does not make it as clear as he should that reactions against these doctrines were already common in the pre-Christian Roman empire. But at least he moves beyond reciting standard objections to offering criticisms of his own:

> The saying, "Who has one virtue has them all, who lacks a particular one has none," is not a divine judgment but only the judgment of human beings – of great cleverness and with time and zeal for learning, to be sure, but still human beings. But I do not know how I can deny that even a woman – to say nothing of a man (*vir*), from whom the word "virtue" (*virtus*) is derived – who remains faithful to her husband, if she does this because of God's commandment and promise and is

faithful to him above all, has chastity; nor would I say that chastity is not a virtue or only an insignificant one. And the same is true of a husband who remains faithful to his wife. Yet there are many such people, none of whom I would say is without some sin, and certainly that sin, whatever it is, comes from some vice. Hence conjugal chastity in devout men and women is unequestionably a virtue – for it is neither nothing nor is it a vice, and yet it does not have all the virtues with it. For if all the virtues were present, there would be no vice; if no vice, absolutely no sin; but who is without some sin? Who, then, is without some vice . . . ?[79]

From Augustine's perspective, ancient philosophers are mistaken in thinking that any human being can be morally flawless. They are equally mistaken in believing knowledge or wisdom the foundation of all moral virtues. Virtues are not unified through wisdom; they are unified through charity. The more charity someone has, the more virtue; the more virtue, the less vice; yet no one can attain complete charity in the present life.[80] The passage from James, then, can be explained: it means that all sins are contrary to charity, and because the whole law of God depends on charity, any sin represents a failure to keep the law.[81]

We cannot be surprised that Augustine should reach such a conclusion, when he had already come to regard St. Paul as less than the flawless moral paragon he originally believed. Consider the implication: if even the saints among us are morally flawed, then we never meet virtues except in the company of vices. Moral progress for every one of us accordingly becomes what R. A. Markus aptly describes as as "a lifelong process of convalescence," never entirely complete in our mortal lives.[82] This may help to shed light on Augustine's description of the virtue of temperance in *De civitate Dei*:

> . . . What is the activity of virtue in this life but a perpetual battle with vices, and those not external vices but internal, not vices alien to us but quite clearly our own, our very own? This is the particular struggle of that virtue called *sōphrosynē* in Greek and "temperance" in Latin, which bridles the lusts of the flesh to prevent their gaining the consent of the mind and dragging it into every kind of disgrace . . . What do we want to achieve when we will to be made perfect in the supreme good, other than an end to conflict, so that the desires of the flesh do not oppose the spirit, and there is no vice in us for the spirit to oppose? But will as we may, we lack the strength to achieve this in our present life . . .[83]

Augustine does not mean that the struggle to control one's own emotions is intrinsically good, only that it is an ineliminable feature of our mortal lives. Nor does he adopt the pagan-philosophical conception of virtue in general or of temperance in particular, merely postponing its achievement to the afterlife. Pagan virtue is what makes a person *excellent* or *perfect*; by its very nature, only an elite few will ever attain it, and those who do will attain it only after the long years of study and self-development necessary to acquire practical wisdom. The core notion is that of successful accomplishment, founded on superior intellectual insight. Augustine, in contrast, regards virtue as that which makes us *good*, albeit well short of perfect. Virtue is a threshold, not the end of the road of moral development, so that we are justified in considering people virtuous if they are only moving in the right direction, are steadily *trying*, and have already made noteworthy progress. The unity of the virtues in charity is a motivational unity, a unity of love, belonging far more to the will (or the "heart") than to the mind.

Where ancient philosophers typically regard habit as the genus of virtue, Augustine tends to regard it as the enemy of virtue.[84] Moral character is not the combined product of native aptitude and appropriate habituation, much less an expression of one's success or failure in attaining wisdom. Nor does moral development follow the horticultural model, where good "root stock," appropriate soil and climate, and other fortunate circumstances prove indispensable for the production of an outstanding, flourishing specimen. Character depends on the will, by which one might break the bonds of habit and turn away from one's own past. Hence the importance of conversion, the "turning around" that marks the decisive moment in a Christian's life.

Although the mature Augustine believed that God alone can turn someone away from her own dismal past and produce the correct orientation, he still saw in human beings a power ever capable of responding to God. We are by our very nature suprising creatures: never completely past hope of salvation, never completely beyond danger of degeneration, never thoroughly predictable to mortal observers. Given the vast human penchant for self-deception, we can never even be sure that we know ourselves, much less feel confident in predicting our own moral futures.

Augustine himself sees nothing anxiety-producing in his vision of humanity's moral condition. Were God committed to judging brute performance, as Pelagians teach, we would surely all be doomed. But because God is loving and gives full credit for progress and having "one's heart in the right place," every one of us has reason to try her best and to hope for God's grace. The strangely democratic aspect of Augustine's ethics, often unnoticed, is that neither native intelligence, nor wealth, nor sound "parenting," nor a well-ordered political community, nor any combination of these makes any great difference to whether we shall eventually become virtuous and attain true happiness. Without God's grace, the most brilliant, aristocratic philosophers and the most illiterate, penurious peasants are all in the same boat; and those with God's grace have no reason to feel proud.

NOTES

1 *De civ. Dei* 8.8. All translations in this essay are my own.
2 Ibid. 19.1–3.
3 Ibid. 19.1.

4 The three most influential schools of Hellenistic philosophy were Epicureanism, Stoicism, and Skepticism, with the last divided between Academics and Pyrrhonists. For translations of the sources and helpful commentary, see Long and Sedley 1987.

5 Acts 17.18–32.

6 Probably the best introduction to this vast topic is given in Nock 1988, esp. ch. 11–14.

7 Illuminating essays concerning the complex relations between Christianity and Neoplatonism can be found in Armstrong 1979. See also Frede 1997.

8 For insightful, detailed analysis of Hellenistic ethics see Annas 1993.

9 "Beati certe esse volumus," a line from Cicero's lost dialogue, the *Hortensius* (frg. 36), is quoted by Augustine in *C. Acad.* 1.2.5. Recall his report in the *Confessions* (3.4) that it was reading the *Hortensius* that converted him to philosophy.

10 This lesson, too, can be found in the *Hortensius* (frg. 39), quoted by Augustine in *De beata vita* 2.10, and again in *De Trin.* 13.5.8.

11 *De beata vita* 2.14.

12 *Retract.* 1.1.2.

13 Ibid. 1.1.4, 1.3.2, 1.10.1.

14 Ibid. 1.6.5, 1.2.

15 See e.g. *De Trin.* 13.7.10.

16 See e.g. *Conf.* 7.9; *De civ. Dei* 8.8–10.

17 Epicurus, *Letter to Menoeceus*, A124–127, in Long and Sedley 1987, 149–150.

18 *De Trin.* 13.8.11.

19 See e.g. *De lib. arb.* 3.8.

20 Augustine's repeated contrast between Stoics and Epicureans unfairly presents the Epicureans as sensualists. This calumny was, however, quite common among the pagan authors Augustine read. He repeats it but hardly invented it.

21 Although Augustine explains in many works what he takes to be the differences between Epicureans and Stoics, his briefest, most eloquent account is given in *Sermons* 150.

22 *De civ. Dei* 19.20: "non absurde dici etiam nunc beatus potest, spe illa potius quam re ista."

23 *De civ. Dei* 22.24.

24 *De civ. Dei* 11.16.

25 *De lib. arb.* 3.5. What some would now consider the radical devaluing of animals was common in Hellenistic philosophy. For background see Sorabji 1993.

26 *De civ. Dei* 11.16.

27 In some places, as in *De civ. Dei* 11.16, and *De lib. arb.* 3.5, Augustine refers explicitly to the intrinsic worth (*dignitas*) of human beings. In other places, he uses a passive participle, such as *amandum*, to signify more generally what is worthy or deserving of love. For an example see *De civ. Dei* 15.22 (below, n. 32).

28 *De vera relig.* 46, 87.

29 Ibid. 46, 88.

30 *De doct. christ.* 1.22.20.

31 *De Trin.* 9.8.13.

32 *De civ. Dei* 15.22: "Nam et amor ipse ordinate amandus est, quo bene amatur quod amandum est, ut sit in nobis virtus qua vivitur bene. Unde mihi videtur, quod definitio brevis et vera virtutis ordo est amoris; propter quod in sancto cantico canticorum [2.4] cantat sponsa Christi, civitas Dei: 'Ordinate in me caritatem.'"

33 *De civ. Dei* 5.19.20; *Sermons* 150.5–9.

34 See e.g. *Ep.* 130.2.3.

35 *De doct. christ.* 1.26.27; *Sermons* 179A, 4; *Ep.* 155.
36 *De civ. Dei* 21.27; *Enchiridion de fide, spe et caritate* 76.
37 *Conf.* 2.8.
38 *De civ. Dei* 14.11; see also 1 Timothy 2.14.
39 *De civ. Dei* 10.5.
40 Matthew 26.39; *De vera relig.* 16.31–32.
41 See e.g. O'Donovan 1980, 93–97.
42 *De civ. Dei,* 14.28: "Fecerunt itaque civitates duas amores duo, terrenam scilicet amor sui usque ad contemptum Dei, caelestem vero amor Dei usque ad contemptum sui. Denique illa in se ipsa, haec in Domino gloriatur. Illa enim quaerit ab hominibus gloriam; huic autem Deus conscientiae testis maxima est gloria."
43 *De civ. Dei* 19.14: "Iam vero quia duo praecipua praecepta, hoc est dilectionem Dei et dilectionem proximi, docet magister Deus, in quibus tria invenit homo quae diligat, Deum, se ipsum, et proximum, atque ille in se diligendo non errat, qui Deum diligit . . ." See also *Sermons* 179A, 4.
44 *De civ. Dei* 12.8–9, 15.5, 15.7.
45 *De Trin.* 8.8.12; *De civ. Dei* 19.17.
46 Ibid. 4.5, 19.21.
47 See especially *Leviathan* I, chs. 13 and 17.
48 For an example see *Epistola de malis doctoribus et operibus fidei et de iudicio futuro* 15, where Pelagius (or possibly one of his early disciples) offers a memorable description of the unquenchable fires and the gnawing of immortal worms that sinners will ultimately suffer.
49 *Ep.* 145, 4: "Inimicus ergo iustitiae est, qui poenae timore non peccat, amicus autem erit, si eius amore non peccet; tunc enim vere timebit peccare. Nam qui gehennas metuit, non peccare metuit sed ardere . . ."
50 Augustine reports in *Retract.* 2.43 that he wrote Books 6–10 of *De civitate Dei* partly just to debunk the idea that sacrifices to pagan gods would improve one's fortunes after death. Regarding popular belief in divine punishments in the afterlife Nock (1988) remarks, "It was not a wholly imaginary bogy from which the Epicureans sought to free mankind" (ch. 7, esp. 103); see also Brunt 1989.
51 In his later works, where Augustine worries that the Pelagians are exacerbating popular fears of divine punishment, he returns again and again to the profound differences between love and fear. Some examples: *De spiritu et littera* 26; *De civ. Dei* 14.9; and esp. *Sermons* 156.14–15.
52 *Conf.* 8.5.
53 *Conf.* 8.10: "Ego cum deliberabam, ut iam servirem domino deo meo, sicut diu disposueram, ego eram, qui volebam, ego, qui nolebam; ego eram. Nec plene volebam nec plene nolebam. Ideo mecum contendebam et dissipabar a me ipso, et ipsa dissipatio me invito quidem fiebat, nec tamen ostendebat naturam mentis alienae, sed poenam meae."
54 For detailed discussion see Kahn 1988.
55 *De civ. Dei* 14.6: "Interest autem qualis sit voluntas hominis; quia si perversa est, perversos habebit hos motus; si autem recta est, non solum inculpabiles, verum etiam laudabiles erunt. Voluntas est quippe in omnibus; immo omnes nihil aliud quam voluntates sunt. Nam quid est cupiditas et laetitia nisi voluntas in eorum consensione quam volumus? Et quid est metus atque tristitia nisi voluntas in dissensione ab his quae nolumus?"

56 Ibid. 12.6.

57 Ibid. 12.7–8, 14.11–15.

58 *De lib. arb.* 3.17; see also *De civ. Dei* 12.6.

59 See, for example, Kant's *Grounding for the Metaphysics of Morals* (Kant, trans. Ellington, 1981), sect. III.

60 Augustine's eudaimonism should never be mistaken for utilitarianism or some other form of consequentialism. Important distinctions are explained in Kirwan 1999.

61 Romans 7.18–25. In *De pecc. merit. et remis.*, written in 412 AD, Augustine asserts that Paul speaks in his own voice in Romans 7. Augustine acknowledges the change in his thinking about this text in *Retract.* 1.22. For more detailed discussion see Burns 1979.

62 *De nuptiis et concupiscentia* 1.30–31; *Contra Julianum* 6.23.70–73.

63 Matthew 5.48.

64 The Pelagian proposition that "If a person ought to be without sin, he can be," formulated with impressive succinctness by Caelestius, is quoted and criticized by Augustine in *De perfectione justitiae hominis* 3.5. For a helpful survey of Pelagian teachings see Brown 1967, 340–352, 365–397.

65 Augustine quotes Julian's remark in *Contra Julianum opus imperfectum* 1.78. In Roman family law, a son was "emancipated" from his father when he came of age; hence Augustine's retort (ibid.) that if a man is emancipated from God, he is no longer within the father's family.

66 *De pecc. merit. et remis.* 2.6–7, 12–17. While Augustine grants the possibility that someone could be perfect in this life through the grace of God, he insists that no one ever has been.

67 Augustine's favorite example is the lust felt by St. Paul against his own wishes, and to which Paul did not consent (see e.g. *De perfectione justitiae hominis* 11.28). Related philosophical problems are explored in Mann 1998.

68 *Conf.* 1.7.

69 *De perfectione justitiae hominis* 3.6.

70 *De pecc. merit. et remis.* 2.13, 2.15–16.

71 Ibid. 2.6.

72 Ibid. 2.16.

73 Our "oneness in Adam" runs like a leitmotif through Augustine's anti-Pelagian writings. An excellent analysis, with extensive citations of secondary literature as well as sources, is provided in Rist 1994, 121–140.

74 For an example of the powerful connection between Augustine's understanding of Christ and his doctrine of original sin, see *De perfectione justitiae hominis* 7, where he claims that if a man can live without sin strictly through his own efforts, Christ died in vain.

75 Excerpts from scholastic texts on the inseparability of the virtues are published in Lottin 1942–1960, 3, pt. 2, 197–252; 4, pt. 3, 551–663.

76 For further discussion see Irwin 1996.

77 *Ep.* 167. Much of this letter is summarized in Langan 1979.

78 *Retract.* 2.45.

79 *Ep.* 167, 3.10: "Non enim et ista divina sententia est, qua dicitur: Qui unam virtutem habuerit, omnes habet eique nulla est, cui una defuerit. Sed hominibus hoc visum est multum quidem ingeniosis, studiosis, otiosis sed tamen hominibus. Ego vero nescio, quem ad modum dicam non dico virum, a quo denominata dicitur virtus, sed etiam

mulierem, quae viro suo servat tori fidem, si hoc faciat propter praeceptum et pro
missum dei eique primitus sit fidelis, non habere pudicitiam aut eam nullam vel
parvam esse virtutem; sic et maritum, qui hoc idem servat uxori. Et tamen sunt
plurimi tales, quorum sine aliquo peccato esse neminem dixerim, et utique illud
qualecumque peccatum ex aliquo vitio venit. Unde pudicitia coniugalis in viris fem-
inisque religiosis cum procul dubio virtus sit – non enim aut nihil aut vitium est –,
non tamen secum habet omnes virtutes. Nam si omnes ibi essent, nullum esset
vitium; si nullum vitium, nullum omnino peccatum; quis autem sine aliquo peccato?
Quis ergo sine aliquo vitio . . . ?" See also *De pecc. merit. et remis.* 2.15.

80 *Ep.* 167.3.11.
81 Ibid. 167.5.16.
82 Markus 1990, 54.
83 *De civ. Dei* 19.4: "Quid hic agit [virtus] nisi perpetua bella cum vitiis, nec exteriori-
bus, sed interioribus, nec alienis, sed plane nostris et propriis, maxime illa, quae
Graece *sōphrosynē*, Latine temperantia nominatur, qua carnales frenantur libidines,
ne in quacque flagitia mentem consentientem trahant? . . . Quid autem facere
volumus, cum perfici volumus fine summi boni, nisi ut caro adversus spiritum non
concupiscat, nec sit in nobis hoc vitium, contra quod spiritus concupiscat? Quod in
hac vita, quamvis velimus, facere non valemus . . ."
84 Augustine's views on *consuetudo* are analyzed in detail in Prendiville 1972.

16

PAUL WEITHMAN

Augustine's political philosophy

The topic of Augustine's political philosophy must be approached with care.[1] Augustine never devoted a book or a treatise to the central questions of what we now call "political philosophy." Unlike Aristotle, he did not attempt serially to address them and to draw out the institutional implications of his answers. Unlike Thomas Hobbes, he did not elaborate a philosophical theory of politics, if by that is meant a synoptic treatment of those central questions which relies on theoretical devices contrived for the purpose. Discussions of politics can be found in a number of Augustine's writings, but these are generally conducted in service of conclusions which neither we nor he would regard as philosophical. Indeed it is questionable whether Augustine thought that political philosophy has a subject-matter which should be sharply distinguished from the subject-matters of other areas of philosophy or of political enquiry. His own treatments of political subjects draw heavily upon ethics, social theory, the philosophy of history, and, most importantly, psychology and theology. It is possible to recover a distinctive set of political views from Augustine's texts. That set constitutes not a political philosophy, but a loose-jointed and heavily theological body of political thought which Augustine himself never assembled. It does not fit comfortably into any one of the disciplinary categories now standardly associated with the study of politics.

Though Augustine did not draw his own political views together into a coherent whole, subsequent generations of readers have seen unity and power in his political thought. In the sixteen centuries since Augustine's death, the body of work he left behind has proven a perennially rewarding source for philosophers and theologians concerned with the nature and purposes of government, the relations between Church and state, the implications of religious and moral pluralism for political society, and the conditions of just war. Its importance for medieval political theory would be difficult to overstate. In the twentieth century, creative social thinkers as different as Reinhold Niebuhr, Alasdair MacIntyre, and John Milbank have returned to it with profit.[2] Unfortunately it is not possible to trace the gestation of that body of thought through Augustine's many writings, to describe in any detail the classical and Christian political views on which it was nourished, or to discuss its subsequent influence. My primary aim is simply to sketch its profile as it appeared at maturity.

Love, the two cities, and the *saeculum*

The richest source of political material in Augustine's literary corpus is *De civitate Dei*, a book Augustine undertook to answer those who blamed the christianization of the Roman empire for the sack of Rome in 410. There he argues that despite the great diversity of human cultures, nations, and languages, the most fundamental cleavage in humanity is that between the two groups he calls the City of God and the Earthly City.[3] It is significant that Augustine employs a concept which denotes a discrete political entity, a city, to describe these two groups. His use of it suggests, correctly, that he thinks the internal dynamics of the two groups are to be explained using the same concepts appropriate for explaining the behavior of more familiar political entities like Rome. It also suggests, misleadingly, that each of the two cities can be identified with one political society or another. To see why this is mistaken and to see how the motif of the two cities structures Augustine's political thought, it is necessary to begin with his psychology and the central place of theology within it.

According to Augustine, human beings are moved by what he calls their "loves." He uses this term to embrace a variety of attitudes toward things we possess, as well as a wide range of human appetites and aversions toward things we do not possess.[4] These loves may be transient motives which explain isolated actions, engrained traits of character that motivate habitual action, or fundamental orientations of the person that unite her traits and unify her character. Two ways of loving are especially important for Augustine: what he calls "use," and "enjoyment." To enjoy something is to love it for its own sake; he contrasts this with regarding things as useful for securing something else.[5] Something that is worthy of being loved entirely for its own sake is the sort of thing that is capable of conferring true happiness.[6] Its secure possession brings about the quiescence of desire. Only God is worthy of being loved in this way and, as Augustine famously says to God in the first paragraph of his *Confessions*, "our hearts find no peace until they rest in you."[7] On the other hand, no creature, whether animate or inanimate, ought to be loved entirely for its own sake; no created good can completely quiet the appetites and confer the happiness and peace that the enjoyment of God can bring.

Perfect justice, Augustine thinks, would consist in an enduring disposition to love objects, including God, according to their worth.[8] Sin, the condition of humanity since the fall of Adam and Eve, is a turn away from God that causes psychological disarray. It introduces disorder into our loves so that we give ourselves and the satisfaction of our own desires undue importance, a disorder Augustine associates with the sin of pride.[9] Because of this prideful exaltation of self, the way we love things is at odds with what their nature merits.[10] We are prone to enjoy objects which ought to be used and to use goods which ought to be enjoyed. We are also prone to seek happiness in the possession of things that cannot confer it, including pleasures of the flesh, transient glory, enduring reputation, and, especially, power over others. Despite the disordered loves that sin causes, Augustine thinks that we also retain some desire to do what we ought. This puts human beings at odds with themselves. It explains why Augustine was so impressed with St. Paul's famous lament "the good that I will to do I do not do; but the evil I will not to do, that I do."[11] As a consequence of our turn away from God, even the best human lives are beset by inner conflict[12] and conflicts with other people, conflicts evident in even the most intimate human relationships.[13]

In *De civitate Dei*, Augustine relies on this account of love to explain the origin of the two cities and their progress through time. The loves to which he appeals are not transient motives; they are fundamental orientations of the members of the two cities. The City of God consists of those who glory in God and love God rightly. Its members are unified by their common love of God, "a love," he says, "that rejoices in a common and immutable good: a love, that is, that makes 'one heart' out of many."[14] The Earthly City, Augustine asserts, was created "by love of self extending even to contempt of God."[15] It consists of those who exalt themselves and love dominion. Fractious though it is,[16] it has a certain unity since its members look for glory, revel in the strength of their rulers and subjugate nations.[17] Because each of the two cities includes all those who are alike in their deepest loves, it follows that the members of the cities are dispersed in time and space. Augustine traces the founding of the Earthly City to Cain, the son of Adam and Eve who is said by the scriptures to have killed his brother Abel and founded a city.[18] The City of God, he says, includes the saints and the angels;[19] only some of its citizens are in the world and they are spread throughout it. Augustine speaks evocatively of them as being "on pilgrimage" in this life. He spells out the implications of this poignant image using technical language he introduced in his discussion of love. Members of the City of God, he says, merely use the world while they are in it; they do not enjoy it.[20]

Augustine sometimes speaks as though the City of God is the Church.[21] His considered view, however, is that "many reprobate are mingled in the Church with the good. Both are, as it were, collected in the net of the Gospel; and in this world, as in a sea, both swim without separation, enclosed in the net until brought ashore."[22] Thus members of the two cities exist side by side in the visible Church.[23] Every political society also includes citizens of each. Indeed Augustine is emphatic that before the coming of Christ members of the City of God were to be found even outside the society of Israel, as the example of Job makes clear.[24] Therefore no visible society or institution can be identified with either the City of God or the Earthly City. The distinction between the two cities is an eschatological rather than a political one. It is a distinction between those who are and are not destined for eternal life with God, rather than one between those who are and are not members of a given society. The members of the two cities are intermingled in what Augustine calls the *saeculum*, the realm of temporal existence in which politics takes place.[25]

In *De civitate Dei* Augustine seizes on the lust for domination which he says characterizes the Earthly City. There he poses a question which seems an obvious counterpoint to his remark in the *Confessions* that the human heart finds true rest only in God. "But, once established in the minds of the powerful, how," he asks, "can that lust for mastery rest until, by the usual succession of offices, it has reached the highest power?"[26] The answer, as we shall see, is the arrogant do not rest until they have achieved dominion. This restless love for power explains the sway of history's great empires and Rome's hegemony over Augustine's own world. Indeed love and conflict are central to Augustine's discussions of politics. Augustine's identification of a love which defines one of the cities with one of the driving forces in political history suggests that history unfolds as a result of a contest between the Earthly City and the City of God. In fact nothing could be further from Augustine's view than this facile dualism. Though people may differ in their most fundamental orientations, every human being has a divided will. Even those who are destined to spend eternity with God are to some extent responsible for the conflicts of temporal life. Even they therefore need the restraint that, as we shall see, Augustine thinks government exists to provide.

Slavery, government, and property

Augustine is relatively uninterested in a question about government that was of central concern to both Plato and Aristotle: Which form of government is best? In an early passage Augustine remarks perfunctorily that if a people are committed to the common good they ought to be allowed to choose their own rulers. He does not give the matter further consideration.[27] Again unlike Plato and Aristotle, Augustine is uninterested in the historical and social processes by which one regime – kingship, for example – is typically transformed into another. He is far more interested in how God's providence works through political history than he is in how that history depends upon the social forces characteristically set in play by one or another institutional form.

To see this, it is helpful to see exactly what questions his discussion of government is intended to answer. Augustine seems not to have had a clear concept of the state, understood as a society's governing political apparatus. Thus when he speaks of Rome, as he often does in *De civitate Dei*, he sometimes has in mind the city of Rome, sometimes the Roman republic, sometimes the empire and sometimes the society of Roman citizens together with their traditions, laws, and mores, but never the set of institutions which collectively administered Rome's political affairs. Augustine's remarks about the origin and purposes of government are therefore not answers to questions about the origin or purposes of the state.

Crudely put, Augustine is interested not in a political institution, but in the rationale for a human relationship. He observes that some human beings have the authority to govern or, better, to control the actions of others by the use of coercion. This he regards as unnatural, at least outside the family. He then asks how such an authority relationship came to be and what ends it serves. His answer is that it exists only because human beings are sinful creatures who need to be humbled and restrained by force and the threat of force. This conclusion depends crucially upon the fact that Augustine does not distinguish clearly between a relationship which is specifically political and other relationships of authority and subjection, especially the relationship between a master and slaves.

The qualified assimilation of political subjection to slavery is the key to Augustine's views about the purposes of political authority and its origins in human sinfulness. His argument that slavery is unnatural and results from sin does not add significantly to views he inherited from the Patristic tradition. He enjoins masters to treat their slaves kindly and reiterates St. Paul's injunction that slaves should obey their masters. What is significant is Augustine's use of traditional ideas about slavery to explain government. Augustine says that human beings are naturally social. They have a common origin in Adam and because of this common origin they are naturally drawn together by bonds of sympathy and kinship.[28] Indeed he remarks that there is no species so naturally social as humanity.[29] Augustine also intimates that, had original sin not been committed, sinless human beings would have reproduced and multiplied to fill the earth.[30] Because of their natural sociability, they would have lived in groups and those groups would presumably have needed direction. At issue is whether that direction would most aptly be described as an exercise of political authority. Analyzing the argument that it would not brings to light Augustine's assimilation of political authority to the mastership of slaves.

Augustine closes *De civitate Dei* 19.14 by talking briefly about the authority exercised by a benevolent father and husband. He opens chapter 15 by saying that "this is prescribed by the order of nature: it is thus that God created man." God, Augustine continues, intended human beings to exercise dominion *only* over irrational creatures and members of their families. He adduces two scriptural passages as evidence of God's intent. First, he quotes Genesis 1.26 to show that God gave Adam dominion only over the fish, the birds, and things that crawl on the earth. Later he refers to the patriarchs, saying that they were shepherds rather than kings. "This was done," he says, "so that in this way also God might indicate what the order of nature requires, and what the desert of sinners demands. For we believe that it is with justice that a condition of servitude is imposed on the sinner."[31] The closing discussion of chapter 15 and the second of Augustine's scriptural allusions suggest that he thinks if original sin had not been committed, human groups would have been guided by paternal authority akin to that exercised by a Roman *paterfamilias* or a biblical patriarch. It is this, in turn, which suggests that he thinks political authority is a result of human sinfulness. But what is it about political authority that makes Augustine think it would not have existed if human beings were not sinful? And what is it about sin that makes Augustine think political authority exists because of it?

Let us take the second question first. As we saw, Augustine observes that human beings are the most social of species by nature; he completes the thought by saying that human beings are also the most "quarrelsome by perversion."[32] Human beings, Augustine says, never lose their desire for peace. Indeed, he implies, we crave peace. But the psychological disorder which is symptomatic of our sinfulness makes it difficult for any of us to live in peace with ourselves and others.[33] The human tendency to conflict is so strong that peace could not be brought about if groups were governed only by parental power. After the commission of original sin, political power is required.

Because of the distorted loves of sinful human beings and the conflicts that arise among them, the aims of political authority must be limited. Augustine says "the earthly city . . . desires an earthly peace, and it limits the harmonious agreement of citizens concerning the giving and obeying of orders to the establishment of a kind of compromise between human wills about the things relevant to mortal life."[34] In answer to the question of why those who have the power to establish peace also have the authority to do so, Augustine would reply that their authority comes ultimately from God, who ordained political authority as a remedy for sin.

Augustine's treatment of property follows the pattern laid down by his treatment of political authority. He follows other Patristic writers in thinking that the division of property is not natural.[35] What he means can be teased out of a passage in one of his letters, where he suggests that those who make bad use of their property, or acquire it unjustly, possess it unjustly.[36] We might expect Augustine to suggest that those who hold property unjustly would be deprived of it under a just system of property law. A thinker more interested in institutional questions might go on to say what those laws should be. Instead Augustine continues, surprisingly, that one of the functions of laws of property is to protect unjust possession so that "those using their [their property] badly become less injurious"[37] than they would otherwise be. Presumably what he has in mind is that those who make bad use of the property to which they are legally entitled do so because of their strong attachment to material goods. Their attachment is so powerful that they would steal or illegally retain the things they wanted if the laws required them to give them up when they used them badly. Laws which allow the unjust to retain possession of property thus keep them from "obstruct[ing the faithful] by their evil deeds." As should be apparent from his discussion of love, Augustine thinks that so strong an attachment to finite goods is an affective disorder that results from human sinfulness. Therefore the fact that sinful human beings have an undue love for material things is what explains the feature of private property Augustine regards as the most salient and unnatural: the fact that laws which establish property protect the claims of those who should not own it. Like political authority, it providentially works to the benefit of all by allowing us to live together more peacefully than we otherwise could.

This brings us back to the first question: what is it about political authority that makes Augustine think it would not have existed if human beings were not sinful? The answer is that for Augustine, the most salient feature of political authority is just that feature an authority would have to have in order to govern a society of people all of whom are constitutionally prone to conflict: the authority to coerce them. This authority is common to those in positions of political power and the masters of slaves. Augustine also insists that subjection to political authority, like the subjection to a slave-master, is morally improving because both foster humility, particularly when the good are subjected to the bad.[38] Thus political authority and the mastery of slaves both rely on coercion, and both teach humility to sinfully proud human beings. It is because of these fundamental similarities that Augustine assimilates the former type of authority to the latter, easily moving back and forth between the two in chapter 15 of De civitate Dei and elsewhere.[39]

Augustine, Cicero, and Rome

The claim that political subjection is fundamentally akin to slavery seems prey to a number of obvious objections. First, no, or very few, societies maintain peace through forms of coercion that bear any resemblance to the treatment of slaves. Augustine's study of history should have taught him that peace in any society depends on a large measure of voluntary, if sometimes grudging, compliance. Secondly, political society arguably exists to bring about some degree of justice. The fact that societies are perceived by their members to do so helps to explain why the members of those societies comply with the demands of the social order. Thirdly, it might be thought, it is precisely because political societies effectively aim at justice that citizens, especially citizens who are active in political affairs, realize important elements of the human good. They develop and exercise virtues like justice, patriotism, and self-sacrifice which both are good for them and help to sustain their society. These second and third of these points are stressed by Cicero, who, by defending the second of them, placed himself in a tradition of political thought which had its origins in classical Athens. By setting out to refute these claims, Augustine takes a firm stand against that tradition.

Cicero raises these points in his dialogue *De Re Publica*, a work well known to Augustine. One of the participants in the dialogue is Scipio Africanus, who claims that a society is "not every assembly of the multitude, but an assembly united in fellowship by common agreement as to what is right and a community of interest."[40] Scipio later asks rhetorically "what is a society except a partnership in justice?";[41] still later he praises those who dedicate themselves to public service, implying that they are the most virtuous of citizens.[42] Augustine mentions the first two of these remarks early in *De civitate Dei*[43] and returns to them in Book 19. There he makes the traditional claim that justice prevails only where each is given his due. It therefore demands, he says, the worship of the true God. Since God was not worshiped in Rome, justice never prevailed there. Since it is granted all around that Rome is a society, it follows that Scipio's definition of a society must be wrong.[44]

Augustine began writing *De civitate Dei* to answer the charge that the abandonment of the Roman deities for the God of Christianity was an injustice to the gods which had led to Rome's sack by the barbarians. The argument that Rome was unjust because the Christian God was not worshiped there would therefore have struck many of Augustine's intended readers as high-handed provocation at best and question-begging at worst. Augustine therefore supports his reply to Cicero by several more sophisticated strands of thought which he deftly interweaves. One is a highly polemical version of Roman history. Augustine reminds his readers that the founder of Rome was a fratricide who could not bear to share the glory of the founding with his brother.[45] He recounts the Roman abduction of the Sabine women with a gleeful sarcasm aimed at the Roman historian Sallust, who boasted of the justice of the early Romans.[46] Worship of the Roman gods, Augustine says, was characterized by "horrible and detestable evils,"[47] particularly in the theaters where the deeds of the gods were re-enacted.[48] He quotes Sallust himself on the efforts of the Roman rich to suppress the poor before the destruction of Carthage, and on the moral decline of Rome afterwards.[49] In reply to those who would blame Christianity for the fall of Rome, Augustine writes:

> Rome was founded and extended by the labors of those men of old; their descendants made Rome more hideous while it stood than when it fell. For in that ruin there fell only stones and wood; whereas by these men's lives were overthrown, not her walls, but her moral defenses and adornments. More fatal than the flames which consumed the city's houses were the lusts that burned in their hearts.[50]

Augustine furnishes this narrative to support his claim that if Rome was a society, this was not because justice prevailed there but in spite of the fact that it did not. But Augustine uses history in service of another and more subtle point. The upshot of his narrative is that because of Rome's injustice, the city never was worthy of the place its patriotic citizens gave it in their loves. Augustine believes, as we saw, that justice requires us to love things as their nature merits. This claim, together with his historical narrative, strengthens his case that justice never prevailed in Rome, for it implies that even the noblest citizens of the Roman republic were not just, his passing remark about "moral adornments" notwithstanding. This conclusion, in turn, allows him to advance two further arguments. It enables him to rebut Cicero's contention that devoted citizenship draws on genuine human excellence by replying that even when Rome was at its apogee, the noblest of its citizens developed qualities which merely bore outward resemblances to the virtues. It also enables him to rebut the related thesis that the stability and power of Rome in this period were to be explained by the civic virtues of its citizens. Augustine can be at his most shocking and effective when he impugns the virtue of venerable figures in Roman history. The passages in which he does so lend his position considerable rhetorical force,[51] especially when conjoined with his view that Christians are the best subjects and office-holders a society could have.[52] The real burden of his case against the moral superiority of the great Romans of the past depends, however, upon his account of what the virtues are and are not. As we should expect, claims about the right order of love lie at the heart of that account.

Some of Augustine's most extreme claims about the conditions of virtue, and his most extreme conclusions about the noble Romans' lack of it, are to be found in De civitate Dei. There Augustine writes of the ancient Romans:

> glory they loved most ardently. They chose to live for it, and they did not hesitate to die for it . . . Because they deemed it ignoble for their fatherland to serve and glorious for it to rule and command, the first object of all their desire was freedom, and the second, mastery . . . It was, therefore, this avidity for praise and passion for glory that accomplished so many wonderous things; things which were doubtless praiseworthy and glorious in the estimation of men.[53]

Since Augustine thinks that justice requires loving things according to their nature, he goes on to deny that it is "a true virtue unless it tends toward that end where the good of man is."[54] Earthly glory, for oneself or one's city, is not "where the good of man is." Therefore the Romans' passion for glory was not a virtue, a genuine human excellence, regardless of the achievements it brought to the city they loved. Augustine does not deny that "those men of old" who "founded and extended" Rome exhibited a self-discipline which "their descendants" did not. They "overcame the desire for riches and many other vices";[55] this suppression is presumably what he means by speaking of Rome's "moral adornments." To determine whether such self-restraint is genuinely virtuous, however, Augustine argues that it is necessary to look at the loves – the underlying family of desires and aversions – which constitute its characteristic motive.

Augustine argues that acts of self-restraint are sinful if performed from fear of punishment[56] and that abstinence "is only good when it is practiced in accordance with faith in the Supreme Good, which is God."[57] He claims that the self restraint of the ancient Romans was rooted not in such faith, but in fear of destruction by the enemy city of Carthage[58] and in desires for Rome's freedom, dominion, and the ersatz immortality that comes from lasting glory. As Augustine says, "What else was there for them to love, then, but glory, by which they sought to find even after death a kind of life in the mouths of those who praised them?"[59] He concludes that neither these loves nor the self-restraint they motivated made the Romans virtuous. They only made them "less vile."[60]

Elsewhere Augustine is more measured. In a letter written about the time he began *De civitate Dei*, he grants that those who founded and preserved Rome had "a certain characteristic rectitude" which he refers to as "civic virtue."[61] The notion of a civic virtue assumed great importance in civic republicanism, a tradition of political thought which has its origins in Cicero.[62] According to this tradition, true excellences are traits that orient their possessor toward their city's common good. In Augustine's writing, however, there is no implication that this probity is a genuine virtue. As if to make this point, Augustine hastens to add that the Romans had these traits "without true religion." Thus Augustine's remark about civic virtue should not blind us to the radical character of his political thought. His arguments that political authority is exercised because of human sinfulness, that it is fundamentally akin to slavery, that it exists to restrain and humble those subject to it, and that citizens do not develop the virtues by dedicating themselves to political life, together constitute a sustained assault on the tradition of political thinking which locates "the good for man" in the common good of an earthly rather than a heavenly city.

The assault culminates in Augustine's alternative definition of a commonwealth, which he offers in Book 19 of *De civitate Dei*. "A people," Augustine famously says there, "is an assembled multitude of rational creatures bound together by common agreement on the objects of their love."[63] Political societies will enjoy the voluntary support of their members as long as their members love the same things. For present purposes, what is most important about Augustine's definition of a people is that what sustains a society need not be a common love of or aspiration for justice. Instead what sustains societies may be nothing more than that their citizens love the limited peace their governments establish.

Augustine is sometimes labeled a "positivist" about politics or, more commonly, a "political realist."[64] His definition of a people lends some credence to the charge of positivism. Positivists in the philosophy of law maintain that some precept counts as a law in virtue of having been enacted or posited in the right way. It is no less so because it does not stand in the right relationship to natural or moral law. Similarly, Augustine thinks that some groups count as a people in virtue of having a common object of love. They are no less so because the object of their love is not just; indeed Augustine intimates in one place that robber bands count as societies.[65] There are also ample grounds for describing Augustine as a political realist. He recognizes that those in authority must sometimes do things they deeply regret, like torturing the innocent.[66] He recounts embarrassing details about Roman history and demolishes the myths latter-day Romans tell themselves about their city's past. He is clear-eyed about the loves of power and glory that actually move human beings and that, as we have seen, explain why political authority and subjection exist in the first place.

Augustine's positivism and realism do not imply, however, that he thinks any state of affairs is as good as any other, that any society is as good as any other, or that whatever those in political authority do to ensure peace is acceptable. He would surely recognize that earthly peace can be established on terms that are better or worse. Though he believes ideal justice cannot be realized in political society, he would certainly recognize the possibility of incremental improvements. Augustine says at one point that human law must conform to divine law, though this commitment is absent from his more mature work.[67] He suggests that the world would be better off if it were partitioned into small kingdoms rather than far-flung empires.[68] Immediately after offering his own definition of a people as a multitude in agreement on the objects of their love, Augustine continues "and, obviously, the better the objects of this agreement, the better the people; the worse the objects of this love, the worse the people."[69] Having remarked that those who are devoted to glory cannot have real virtue, he grudgingly concedes that those whose passions are checked by this devotion "are more useful to the earthly city when they have even that imperfect kind of virtue than they would be if they did not have it."[70] Finally, as we shall see below, he holds out an ideal or "mirror" for Christians in positions of political authority.[71] Augustine does not, therefore, believe that various aspects of political life are beyond any ethical assessment. What he does believe is that the moral assessment of political authorities turns crucially on how they try to bring about earthly peace. The moral assessment of the peace they establish depends upon its terms. The claims that Augustine has a "negative" view of politics or that he thinks politics is "morally neutral" are therefore overstated.[72] They emphasize Augustine's departure from a tradition of thought according to which politics is an integral part of genuine human flourishing. In doing so, they obscure the fact that even those whose loves are properly ordered can attach some instrumental value to the end political authority exists to secure.[73]

The instrumental value of earthly peace opens the possibility of a positive this purpose? Augustine's attitude toward the christianization of the Roman empire and the duties of Christian rulers is complex and I can only touch upon it here. He is certainly less enthusiastic about the conversion of the empire than some of his contemporaries and less sanguine about what it will bring. To those who argue that imperial power can be used to advance Christianity he replies that pagan Rome advanced the cause of Christ by creating the martyrs.[83] In his most famous piece of writing on the duties of Christian rulers, the "mirror for princes" in De civitate Dei Book 5, Augustine does say that they are to "make their power the handmaid of his majesty by using it to spread his worship to the greatest possible extent."[84] As a result of his protracted involvement in the Donatist controversy in northern Africa during the closing decade of the fourth century and Donatist violence against Catholics, Augustine abandoned his opposition to religious coercion.[85] While he never endorsed coercing pagans or Jews, he came to believe that as a result of official sanctions, members of what he thought a heretical sect of Christianity could be brought to sincere and ortho- dox conviction.

This conclusion is, however, hard to reconcile with Augustine's insistence on the opacity of the human heart and on how little we know of our own and others' motives. Augustine takes this opacity and ignorance to have political implications, as he makes clear late in De civitate Dei. There Augustine writes that Christian judges must sometimes torture innocent witnesses in an attempt to uncover the truth, even though they may never learn whether they have attained it.[86] Thus, he concludes sadly, "the ignorance of the judge is very often a calamity for the innocent."[87] This suggests that Augustine had modest hopes about what public officials can accomplish and so he has modest hopes for pol- itics. The suggestion draws some support from his description of earthly peace as a mere compromise. It draws still more from a rhetorical question Augustine poses earlier in City of God. "As far as this mortal life is concerned," he asks, "which is spent and finished in a few days, what difference does it make under [whose] rule a man lives, who is so soon to die?"[88]

Augustine is sometimes said to have "interiorized" personal ethics by moving the focus of ethical evaluation of an agent from the agent's action and its effect on the world to the psychological dispositions from which the agent's actions proceed.[89] This gains some credence from his discussions of Christian office- holders. Despite his remarks about putting imperial power at God's service, Augustine's mirror for princes is really an extended paean to the Christian emperor who loves and fears God and who acts from the virtues of clemency, mercy, compassion, humility, piety, and generosity.[90] This, conjoined with his warning that Christian emperors may be deposed,[91] and his argument that judges must proceed though they cannot be sure they will ascertain the truth, suggests that public officials, at least, will not be judged by their effectiveness. A assessment of Rome's political and military accomplishments. That, in turn, raises the question of why Rome accomplished what it did. This is just the question to which Roman historians hoped to provide a persuasive answer by citing the virtues of the ancient Romans[74] or the wisdom of the Roman constitution.[75] Augustine would not deny that the self-restraint, military discipline, and patriotism of the Romans strengthened Rome and extended its sway.[76] By denying that these qualities are virtues, and later by denying that we can "by clear inspection . . . give judgment as to the merits of kingdoms,"[77] Augustine robs the explanation of its intended force. Furthermore, to seize on this explanation of Roman success is to miss what is most important in Augustine's discussion of the rise and fall of empires.

As we saw earlier, Augustine's analysis of politics departs from the fact that some human beings can guide the lives of others by the threat and employment of force. Their authority to do so is ordained by God, Augustine says, to humble those who are subject to it and to control their desires for earthly happiness. Even the good need this discipline, Augustine thinks. Sometimes it is imposed by subjecting them to the bad; to this end, God makes use even of men like Nero.[78] What is true of the subjection of some people to others is equally true, Augustine thinks, of the subjection of populations to empires. He says:

> God, therefore, the author and giver of happiness, because he is the only true God, himself gives earthly kingdoms to both good men and bad. He does not do this rashly, or as it were at random, for he is God, not Fortune. Rather he acts in accordance with an order of things and times which is hidden from us, but entirely known to him.[79]

History does not provide evidence that Rome or any other empire is favored by Fortune or destiny, nor can Roman ascendancy be understood simply by appealing to the moral qualities of the Romans. It was God who gave power to Assyria and to Persia.[80] It was God who made use of Roman patriotism and discipline "to suppress the evils of many nations."[81] Political history is governed by God's providence. To the extent that historical explanations are possible, they must refer to it. But for Augustine, such explanations must always be tentative. He can conjecture about God's reasons for giving power to Rome,[82] but his considered view seems to be, as he says in the quoted passage, that the reasons history unfolds as it does are "hidden from us."

Justified violence

Even if no political society can be the City of God, should not the Christian ruler try to approximate it in his realm? Despite the difficulty of discerning God's action in history, is it not likely that God raised up Christian rulers for precisely fully interiorized ethic would hold not only that persons will not be judged by the effectiveness of what they do, but also that they will not be judged negatively even if what they do seems on its face to be bad. This is what is required to give full force to Augustine's famous remark "love and do what you will."[92] To find such an ethic in Augustine, it is necessary to turn from his treatment of the duties of office or his remarks about peace to his discussion of war.

It is ironic that an author who writes so eloquently about the good of peace should have played a pivotal role in the emergence of a body of Christian thought justifying warfare. Many in the early Church had interpreted the Gospel's injunction to "turn the other cheek" as forbidding the use of force to defend oneself or others and forbidding participation in warfare. In reply to the pacifist interpretation of this injunction, Augustine points out that Christ challenged the temple officer who hit him rather than turning his other cheek toward him.[93] He maintains that what Christ requires "is not a disposition of the body but of the heart, for there," he continues, "is the sacred resting place of virtue."[94] This suggests that at least some forms of violence may be justifiable if they proceed from a heart which loves rightly.

In an early work, Augustine argues that laws which permit the use of force to defend oneself, and perhaps another, against unjust attack are not unjust laws. He does so on the grounds that laws may permit lesser evils to prevent greater ones.[95] As he hastens to add, however, this leaves open the possibility that actions of this kind are in conflict with a higher law even if the law which permits them is not. He does not assert that it is morally permissible for private persons to use force to defend others. In one of his letters he seems to claim just the opposite,[96] despite saying elsewhere that the law which permits them to do so is unexceptionable. He reaches a different conclusion, however, about soldiers. To see how he does so, note that legal actions declaring war do not typically *permit* soldiers to fight; they *require* it. It would be paradoxical for Augustine to assert that legal actions declaring war are justifiable but that all the subjects to whom they apply are obliged to disobey them. Therefore if Augustine is to argue that Christians may participate in war, he must argue both that the legal actions declaring war are morally acceptable and that Christians are permitted or obliged to obey them. The first he establishes by arguing that wars may be waged in self-defense, if another nation refuses to return property it has unjustly appropriated or if it refuses to rectify injustices.[97] The second he establishes with the qualified assertion that soldiers are obliged to fight a war that has been declared by lawful authority.[98] The qualification he adds is that soldiers engaged in warfare should not be motivated by cruelty, bloodlust, or desire for vengeance. Augustine thinks that we can never be certain of our own motives. So long as they try not to act from these motives, Christians may fight in wars despite Christ's seeming command to the contrary.

The continuing significance of Augustine's political thought

The division of the world into two cities does not originate with Augustine. It is an image that he found in other writers and adapted to his own purposes.[99] Why does he do so? Why, that is, does he assert that those who love God constitute a single city composed of the angelic, the living, and the dead? The notion of a communion of saints has theological implications that Augustine draws out to explain how heavenly denizens of the City of God help those of its members who are still on pilgrimage.[100] But what does this assertion add to his political thought?

I noted earlier that Augustine does not place politics beyond ethical assessment. Still less does he believe it beyond theological critique. The force of that critique depends crucially upon the alternative social model that he develops, the City of God. That city serves as a social ideal the rightly ordered love, peace, and justice of which no earthly society can realize. It is an ideal by comparison with which every earthly city must suffer. Thus Augustine compares the riches of Rome with the treasury of the City of God.[101] He juxtaposes the specious immortality sought by Roman heroes with the eternal life gained by the Christian martyrs.[102] He contrasts Rome with the City of God by comparing it to the Earthly City, reminding his readers that both were founded by fratricides.[103] He therefore uses the City of God as a standard against which actual political societies, especially the great empires,[104] can be measured and found wanting. This enables Augustine to expose the vanity of their moral pretensions and to heighten his readers' desire to be members of that city where the "Supreme Good is to be found."[105] As he says early in *De civitate Dei*:

> Of the rise and progress and appointed end [of the two cities], then, I shall now speak . . . I shall do so as far as I judge it expedient to the glory of the City of God, which shall shine forth all the more brightly when compared with the other city.[106]

I mentioned at the outset that Augustine's political thought does not fit comfortably into the contemporary categories of political enquiry. Like Augustine's work, the disciplines which now study politics – political theory, political philosophy and political science – have critical implications. Political theory and political philosophy articulate norms by which actual societies are to be judged. The same is true of some political science. Where their practitioners part company with Augustine is in their view that political activity can be made or shown to be a rational undertaking. They attempt to understand political behavior in terms of rational choice theory; to rationalize decisions among policy options according to their expected risks, costs, and benefits; to locate rational preferences and procedures for their rational aggregation; to defend deliberative procedures for the rational exchange of opinion so that citizens will respect one another and become attached to their common good; to frame institutions which encourage progress by liberating human reason, and to find principles of justice the rational authority of which will stabilize and legitimize institutions conforming to them. By contrast, what seems to interest Augustine about politics is what it shows about the divine and psychological forces which govern human life but which human reason cannot fully penetrate or control.

We have seen that in Augustine's hands, an analysis of political life invariably reveals the work of those forces he calls "loves." He appeals to the loves of self, glory, immortality, and peace to explain why human beings need a regime of private property and coercive authority, why they build and maintain empires, how societies remain stable. Augustine allows for the possibility that, as with the Romans, political life will discipline the less desirable human loves. But he would deny that politics can eradicate or redirect those fundamental loves, or that those loves can be enduringly subjected to our reason by felicitous institutional design. Instead, he offers an explanation of political stability that interestingly rivals explanations appealing to rationalist accounts of mutual respect, justice, and institutional legitimacy. He thereby promises a corrective to political theories which exaggerate the role that reason can or should play in ordering political life.

That promise can be made good only if he can persuasively undercut alternative theories of the way human beings do or could behave in politics. In a sustained attempt to do so, Augustine recalls episodes that apologist historians either paper over or neglect. He tirelessly probes what purports to be virtuous behavior, exposing the operation of misdirected loves and showing how frequently they masquerade as nobler motives with the connivance of self-deception and ideology. After the close of what Isaiah Berlin once called "our terrible century" [107] it might seem doubtful that we need Augustine to teach us about either brutality or hypocrisy. Yet many of the best political theories now on offer are premised on psychologies that are extremely optimistic. They leave us without the conceptual resources necessary to understand the evil which human beings visit on one another. Peter Brown once wrote that for Augustine, "political activity is merely symptomatic: it is merely one way in which men express orientations that lie far deeper in themselves."[108] Augustine's account of those deep human orientations provides a set of concepts with which religious thinkers can make sense of political evil. This account is among his most enduring and valuable contributions to political thought.

NOTES

1 I am grateful to Brian Daley, S.J., Robert Markus, Brian Shanley, O.P., and Eleonore Stump for helpful comments on an earlier draft.
2 See Niebuhr 1953; MacIntyre 1988; Milbank 1990.
3 On human diversity, see De civ. Dei 14.1. Unless otherwise noted, quotations of De

civitate Dei are from Dyson 1998. Of the available English editions, this is generally to be preferred for its literalness and economy of translation, and for the briskness of its prose. On occasion, I have followed Bettenson 1972 or have retranslated passages myself. Unless otherwise noted, all translations from other of Augustine's works are my own.

4 *De civ. Dei* 14.7.
5 *De doct. christ.* 1.31.
6 *De civ. Dei* 8.8.
7 *Conf.* 1.1.
8 *De vera relig.* 48.93.
9 *De civ. Dei* 14.13.
10 Ibid. 15.22.
11 Romans 7.19.
12 *De civ. Dei* 14.7.
13 Ibid. 19.5, 19.8.
14 Ibid. 15.3.
15 Ibid. 14.28.
16 Ibid. 15.4.
17 Ibid. 14.28.
18 Ibid. 15.2.
19 For the angels, see ibid. 10.7.
20 Ibid. 15.7.
21 Ibid. 13.16.
22 Ibid. 18.49; see also 18.54.
23 Ibid. 1.35.
24 Ibid. 18.47.
25 For a fine discussion of this notion in Augustine's thought, see Markus 1970.
26 *De civ. Dei* 1.31.
27 *De lib. arb.* 1.6.
28 *De civ. Dei* 12.23–24, 14.1.
29 Ibid. 12.28.
30 Ibid. 13.24, 14.26.
31 Ibid. 19.15.
32 *De civ. Dei* 12.28 (following Bettenson).
33 *De civ. Dei* 21.15.
34 *De civ. Dei* 19.17 (following Bettenson).
35 See generally Deane 1963, 104–105.
36 *Ep.* 153.
37 Ibid.
38 *Enarr. in Ps.* 124.8.
39 Ibid.
40 *De civ. Dei* 2.21; cf. Cicero, *De Re Publica* 1.25.
41 Ibid. 1.39.
42 Ibid. 6.26.29.
43 *De civ. Dei* 2.21.
44 Ibid. 19.24.
45 Ibid. 15.5.
46 Ibid. 2.17.

47 Ibid. 2.6.
48 Ibid. 1.32.
49 Ibid. 2.18.
50 Ibid. 2.2. In the first sentence, I have followed Bettenson's translation, which gives a more accurate rendering of Augustine's word "foediorem."
51 Ibid. 1.19.
52 *Ep.* 138.
53 *De civ. Dei* 5.12.
54 Ibid. (my translation).
55 Ibid. 5.13.
56 Ibid. 14.10; *De moribus ecclesiae catholicae* 30.
57 *De civ. Dei* 15.20.
58 Ibid. 1.30–31.
59 Ibid. 5.14.
60 Ibid. 5.13.
61 *Ep.* 138.
62 On republicanism, see Pettit 1997.
63 *De civ. Dei* 19.24.
64 See Deane 1963, 221–243 and Niebuhr 1953, chapter 9.
65 *De civ. Dei* 4.4.
66 Ibid. 19.6.
67 *De vera relig.* 31.58. For the claim that this commitment is not found in later works, see Markus 1970, 89.
68 *De civ. Dei* 4.15.
69 Ibid. 19.24.
70 Ibid. 5.19.
71 Ibid. 5.24; *Ep.* 155.
72 See the literature cited in Burnell 1992.
73 Cf. *De doct. christ.* 2.25.
74 See the remarks about Cato and Sallust at *De civ. Dei* 5.12.
75 See, for example, Polybius, *The Rise of the Roman Empire*, Book 6.
76 *De civ. Dei* 5.12.
77 Ibid. 5.21.
78 Ibid. 5.19.
79 Ibid. 4.33.
80 Ibid. 5.21.
81 Ibid. 5.13 (following Bettenson)
82 *De civ. Dei* 18.22.
83 For a nuanced discussion see Markus 1970, chapter 3.
84 *De civ. Dei* 5.24.
85 The best study of this matter is Brown 1964.
86 *De civ. Dei* 19.6.
87 Ibid.
88 *De civ. Dei* 5.17.
89 For a sophisticated treatment see Taylor 1989, chapter 7.
90 *De civ. Dei* 5.24.
91 Ibid. 5.25.
92 *In Johannis epistulam ad Parthos tractatus* 7.8.

93 John 18.23.
94 *C. Faust.* 22.76.
95 *De lib. arb.* 1.5.
96 *Ep.* 47, cited at Deane 1963, 311 n. 22.
97 Here I follow Deane 1963, 160.
98 *C. Faust.* 22.74.
99 *De doct. christ.* 3.34.
100 See the remarks about the ministry of the angels at *De civ. Dei* 10.7.
101 Ibid. 5.16.
102 Ibid. 5.14.
103 Ibid. 15.5.
104 Ibid. 18.2.
105 Ibid. 19.11.
106 Ibid. 1.35.
107 Berlin 1991, 127.
108 Brown 1965, 9.

17

M. W. F. STONE

Augustine and medieval philosophy

One of the reasons why it is so difficult to introduce the problems and issues of medieval philosophy by means of highly general labels as "Aristotelian," "Neoplatonist," and "Augustinian" is that such markers so often obscure as much as they explain. This is certainly the case with regard to the general term "medieval Augustinianism."[1] For some historians, however, this term is uncontroversial. They maintain that there was an identifiable and continuous tradition of reflection and commentary on Augustine's work throughout the Middle Ages.[2] Evidence for this view is not hard to find. Augustine has had an enormous influence on Western philosophical thought.[3] In medieval times, Neoplatonism and Aristotle exceeded his influence only in extent, variation and chronology. Augustine was also *the* authority in Latin-speaking Christian theology and philosophy, enjoying an honorific status. In virtue of these facts, it is unsurprising that his imprint and legacy are to be found in the work of so many medieval thinkers.[4]

If this is the case, why then is the term "medieval Augustinianism" controversial? In the first instance, the very idea that there existed a homogeneous and continuous tradition of thought in the Middle Ages that was distinctively "Augustinian" is open to question. It is difficult to find philosophers, at least before the fourteenth century, whose work is parasitic on Augustine's own ideas, or who believe themselves to be members of an "Augustinian school." Most medieval thinkers were in one sense or other influenced by some of Augustine's theories, but their actual ideas cannot be said to be completely dependent on his work. Further to this, any appreciation of Augustine's influence on medieval thought must take into account that not all of his works were always available to philosophers throughout the Middle Ages. Thus, we can note that there are marked differences in the ways in which Augustine's philosophical inheritance is used by early medieval philosophers, by thirteenth-century thinkers, and by self-styled "Neo-Augustinian" theologians in the later Middle Ages. Any serious study of medieval thought will reveal not one but many different readings of Augustine.[5] These readings exhibit not only the saint's authoritative status among philosophers within the Christian tradition, but also the breadth, depth, and variety of the Augustinian corpus itself.

Early medieval thought

Writing a century after the death of Augustine, Boethius (c. 480–c. 526 AD) advanced a system of thought in which Augustinian theses are assimilated to the later Platonic tradition of Proclus (410–485 AD) and Ammonius (fl. 550 AD).[6] Many of Boethius' doctrines are demonstrated according to the Aristotelian logic of those Platonic schools. This is significant since it shows Boethius building on a style of purely philosophical argument latent in parts of Augustine's work. Unlike other Fathers of the Latin West – here one thinks of Hilary of Poitiers (c. 315–367/8) and Ambrose of Milan (c. 339–397) – Augustine had used not only arguments that were based on scriptural authorities (*auctoritates*), but also those that made direct appeal to reason alone (*sola ratione*).[7] Boethius' enthusiasm for Aristotelian logic enabled him to endorse and further refine this element in Augustine. His efforts helped to strengthen the place of discursive thought and rational reflection within Christian theology, an activity to which Augustine was by no means ill disposed.[8]

More explicitly, the doctrines of Augustine were brought into formal contact with the central tenets of later Neoplatonism in the works of John Scottus Eriugena (c. 810–c. 877). Eriugena derived his understanding of the themes and issues of Neoplatonism from his reading and translations of Pseudo-Dionysius (fl. 500).[9] That influence aside, many elements of Eriugena's theology, especially the works *Periphyseon*, *De divisione naturae*, and *De praedestione*, exhibit the influence of Augustine.[10]

The distinctive portraits of Augustine to be found in the work of Boethius and Eriugena were widely influential (along with other Neoplatonic and Greek Patristic sources) in the great revival of Neoplatonic philosophy that occurred in the so-called "Renaissance of the Twelfth Century."[11] The work of Honorius Augustodunensis (1075/1080–c. 1156), whose *Clavis physicae* is indebted to Eriugena,[12] still drew very heavily on Augustinian theology. In the early twelfth century, the writings of Anselm of Canterbury (1033–1109) distinguished themselves by their unique appropriation, revision, and extension of so many elements in Augustine's philosophical and theological thought. Anselm is certainly indebted to Augustine, but the nature and extent of his debt are sometimes difficult to gauge.

In the *Proslogion*, we find strong evidence both of Anselm's commitment to a number of Augustinian themes and objectives and of his independent development of them. While the definition from which Anselm begins his famous *a priori* argument for the existence of God ("id quo maius cogitari non potest") has precedents in Augustine and Boethius, none of his Christian predecessors had thought to find in it an argument that could demonstrate divine existence.[13] The *ratio Anselmi*, as the argument was known to the medievals, is certainly "Augustinian," in the sense that the *fidelis*, the one who believes, is illumined by reason and finds a self-authenticating truth within his own thought. It is also "Boethian" in its confidence that a logical explication of the very concept of God can constitute a bona fide demonstration of God's actual existence. But in many ways, the argument is original to Anselm, since he was the first in the medieval Christian tradition to draw out completely the implications of those earlier suppositions.

The work of Anselm by no means exhausts twelfth-century interest in the many facets of Augustine's philosophical and theological legacy. Hugh of St. Victor (d. 1141) is certainly faithful to Augustine, but his interest in the explanation of the phenomenal world and natural science led him to embrace Eriugena's brand of Christian Neoplatonism.[14] Of further interest is the aforementioned Honorius Augustodunensis. A Benedictine monk like Anselm, his work exhibits a profound theological debt to Augustine, but as with Hugh, certain elements in his writings abound with Eriugenist doctrine and imagery.[15] Rupert of Deutz (1075/1080–1129), a younger contemporary of Anselm and a stalwart defender of traditional Benedictine monasticism, divides himself from Anselm in his insistence upon the exegetical character of theology, and in his development of an "Augustinian" theology of history.[16] Rupert's symbolic exegesis is developed out of Augustine's commentaries on scripture. Augustine remains for him the "pillar and firmament of truth, truly the pillar of cloud, in which the wisdom of God has set his throne."[17]

Differences among twelfth-century authors aside, there is a sense in which that century did much to push Augustine's theology and philosophy to the forefront of medieval intellectual culture. For Augustine's works were given pride of place in that influential codification of theology, the *Sententiae in IV libris distinctae* (Four Books of Sentences) by Peter Lombard (c. 1095–1160).[18] As this book was to dominate the theological curriculum for the next 450 years, becoming a set text in the theology faculties of newly established universities, it ensured the continuing presence of Augustinian theories and precepts in all aspects of medieval philosophy and theology.

The thirteenth century

Thirteenth-century philosophers and theologians knew Augustine primarily through a few standards treatises – *Confessiones, De civitate Dei, De libero arbitrio, De doctrina christiana, De vera religione,* and *De Genesi ad litteram libri duodecim* – and through the abundant quotations that circulated under his name in *florilegia*, canon law, and Lombard's *Sententiae*. In thirteenth-century works, the precise source of a quotation from one of Augustine's works is seldom acknowledged beyond his name, although later and more systematic authors such as Bonaventure (1221–1274), Albert the Great (1200–1280), and Thomas Aquinas (1224–1274) did produce more accurate citations of his work.

The introduction of the works of Aristotle into the universities, as well as into the hearts and minds of so many thirteenth-century thinkers, can be said to complicate any account of Augustine's influence upon the philosophy of the period.[19] It has long been commonplace among historians of medieval philosophy to describe the principal events and developments from the middle of the thirteenth century onwards in terms of a dispute between so-called "Augustinians" and "Aristotelians."[20] It is argued that evidence of such a contest can be found in the struggles that led to the infamous condemnations of certain philosophical theses at the universities of Paris and Oxford in 1270 and 1277.[21] The "Aristotelians," in this story, were not just the infamous members of the Arts Faculties such as Siger of Brabant (c. 1240–1281/1284) and Boethius of Dacia (fl. 1260), whose theories concerning the immortality of the soul and the eternity of the world were thought to challenge the authority of Christian doctrine in philosophy,[22] but also Dominican theologians such as Albert and Aquinas. The "Aristotelianism" of these other thinkers is often thought to consist in their approval of Aristotelian doctrines, and in their application of those doctrines to a number of theological discussions.[23]

By contrast, the "Augustinians" in this standard narrative were not simply reactionary theologians, but thinkers who found the growing use of Aristotle not only detrimental to the defense of the Christian faith but also to the practice of philosophy. Among these individuals, Franciscans such as Alexander of Hales (c. 1185–1245), Bonaventure, and John Pecham (c. 1230–1292), are cited as exemplars of an "Augustinian" school.[24] Because of the affiliation of the protagonists to different religious orders, the quarrel is often presented as an on-going dispute between the Dominicans and Franciscans.

In many ways this analysis of the principal controversies of thirteenth-century philosophy reduces them to a set of unhelpful caricatures. A simple point that is often lost sight of is that both Aristotle and Augustine were studied, cited, and defended at great length by philosophers and theologians on both sides of the putative divide. Some of the best-known "Augustinians," such as Bonaventure, expended much labor explicating the texts of Aristotle, thereby offering exacting interpretations of his philosophy precisely in order to resist attempts to "baptize" his system of thought.[25] Bonaventure's work also reveals an acquaintance with the work of Avicenna (980–1037) and Averroës (c. 1126–1198), thereby reflecting the complexity and dynamism of philosophical discussion at the University of Paris during the 1250s and 1260s. Contrary to received wisdom,

Bonaventure is not hostile to the practice and institution of philosophy: his work exhibits an erudite and informed knowledge of the Aristotelian philosophy of his time.[26]

On the other side, leading "Aristotelians," such as Albert and Aquinas, frequently cited Augustine as *the* Christian authority (*auctoritas*). In particular, Aquinas was careful to remain within the guidelines he had laid down for the correct appropriation of pagan philosophy by Christian thinkers.[27] These observations alone bear testimony to the fact that one has to be extremely careful when using the terms "Aristotelian" and "Augustinian" to describe the complex events and positions of philosophy in the second half of the thirteenth century.

Caution aside, it is true that some members of the Franciscan order did champion certain elements of Augustine's thought insofar as they saw his work as central to the preservation of doctrinal fidelity. Important aspects of the work of Bonaventure can be appreciated in this context. With his fellow Franciscans he sought to maintain, albeit with certain modifications and definite amendments, Augustine's teaching on divine illumination, the powers of the soul and seminal reasons.[28] Augustine was understood to have held that all knowledge was made possible by "illumination," that is, by the intelligible presence of divine rules and reasons in the workings of the human mind.[29] Such rules and reasons were taken to constitute God's very own patterns and powers of creation. On most accounts of divine illumination, this did not entail that a human mind in its present life could ever see the divine essence, or could know anything just by relying on divine illumination. Bonaventure, for one, was clear that the presence of the divine ideas is ordinarily a necessary but not a sufficient cause for cognition.[30] Similar, but more nuanced, accounts of divine illumination can be found in Alexander of Hales and John Pecham.[31] The theory also found support outside the Franciscan order in the work of a secular master like Henry of Ghent (d. 1293).[32]

With regard to the powers of the soul, some authors claimed to follow Augustine by holding that such powers were nothing more than relations to certain acts. For this reason, they held that there could be no essential distinctions among the powers of the soul, since the soul had a single essence. This argument was often directed at philosophers who followed Aristotle in holding that because the powers inhered in the soul as accidents in a substance, such powers were distinct. Others, like Bonaventure, sought to enlist the authority of Augustine in order to argue for an intermediate position between the two extremes. On this view, the soul's powers are only analogically located in the category of substance. Thus, the powers of the soul can be considered as really different – not as separate essences are different, but as powers of a *single* essence can be viewed as different.[33]

Augustine's account of seminal reasons was derived, in part, from Stoic natural philosophy.[34] Many of his Franciscan supporters were unaware of this genealogy, and thus construed the doctrine as affirming the superiority of the completeness of divine creation over the Aristotelian conception of the pure potency of matter. They understood Augustine to teach that God had infused into matter, at the moment of creation, intelligible patterns that could be actualized over time. Bonaventure, for example, held that the souls of non-rational animals and of plants were created not *ex nihilo* and not simply out of pre-existing matter, but rather in the manner of a seed. In other words, these souls were created by actualizing an active potency in matter. After the moment of creation, animal souls were reproduced without divine intervention by the natural actualization of these "seminal reasons."[35]

Another way in which Augustine is taken to influence thirteenth-century philosophy is in the development at that time of the theory in moral psychology known as "voluntarism." By no means a homogenous intellectual movement, voluntarism sought to describe the genesis of human action by identifying the will as the prominent cause and explanation of action. Voluntarism is so often described as opposing "intellectualism," a view associated with the work of philosophers like Aquinas who had argued that reason or intellect was more active than will in the commission of human acts. While both Augustine and Aristotle are conspicuous in the disputes over *liberum arbitrium* (freedom of decision), this being the main forum in which discussions about reason and will took place, it is difficult to determine precisely the extent of the debt such discussions owe to these philosophers. For it is often the case that what separates an "intellectualist" from a "voluntarist" in discussions of *liberum arbitrium* prior to the 1277 condemnations is more a matter of emphasis than a profound difference in moral psychology.[36]

Towards the end of the thirteenth century, Henry of Ghent and John Duns Scotus (c. 1226–1308) brought to bear "Augustinian" arguments relating to the powers of the soul and the nature of human knowledge and action in original and interesting ways. Henry, for instance, refined existing thinking on divine illumination. He held that since knowledge of natural things depends in part upon divine illumination, there could be no purely natural way of knowing things about the natural order.[37] In Scotus' thesis that the will does not necessarily choose the *summum bonum*, even when it discerns it intellectually, we find distinct echoes of Augustine's moral psychology.[38]

It is sometimes claimed that we find the first signs of a self-conscious philosophical Augustinianism in the works of writers from the religious order known as the Augustinian friars. Forged out of existing monastic communities in the middle of the thirteenth century, the order's constitution was ratified in 1290. Some historians have wanted to see in the writings of this order an institutional home for an "Augustinian school" (*schola Augustiniana*) of philosophy and theology,[39] but as with most matters pertaining to developments within thirteenth-century thought the matter is far from simple. Giles of Rome (c. 1247–1316), the first Parisian master of the order and later its Prior General, had been a student of Aquinas. As a consequence, his philosophical work is heavily indebted to Thomism.[40] Despite the fact that he was later claimed by members of his order to have founded a new school of philosophy, the *schola Aegidiana*, there is no unequivocal evidence that Giles was ever a thoroughgoing Augustinian or that his *schola* was set up in order to further the aims and objectives of an "Augustinian philosophy."

A good illustration of this last point can be seen in the work of Giles's successor as Prior General, James of Viterbo (c. 1255–1308). Among other things, James is known for his writings on politics, especially his *De regimine christiana*. If there had been a genuine *schola Augustiniana* or *schola Aegidiana* in existence at this time, one would have expected James's work to resonate with Augustinian precepts and theories. However, when one actually examines *De regimine*, one finds something altogether different. True enough, the influence of Augustine's work, especially *De civitate Dei*, is apparent in its pages, but the work is more directly influenced by the political writings of Aquinas, combining genuine moments of originality with sagacious commentary. Of particular interest is James's argument that while the Church does possess some temporal jurisdiction over the civil powers, it ought to exercise that power infrequently and only out of necessity. Recalling the growing dispute at that time between Pope Boniface VII and Philip IV ("the Fair") of France, one is struck by the prudent nature of the advice.[41]

The fourteenth and fifteenth centuries

The fourteenth century can be said to have witnessed a profound change in the use and discussion of the works of Augustine by medieval philosophers. To begin with, one finds a greater variety of works being cited, accompanied by longer and more exact quotations. Further to this, there is an earnest effort on the part of scholars to maintain the highest standards of accuracy in their critical presentation of Augustine's views. A good deal of this more rigorous approach to the work of Augustine can be said to be derived from the dissemination of humanist practices of citation and commentary that are a particular feature of scholasticism in the middle to late fourteenth century.[42]

The first major figure of the fourteenth century is William of Ockham (1285–1347). Ockham is an original philosopher whose thought does not lend itself to a concrete characterization in terms of "Augustinianism." His innovations in logic and epistemology owe much to a sustained reflection on Aristotle, whereas his nominalism in metaphysics was certainly opposed to the more standard realism that is often found in fourteenth-century members of the Augustinian order. It is only perhaps in Ockham's ethics and soteriology that vestiges of the Augustinian tradition are present.

In the fourteenth century we finally meet philosophers deserving of the title "Neo-Augustinians." Thanks to the pioneering work of scholars such as Damascus Trapp OSA,[43] Adolar Zumkeller OSA,[44] and William Courtenay,[45] some aspects of this tradition are now accessible to modern readers. The members of the Neo-Augustinian movement combined fidelity to Augustine's texts with a definite set of philosophical and theological motives, which led them to reappropriate Augustine's teaching. They wanted to understand and rehabilitate that teaching in response to the issues provoked by the growing influence of the so-called *via moderna* or "modern way" in philosophy.[46] Among this group of thinkers Thomas Bradwardine (c. 1300–1349) and Gregory of Rimini (c. 1300–1358) stand out as most worthy of comment.

Bradwardine was a prominent member of the "Oxford Calculators," a group of Masters of Arts who were based in Merton College in the second and third decades of the century.[47] He wrote important works on logic and the philosophy of language. He also composed one of the most important works of the Neo-Augustinian movement, the *Summa de causa Dei contra Pelagium et de virtute causarum* ("On God's Cause against Pelagius and on the Power of Causes").[48] This work was inspired by Augustine's anti-Pelagian writings and directed at a number of Bradwardine's contemporaries such as Robert Holcot (c. 1290–1349), Adam Wodeham (d. 1358) and Thomas Buckingham (c. 1290–1351), whom he suspected of fostering Pelagian thoughts.[49]

Gregory was a member of the Augustinian friars and was elected Prior General of the order in 1357, having earlier taught in Paris and Italy.[50] His philosophical appropriation of Augustine is wider than that of Bradwardine and certainly more nuanced. Augustine's direct influence on Gregory, especially through works such as *De libero arbitrio*, is revealed in Gregory's thesis that intelligible knowledge depends on innate ideas that direct the soul to rational and moral ends.[51] This is but one instance in which Gregory tackles current problems in fourteenth-century philosophy by bringing to bear positions and arguments he has retrieved from the texts of Augustine.[52]

The most distinctive feature of the Neo-Augustinian movement of the fourteenth century, however, was its sustained philosophical and theological attack on Pelagianism. Bradwardine and Gregory broke new ground in the ensuing debate about these issues by limiting the significance of created grace (*gratia creatura*). According to Bradwardine, grace is a habit given by God and united to the human will, by which the will loves God, above all else, on account of God himself. Yet the will and the habit of grace do not co-operate as coefficient causes in the performance of a good act. Grace alone is the efficient cause.[53] Thus

Bradwardine accepted the existence of created grace but denied the existence of co-operative grace (*gratia cooperans*). He then argued that created grace has only limited efficacy; so, for example, the will cannot rise above temptation by virtue of created grace alone, it must possess an *auxilium Dei speciale*.[54] This assistance is actually God's own will.[55] For Bradwardine, then, the modern Pelagians were not at fault in their teaching on the doctrine of created grace, but rather were guilty of minimizing God's personal involvement in the commission of acts of moral goodness.

Gregory also advanced the view that God influences *immediately* the performance of a good deed. He taught that a general divine influence enables the will to function. An additional influence, however, provides what the will lacks in itself – the ability to love God on account of himself. Although Gregory could call the co-operation of the human will with this special additional influence a "coefficiency," he did not hold that the *auxilium speciale* effected a moral and spiritual restoration of fallen human nature. Even under the reforming aspect of spiritual grace, the will is unable to love God above all else. The *auxilium* is only applied to particular acts; as a supernatural cause it ameliorates the moral nature of the act that is to be done. The will can either comply with this process or else resist its influence.[56]

It is sometimes argued that Neo-Augustinian thinkers such as Bradwardine and Gregory exerted a profound influence on members of the Augustinian order in the later decades of the fourteenth century, and that their anti-Pelagianism became a distinctive hallmark of that order's intellectual output. It is difficult, however, to sustain a clear and coherent connection between the Neo-Augustinians and members of the Augustinian school. Of course, the work of Gregory of Rimini, a former prior of the order, was taken up in a revised form by friars such as Hugolin of Oriveto,[57] Johannes Klenkok,[58] Johannes Hitalingen,[59] Angelus Dobelinus,[60] and Johannes Zacharie,[61] but the anti-Pelagian polemics of Bradwardine by no means attracted unanimous support. His work was often criticized by the Augustinian friars for the constraints he had placed upon the efficacy of human choice.[62] Further, when one examines the work of another prominent philosopher of the Augustinian order, Alfonsus Vargas (d. 1366), who flourished in Paris and Seville in the late 1340s, one finds that he did not consider the campaign against the so-called modern "Pelagians" to be the *causa sine qua non* of modern Augustinian philosophy.[63]

The most important work of Augustinian scholarship of this period was the *Milleloquium Sancti Augustini* compiled by Bartholomew of Urbino (fl. 1340) in 1345. This work consisted of approximately 1500 passages taken from Augustine's corpus, arranged alphabetically in 1081 entries.[64] The *Milleloquium* is a fine piece of scholarship that bears testimony to the exegetical rigour and sophistication of late medieval philosophical and literary culture. It is not a random collection of Augustinian *dicta*, but rather a well-researched and comprehensive document composed with the intention of making Augustine's thought attractive and accessible to a new generation of readers.

Besides the above individuals, Augustine's work also was a major influence on the writings of Jean Gerson (1363–1429) and John Wyclif (before 1330–after 1380). Gerson developed a view of the Fall, original sin, and justification that was shaped profoundly by his reading of Augustine's texts. Some of the pessimistic aspects of his moral theory are directly attributable to the influence of the late Augustine.[65] The work of Wyclif, especially in its opposition to nominalism in metaphysics and its concern with scriptural fidelity, presents yet one more window on Augustine's influence on late fourteenth-century Oxford philosophy.[66]

A further feature of fourteenth-century "Augustinianism" was the commentary. Many of these derived from scholars based at Oxford. In the early part of the century Nicholas Trevet (c. 1258–after 1334) wrote a commentary on *De civitate Dei*.[67] This was followed by, among others, a short commentary on that same work by John Baconthrop (c. 1290–1346?) as well as his commentary on the *De Trinitate*.[68] By the end of the fourth decade of the century Richard Fitzralph (c. 1295–1360) had composed *Glossulae super de Trinitate*, a work now lost but cited by Adam Wodeham.[69] Finally, the Dominican Thomas Walleys (fl. 1340) and the Franciscan John Ridevall (fl. 1330) both wrote commentaries on *De civitate Dei*, with the latter also composing a commentary on the *Confessiones*.[70]

The influence of Augustine remained strong throughout the fifteenth century. His work was a constant source of stimulation for both "humanist" and "scholastic" philosophers. Renaissance *savants* like Marsilio Ficino (1433–1499) saw in Augustine's work an appealing prototype of a "Christian Platonism."[71] Other writers touched by humanism as diverse as Jean Calvin (1509–1564), Philip Melanchthon (1497–1560), Lorenzo Valla (c. 1407–1457), Desiderius Erasmus (1446–1536), and Pietro Pomponazzi (1462–1522), all found inspiration in Augustine's vision of humanity.[72]

During the Reformation the philosophical and theological theories of Augustine loomed large. Stimulated by the publication of the first critical edition of his work, completed by Johannes Amerbach in 1506, the Reformers had direct access to the Augustinian corpus. However, most of them tended to read Augustine selectively. Thus great emphasis is placed on Augustine's theory of election and reprobation, justification and volition, while the more positive elements of his anthropology and theory of grace are underplayed or ignored. It is well known, for instance, that Martin Luther (1483–1546) was strongly influenced by the work of Johannes von Staupitz (after 1460–1524).[73] Staupitz's work bequeathed to Luther the seeds of his future theories of grace and justification, theories that would not have been unfamiliar to many fifteenth-century

Neo-Augustinian thinkers in Northern Europe. That said, while Luther's interpretation of these facets of late Augustinian theology helps us to understand Luther's own theological predilections, they do not throw much light on late medieval Augustinianism *per se*.

Here again we return to the abiding theme of this chapter: the many faces of Augustine and their representation in medieval thought. Given the length, complexity, and variety of his extant writings, we ought not to be surprised that each generation of medieval thinkers gave expression to that element in Augustine's work that helped them to understand the theological and philosophical problems of their own times. Indeed, the very universality of Augustine's corpus, and its relevance to the demands of everyday life, were ever present in the minds of his medieval interpreters. For them Augustine, the supreme *auctoritas* of the Christian tradition, provided indispensable instruction not only in speculative thought and practical action, but also in the more intimate spheres of the call to holiness and sanctity.

NOTES

1 The very same point is made by Jordan (1998). Jordan goes on to specify three senses of the term "Augustinian" in the history of philosophy: (i) a comprehensive dependence on the work of Augustine; (ii) a specific defense of Augustine's teaching in the face of rival philosophical theories; and (iii) a reappropriation of Augustinian principles to address new questions and issues in philosophy and theology. Jordan argues, rightly to my mind, that all three senses of the term are to be found in the medieval period. I am grateful to Eleonore Stump for drawing my attention to Jordan's article. The present study was written before I became acquainted with this intelligent paper.

2 The first to coin the term "Augustinianism" in connection with the study of the thirteenth century was Ehrle (1889). This method of classifying the philosophical positions of the thirteenth century was continued by De Wulf (1901) and developed by Mandonnet (1911), who argued that there was a tradition of "Augustinian Platonism," a thesis later supported and developed by Gilson (1924 and 1929). Gilson sought to clarify Mandonnet's "Augustinian Platonism" by arguing that it could be separated into several streams, of which "Franciscan Augustinianism," represented by Bonaventure, was the most prominent. Some years later, Gilson coined the phrase "the Second Augustinian School" to describe the work of Henry of Ghent and Duns Scotus: see Gilson 1955, 446–471.

3 On Augustine's appeal throughout the ages see Marrou 1955; O'Donnell 1991; Matthews (ed.) 1999; Fitzgerald (ed.) 1999.

4 For a discussion of the general impact of Augustine's work on philosophical, theological, and literary thought in medieval times, see Schaefer 1988.

5 The point is well put by Damasus Trapp, who says: "What happened in the Early, in the High, and in the Late Middle Ages may, who knows, be pressed into the following, somewhat daring formula: early scholasticism had both an Augustine and an Augustinianism of its own; Aristotelic Thomism had an Augustine but no Augustinianism; late scholasticism rediscovered Augustine within an Augustinianism of its own!" (Trapp 1965b, 150).

6 On Boethius' use of Augustinian ideas and terminology see Crouse 1980 and Obertello 1983.
7 Thomas Aquinas observes that there are two ways of treating a subject, by authorities and by reasons. He notes that Augustine used both ways, while Ambrose and Hilary only used the way of authorities. See *Expositiones super librum Boethii de Trinitate*, ed. Decker, pp. 46–47.
8 Kretzmann 1990.
9 For a helpful discussion of this element of Eriugena's work see Roques 1973; Steel 1983; D'Ouforio 1994.
10 Mathon 1954; R. Russell 1973. Some have held that Eriugena's use of Augustine in this work is somewhat eccentric and unfaithful to Augustine's intentions, see Sheldon-Williams 1973.
11 Chenu 1957; Dronke (ed.) 1988.
12 Honorius Augustodunensis, *Clavis Physicae*, ed. Luceutini.
13 See Augustine, *De doct. christ.* 1.7; *De lib. arb.* 2.6.14; *Conf.* 7.4; Boethius, *De consolatione philosophiae*, III, pr. 10.
14 Baron 1957, 1–18; 41–42; 172–181.
15 Garrigues 1977; Crouse 1978.
16 Van Engen 1983, ch. 3.
17 Rupert of Deutz, *De sancta trinitate et operibus eius* 40.19, ed. Haake, "Augustinus, columna et firmamentum veritatis, et vere columna nubis, in qua thronum suum posuit sapientia Dei."
18 Colish 1994.
19 See Lohr 1982.
20 Gilson 1955, Part 8; Copleston 1964, Part 4, 212ff.
21 For a helpful discussion of these famous episodes see Wippel 1977. The standard work on the 1277 condemnations is Hissette 1977.
22 Van Steenberghen 1980.
23 Van Steenberghen 1991, 277–320.
24 Gilson 1924, 1955.
25 This element in Bonaventure's work is the subject of an intelligent essay by Andreas Speer: see his "Einleitung" to his edition of Bonaventure's *Questiones disputate de scientia Christi*, pp. XI–L. See also Bougerol 1973.
26 Van Steenberghen 1991, 203–222.
27 See the "Prologus" to *Summa Theologiae*.
28 J. Quinn 1973, 101–319.
29 See *De Trin.* 9.7.12, 12.14.23; *In Johannis evangelium tractatus*, 25.4; *De doct. christ.* 11.27.2, 46.2; *De diversis quaestionibus octoginta tribus*, "De ideis."
30 Bonaventure, 4 *Sent.* 50.2.12 and 1 *Sent.* vols. 1 and 4 of *S. Bonaventura Opera omnia*.
31 On Alexander see Principe 1967, chs. 1 and 5. On Pecham see Little 1926 and Sharp 1930.
32 Macken 1972.
33 For a discussion of these issues see Dales 1995, 99f.
34 Boyer 1931, ch. 3.
35 J. Quinn 1973, 120ff.
36 For a general account of the so-called voluntarist school at this time see Korolec 1982; 1995, 94–149; Stone 2001.
37 Macken 1972; Pasnau 1995. Henry's general debt to Augustine is explored in Macken 1992.

38 Ingham 1989, Part II; Adams 1995.
39 This is true in part of the work of Trapp and Zumkeller. For a dissenting voice, which draws upon the work of English theologians, see Courtenay 1987, 307–324.
40 Nash 1956; 61–92; Murray, "Introduction" to Giles of Rome, *Theorems on Existence and Essence* (*Theoremata de esse et essentia*).
41 For a discussion of James's work see Wilks 1964.
42 Smalley 1960; Courtenay 1987, 311ff.
43 Trapp 1954, 1956, 1963a, 1963b, 1964; 1965a, 1965b.
44 Zumkeller 1953, 1954, 1978, 1980.
45 Courtenay 1980, 1987, 1990, 1991.
46 For a full discussion of this development see Zimmermann (ed.) 1974.
47 Oberman 1958; Dolnikowski 1995.
48 Bradwardine, *De causa Dei*, ed. H. Saville.
49 Leff 1958; Obermann 1958, 95–186. For a more recent discussion of some of these issues see Genest 1992.
50 Gregory of Rimini (Gregorius Arminensis OSA), *Lectura super primum et secundum Sententiarum*, ed. Trapp and Marcolini.
51 *Lectura* I. 6.
52 Gregory's general debt to Augustine is brought out in explicit detail by Leff 1961; Eckermann 1978; and Oberman (ed.) 1981.
53 Bradwardine, *De causa Dei*, I., 39, pp. 329; I. 40, p. 64.
54 Ibid. II. 4 and 5, pp. 477ff. Cf. II. 6, pp. 491–497; II. 9, p. 498.
55 Ibid. II. 6, p. 489. A concise explanation of Bradwardine's theory of causality can be found in Oberman 1958, 78–83.
56 Gregory of Rimini, *II Sent.*, dd. 26–28, a. 3, ed. Trapp and Marcolini, vol. 6, p. 77.
57 Hugolin of Oriveto lectured at Paris in the late 1340s and early 1350s. He later lectured at Perugia and in the provincial school at Rome. See Zumkeller 1941.
58 Johannes Klenkok lectured at Oxford from 1359 to about 1361. He later lectured in convent schools in Marburg and Erfurt in the late 1360s, and in the early 1370s at the University of Prague. See Trapp 1964; Zumkeller 1984.
59 Johannes Hitalingen taught in a *studium generale* in Avignon in the late 1350s and early 1360s, followed by a period in that same decade at the University of Paris; see Zumkeller 1980.
60 Angelus Dobelinus lectured in the University of Paris from 1374 to 1375, and later at Erfurt, first at the *studium generale* and then in the newly founded University. See Zumkeller 1984, 136ff.
61 Johannes Zacharie lectured in the University of Oxford from 1389 to roughly 1392. He subsequently moved to the University of Erfurt in about 1400. See Zumkeller 1984, 215.
62 Ibid. 153, 196, 298ff, 503. The reaction to this aspect of Bradwardine's work was by no means unique to the Augustinian friars. John Wyclif, although in general agreement with Bradwardine, also censured his determinism. See Robson 1961, 47ff., 198. Such criticism of Bradwardine, however, did not preclude his enjoying a distinct intellectual legacy in the later years; see Oberman 1981, 64–71.
63 See Kürzinger 1930, 55ff, for a discussion of Alfonsus' distinctive philosophical concerns.
64 Arbesman 1980.
65 See his *Le Miroir de l'âme* and *Definitiones terminorum theologiae moralis* in volumes 7 and 9 of his *Œuvres complètes*, ed. Glorieux. Brown 1987, 194, provides a stimulating commentary on this aspect of Gerson's work.

66 See Robson 1960; Courtenay 1987, 348–355.
67 Smalley 1960, 58–65; Zumkeller 1964, 172.
68 Xiberta 1931.
69 Courtenay 1978, 79.
70 Smalley 1960, 88–100, 121–132.
71 Vasoli 1998.
72 Bouwsma 1975, 3–60.
73 Steinmetz 1968. For a more general discussion of late medieval philosophy and its influence upon the events of the Reformation see Oberman 1963.

18

GARETH B. MATTHEWS

Post-medieval Augustinianism

By "post-medieval Augustinianism" I shall mean characteristically Augustinian concepts, questions, arguments, responses, and ways of thinking that are prominent in various modern philosophers, whether or not those philosophers ever acknowledge the Augustinian provenance of these aspects of their own thinking. On this way of understanding "Augustinianism" Descartes is perhaps the most Augustinian of modern philosophers, even though Descartes himself declined to acknowledge that there was any significant affinity between his own thought and that of Augustine (let alone that Augustine had actually influenced his thinking!). Both because Descartes was so profoundly Augustinian in his ways of thinking and because he inaugurated the "post-medieval" period in Western philosophy, I shall begin with him.

René Descartes (1596–1650)

Augustine was the very first important philosopher in our Western tradition to develop his thought from a first-person point of view. This remarkable truth is flagged by the fact that Augustine's *Confessions*, which is a philosophical as well as a theological work, is also the first autobiography of importance in Western literature. It is further underlined by the fact that his *Soliloquies*, even though it is a dialogue, is a dialogue between Augustine and reason; in effect, it is a philosophical monologue.

Augustine's commitment to thinking from a first-person perspective is, however, much more significant than a mere stylistic preference. One consequence of this commitment is the fact that many of his most interesting and important ideas focus on what we might call the "ego of thought." The ego of thought is what seems to be referred to by the second occurrence of "I" in sentences like the following:

> I know that I exist.
> I think that I am dreaming.
> I wonder whether there are minds in addition to the one I have.

The fact that what I seem to be referring to in these embedded uses of the first-person pronoun is thought's "I," or thought's ego, is shown by the fact that I can, for example, know that I exist without knowing that Geraldo exists even if, unknown to me, I am Geraldo.[1]

Descartes's famous reasoning, *cogito ergo sum*,[2] focuses on the "I" known to thought. I can know that I exist, Descartes argues, even if I do not know whether I am now dreaming, or even whether my "perceptions" of the physical world have any more reality than the illusions of my dreams. But when Descartes writes that "even the most extravagant suppositions of the skeptics were incapable of shaking" the truth of the *cogito*,[3] he is echoing, whether consciously and deliberately or not, Augustine's assurance that "the quibbles of the skeptics lose their force" in the face of the truth of "I know that I am." "Because therefore I, the one who might be mistaken, would have to exist, even if mistaken," writes Augustine, "without doubt I am not mistaken in recognizing myself to exist" (*De civ. Dei* 11.26).

Descartes's characterization of what a mind is is also remarkably Augustinian. Here is Descartes:

> But when then am I? A thing that thinks. What is that? A thing that doubts, understands, affirms, denies, is willing, is unwilling, and also imagines and has sensory perceptions.[4]

Augustine, "investigating the nature of the mind," admonishes us "not to take into consideration any knowledge that is obtained from without, through the senses of the body" (*De Trin.* 10.10.14). After saying a little about what one can doubt concerning oneself as a mind, he asks, rhetorically, "Who would doubt that he lives, remembers, understands, wills, thinks, knows, and judges?" (ibid.).

A crucial difference between the two lists is the fact that Augustine includes *living* as a function of the mind, whereas Descartes does not. Thus Augustine thinks of a mind (*mens*) as a rational animator (*animus*). It can be an animator, on his view, even when, after death and before the resurrection, it has nothing to animate. By contrast, Descartes insists that the mind has nothing essential to do with life. Thus he writes:

> But I, perceiving that the principle by which we are nourished is wholly distinct from that by means of which we think, have declared that the name *soul (anima)*, when used for both is equivocal . . . I consider the mind not as part of the soul, but as the whole of that soul which thinks.[5]

Behind this difference lie important metaphysical considerations. Descartes, in his foundational project of reconstructing knowledge on a basis of certainty, first establishes his own existence, that is, the existence of his mind, in the explicit realization that at this stage of the reconstruction, he doesn't even know whether there are bodies of any kind, whether living or not. For all he has yet established, his perceptions of bodies, even of his own body, may have no more reality than the illusions of his dreams. If he can nevertheless know, at this stage, that a mind exists, and also know its essence without knowing whether any bodies exist, then the animation of a body is not essential to mind.

Although Augustine, like Descartes, raises the question "How do I know that I am not now dreaming?", he considers only fleetingly the possibility that all life might be a dream. The one place in his writing where he does raise this possibility is the following passage from the earliest piece of writing from him that we have:

"How do you know that this world exists," says [the Academician], "if the senses are mistaken?" . . .
". . . I say I call 'the world' this whole thing, whatever it is, which encloses us and nourishes us, this thing which appears to my eyes and seems to me to make up earth and heaven, or ostensible earth and ostensible heaven . . .
You ask me, "Is what you see still the world, even if you're asleep?" It has already been said that I call "the world" whatever seems to me to be such." (C. Acad. 3.11.24–25)

Whereas Descartes makes it a central part of his reconstruction of knowledge to deal with the "problem of the external world" – that is, to show how one can know that a physical world, independent of one's thoughts and sensory images, exists – Augustine asks this most radical dream question only to make a much more limited point. He aims only to defeat global skepticism by presenting various unassailable truths, including the tautology like assertion "either there is one world or there is not" (C. Acad. 3.10.23).

Taking seriously the question "How do I know that I am not dreaming?" seems to require that one take seriously the possibility that I am my dream self. Taking this possibility seriously provides a basis for raising the "moral dream problem," that is, for asking whether I am morally responsible for the acts of my dream self. Augustine agonizes over this problem, perhaps most eloquently in his Confessions at 10.30.41. Clearly he wants to say it would be unfair to hold him responsible for what he thinks and does in the privacy of his dreams; but he is unsure about what absolves him of responsibility.

Descartes seems to identify himself with his dream self as well. He discusses the moral dream problem in a letter to Elizabeth.[6] His primary response to this problem seems to be the excuse that, in our dreams, our mind is not at liberty and we are therefore not entirely within our own power. One might argue that Descartes is not entitled to this excuse, since in Meditation IV he explains freedom of choice as the ability to affirm or deny, pursue or avoid, when "we do not feel we are determined by any external force."[7] He surely would have realized that I can pursue or avoid something in a dream without feeling that I am determined by any external force.[8]

Augustine has been credited (or debited!) with being the first philosopher to develop the concept of the will.[9] Certainly the idea of the will is prominent in his thought. Of the many ways in which Augustine makes philosophical use of the notion, one of the most important is his development of what has come to be called the "free-will defense" in response to the problem of evil. Augustine understands the "movement of the will when it turns from the immutable to the mutable good" to be an "aversion," a "defective movement," whose cause is nothing. Thus God, who has given human creatures the good gift of free will, without which we cannot "live aright," is not responsible for our misuse of this gift (*De lib. arb.* 2.20.54).

As Stephen Menn has recently made perspicuous,[10] Book IV of Descartes's *Meditations* can be seen as an Augustinian theodicy focused on what Menn calls "cognitive evil," that is, the error of human judgment. Here is Descartes:

> I must not complain that the forming of those acts of will or judgments in which I go wrong happens with God's concurrence. For in so far as these acts depend on God, they are wholly true and good . . . As for the privation involved – which is all that the essential definition of falsity and wrong consists in – this does not in any way require the concurrence of God, since it is not a thing; indeed, when it is referred to God as its cause, it should be called not a privation but simply a negation.[11]

Hugo Grotius (1583–1645) and the just war tradition

In keeping with his first-person approach to philosophy more generally, Augustine brings to Western ethics an new emphasis on the "inner life" of the moral agent.[12] Sin, Augustine supposes, arises not from the "external" consequences of an agent's evil action, but rather from the soul's "consent" to try to satisfy an evil desire. The soul's "consent" may result in the formation of an intention to perform a certain action, but it need not (*De serm. Dom. in monte* 1.12.34). As Jesus puts it in his Sermon on the Mount, one may commit adultery simply in one's heart (Matthew 5.27–28). And even if one forms an intention to act, the sin may be committed quite independently of whether the "bodily" action one intends to perform is actually carried out. Someone who has "consented" inwardly to an evil desire, Augustine tells us, although he has not done anything with his hand or with any other part of the body, is already guilty in accordance with the laws of God, even if what he has done is invisible to human eyes (*De continentia* 2.3).

No doubt Augustine's intentionalism and his preoccupation with the agent's "inner life" find some echo in modern deontological theories of ethics. Surprisingly, however, the most clearly influential aspect of his ethical thought concerns issues about what counts as a just war. Augustine is, in fact, often considered the father of just war theory.[13] There is, however, a deep irony in this recognition. For one thing, Augustine was not very original in developing his theory of what makes a war a just one. He drew heavily on Cicero and St. Ambrose. Moreover, his comments on what makes a war just or unjust are scattered.[14] And, finally, some of his views on warfare seem surprisingly "external" in a philosopher preoccupied with "interiority." For example, he contends that a soldier is not responsible for the death he causes if he is carrying out the order of a legitimate superior; he is in that case, Augustine maintains, nothing but a "sword" in the hand of his ruler (*De civ. Dei* 1.21). In mitigation of this last irony it should, however, be pointed out that Augustine does condemn conduct, even in a fully legitimate war, that expresses a love of violence, or a vengeful cruelty (*C. Faust.* 22.74).

Hugo Grotius, the pioneering theorist of international law and the most influential just war theorist in the modern period, distinguishes between the requirements for entering into war justly (*jus ad bellum*) and the requirements for conducting war justly, once hostilities have begun (*jus in bello*). Augustine had much more to say about the former, although Aquinas' interpretation of his views, insofar as they figure in the development of the ethical principle of "double effect," have also played some role in modern conceptions of justice in the conduct of war. In any case, Grotius acknowledged his indebtedness to Augustine by citing, referring to, or alluding to his writings over one hundred and fifty times in his great treatise on justice in war and peace, *De jure belli ac pacis*.

There has been no later just war theorist of the stature of Grotius. Nevertheless, the tradition to which he contributed so significantly, a tradition which Augustine helped to initiate, flourishes even today.[15]

Nicolas Malebranche (1638–1715)

Unlike Descartes, Malebranche happily, even insistently, acknowledges his debt to Augustine, as well as, of course, to Descartes. "I avow that it is principally [St. Augustine's] authority which has given me the desire to put forth the new philosophy of ideas," he writes.[16]

Malebranche's frequent and wholehearted expressions of reliance on Augustine do not keep him from pointing out differences between their respective views. Thus Book II, Part Two, Chapter 6, of his *Recherche* (*Search After Truth*), which is subtitled "That we see all things in God," includes a substantial quotation from Book 14 of Augustine's *De Trinitate*. The passage Malebranche quotes expresses the Augustinian idea of illumination. Malebranche then comments:

> Saint Augustine has an infinity of such passages by which he proves that we already see God in this life through the knowledge we have of eternal truths. The truth is uncreated, immutable, immense, eternal, and above all things . . . Only God can have all these perfections. Therefore, truth is God. We see some of these immutable,

eternal truths. Therefore, we see God. These are the arguments of Saint Augustine – ours are somewhat different, and we have no wish to make improper use of the authority of so great a man in order to support our own view. We are of the opinion, then, that truths (even those that are eternal, such as that twice two is four) are not absolute beings, much less that they are God Himself. For clearly, this truth consists only in the relation of equality between twice two and four. Thus, we do not claim, as does Saint Augustine, that we see God in seeing truths, but in seeing the *ideas* of these truths ... Thus, our view is that we see God when we see eternal truths, and not that these truths are God, because the ideas on which these truths depend are in God.[17]

Characteristically, Malebranche adds the comment, "it might even be that this was Saint Augustine's meaning."

In fact, Malebranche's notion that the soul can see ideas in God provided him not only with an assurance of the objectivity of mathematical truths such as "twice two equals four," but also a way of grounding the objectivity of our perception of sensible objects in the physical world. Steven Nadler presents this development of Augustine's view this way:

Augustine's explicit view, as Malebranche reads him, is that we see in God only eternal laws and truths, mainly mathematical objects and principles and moral rules. [According to Malebranche,] "He [that is, Augustine] never asserted that we see in God corruptible things or things subject to change, such as all the bodies which surround us ..." Malebranche's view, on the other hand, is that we *do*, in fact, perceive and know bodies in God. But this does not mean that the immediate objects of knowledge in God are themselves changeable, corruptible things. What we see in God are the *ideas* of bodies, "their essences, which are immutable, necessary, and eternal." Thus to Augustine's doctrine of illumination, which is basically a theory concerning our knowledge of eternal truths alone, Malebranche's vision in God adds a second dimension: it is also a theory concerning our knowledge of the nature (but not the existence) of corporeal bodies, of the material world surrounding us. What makes this knowledge possible is the Augustinian thesis that the ideas in God are the archetypes which God employed in creating the world.[18]

In fact, Malebranche's "addition" may not be an addition at all, but part of Augustine's own conception of divine illumination. (See discussion of "Illumination," pp. 180–183 above).

Gottfried Wilhelm Leibniz (1646–1716)

"Where then does evil come from," Augustine asks in Book 7 of his *Confessions*, "since a good God made all things good?" To block the Platonic response that God was limited in his creation to the use of recalcitrant matter, Augustine then adds: "Is it that, although he is omnipotent, he was impotent to alter and change the whole so that nothing evil remained?" (*Conf.* 7.5.7).

Although Augustine was not the first philosopher to state the philosophical problem of evil,[19] it is his preoccupation with this problem, more than anyone else's, that has shaped later discussion in Western philosophy, both medieval and modern. Among Augustine's responses to this problem are the following:

(i) Evil is a privation, a lack, a "nothing." It is a mistake to look for the cause of nothing.

(ii) Natural evil, though in itself ugly, fits into an ordered design that is, as a whole, beautiful.

(iii) Moral evil is the result of the exercise of free will, without which there would be no moral goodness.

Leibniz picks up and develops each of these points, often with the recognition that he is developing Augustinian ideas. Thus, when in his *Theodicy* he comments, "I have already pointed out more than once in this work that evil is a consequence of privation," he is quick to add, "St. Augustine has already put forward this idea."[20] And when he summarizes his views on how to deal with this problem, he makes these comments:

> I have proved this in further detail in this work by pointing out, through instances taken from mathematics and elsewhere, that an imperfection in the part may be required for a greater perfection in the whole. I have followed therein the opinion of St. Augustine, who said a hundred times that God permitted evil in order to derive from it a good, that is to say, a greater good . . .[21]

Something similar is true of the problem of God's foreknowledge and human free will. Although this problem is already foreshadowed in Cicero's discussion of fate, it is Augustine's discussion, in his *De libero arbitrio*, that has echoed in the writings of philosophers and philosophical theologians down to the present day. Evodius, Augustine's interlocutor, says he wants to know "how it can be that God foreknows everything in the future and that, nevertheless, we do not sin by any necessity." Evodius adds: "Since God foreknew that man would sin, that which God foreknew must necessarily happen. How then is the will free when there is apparently this unavoidable necessity?" (*De lib. arb.* 3.2.4).

One of Leibniz's preliminary points depends on distinguishing between hypothetical and absolute necessity:

> They say that what is foreseen cannot fail to exist, and they say so truly; but it follows not that what is foreseen is necessary, for *necessary truth* is that whereof the contrary is impossible or implies a contradiction. Now this truth which states that I shall write tomorrow is not of that nature, it is not necessary. Yet supposing that God foresees it, it is necessary that it come to pass; that is, the consequence is necessary, namely, that it exist, since it has been foreseen; for God is infallible. This is what is termed a *hypothetical necessity*. But our concern is not this necessity; it is an *absolute necessity* that is required, to be able to say that an

action is necessary, that it is not contingent, that it is not the effect of a free choice.[22]

Augustine makes a similar distinction, but not so elegantly:

The same applies when we say that it is necessary that when we will, we will by free choice. Doubtless what we say is true; and it [certainly] does not mean that we are subjecting our free will to a necessity which takes away our freedom. (*De civ. Dei* 5.10)

Leibniz goes on to say that this solution reaches only so far. One might still worry that God's foreknowledge must "have its foundation in the nature of things, and this foundation, making the truth *predeterminate*, will prevent it from being contingent and free."[23]

John Stuart Mill (1806–73)

In developing a rational reconstruction of knowledge from his own first-person point of view, Descartes recognizes that he needs to offer a justification for his belief that there is a physical world distinct from and independent of his own representations of such a world. He undertakes to do that in *Meditation* VI. However, from this same first-person point of view, Descartes also needs to offer a justification for his belief that there are other finite minds, that is, other first-person points of view besides God's. Descartes never recognizes that he has this obligation.[24] And so he has nothing directly to say about what has come to be called "the problem of other minds."

In Part V of his *Discourse* Descartes does consider what reason we have for supposing that only human beings have minds and not, say, monkeys or automata. But he assumes, without argumentation, that there are other finite minds – in fact, human minds – in addition to his own.

Malebranche, however, does recognize the problem of other minds and he offers a solution to it.[25] George Berkeley (1685–1783), who was taken by many of his contemporaries to be a follower of Malebranche, also takes the problem of other minds seriously. But among modern philosophers who recognize and try to deal seriously with the problem, perhaps no one is more often cited than John Stuart Mill. Mill's solution to the problem, the notorious "argument from analogy," goes this way:

I conclude that other human beings have feelings like me, because, first, they have bodies like me, which I know, in my own case, to be the antecedent condition of feelings; and because, secondly, they exhibit the acts, and other outward signs, which in my own case I know by experience to be caused by feelings. I am conscious in myself of a series of facts connected by an uniform sequence, of which the beginning is modifications of my body, the middle is feelings, the end is outward demeanour. In the case of other human beings I have the evidence of my senses for the first and last links of the series, but not for the intermediate link ... Experience, therefore, obliges me to conclude that there must be an intermediate link, which must be the same in others as in myself, or a different one: I must either believe them to be alive, or to be automatons; and by believing them to be alive, that is, by supposing the link to be of the same nature as in the case of which I have experience, and which is in all other respects similar, I bring other human beings, as phenomena, under the same generalizations which I know by experience to be the theory of my own existence.[26]

Mill's argument is a close relative of this argument from Augustine's *De Trinitate*:

> For we also recognize, from a likeness to us, the motions of bodies by which we perceive that others besides us live. Just as we move [our] body in living, so, we notice, those bodies are moved. For when a living body is moved there is no way to open our eyes to see the mind (*animus*), a thing which cannot be seen by the eyes. But we perceive something present in that mass such as is present in us to move our mass in a similar way; it is life and soul (*anima*).[27] Nor is such perception something peculiar to, as it were, human prudence and reason. For indeed beasts perceive as living, not only themselves, but also each other and one another, and us as well. Nor do they see our soul (*anima*), except from the motions of the body, and they do that immediately and very simply by a sort of natural agreement (*quadam conspiratione naturali*). Therefore we know the mind (*animus*) of anyone at all from our own; and from our own case we believe in that mind which we do not know (*ex nostro credimus quem non novimus*). (*De Trin.* 8.6.9)

One important difference between these two passages is that Augustine attributes to non-human animals an instinctive recognition of human minds that is, so to speak, the functional equivalent of a human being's use of the argument from analogy to justify a belief in other human minds. Mill makes no similar move.

One striking point is the close connection Mill sees between attributing feeling to another being and supposing that that being is alive, that is, that its movements are those of a living being. Unlike Descartes, but like Augustine, Mill thus seems to understand mind as a "rational" form of animation.

Wittgenstein's Augustine

I conclude this survey of post-medieval Augustinianism with a brief discussion of the figure of Augustine in Ludwig Wittgenstein (1889–1951). Although Wittgenstein offers a trenchant criticism in his *Blue Book* of Augustine's discussion of time in *Confessions* Book 11,[28] and uses a direct quotation from Augustine's *Confessions* (1.8.13) to identify a conception of language he wants to discuss and criticize in *Philosophical Investigations*, he shows no real interest in using the techniques of a historian of philosophy to isolate or interpret the Augustinian passages. In the *Blue Book* passage he uses Augustine to illustrate a mistake he supposes many philosophers make. It is the mistake of supposing that coming up with an adequate definition of a philosophically problematic term, in this case, the term "time," will clear away the problem. Instead, Wittgenstein suggests, a definition, if it is adequate, will simply reproduce what we found problematic about the term in the first place.

Perhaps Wittgenstein thought that he himself was once guilty of making the mistake he attributes to Augustine. Whether or not that is so, there can be no doubt that his use of Augustine in the *Philosophical Investigations* is, in part, a way of getting at a mistake, or a family of mistakes, he had made earlier on in his philosophical career. Thus he wants to focus attention on what G. P. Baker and P. M. S. Hacker, in their influential commentary, have called "Augustine's picture of language" – a picture that Wittgenstein seems to link with Gottlob Frege (1848–1925), Bertrand Russell (1872–1970), and, perhaps especially, with his own early work, the *Tractatus*. The Augustinian picture of language as it emerges in the *Philosophical Investigations* is thus, it seems, primarily a device for presenting, assessing, and criticizing views on the nature of language prominent in the first half of the twentieth century, even though the philosophers who made those views prominent, including presumably Wittgenstein himself when he wrote the *Tractatus*, did not think of themselves as Augustinians.

Among the rather large number of theses that Baker and Hacker identify in Wittgenstein's "Augustinian picture of language" are these:

(i) Any significant word signifies something. Its meaning is what it stands for or signifies. It is assigned a meaning by correlating it with an object. Such a correlation gives it a meaning by making it into a name of an object. It represents the object it stands for . . . .

(ii) Since verbal definitions merely explain one expression by means of others and hence constitute connections within language, ostensive definitions provide the only possible means for correlating words with things . . .

(iii) The thesis that all words are names is equivalent to the thesis that the fundamental form of explanation of words is ostensive definition, that ostensive definitions are the foundation of language . . .

. . .

(vi) An ostensive definition . . . forges a timeless link between a word and a thing. . . . This is independent of whether we can settle this question, of whether we can reidentify this object . . .[29]

The first item in this list of theses squares very well with what Augustine says about language in various of his works. In the early dialogue *De magistro*, for example, he announces that words are signs and that a sign can't be a sign without signifying something (2.3). Oddly, Baker and Hacker attribute to Augustine the claim that "one cannot point to objects signified by prepositions," for example, the object signified by "from" (*ex*), and that this "observation" is "*prima facie* at odds with the *Urbild*,"[30] that is, with what they call "Augustine's picture of language."

In fact, Augustine's views on ostention, as expressed in *De magistro*, are much more complicated than Baker and Hacker suggest. In that dialogue Augustine stands by his assertion that words are signs and that signs signify something. The "something" that "from" signifies, he decides, is separation (2.4). According to Adeodatus, Augustine's son and interlocutor in that dialogue, "if" signifies doubt (2.3), and the word "nothing," Augustine finally concludes, signifies a certain state of mind, roughly, the state of mind of one who is looking for something and doesn't find it.

Lest one conclude that Augustine's discussion in *De magistro* is too primitive to be worth discussing, let me say that Russell was not averse to thinking of the meaning of a word as a state of mind of someone who might be using the word. Consider this passage from Russell:

> Suppose I see an animal and say, "that was a stoat or a weasel." My statement is true if it was a stoat, and true if it was a weasel; there is not some third kind of animal, stoat-or-weasel. In fact, my statement expresses partial knowledge combined with hesitation; the word "or" expresses my hesitation, not something objective.[31]

This passage from Russell should count as some evidence that Wittgenstein was right to link Russell to Augustine's picture of language.

Contrary to what Baker and Hacker suggest, however, Augustine does not, in his *De magistro*, simply deny that what the preposition "from" signifies is an "object" that can be pointed to. What he and Adeodatus do is, in fact, something far more drastic. They consider a whole range of objects signified by words that cannot be pointed to. Here is Adeodatus:

> I admit that sound, smell, flavor, weight, heat, and other things that pertain to the rest of the senses, despite the fact that they can't be sensed without bodies and consequently are corporeal, nevertheless can't be exhibited through [pointing] a finger. (3.5)

There follows a very interesting discussion of the ambiguity of ostention – where "ostention" is understood very broadly to include, say, showing someone what walking is by walking. They conclude that there is no way to rule out the possibility that the learner will misunderstand the demonstration and take walking to be hurrying, or taking only as many steps as the demonstrator has taken.

Perhaps I have said enough to make clear that there are certain ironies in the use to which Wittgenstein puts his quotation from Augustine's *Confessions*. The quotation does indeed suggest a picture of language acquisition by ostensive learning. But when Wittgenstein goes on to criticize this picture by, for example, bringing up worries about the ambiguity of ostention, he echoes a worry Augustine himself expresses in one of his earliest writings. Although Augustine's response to this worry is quite different from Wittgenstein's, it is interesting that they were both attracted to the idea that learning by ostention is the foundation of language acquisition and that they both came to reject that view as unsatisfactory.

NOTES

1 The example is not purely fanciful. "Geraldo" is, indeed, a name given me on my Argentine birth certificate; but I might well not have known anything about that birth certificate, or about the fact that I was given, at birth, two sets of names.
2 *Discourse on Method*, Part IV.
3 Ibid.
4 *Méditation* II, VII. 28 (*Œuvres de Descartes*, ed. Adam and Tannery, CSM II 19, vol. 7, p. 28), Cottingham *et al.*, trans., 1984–85, vol. 2, p. 19.
5 Fifth Set of Replies to Objections to the *Meditations*, AT VII. 356, CSM II. 246.
6 Letter to Elizabeth, 1 September 1645, K 167–168 (Kenny 1980).
7 AT VII, 57, CSM II 40.
8 Cf. Matthews 1992, chapter 8.
9 Dihle 1982.
10 Menn 1998. See especially chapter 7, "Theodicy and Method."
11 AT VII 60–61, CSM II 42.
12 Mann 1999.
13 Christopher 1994, 30.
14 Holmes (1999, esp. fn. 5, 339) follows David Lenihan in identifying these as the chief passages in which Augustine discusses war: *De lib. arb.* 1.5; *C. Faust.* 22; *Ep.* 138, 189, 222; *Quaestiones in Heptateuchum* 6.10; *De serm. Dom. in monte* 30; *De civ. Dei.* But it is worth noting that Hugo Grotius (*De jure belli ac pacis*, trans. Kelsey) quotes or alludes to no fewer than 34 of Augustine's works.
15 Holmes 1989; Christopher 1994.
16 Cited in Nadler 1992, 101. Whether Malebranche got his idea of the "vision in God" from reading Augustine, or whether he arrived at this idea independently and simply found confirmation in Augustine, is a matter of scholarly discussion. Cf. ibid., 101, fn. 6.
17 Nicolas Malebranche, *The Search After Truth*, trans. Lennon and Olscamp, 233–234.
18 Nadler 1992, 105–6.
19 It is found in Book II of Plato's *Republic* at 379c.
20 Leibniz, *Theodicy*, trans. E. W. Huggard, §378, p. 352.
21 Ibid. 378.
22 Ibid. §37, p. 144.
23 Ibid.§38, p. 144.
24 Some readers have thought, mistakenly, that he does so in the famous "hats-and-cloaks" passage at the end of *Meditation* II, but this is not so. See chapter 9 of Matthews 1992.

25 Malebranche, *Search After Truth*, 3.7.5 ("How we know other men's souls").
26 Mill 1889, pp. 243–244.
27 Augustine thinks of the human soul [*anima*] as a rational soul [*animus*] or mind [*mens*].
28 Wittgenstein 1960, 26–27.
29 Baker and Hacker 1980, 36–37.
30 Ibid. 61.
31 Russell 1948, 126.

BIBLIOGRAPHY

PRIMARY SOURCES

Aetius, *Placita*, in *Doxographi Graeci*, ed. H. Diels, Berlin, 1879.

Anselm, *Opera omnia*, 6 vols, ed. F. S. Schmitt, Edinburgh: Nelson, 1946–61.

Aquinas, Thomas, *Expositiones super librum Boethii de Trinitate*, ed. B. Decker, Leiden: Brill, 1965.

Aristotle, *Categoriae et Liber de Interpretatione*, ed. L. Minio-Paluello, Scriptorum Classicorum Bibliotheca Oxoniensis, Oxford: Clarendon Press, 1989.

De Arte Poetica, ed. I. Bywater, 2nd edn., Oxford, 1911.

De caelo, ed. D. J. Allan, Scriptorum Classicorum Bibliotheca Oxoniensis, Oxford: Clarendon Press, 1936.

Metaphysics, a revised text with introduction and commentary by W. D. Ross, 2 vols., Oxford: Clarendon Press, 1924.

Physics, a revised text with introduction and commentary by W. D. Ross, Oxford: Clarendon Press, 1936.

Augustine, *Confessionum libri XIII*, ed. Pius Knöll, CSEL 33, Vienna: F. Tempsky, Leipzig: G. Freytag, 1896. Also *Confessiones libri XIII*, ed. Lucas Verheijen, CCSL 27, Turnhout: Brepols, 1981.

Augustine: Confessions, trans. H. Chadwick, Oxford University Press, 1991. (Chadwick 1991.)

Augustine: Confessions, trans. J. J. O'Donnell, Oxford: Clarendon Press, 1992 (3 vols.). (O'Donnell 1992a.)

Augustine: Confessions, trans. R. S. Pine-Coffin, Harmondsworth: Penguin, 1961. (Pine-Coffin 1961.)

Contra Academicos, ed. W. M. Green, CCSL 29, Turnhout: Brepols, 1970. Also T. Fuhrer, ed., *Augustin contra Academicos: vel De Academicis Bücher 2 und 3*. Patristische Texte und Studien, vol. 46. Berlin and New York: de Gruyter, 1997. (Fuhrer 1997.)

Against the Academics, trans. J. J. O'Meara, Ancient Christian Writers, vol. 12. New York and Ramsey, NJ: Newman Press, 1951. (O'Meara 1951.)

Contra Faustum, ed. Josephus Zycha, CSEL 25, Vienna: F. Tempsky, Leipzig: G. Freytag, 1891/92.

Contra Gaudentium, ed. Michael Petschenig, CSEL 53, Vienna: F. Tempsky, Leipzig: G. Freytag, 1910.

Contra Iulianum, ed. J.-P. Migne, *PL* 44, Paris: In Via Dicta D'Amboise, Près la Barrière D'Enfer, 1845.

Contra Julianum opus imperfectum, ed. M. Zelzer, CSEL 85.1, Vienna: Hoelder-Pichler-Tempsky, 1974 (Books 1–3).

De beata vita, ed. W. M. Green, CCSL 29, Turnhout: Brepols, 1970.

De civitate Dei, ed. B. Dombart and A. Kalb, CCSL 47 48, Turnhout: Brepols, 1955.

Concerning the City of God against the Pagans, trans. H. Bettenson, New York: Penguin, 1972. (Bettenson 1972.)

Augustine: The City of God against the Pagans, trans. R. W. Dyson, Cambridge University Press, 1998. (Dyson 1998.)

De correptione et gratia, ed. J.-P. Migne, *PL* 44, Paris: In Via Dicta D'Amboise, Près la Barrière D'Enfer, 1845.

De dialectica, trans. with introduction and notes by B. Darrell Jackson from the text edited by J. Pinborg, Dordrecht: Reidel, 1975. (Jackson 1975.)

De diversis quaestionibus ad Simplicianum, ed. A. Mutzenbecher, CCSL 44, Turnhout: Brepols, 1970.

De diversis quaestionibus LXXXIII, ed. A. Mutzenberger, CCSL 44A, Turnhout: Brepols, 1975.

De doctrina Christiana, ed. J. Martin, CCSL 32, Turnhout: Brepols, 1982.

De dono perseverantiae, ed. J.-P. Migne, *PL* 45, Paris: In Via Dicta D'Amboise, Près la Barrière D'Enfer, 1845.

De fide et symbolo, ed. J. Zycha, CSEL 41, Vienna: F. Tempsky, Leipzig: G. Freytag, 1900.

De Genesi ad litteram, ed. J. Zycha, CSEL 28.1, Vienna: F. Tempsky, Leipzig: G. Freytag, 1894.

De Genesi ad litteram imperfectus liber, ed. J. Zycha, CSEL 28.1, Vienna: F. Tempsky, Leipzig: G. Freytag, 1894.

De Genesi contra Manichaeos, ed. D. Weber, CSEL 91, Vienna: Verlag der Österreichischen Akademie der Wissenschaften, 1998.

De gratia Christi et de peccato originali, ed. C. F. Urba and J. Zycha, CSEL 42, Vienna: F. Tempsky, Leipzig: G. Freytag, 1902.

De gratia et libero arbitrio, ed. J.-P. Migne, *PL* 44, Paris: In Via Dicta D'Amboise, Près la Barrière D'Enfer, 1845.

De libero arbitrio, ed. W. M. Green, CCSL 29, Turnhout: Brepols, 1970.

Augustine: On the Free Choice of the Will, trans. T. Williams. Indianapolis/Cambridge: Hackett Publishing Company, 1993. (T. Williams 1993.)

De natura et gratia, ed. C. F. Urba and J. Zycha, CSEL 60, Vienna: F. Tempsky, Leipzig: G. Freytag, 1913.

De nuptiis et concupiscentia, ed. J. Zycha, CSEL 42, Vienna: F. Tempsky, Leipzig: G. Freytag, 1902.

De peccatorum meritis et remissione et de baptismo parvulorum, ed. C. F. Urba and J. Zycha, CSEL 60, Vienna: F. Tempsky, Leipzig: G. Freytag, 1913.

De perfectione iustitiae hominis, ed. J. Zycha, CSEL 42, Vienna: F. Tempsky, Leipzig: G. Freytag, 1902.

De praedestinatione sanctorum, ed. J.-P. Migne, *PL* 44, Paris: In Via Dicta D'Amboise, Près la Barrière D'Enfer, 1845.

De spiritu et littera, ed. C. F. Urba and J. Zycha, CSEL 60, Vienna: F. Tempsky, Leipzig: G. Freytag, 1913.

De Trinitate, ed. W. J. Mountain, CCSL 50, Turnhout: Brepols, 1970.

La Trinité (Livres VIII–XV), trans. P. Agaësse, SJ, notes by J. Moingt, SJ, Bibliothèque Augustinienne 16. Paris: Brouwer, 1955. (Agaësse 1955.)

The Trinity, trans. S. McKenna, Washington, DC: Catholic University of America Press, 1963. (McKenna 1963.)

The Trinity, trans. E. Hill. Brooklyn, NY: New City Press, 1990.

De vera religione, ed. J. Martin, CCSL 32, Turnhout: Brepols, 1982.

Enchiridion ad Laurentium de fide et spe et caritate, ed. E. Evans, CCSL 46, Turnhout: Brepols, 1969.

Epistulae, ed. A. Goldbacher, CSEL: Epp. 1–30 vol. 34/1; Epp. 31–123 vol. 34/2; Epp. 124–84 vol. 44; Epp. 185–270 vol. 57; *Praefatio et indices* vol. 58. Vienna: F. Tempsky, Leipzig: G. Freytag, 1895–1923.

Œuvres de saint Augustin: Lettres 1*–29*, ed. J. Divjak, Paris: Etudes Augustiniennes, 1987. (Divjak 1987.)

Saint Augustine: Letters 1*–29*, trans. R. B. Eno, Washington, DC: The Catholic University of America Press, 1989. (Eno 1989.)

In Iohannis evangelium tractatus CXXIV, ed. R. Willems, CCSL 36, Turnhout: Brepols, 1954.

Retractationum libri duo, ed. Pius Knöll, CSEL 36, Vienna: F. Tempsky, 1902.

Retractationes, ed. A. Mutzenbecher, CCSL 57, Turnhout: Brepols, 1984.

Retractations, trans. M. I. Bogan, Washington, DC: The Catholic University of America Press, 1968. (Bogan 1968.)

Sermones, ed. J.-P. Migne, *PL* 38, Paris: In Via Dicta D'Amboise, Près la Barrière D'Enfer, 1841.

Newly Discovered Sermons, ed. E. Hill, in series *The Works of Saint Augustine: A Translation for the 21st Century*. Hyde Park, NY: New City Press, 1997. (Hill 1997.)

Bartholomew of Urbino, *Milleloquium Sancti Augustini*, Lyons: 1555.

Bonaventure, *Opera omnia*, 10 vols., Quarachi: Collegi a S. Bonaventura, 1882–1902.

Quaestiones disputatae de scientia Christi, ed. A. Speer, Hamburg: Felix Meiner Verlag, 1992.

Bradwardine, Thomas, *De causa Dei*, ed. H. Saville, London: 1618; reprinted Frankfurt: Minerva, 1964.

Cicero, *De natura deorum*, ed. W. Ax, Stuttgart: Teubner, 1968.

De re publica. Cambridge, MA: Harvard University Press, 1977.

Descartes, René, *Œuvres*, ed. C. Adam and P. Tannery, Paris: Vrin, 1964–1976.

The Philosophical Writings of Descartes, trans. J. Cottingham, R. Stoothoff, and D. Murdock, Cambridge University Press, 1984–85. (Cottingham *et al.*, trans., 1984–85.)

Philosophical Letters, trans. A. Kenny, Oxford University Press, 1980. (Kenny 1980.)

Gellius, Aulus, *Noctes Atticae*, ed. P. K. Marshall, Scriptorum Classicorum Bibliotheca Oxoniensis, Oxford: Clarendon Press, 1968.

Gerson, Jean, *Œuvres Complètes*, ed. M. Glorieux, 10 vols., Paris: Desclée, 1960–73.

Giles of Rome, *Theorems on Existence and Essence (Theoremata de esse et essentia)*, introduction by M. V. Murray, Medieval Philosophical Texts in Translation 7, Milwaukee: Marquette University Press, 1973.

Gregory of Rimini (Gregorius Arminensis), *Lectura super primum et secundum Sententiarum*, 6 vols., ed. D. Trapp and V. Marcolini, Berlin: de Gruyter, 1978–84.

Grotius, Hugo, *De jure belli ac pacis*, trans. T. W. Kelsey, Oxford: Clarendon Press, 1925.

Hobbes, T., *Leviathan*, ed. R. Flathman and D. Johnson, New York and London: Norton, 1997.

Honorius Augustodunensis, *Clavis Physicae*, ed. P. Lucentini, Rome: Edizioni di Storia Letteratura, 1974. Also ed. J.-P. Migne, *PL* 172, Paris, 1854.

Hugh of St. Victor, *De theophania multiplici*, ed. J.-P. Migne, *PL* 177, Paris, 1854.

Laertius, Diogenes, *Lives of the Philosophers*, text and translation by R. D. Hicks, 2 vols., Cambridge, MA: Harvard University Press, 1958.

Leibniz, G. W., *Theodicy*, trans. E. M. Huggard, New Haven: Yale University Press, 1952.

Lucretius, *De rerum natura*, ed. C. Bailey, Oxford: Clarendon Press, 1922.

Malebranche, Nicolas, *The Search After Truth*, trans. T. M. Lennon and P. J. Olscamp, Columbus, OH: Ohio State University Press, 1980.

Origen, *Commentariorum series in Matthaeum*, ed. J.-P. Migne, *Patrologia Graeca* 13, Paris: In Via Dicta D'Amboise, Prope Portam Lutetiaè Parisiorum Vulgo D'Enfer Nominatum, 1857.

   De principiis, ed. H. Görgemanns and H. Karpp, Darmstadt: Wissenschaftliche Buchgesellschaft, 1976.

Pelagius, *Epistola de malis doctoribus et operibus fidei et de iudicio futuro*, in *PL Supplementum*, vol. 1. Paris: Garnier, 1958.

Plato, *Opera*, ed. J. Burnet, Scriptorum Classicorum Bibliotheca Oxoniensis, Oxford University Press, 1900–07.

   Platonis Opera, vol. 1, ed. E. A. Duke *et al.*, Oxford University Press, 1995.

Plotinus, *Opera* I–III, ed. P. Henry and H. R. Schwyzer, Scriptorum Classicorum Bibliotheca Oxoniensis, Oxford: Clarendon Press, 1964–82.

Polybius, *The Rise of the Roman Empire*, trans. I. Scott-Kilvert, New York: Penguin, 1978.

Rupert of Deutz, *De sancta trinitate et operibus eius*, ed. H. Haacke, *Corpus Christianorum, Continuatio Medievalis*, vol. XXIV, Turnhout: Brepols, 1972.

Sextus Empiricus, *Adversus mathematicos*, text and translation (*AM* 8 is "Against the Logicians" II), ed. R. G. Bury, vols. 2–4, Cambridge, MA: Harvard University Press, and London: Heinemann Ltd., 1983–87.

Tertullian, *De cultu feminarum*, ed. A. Kroymann, CCSL 1, Turnhout: Brepols, 1954.

Victorinus, Marius, *Theological Treatises on the Trinity*, trans. M. T. Clark, Washington, DC: Catholic University of America Press, 1981. (Clark 1981.)

SECONDARY SOURCES

Adams, M. M. 1995. "Duns Scotus on the Will as Rational Power," in Leonard Sileo, ed., *Via Scoti. Methologia ad Mentem Joannis Duns Scoti*, Rome: Antonianum, 839–854.

Agaësse, P. 1955. *See* Primary Sources (*De Trinitate*).

Agaësse, P. and Solignac, A. (eds.) 1972. *La Genèse au sens littéral VIII–XII*, Bibliothèque Augustinienne 49, Paris: Brouwer.

Alfaric, P. 1918. *L'évolution intellectuelle de saint Augustin, 1: Du Manichéisme au Néoplatonisme*, Paris: Nourry.

Anderson, J. G. 1965. *St. Augustine and Being: A Metaphysical Essay*, The Hague: Nijhoff.

Annas, J. 1993. *The Morality of Happiness*, Oxford and New York: Oxford University Press.

Arbesmann, R. 1980. "The Question of the Authorship of the *Milleloquium Veritatis Sancti Augustini*," *Analecta Augustiniana* 43, 165–186.

Armstrong, A. H. 1979. *Plotinian and Christian Studies*, London: Variorum Reprints.

Atherton, C. 1993. *The Stoics on Ambiguity*, Cambridge University Press.

Ayres, L. 1998. "The Christological Context of *De Trinitate* XIII," *Augustinian Studies* 29, 111–139.

Ayres, L. (ed.) 1999. *The Trinity: Classical and Contemporary Readings*, Oxford: Blackwell.

Babcock, W. S. 1988. "Augustine on Sin and Moral Agency," *Journal of Religious Ethics* 16, 28–55, reprinted in W. S. Babcock, ed., *The Ethics of St. Augustine*, Atlanta, GA: Scholars Press, 87–114.

Baker, G. P. and Hacker, P. M. S. 1980. *Wittgenstein: Understanding and Meaning, An analytical commentary on the Philosophical Investigations*, vol. 1, Chicago: University of Chicago Press, and Oxford: Blackwell.

Barnes, M. R. 1993. "The Arians of Book V and the genre of *De Trinitate*," *Journal of Theological Studies*.

Barnes, M. R. 1995a. "The Use of Augustine in Contemporary Trinitarian Theology," *Theological Studies* 56, 237–251.

Barnes, M. R. 1995b. "De Régnon Reconsidered," *Augustinian Studies* 26, 51–79.

Barnes, M. R. 1999. "Rereading Augustine's Theology of the Trinity," in Davis *et al.*, *The Trinity*, Oxford University Press.

Barnes, M. R. and D. H. Williams (eds.) 1993. *Arianism after Arius: Essays on the Development of the Fourth Century Trinitarian Conflicts*, Edinburgh: T. & T. Clark.

Baron, R. 1957. *Science et sagesse chez Hugues de Saint Victor*, Paris: Lethielleux.

Bearsley, P. 1983. "Augustine and Wittgenstein on Language," *Philosophy* 58, 229–236.

Berlin, I. 1991. *The Crooked Timber of Humanity*, New York: Knopf.

Bettenson, H. (trans.) 1972. *See* Primary Sources (*De civitate Dei*).

Bogan, M. I. (trans.) 1968. *See* Primary Sources (*Retractationes*).

Bonhoeffer, A. 1890. *Epictet und die Stoa*, Stuttgart: Ferdinand Enke.

Bonnardière, A.-M. 1960. *Biblia Augustiniana*, Paris: Etudes Augustiniennes.

Bonnardière, A.-M. (ed.) 1986. *S. Augustin et la Bible*, Paris: Editions Beauchesne.

Bonner, G. 1984. "Christ, God and Man in the Thought of Saint Augustine," *Angelicum* 61, 268–294.

Bonner, G. 1992. "Augustine and Pelagianism," *Augustinian Studies* 23, 33–51.

Bonner, G. 1993. "Augustine and Pelagianism," *Augustinian Studies* 24, 27–47.

Bougerol, J. G. 1973. "Dossier pour l'etude des rapports entre Saint Bonaventure et Aristote," *Archives d'Histoire Doctrinale et Littéraire du Moyen Age* 40, 135–222.

Bourke, V. J. 1954. "St. Augustine and the Cosmic Soul," *Giornale de Metafisica* 9, 431–434.

Bourke, V. J. 1992. *Augustine's Love of Wisdom: An Introspective Philosophy*, West Lafayette: Purdue University Press.

Bouwsma, W. J. 1975. "Two Faces of Humanism. Stoicism and Augustinianism in Renaissance Thought," in H. Oberman and T. A. Brady, eds., *Itinerarium Italicum: The Profile of the Italian Renaissance in the Mirror of its European Transformations*, Leiden: Brill, 3–60.

Boyer, C. 1931. *La théorie augustinienne des raisons séminales*, Rome: Miscellanea Agostiniana.

Brown, D.C. 1987. *Pastor and Laity in the Theology of Jean Gerson*, Cambridge University Press.

Brown, P. 1964. "St. Augustine's Attitude to Religious Coercion," *Journal of Roman Studies* 54, 107–116.

Brown, P. 1965. "Saint Augustine," in Beryl Smalley, ed., *Trends in Medieval Political Thought*, Oxford: Oxford University Press.

Brown, P. 1967. *Augustine of Hippo*, Berkeley: University of California Press.

Brunt, P. A. 1989. "Philosophy and Religion in the Late Republic," in M. Griffin and J. Barnes, eds., *Philosophia Togata*, Oxford: Clarendon Press.

Bubacz, B. 1981. *St. Augustine's Theory of Knowledge: A Contemporary Analysis*, New York: Edwin Mellen Press.

Burnaby, J. 1938. *Amor Dei: A Study of the Religion of St. Augustine*, London: Hodder and Stoughton.

Burnell, P. J. 1992. "The Status of Politics in St. Augustine's *City of God*," *History of Political Thought* 13/1, 13–29.

Burns, J. P. 1979. "The Interpretation of Romans in the Pelagian Controversy," *Augustinian Studies* 10, 43–54.

Burns, J. P. 1980. *The Development of Augustine's Doctrine of Operative Grace*, Paris: Etudes Augustiennes.

Burnyeat, M. F. 1982. "Idealism and Greek Philosophy: What Descartes Saw and Berkeley Missed," *The Philosophical Review* 91, 3–40.

Burnyeat, M. F. 1987. "Wittgenstein and Augustine's *De Magistro*," *Proceedings of the Aristotelian Society*, Supplementary volume 61, 1–24; reprinted in Matthews, ed., 1999, 286–303.

Burnyeat, M. F., and Frede, M. (eds.) 1997. *The Original Skeptics: A Controversy*, Indianapolis and Cambridge: Hackett Publishing Company, Inc.

Callahan, J. F. 1948. *Four Views of Time in Ancient Philosophy*, New York: Greenwood Press.

Callahan, J. F. 1967. *Augustine and the Greek Philosophers*, Villanova University Press.

Chadwick, H. 1983. "Freedom and Necessity in Early Christian Thought about God," in D. Tracy and N. Lash, eds., *Cosmology and Theology*, New York: Seabury Press.

Chadwick, H. 1991. "Christian Platonism in Origen and Augustine," in H. Chadwick, *Heresy and Orthodoxy in the Early Church*, Aldershot: Variorum XII.

Chadwick, H. (trans.) 1991. See Primary Sources (*Confessions*).

Chenu, M. D. 1957. *La théologie au douzième siècle*, Paris: Vrin.

Christopher, P. 1994. *The Ethics of War and Peace*, Englewood Cliffs, NJ: Prentice Hall.

Clark, M. T. 1958. *Augustine: Philosopher of Freedom*, New York: Desclee.

Clark, M. T. (trans.) 1981. See Primary Sources (Victorinus).

Clark, M. T. 1989. "The Trinity in Latin Christianity," in *Christian Spirituality: Origins to the Twelfth Century*, New York: Crossroad, 276–290.

Clark, M. T. 1994. *Augustine*, London: Geoffrey Chapman, and Washington, DC: Georgetown University Press.

Colish, M. 1994. *Peter Lombard*, 2 vols., Leiden: Brill.

Conen, P. F. 1964. *Die Zeittheorie des Aristoteles* (*Zetemata* 35), Munich: Beck.

Copleston, F. 1964. *A History of Philosophy, Vol. II: Augustine to Scotus*, London: Burns and Oates.

Cottingham, J., et al. (trans.) 1984–85. See Primary Sources (Descartes).

Courcelle, P. 1950. *Recherches sur les Confessions de saint Augustin*, Paris: Boccard.

Courcelle, P. 1963. *Les Confessions de saint Augustin dans la tradition littéraire*, Paris: Etudes Augustiniennes.

Courcelle, P. 1968. *Recherches sur les Confessions de Saint Augustin*, Paris: Boccard.

Courtenay, W. J. 1978. *Adam Wodeham: An Introduction to His Life and Writings*, Leiden: Brill.

Courtenay, W. J. 1980. "Augustinianism at Oxford in the Fourteenth Century," *Augustiniana*, 30, 58–70.

Courtenay, W. J. 1987. *Schools and Scholars in Fourteenth-Century England*, Princeton University Press.

Courtenay, W. J. 1990. "Between Despair and Love: Some Late Medieval Modifications of Augustine's Teaching on Fruition and Psychic States," in Kenneth Hayen, ed., *Augustine, the Harvest and Theology (1300–1650): Essays Dedicated to Heiko Augustinus Oberman in Honor of his 70th Birthday*, Leiden: Brill.

Coward, H. G. 1990. "Memory and Scripture in the Conversion of St. Augustine," in H. Meynell, ed., *Grace, Politics and Desire: Essays on Augustine*, Calgary: University of Calgary Press, 19–30.

Craig, W. L. 1984. "Augustine on Foreknowledge and Free Will," *Augustinian Studies* 15, 41–67.

Crawford, D. D. 1988. "Intellect and Will in Augustine's *Confessions*," *Religious Studies* 24, 291–302.

Crouse, R. D. 1978. "*Intentio Moysi*: Bede, Augustine, Eriugena and Plato in the *Hexaemeron* of Honorius Augustodunensis," *Dionysius* 2, 137–157.

Crouse, R. D. 1980. "*Semina rationum*: St. Augustine and Boethius," *Dionysius* 4, 75–86.

Crouse, R. D. 1985a. "St. Augustine's *De trinitate*: Philosophical Method," *Studia Patristica* 16, 501–510.

Crouse, R. D. 1985b. "The Doctrine of Creation in Boethius: The *De Hebdomadibus* and *Consolatio*," *Studia Patristica* 16, 501–510.

Crouse, R. D. 1987. "A Twelfth-Century Augustinian: Honorius Augustodunensis," *Studia Ephemeridis Augustinianum* 26, 167–177.

Dales, R. C. 1995. *The Problem of the Rational Soul in the Thirteenth Century*, Leiden: Brill.

Davis, S. T., D. Kendall, and G. O'Collins (eds.) 1999. *The Trinity*, Oxford and New York: Oxford University Press.

Deane, H. A. 1963. *The Political and Social Ideas of St. Augustine*, New York: Columbia University Press.

De Wulf, M. 1901. "Augustinisme et aristotélisme au XIIIe siècle," *Revue Néo-Scolastique* 8, 151–166.

Diels, H. (ed.) 1929. *Doxographi Graeci*, Berlin: De Gruyter.

Dihle, A. 1982. *The Theory of Will in Classical Antiquity*, Berkeley: University of California Press.

Dillon, J. M. 1977. *The Middle Platonists*, Ithaca: Cornell University Press, and London: Duckworth.

Dillon, J. M. 1988. "'Orthodoxy' and 'Eclecticism': Middle Platonists and Neo-Pythagoreans," in J. M. Dillon and A. A. Long, eds., *The Question of "Eclecticism": Studies in Later Greek Philosophy*, Berkeley, Los Angeles, London: University of California Press, 103–125.

Divjak, J. (ed.) 1987. *See* Primary Sources (*Epistulae*).

Djuth, M. 1990. "Stoicism and Augustine's Doctrine of Human Freedom after 396," in J. C. Schnaubelt and F. van Fleteren, eds., *Collectanea Augustiniana*, New York: Lang, 387–401.

Dobbin, R. "Prohairesis in Epictetus," *Ancient Philosophy* 11, 111–135.

Dolbeau, F. 1996. *Augustin d'Hippone: Vingt-six sermons au peuple d'Afrique*, Paris: Etudes Augustiniennes.

Dolnikowski, E. 1995. *Thomas Bradwardine: A View of Time and a Vision of Eternity in Fourteenth Century Thought*, Leiden: Brill.

D'Ouforio, G. 1994. "The *concordia* of Augustine and Dionysius: Toward a Hermeneutic of the Disagreement of Patristic Sources in John the Scot *Periphyseon*," in Bernard McGinn and Willemien Offen, eds., *Eriugena: East and West*, Notre Dame: University of Notre Dame Press, 115–140.

Dronke, P. (ed.) 1988. *A History of Twelfth Century Western Philosophy*, Cambridge University Press.

Dyson, R. W. (trans.) 1998. *See* Primary Sources (*De civitate Dei*).

Eckermann, W. 1978. *Wort und Wirklichkeit: Der Sprachverständnis in der Theologie Gregors von Rimini und sein Weiterwirken in der Augustinerschule*, Wurzburg: Augustinus Verlag.

Effe, B. 1970. *Studien zur Kosmologie und Theologie der Aristotelischen Schrift "Über die Philosophie"* (*Zetemata* 50), Munich: Beck.

Ehrle, F. 1889. "Beiträge zur Geschichte der mittelalterlichen Scholastick: II, Der Augustinismus und der Aristotelismus in der Scholastick gegen Ende des 13. Jahrhunderts," *Archiv für Literatur und Kirchengeschichte des Mittelalters* 5, 603–635.

Eno, R. B. (trans.) 1989. *See* Primary Sources (*Epistulae*).

Etzkorn, G. J. 1977. "Walter Chatton and the Absolute Necessity of Grace," *Franciscan Studies* 33, 39–63.

Evans, M. G. J. 1982. *The Varieties of Reference*, Oxford and New York.

Everson, S. (ed.) 1994. *Language, Companions to Ancient Thought* 3, Cambridge University Press.

Fischer, J. M. 1994. *The Metaphysics of Free Will: An Essay on Control*, Aristotelian Society Series 14, Oxford: Blackwell.

Fischer, J. M., and Ravizza, M. 1998. *Responsibility and Control: A Theory of Moral Responsibility*, Cambridge University Press.

Fitzgerald, A. D. (ed.) 1999. *Augustine Through the Ages: An Encyclopaedia*, Grand Rapids, MI: Ecrdmans.

Flasch, K. 1993. *Was Ist Zeit?* Frankfurt am Main: Klostermann.

Frankfurt, H. 1969. "Alternate Possibilities and Moral Responsibility," *Journal of Philosophy* 66, 829–839; reprinted in Harry Frankfurt, *The Importance of What We Care About*, Cambridge University Press, 1988, 1–10.

Frankfurt, H. 1971. "Freedom of the Will and the Concept of a Person," *Journal of Philosophy* 68, 5–20; reprinted in Harry Frankfurt, *The Importance of What We Care About*, Cambridge University Press, 1988, 11–25.

Frede, M. 1997a. "The Skeptic's Two Kinds of Assent and the Question of the Possibility of Knowledge," in Burnyeat and Frede 1997, 127–51 (first published in R. Rorty, J. B. Schneewind, and Q. Skinner, eds., *Philosophy in History: Essays on the Historiography of Philosophy*, Cambridge University Press, 1984, 255–278).

Frede, M. 1997b. "Celsus' Attack on the Christians," in J. Barnes and M. Griffin, eds., *Philosophia Togata II*, Oxford: Clarendon Press.

Fredriksen, P. 1978. "Augustine and his Analysts," *Soundings* 51, 206–227.

Frend, W. H. C. 1985. *The Donatist Church*, Oxford: Clarendon Press (3rd edn).

Fuhrer, T. 1997. *See* Primary Sources (*Contra Academicos*).

Garrigues, M. O. 1977. "Honorius Augustodunensis, *De anima et de Deo*," *Recherches Augustiniennes* 12/2, 212–279.

Genest, J. F. 1992. *Prédétermination et liberté créée au XIVe siècle. Buckingham contra Bradwardine*, Paris: Vrin.

Gilson, E. 1924. *La philosophie de saint Bonaventure*, Paris: Vrin.

Gilson, E. 1929. "Les sources gréco-arabes de l'augustinisme avicennisant," *Archives d'Histoire Doctrinale et Littéraire du Moyen Age* 4, 5–149.

Gilson, E. 1955. *History of Christian Philosophy in the Middle Ages*, New York: Random House.

Gilson, E. 1960. *The Christian Philosophy of Saint Augustine*, trans. L. E. M. Lynch. New York: Random House, New York: Vintage Press, 1960; London: Gollancz, 1961.

Glucker, J. 1978. *Antiochus and the Late Academy*, Hypomnemata, vol. 56. Göttingen: Vandenhoeck & Ruprecht.

Glucker, J. 1995. "*Probabile, Veri Simile*, and Related Terms," in J. G. F. Powell, ed., *Cicero the Philosopher*, Oxford: Clarendon Press, 115–43.

Gorman, M. 1987. "The Manuscript Traditions of St. Augustine's Major Works," in *Congresso Internazionale su s. Agostino nel XVI Centenario della Conversione. Atti I*, Rome: Augustinianum, 381–412.

Hadot, I. 1984. *Arts libéraux et philosophie dans la pensée antique*, Paris: Etudes Augustiniennes.

Hanson, R. C. 1988. *The Search for the Christian Doctrine of God*, Edinburgh: T. & T. Clark.

Hennings, R. 1994. *Der Briefwechsel zwischen Augustinus und Hieronymus und ihr Streit um den Kanon des Alten Testaments und die Auslegung von Gal. 2, 11–14*, Leiden: Brill.

Herrera, R. A. 1998. "A Further Beating of a Nearly Dead Horse: Augustine's Presence in Anselm's Thought," *Augustiniana*, 48, 331–343.

Hill, E. 1985. *The Mystery of the Trinity*, London: Geoffrey Chapman.

Hill, E. 1991. *The Trinity*, New York: New City Press.

Hill, E. 1997. *See* Primary Sources (*Sermones*).

Hissette, R. 1977. *Enquête sur les 219 articles condamnés a Paris le 7 mars 1277*, Louvain: Publications Universitaires.

Holmes, R. L. 1989. *On War and Morality*, Princeton University Press.

Holmes, R. L. 1999. "St. Augustine and the Just War Theory," in Matthews, ed., 1999, 323–344.

Holte, R. 1962. *Béatitude et Sagesse. Saint Augustin et le problème de la fin de l'homme dans la philosophie ancienne*, Paris: Etudes Augustiniennes.

Hume, D. 1896. *A Treatise of Human Nature* (1739–1740), ed. L. A. Selby-Bigge, Oxford: Clarendon Press.

Husserl, E. 1966. *Zur Phänomenologie des inneren Zeitbewusstseins (1893–1917)*, ed. R. Boehm, Husserliana 10, The Hague: Nijhoff. English translation in E. Husserl, *Collected Works*, vol. 4, Dordrecht: Kluwer, 1991.

Incandela, J. 1994. Review of William Anglin's *Free Will and the Christian Faith*, *The Thomist* 58, 148–153.

Ingham, M. E. 1989. *Ethics and Freedom. An Historical-Critical Investigation of Scotist Ethical Thought*, Lanham, MD: University of America Press.

Inwood, B. unpublished. "The Will and the Self in Seneca."

Inwood, B. and Mansfield, J. (eds.) 1997. *Assent and Argument: Studies in Cicero's Academic Books*, Leiden, New York, Cologne: Brill.

Irwin, T. H. 1996. "The Virtues: Theory and Common Sense in Greek Philosophy," in R. Crisp, ed., *How Should One Live?* Oxford: Clarendon.

Itard, J. M. G. 1894. *Rapports et memoires sur le sauvage de l'Aveyron*, Paris: Bureaux du Progrès Médical.

Jackson, B. D. 1972. "The Theory of Signs in *De Doctrina Christiana*," *Revue des Etudes Augustiniennes* 15 (1969), 9–49; reprinted in *Augustine: A Collection of Critical Essays*, ed. R. A. Markus, Garden City, NY: Anchor, 1972, 92–137.

Jackson, B. D. 1975. *See* Primary Sources (*De dialectica*).

Jeauneau, E. 1973. "*Lectio Philosophorum*," *Recherches sur l'Ecole de Chartres*, Amsterdam: Hakkert.

Jeck, U. R. 1994. *Aristoteles contra Augustinum. Zur Frage nach dem Verhältnis von Zeit und Seele bei den antiken Aristoteleskomentatoren, im arabischen Aristoteles und im 13. Jahrhundert*, Bochumer Studien zur Philosophie, 21, Amsterdam/Philadelphia.

Jordan, M. D. 1998. "Augustinianism," in E. Craig, ed., *The Routledge Encyclopedia of Philosophy*, 10 vols., vol. 1, New York and London: Routledge, 559–565.

Jungel, E. 1976. *The Doctrine of the Trinity*, Edinburgh: Scottish Academic Press.

Kahn, C. H. 1988. "Discovering the Will: From Aristotle to Augustine," in J. M. Dillon and A. A. Long, eds., *The Question of "Eclecticism": Studies in Later Greek Philosophy*, Berkeley: University of California Press, 234–259.

Kane, G. S. 1981. *Anselm's Doctrine of Freedom and the Will*, New York/Toronto: Edwin Mellen Press.

Kane, R. 1993. *The Significance of Free Will*, Oxford University Press.

Kant, I. 1981. *Grounding for the Metaphysics of Morals*, trans. J. Ellington, Indianapolis: Hackett.

Kenny, A. (trans.) 1980. *See* Primary Sources (Descartes).

Kenny, A. 1993. *Aquinas on Mind*, London: Routledge.

Kent, B. 1995. *The Virtues of the Will*, Washington, DC: Catholic University of America Press.

King, E. B. and Schaefer, J. T. 1988. *Saint Augustine and His Influence in the Middle Ages*, Sewanee: The Press of the University of the South.

Kirwan, C. 1989. *Augustine*, London and New York: Routledge.

Kirwan, C. 1999. "Avoiding Sin: Augustine against Consequentialism," in Matthews, ed., 1999.

Knauer, G. 1957. "Peregrinatio Animae: Zur Frage der Einheit des augustinischen Konfessionen," *Hermes* 85, 216–248; reprinted in Knauer, G. *Three Studies*, New York: Garland, 1987.

Kneale, W. and Kneale, M. 1962. *The Development of Logic*, Oxford University Press.

Knuuttila, S. 1993. *Modalities in Medieval Philosophy*, London: Routledge.

Knuuttila, S. 1996. "Duns Scotus and the Foundations of Logical Modalities," in L. Honnefelder, R. Wood, and M. Dreyer, eds., *John Duns Scotus: Metaphysics and Ethics*, Leiden: Brill, 127–143.

Korolec, J. B. 1982. "Free Will and Free Choice" in Kretzmann, Kenny, Pinborg, and Stump, eds., 1982.

Kretzmann, N. 1983. "Goodness, Knowledge, and Indeterminacy in the Philosophy of Thomas Aquinas," *The Journal of Philosophy* 80, 631–649.

Kretzmann, N. 1990. "Faith Seeks, Understanding Finds: Augustine's Charter for Christian Philosophy," in T. P. Flint, ed., *Christian Philosophy*, Notre Dame, IN: University of Notre Dame Press, 1–36.

Kretzmann, N. 1991. "A Particular Problem of Creation: Why Would God Create This World?" in S. MacDonald, ed., *Being and Goodness: The Concept of the Good in Metaphysics and Philosophical Theology*, Ithaca: Cornell University Press, 229–249.

Kretzmann, N., Kenny, A., Pinborg, J. and Stump, E. (eds.) 1982. *The Cambridge History of Later Medieval Philosophy*, Cambridge University Press.

Kroon, M. de. 1972. "Pseudo-Augustin im Mittelalter. Entwurf eines Forschungsberichts," *Augustiniana* 22, 511–530.

Kürzinger, J. 1930. *Alfonsus Vargas Toelantus und seine theologische Einleitungslehre: ein Beitrag zur Geschichte der Scholastik im 14. Jahrhundert*. Beiträge zur Geschichte der Philosophie und Theologie des Mittelalters 22, Münster: Aschendorff.

Langan, J. 1979. "Augustine on the Unity and Interconnection of the Virtues," *Harvard Theological Review* 72, 81–95.

Le Blond, J.-M. 1950. *Les conversions de saint Augustin*, Théologie 17, Paris: Aubier.

Leff, G. 1958. *Bradwardine and the Pelagians: A Study of his "De Causa Dei" and its Opponents*, Cambridge University Press.

Leff, G. 1961. *Gregory of Rimini: Tradition and Innovation in the Fourteenth Century*, Manchester University Press.

Leff, G. 1979–97. "Augustinismus im Mittelalter," *Theologische Realenzyklopädie*, 27 vols., Berlin/New York: de Gruyter, vol. 4, 699–717.

Lepelley, C. 1987. "Spes saeculi: Le milieu social d'Augustin et ses ambitions séculières avant sa conversion," *Congresso Internazionale su S. Agostino nel XVI. Centenario della Conversione*, Rome, vol. 1, 99–117.

Lévy, C. 1992. *Cicero Academicus: Recherches sur les "Académiques" et sur la philosophie cicéronienne*, Rome: Ecole Française de Rome.

Lienhard, J. 1987. "The Arian Controversy: Some Categories Reconsidered," *Theological Studies* 48.

Little, A. G. 1926. "The Franciscan School at Oxford in the Thirteenth Century," *Archivum Franciscanum Historicum* 19, 803–874.

Lohr, C. H. 1982. "The Medieval Interpretation of Aristotle," in Kretzmann, Kenny, Pinborg, and Stump, eds., 1982.

Long, A. A. 1974. *Hellenistic Philosophy*, London: Duckworth.

Long, A. A. and Sedley, D. N. 1987. *The Hellenistic Philosophers, 1: Translations of the Principal Sources with Philosophical Commentary*, Cambridge University Press.

Lottin, O. 1942–60. *Psychologie et morale au XIIe et XIIIe siècles*, 4 vols., Louvain/ Gembloux.

Lovejoy, A. O. 1936. *The Great Chain of Being: A Study of the History of an Idea*, Cambridge, MA: Harvard University Press.

MacDonald, S. 1999. "Primal Sin," in Matthews, ed., 1999, 110–139.

MacIntyre, A. 1988. *Whose Justice? Which Rationality?*, Notre Dame: University of Notre Dame Press.

McLynn, N. 1994. *Ambrose of Milan*, Berkeley: University of California Press.

Macken, R. 1972. "La théorie d'illumination divine dans la philosophie d'Henri de Gand," *Recherches de Théologie Ancienne et Médiévale* 39, 82–112.

Macken, R. 1992. "Henry and Augustine," in Mark D. Jordan and Kent Emery (eds.) *Ad Litteram: Authoritative Texts and Their Medieval Readers*, Notre Dame, IN: University of Notre Dame Press.

Madec, G. 1970. "A propos d'une traduction du De ordine," Revue des Etudes Augustiniennes 16, 179–186.

Mandonnet, P. 1911. Siger de Brabant et l'averroïsme latin au XIIIe siècle, 2 vols., 2nd edn., Louvain: Publications Universitaires.

Mann, W. E. 1999. "Inner-Life Ethics," in Matthews, ed., 1999, 140–165.

Markus, R. A. 1957. "St. Augustine on Signs," Phronesis 2, 60–83; reprinted in Markus, ed., 1972, 61–91.

Markus, R. A. 1967. "Augustine," in A. H. Armstrong, ed., The Cambridge History of Later Greek and Early Mediaeval Philosophy, Cambridge University Press, 341–419.

Markus, R. A. 1970. Saeculum, Cambridge University Press.

Markus, R. A. 1990. The End of Ancient Christianity, Cambridge University Press.

Markus, R. A. (ed.) 1972. Augustine: A Collection of Critical Essays, Garden City, NY: Anchor Books.

Marrou, H. I. 1959. Saint Augustin et l'Augustinisme, Paris: Vrin.

Masai, F. 1961. "Les conversions de Saint Augustin et les débuts du spiritualisme en Occident," Le Moyen Age 67, 1–40.

Mathon, G. 1954. "L'utilisation des textes de saint Augustin par Jean Scot Erigène dans son De praedestinatione," in Augustinus Magister, vol. 3, Paris: Etudes Augustiniennes, 419–424.

Matthews, G. B. 1972. "Si Fallor, Sum," in Markus, ed., 1972, 151–167.

Matthews, G. B. 1992. Thought's Ego in Augustine and Descartes, Ithaca and London: Cornell University Press.

Matthews, G. B. (ed.) 1999. The Augustinian Tradition, Berkeley: University of California Press.

May, G. 1978. Schöpfung aus dem Nichts. Die Entstehung der Lehre von der creatio ex nihilo, Berlin: de Gruyter.

Mayer, C. P. 1996. "Creatio, creator, creatura," in C. P. Mayer, ed., Augustinus-Lexikon, vol. 2, Basel: Schwabe, 56–116.

Mayer, C. P. and Eckermann, W. (eds.) 1975. Scientia Augustiniana. Festschrift für Adolar Zumkeller OSA, Wurzberg: Augustinus Verlag.

Meijering, E. P. 1979. Augustin über Schöpfung, Ewigkeit und Zeit. Das elfte Buch der Bekenntnisse, Philosophia Patrum 4, Leiden: Brill.

Mendelson, M. 1998. "'The Business of Those Absent': The Origin of the Soul in Augustine's De Genesi Ad Litteram 10.6–26," Augustinian Studies 29, 25–81.

Menn, S. 1998. Descartes and Augustine, Cambridge University Press.

Milbank, J. 1990. Theology and Social Theory: Beyond Secular Reason, Oxford: Blackwell (Repr. 1993).

Mill, J. S. 1889. An Examination of Sir William Hamilton's Philosophy, 6th edn., London.

Milne, C. H. 1926. A Reconstruction of the Old Latin Text or Texts of the Gospels used by Saint Augustine, Cambridge University Press.

Miscellanea Agostiniana: Testi e Studi. 1930. Rome: Vatican City Press.

Moltmann, J. 1981. The Trinity and the Kingdom of God, London: SCM Press.

Moreau, M. 1955. "Mémoire et durée," Revue des Etudes Augustiniennes 1, 239–250.

Mourant, J. 1969. Augustine on Immortality. Villanova University Press.

Mourant, J. 1980. Saint Augustine on Memory. Villanova University Press.

Murray, M. V. 1973. "Introduction" to Giles of Rome, Theorems on Existence and Essence (Theoremata de esse et essentia), Medieval Philosophical Texts in Translation, 7, Milwaukee: Marquette University Press.

Nadler, S. 1992. *Malebranche and Ideas*, New York: Oxford University Press.

Nash, P. W. 1956. "Giles of Rome and the Subject of Theology," *Medieval Studies* 18, 61–92.

Nautin, P. 1973. "Genèse 1, 1–2, de Justin à Origène," in C. Mayer, ed., *In principio. Interprétations des premiers versets de la Genèse*, Paris: Centre d'Etudes des religions du livre, 61–94.

Newman, J. H. 1985. *An Essay in Aid of a Grammar of Assent* (1870), ed. I. T. Ker, Oxford: Clarendon Press.

Niebuhr, R. 1953. *Christian Realism and Political Problems*, New York: Charles Scribner's Sons.

Nock, A. D. 1988. *Conversion: The Old and the New Religion from Alexander the Great to Augustine of Hippo*, Lanham: University Press of America.

Oberman, H. 1958. *Archbishop Thomas Bradwardine, A Fourteenth Century Augustinian: A Study of his Theology in its Historical Context*, Utrecht: Kemink and Zoon.

Oberman, H. 1963. *The Harvest of Medieval Theology: Gabriel Biel and Late Medieval Nominalism*, Cambridge, MA: Harvard University Press.

Oberman, H. 1981a. *Masters of the Reformation*, Cambridge University Press.

Oberman, H. (ed.) 1981b. *Gregor Von Rimini: Werk und Wirkung bis zur Reformation*, Berlin and New York: de Gruyter.

Oberman, H. and James, F. E. (eds.) 1991. *Via Augustini: Augustine in the Later Middle Ages, Renaissance and Reformation, Essays in Honor of Damasus Trapp OSA*, Leiden: Brill.

Obertello, L. 1983. "Boezio e il neoplatonismo. Gli orientamentali attuali della critica," *Cultura e scuolo* 87, 95–103.

O'Carroll, M. 1986. *Trinitas: A Theological Encyclopedia of the Holy Trinity*, Wilmington: Glazier.

O'Connell, R. J. 1968. *St. Augustine's Early Theory of Man, A.D. 386–391*, Cambridge, MA: Belknap Press of Harvard University Press.

O'Connell, R. 1969. *St. Augustine's Confessions: The Odyssey of the Soul*, Cambridge, MA: Belknap Press of Harvard University Press.

O'Connell, R. J. 1987. *The Origin of the Soul in St. Augustine's Later Works*, New York: Fordham University Press.

O'Daly, G. 1974. "Did St. Augustine Ever Believe in the Soul's Pre-Existence?" *Augustinian Studies* 5, 227–235.

O'Daly, G. 1981. "Augustine on the Measurement of Time: Some Comparisons with Aristotelian and Stoic Texts," in H. J. Blumenthal and R. A. Markus, eds., *Neoplatonism and Early Christian Thought*, London: Variorum Press, 171–179.

O'Daly, G. 1986. "Anima, Animus," in *Augustinus Lexikon*, vol. 1, Basel: Schwabe, 315–340.

O'Daly, G. 1987. *Augustine's Philosophy of Mind*, Berkeley: University of California Press and London: Duckworth.

O'Daly, G. 1989. "Predestination and Freedom in Augustine's Ethics," in G. Vesey, ed., *The Philosophy in Christianity*, Cambridge University Press.

O'Donnell, J. J. 1979. "The Demise of Paganism," *Traditio* 35, 45–88.

O'Donnell, J. J. 1991. "The Authority of Augustine," *Augustinian Studies* 22, 7–35.

O'Donnell, J. J. 1992a. *See* Primary Sources (*Confessions*).

O'Donnell, J. J. 1992b. *Confessions II: Commentary on Books 1–7*, Oxford: Clarendon Press.

O'Donovan, O. 1980. *The Problem of Self-Love in St. Augustine*, New Haven and London: Yale University Press.

O'Meara, J. 1951. *See* Primary Sources (*Contra Academicos*).

O'Meara, J. 1954. *The Young Augustine*, London: Longmans, Green.

O'Meara, J. and Bieler, L. (eds.) 1973. *The Mind of Eriugena*: papers of a colloquium, Dublin, 14–18 July, 1970. Dublin: Irish University Press for Royal Irish Academy.

Pasnau, R. 1995. "Henry of Ghent and the Twilight of Divine Illumination," *Review of Metaphysics* 49, 49–75.

Pelzer, A. 1926. "Les 51 articles de Guillaume Occam censurés à Avignon en 1326," *Revue d'Historie Ecclésiastique* 18, 250–270.

Perler, O. 1969. *Les voyages de saint Augustin*, Paris: Ètudes Augustiniennes.

Peters, E. 1984. "What was God doing before He created the Heavens and the Earth?" *Augustiniana* 34, 53–74.

Pettit, P. 1997. *Republicanism*, Oxford University Press.

Pike, N. 1970. *God and Timelessness*, London: Routledge.

Pinc-Coffin, R. S. (trans.) 1961. *See* Primary Sources (*Confessiones*).

Powell, J. G. F. (ed.) 1995. *Cicero the Philosopher*, Oxford: Clarendon Press.

Prendiville, J. 1972. "The Development of the Idea of Habit in the Thought of Saint Augustine," *Traditio* 28, 29–99.

Principe, W. H. 1967. *Alexander of Hales' Theology of the Hypostatic Union*, Toronto: Pontifical Institute of Medieval Studies.

Principe, W. H. 1997. "*Filioque*," in E. Ferguson, ed., *Encyclopedia of Early Christianity*, New York and London: Garland, 426–429.

Quinn, J. F. 1973. *The Historical Constitution of Bonaventure's Philosophy*, Toronto: Pontifical Institute of Medieval Studies.

Quinn, P. L. 1998. "Augustinian Learning," in A. O. Rorty, ed., *Philosophers on Education*, London: Routledge, 81–94.

Quinn, P. L. 1999. "Disputing the Augustinian Legacy: John Locke and Jonathan Edwards on Romans 5:12–19," in Matthews, ed., 1999.

Rappe, S. 1996. "Self-knowledge and Subjectivity in the *Enneads*," in L. P. Gerson, ed., *The Cambridge Companion to Plotinus*, Cambridge University Press, 250–274.

Régnon, T. de. 1892–98. *Etudes de théologie positive sur la Trinité*, 3 vols., Paris: Restaux.

Ricœur, P. 1988. *Time and Narrative*, vol. 3, trans. K. Blamey and D. Pellaeur, Chicago: The University of Chicago Press.

Rist, J. M. 1969. "Augustine on Free Will and Predestination," *Journal of Theological Studies* 20, 420–447.

Rist, J. M. 1969. *Stoic Philosophy*, Cambridge University Press.

Rist, J. M. 1994. *Augustine: Ancient Thought Baptized*, Cambridge University Press.

Robson, J. A. 1961. *Wyclif and the Oxford Schools*, Cambridge University Press.

Roques, R. 1973. "Traduction ou interpretation? Brèves remarques sur Jean Scot traducteur de Denys," in J. O'Meara and L. Bieler, eds., 1973, 59–77.

Ross, D. C. 1991. "Time, the Heaven of Heavens, and Memory in Augustine's *Confessions*," *Augustinian Studies* 22, 191–205.

Russell, B. 1948. *Human Knowledge: Its Scope and Limits*, New York: Simon and Schuster.

Russell, R. 1973. "Some Augustinian Influences in Eriugena's *De divisione naturae*," in J. O'Meara and L. Bieler, eds., 1973.

Russell, R. 1975. "Cicero's Hortensius and the Problem of Riches in Saint Augustine," in P. Mayer and W. Eckermann, eds., 1975, 12–21.

Ryle, G. 1949. *The Concept of Mind*, London: Hutchinson; repr. Harmondsworth: Penguin Books, 1963.

Sage, A. A. 1964. "Voluntas praeparatur a Deo," *Revue des Etudes Augustiniennes* 10, 1–20.

Sharp, D. E. 1930. *Franciscan Philosophy at Oxford in the Thirteenth Century*, London: Oxford University Press.

Sheldon-Williams, I. P. 1973. "Eriugena's Greek Sources," in J. O'Meara and L. Bieler, eds., 1973, 1–14.

Smalley, B. 1960. *English Friars and Antiquity in Fourteenth-Century Oxford*, Oxford: Blackwell.

Solignac, A. 1973. "Exégèse et métaphysique. Genèse 1, 1–3 chez saint Augustin," in C. Mayer, ed., *In principio. Interprétations des premiers versets de la Genèse*, Paris: Centre d'Etudes des religions du livre, 153–171.

Sorabji, R. 1983. *Time, Creation, and the Continuum: Theories in Antiquity and the Early Middle Ages*, Ithaca: Cornell University Press, and London: Duckworth.

Sorabji, R. 1993. *Animal Minds and Human Morals: The Origins of the Western Debate*, Ithaca: Cornell University Press.

Southern, R. 1995. *Scholastic Humanism and the Unification of Europe*, Oxford: Blackwell.

Stark, J. C. 1990. "The Dynamics of the Will in Augustine's Conversion," in J. C. Schnaubelt and F. van Fleteren, eds., *Collectanea Augustiniana*, New York: Lang, 45–64.

Starnes, C. 1977. "St. Augustine and the Vision of Truth," *Dionysius* 1, 85–126.

Steinmetz, D. 1968. *Misericordia Dei: The Theology of Johannes von Staupitz in its Late Medieval Setting*, Leiden: Brill.

Stone, M. W. F. 2001. "Moral Psychology before 1277: 'Intellectualism', 'Voluntarism' and the Concept of *liberum arbitrium* in Bonaventure," in T. Pink and M. W. F. Stone, eds., *Theories of the Will and Human Action: From the Ancients to the Present Day*, London: Routledge.

Striker, G. 1980. "Skeptical Strategies," in M. Schofield, M. Burnyeat, and J. Barnes, eds., *Doubt and Dogmatism: Studies in Hellenistic Epistemology*, Oxford: Clarendon Press, 54–83.

Strobach, N. 1998. *The Moment of Change: A Systematic History in the Philosophy of Space and Time*, The New Synthese Historical Library 45, Dordrecht: Kluwer.

Studer, B. 1993. *Trinity and Incarnation: The Faith of the Early Church*, trans. M. Westerhoff, Collegeville: Liturgical Press.

Studer, B. 1997. "History and Faith in Augustine's *De Trinitate*," *Augustinian Studies* 28, 7–50.

Stump, E. 1988. "Sanctification, Hardening of the Heart, and Frankfurt's Concept of Free Will," *Journal of Philosophy* 85, 395–420; reprinted in J. M. Fischer and M. Ravizza, eds., *Moral Responsibility*, Ithaca, NY: Cornell University Press, 1993, 211–234.

Stump, E. 1989. "Atonement and Justification," in R. Feenstra and C. Plantinga, eds., *Trinity, Incarnation, and Atonement*, Notre Dame, IN: University of Notre Dame Press, 178–209.

Stump, E. 1996a. "Libertarian Freedom and the Principle of Alternate Possibilities," in D. Howard-Snyder and J. Jordan, eds., *Faith, Freedom, and Rationality*, New York: Rowman and Littlefield, 73–88.

Stump, E. 1996b. "Persons: Identification and Freedom," *Philosophical Topics* 24, 183–214.

Stump, E. 1999. "Alternative Possibilities and Moral Responsibility: The Flicker of Freedom," *The Journal of Ethics* 3, 299–324.

Stump, E. and MacDonald, S. (eds.) 1999. *Aquinas' Moral Theory*, Ithaca: Cornell University Press.

Taylor, C. 1989. *Sources of the Self*, Cambridge University Press.

TeSelle, E. 1970. *Augustine the Theologian*, New York: Herder and Herder.

Teske, R. 1983a. "The World Soul and Time in St. Augustine," *Augustinian Studies* 14, 75–92.

Teske, R. 1983b. "Saint Augustine on the Incorporeality of the Soul in *Letter* 166," *Modern Schoolman* 60, 170–188.

Teske, R. 1984. "Platonic Reminiscence and Memory of the Present in St. Augustine," *New Scholasticism* 58, 220–235.

Teske, R. 1996. *Paradoxes of Time in St. Augustine*, Milwaukee: Marquette University Press.

Todorov, T. 1982. *Theories of the Symbol*, trans. by C. Porter of *Théories du symbole* (Paris, 1977); Oxford: Blackwell.

Trapp, D. 1954. "Hiltalinger's Augustinian Quotations," *Augustiniana* 4, 412–449.

Trapp, D. 1956. "Augustinian Theology in the 14th Century: Notes on Editions, Marginalia, Opinions and Book-Lore," *Augustiniana* 6, 146–274.

Trapp, D. 1963a. "The Questiones of Dionysius de Burgo OSA," *Augustinianum* 3, 63–78.

Trapp, D. 1963a. "Angelus de Dobelin, Doctor Parisiensis, and his Lectura," *Augustinianum* 3, 389–413.

Trapp, D. 1964. "Notes on John Klenkok OSA," *Augustinianum* 4, 358–404.

Trapp, D. 1965a. "Notes on Some Manuscripts of the Augustinian Michael de Massa (d. 1337)," *Augustinianum* 5, 58–133.

Trapp, D. 1965b. "Adnotationes," *Augustinianum* 5, 147–151.

Van Engen, J. V. 1983. *Rupert of Deutz*, Publications of the Center for Medieval and Renaissance Studies, University of California Los Angeles, Berkeley/Los Angeles/London: University of California Press.

Van Fleteren, F. E. 1973. "Authority and Reason, Faith and Understanding in the Thought of Saint Augustine," *Augustinian Studies* 4, 33–71.

Van Inwagen, P. 1997. "Against Middle Knowledge," *Midwest Studies in Philosophy* 21, 225–236.

Van Steenberghen, F. 1980. *Thomas Aquinas and Radical Aristotelianism*, Washington, DC: Catholic University Press of America.

Van Steenberghen, F. 1991. *La Philosophie au XIIIe Siècle*, 2nd edn., Philosophes Médiévaux 28, Louvain: Peeters.

Vasoli, C. 1998. "Marsilo Ficino e Agostino," in K. Flasch and D. de Courcelles, eds., *Augustinus in der Neuzeit*, Turnhout: Brepols, 9–21.

Verbeke, G. 1945. *L'évolution de la doctrine du pneuma, du stoïcisme à saint Augustin*, Paris: Brouwer.

Verbraken, P. 1976. *Etudes critiques sur les sermons authentiques de saint Augustin*, Steenbrugge: In abbatia S. Petri.

Wallis, R. T. 1987. "Skepticism and Neoplatonism," in W. Haase and H. Temporini, eds., *Aufstieg und Niedergang der römischen Welt*, vol. 36.1, Berlin and New York: de Gruyter, 911–954.

Weaver, R. H. 1996. *Divine Grace and Human Agency: A Study of the Semi-Pelagian Controversy*, Macon: Mercer University Press.

Wermelinger, O. 1975. *Rom und Pelagius: die theologische Position der römischen Bischöfe im pelagianischen Streit in den Jahren 411–432*, Stuttgart: Hiersemann.

Wetzel, J. 1992. *Augustine and the Limits of Virtue*, Cambridge University Press.

Widerker, D. 1995a. "Libertarian Freedom and the Avoidability of Decisions," *Faith and Philosophy* 12, 113–118.

Widerker, D. 1995b. "Libertarianism and Frankfurt's Attack on the Principle of Alternative Possibilities," *The Philosophical Review* 104, 247–261.

Wilks, M. 1964. *The Problem of Sovereignty in the Later Middle Ages*, Cambridge University Press.

Williams, D. H. 1995. *Ambrose of Milan and the End of the Arian–Nicene Conflicts*, Oxford: Clarendon Press.

Williams, T. (trans.) 1993. *See* Primary Sources (*De libero arbitrio*).

Wills, G. 1999. *Saint Augustine*, New York: Viking/Penguin.

Wippel, J. F. 1977. "The Condemnations of 1270 and 1277 at Paris," *Journal of Medieval and Renaissance Studies* 7, 169–201.

Wittgenstein, L. 1953. *Philosophical Investigations*, Oxford: Blackwell.

Wittgenstein, L. 1958. *The Blue and Brown Books*, Oxford: Blackwell.

Xiberta, B. M. 1931. *De scriptoribus scholasticis saeculi XIV ex ordine Carmelitarum*, Louvain: Presses Universitaires.

Zimmermann, A. (ed.) 1974. *Antiqui und Moderni: Traditionbewusstsein und Fortschrittsbewusstsein im späten Mittelalter*, Miscellanea Medievalia 9, Berlin/New York: de Gruyter.

Zum Brunn, E. 1998. *St. Augustine: Being and Nothingness*, trans. R. Namad, New York: Paragon House.

Zumkeller, A. 1941. *Hugolin von Orvieto und seine theologische Erkenntnislehre*, Würzburg: Augustinus Verlag.

Zumkeller, A. 1953–54. "Hugolin von Orvieto (+1373) über Urstand und Erbsünde," *Augustiniana* 3, 165–193; *Augustiniana* 4, 25–46.

Zumkeller, A. 1964. "Die Augustinerschule des Mittelalters: Vertreter und philosophisch-theologische Lehre," *Analecta Augustiniana* 27, 167–262.

Zumkeller, A. 1978. "Johannes Klenkok OSA (+1374) im Kampf gegen den 'Pelagianismus' seiner Zeit: Seine Lehre über Gnade, Rechtfertigung und Verdienst," *Recherches Augustiniennes* 13, 231–333.

Zumkeller, A. 1980. "Der Augustinermonch Johannes Hiltalinger von Basel (gest. 1392) über Urstand, Erbsünde, Gnade und Verdienst," *Analecta Augustiniana* 43, 57–162.

Zumkeller, A. 1994. *Johannes von Staupitz und seine christliche Heilslehre*, Würzburg: Augustinus Verlag.

INDEX

Index

pride 46–7, 66–7, 69 70, 94, 236
  see also arrogance (*superbia*)
Proclus 254
prohairesis (moral character) 33–4
prolepsis (general idea) of good and evil 34
property 6, 239–40
propositions, truth of 163
punctuation, ambiguity of 69
punishment and reward 222, 223
  see also hell
Pyrrhonists 160, 208
Pythagoras 150

ranking of natures 3
realities, intelligible 66
reality, incorporeal 75
realization, power of 107
reason 2, 46, 120
  acting irrationally 34
  contrasted with faith 30
  discernment as function of 30
  intelligible objects higher than 77
  and objects of pure thought 76
  seminal 257–8
reason and faith 26–7, 37
recollection *see* memory
redemption 49
reflexivity of human higher faculties 116
Reformation scholars 262–3
reincarnation of souls 122
remembering *see* memory
Renaissance scholars 262
reprobation, A's doctrine of 56
res 197–8, 200
responsibility
  (God's) for human rejection of grace 139–41
  moral 54, 56, 131, 137, 222
resurrection of the body 122, 210
revelation, need for written 65–6
reward and punishment 222
Ridevall, John 262
Rist, John 2, 124
Romans, Paul's Epistle to 53–4
Rome
  Augustine and Cicero 235–7
  and the City of God 248
  sack of (410AD) 51–2, 235
Rupert of Deutz 255
Russell, Bertrand 7, 276, 277

Sabellius 96
Sallust 241
sapientia (true judgments) 98–9, 164

sarx see carnal self
Satan *see* Devil
scientia 98–9, 164
scripture 66–8
seeing *see* vision
self-defense 247
self-knowledge 97–8, 176–8
self-restraint 243
semi-Pelagians 51
Seneca, Lucius Annaeus 33, 34
sensation, theory of 5, 165–6
sense perception 4, 98, 163–4, 165–6, 175–6
sense-knowledge 28
Sextus Empiricus 159, 196
Siger of Brabant 256
signification theory 196, 200
  see also words: as signs
Simplicianus of Milan 53, 195
simplicity of God 44, 85–6
simultaneity of creation 103, 104, 105
sin 45–6
  and effect on our loves 235–6
  moral responsibility for 54, 56, 131, 137, 222
  see also original sin
skepticism 5, 27, 28, 159–64, 171–3
slavery 6, 238, 240
Socrates 33, 226
soldiers in war 247, 271
Sorites ("Heap") argument 163, 169 n51
soul 4, 59, 76, 97
  abilities 47
  concentration of power 165–6
  distension of 112
  and divine illumination 181
  and final judgment 56
  image of God in 155
  immortality 122, 256
  incorporeality of 118–19
  knowledge of the 116
  mid-rank position of 116–17
  number of souls 119
  origin of 120–2
  powers of 258
  pre-existence of 121, 148, 150, 179–80
  soul as "breath" 165
  status as a creature 117–18
  three powers of 221
  traducianist view of origin 114 n13
  transmigration of souls 122
  value of 216
  world-soul 119–20
sovereignty of God 41
speech, inner *see* words, inner